A Crown and a Cross

A Crown and a Cross

The Rise, Development, and Decline of the Methodist Class Meeting in Eighteenth-Century England

ANDREW GOODHEAD

WIPF & STOCK · Eugene, Oregon

A CROWN AND A CROSS
The Rise, Development, and Decline of the Methodist Class Meeting
in Eighteenth-Century England

Copyright © 2010 Andrew Goodhead. All rights reserved. Except for brief quotations in critical publications or reviews, no part of this book may be reproduced in any manner without prior written permission from the publisher. Write: Permissions, Wipf and Stock Publishers, 199 W. 8th Ave., Suite 3, Eugene, OR 97401.

Wipf & Stock
An Imprint of Wipf and Stock Publishers
199 W. 8th Ave., Suite 3
Eugene, OR 97401
www.wipfandstock.com

ISBN 13: 978-1-60608-651-3

Manufactured in the U.S.A.

All scripture quotations, unless otherwise indicated, are taken from the Holy Bible, New International Version®, NIV®. Copyright ©1973, 1978, 1984 by Biblica, Inc.™ Used by permission of Zondervan. All rights reserved worldwide.

Contents

Abbreviations vii
Introduction ix

PART ONE

Introductory Comments 3

1. Religion and Society at the Turn of the Eighteenth Century 5
2. The Heritage of John and Charles Wesley 31
3. Religious Societies in England from 1678 76
4. The Fetter Lane Society 101

PART TWO

Introductory Comments 143

5. The Classes of Methodism 145

PART THREE

Introductory Comments 191

6. Routinization 201
7. Totemism 224
8. The One-Generational Meeting 243
9. Conclusion 275

Appendices:
1. The Rules of Anthony Horneck's Savoy Society 289
2. The Poplar Regulations 291
3. Samuel Wesley's Rule for the Epworth Society 295
4. The Rules of the Rev Samuel Walker's Truro Society 298
5. Articles of the Religious Societies at Truro 303
6. The Rules of the Fetter Lane Society (A) 306

7. The Rules of the Fetter Lane Society (B) 309
8. The Rules of the Fetter Lane Society (C) 312
9. Religious Societies from John Wesley's Diary 314
10. The Nature, Design, and General Rules of the United Societies 318
11. Rules of the Band Societies 323
12. Directions given to the Band Societies 325
13. Of the right METHOD of meeting CLASSES and BANDS, in the Methodist-Societies 327

Bibliography 329

Abbreviations

ABBREVIATIONS USED IN THIS BOOK FOR PUBLISHED SERIES OF VOLUMES

Arminian Magazine   *The Arminian Magazine: Consisting of Extracts and Original Treatises on Universal Redemption. 1778, 1779, 1780, 1781, 1782.*

Journal [SE]   J. Wesley. *The Journal of the Rev John Wesley A.M (8 volumes), edited by N. Curnock.* London: Epworth Press, 1938.

Works [BE]   J. Wesley. *The Works of John Wesley, The Bicentennial Edition, edited by F. Baker.* Oxford and Nashville, 1976–2003.

Journal   C. Wesley. *The Journal of the Rev Charles Wesley MA, (two volumes), edited by T. Jackson.* Kansas City: Beacon Hill Press, 1980.

Preachers   T. Jackson, (editor). *The Lives of Early Methodist Preachers Chiefly Written by Themselves, (six volumes).* London: Wesleyan Conference Office, 1872.

Letters [SE]   J. Wesley. *The Letters of the Rev John Wesley AM (ten volumes), edited by J. Telford.* London: Epworth Press, 1931.

ABBREVIATIONS USED IN THIS BOOK FOR JOURNAL SERIES

JEH   *The Journal of Ecclesiastical History, (1987).*

Proceedings   *Proceedings of the Wesley Historical Society,*

Introduction

THIS BOOK IS CONCERNED with the class meeting. In 1742, Captain Foy, a member of the Bristol Methodist Society, suggested that grouping members together into classes and appointing a leader over them to collect one penny per week would assist defraying the debt on the recently built Meeting House in the Horsefair. The class quickly developed from a method of collecting money house to house into an opportunity for the class leader to inquire about the spiritual condition of the society members in his or her class, and thereafter into a weekly meeting for mutually accountable conversation, support, and fellowship.

The class meeting is considered by many, including exponents of cell church theories,[1] the high point of Wesley's organization. Some argue today that the class would revitalize the Church if it could be "rediscovered" and used within churches as a point of entry. It has been romanticized and credited with the force to convert millions. D. Michael Henderson makes this bold assertion when he writes:

> Wesley left nothing to chance. He made sure that those who were serious about leading a new life were channelled into small groups for growth in discipleship. These little meetings were later called "classes" and formed the backbone of the Methodist reformation for the next century. The "class meeting" turned out to be the primary means of bringing millions of England's most desperate people into the liberating discipline of Christian faith.[2]

This rather sweeping statement requires contextualization and evidence will be adduced to show that the "millions of England's most desperate people" suggested by Henderson simply did not exist in the eighteenth, nor indeed the nineteenth century. David Lowes Watson quite properly evinces the reality:

---

1. For a definition of cell hurch see, Croft et al., *A Future for Housegroups*, 5.
2. Henderson, *John Wesley's Class Meeting: A Model for Making Disciples*, 28.

x *Introduction*

> Methodist membership seems . . . to have comprised artisans or tradespeople, persons who were in possession of at least a rudimentary education and who, whilst living in the midst of social unrest, were usually not among those hardest hit by the changes.[3]

Even pre-Wesleyan societies reached the semi-skilled and skilled trades, rather than the illiterate lowest classes. Portus, in *Caritas Anglicana* notes that membership of the early Unitary (Anglican) societies was generally confined to skilled manual trades: occupations such as "Buttonseller, Milliner, Tailor, Salesman, Perfumer, Goldsmith, Confectioner, Perukemaker."[4] Amongst the founders of the Fetter Lane Band were a bookseller, a brazier, a barber, a poulterer, a clog maker, a wine-cooper, a barber, and a retired attorney.[5]

In his 1932 MA dissertation, W. A. Goss evidenced the earliest Bristol Methodists were primarily artisan: John Deschamps was a stuff maker, John Alldin and James Kelson cordwainers, John Tripp was a gunsmith.[6] There was one gentleman, John Dyer,[7] and one freeholder, Thomas Gough.[8]

Clive Field has shown in his comprehensive article, *The Social Composition of English Methodism to 1830: A Membership Analysis*,[9] the social, marital, and gender make up of Methodism in its earliest years

---

3. Watson, *The Early Methodist Class Meeting*, 131. See also Appendix G on 207, which shows a list of the society members, divided into classes of the Bingley Society in 1763. The trades and status of the membership is recorded.

4. Portus, *Caritas Anglicana. Or An Historical Inquiry into those Religious Societies and Philanthropical Societies that Flourished in England Between the Years 1678 and 1740*, 21. Portus is quoting from a manuscript, *Sunday Nights Society meeting att Mr. Bradshaws in Denmarke Street against Tom's Coffee House near Exeter Change in the Strand*. (Rawl. MS. D. 1312, fo.2.) Portus also refers to a document in the Bodleian Library, Oxford, *The Names, Places of abode, Employmts, and Occupacions of the several Societys in and about the Cities of London and Westminster Belonging to the Church of England*, 1694 (Bodleian, MS. Rawl. D. 1312).

5. Trousdale, "The Moravian Society. Fetter Lane–London," 30.

6. Goss, "Early Methodism in Bristol, with Special Reference to John Wesley's Visits to the City, 1739–90, and Their Impression on the People," 65. A copy of this dissertation is held in the archive of The New Room, Bristol

7. Goss, "Early Methodism in Bristol," 54.

8. Goss, "Early Methodism in Bristol," 65.

9. Field, "The Social Composition of English Methodism to 1830: A Membership Analysis," 153–69.

using extant membership records. His study of the occupations of the Methodists evidences that the occupations of the male membership reflected the major "artisan" economy of a locality. In the article, Field notes an issue I highlight in the third section of the book, that of rising social aspirations: "By the end of the eighteenth century there was mounting concern amongst many of the leading Methodist preachers about the growing respectability of the movement as evidenced by 'the steady rise of many of its members in the social scale.'"[10]

As to numbers, in 1742 the membership of the London United societies stood at around eleven hundred.[11] The returns of members for 1790, the year prior to Wesley's death on the 2nd March 1791, indicate that out of a population of 8,216,096 in England and Wales, only 1 percent identified themselves as Methodist, making 53,691 Methodists.[12] By 1901, the Wesleyan Methodists stood at 454,982 members, just 1.2 percent of the population.[13] None of these figures allows for the "millions" suggested by Henderson.

From the cell church perspective, Wesley is credited with having rediscovered "a New Testament pattern to the church of his day."[14] Howard Snyder, a Free Methodist, is quoted thus by William Beckham: "(the) class meeting was the cornerstone of the whole edifice. The classes were in effect house churches (not classes for instruction, as the term might suggest), meeting in the various neighborhoods where people lived."[15]

In one respect, Snyder's statement is true: the class was indeed the "cornerstone" to Wesley's organization from 1742; however, there is no evidence to support the claim that the class was a "house church."

---

10. Field, "The Social Composition of English Methodism to 1830: A Membership Analysis," 167.

11. Wesley, "*Works [BE]*, Vol. 19," 250.

12. See Watson, *The Early Methodist Class Meeting*, 131. See also Turner, *Conflict and Reconciliation Studies in Methodism and Ecumenism in England. 1740–1982*, 63–65. Although Turner dates Wesley's death to 1792 (rather than the correct year of 1791) he clearly shows the increase of population and membership from 1792 to the mid nineteenth century.

13. Rack, "Wesleyan Methodism 1849–1902," 123. The figures quoted represent the population of Great Britain, excluding Ireland.

14. Beckham, *The Second Reformation: Reshaping the Church for the 21st Century*, 119.

15. Beckham, *The Second Reformation*" 119. (Word in brackets mine) the original quotation can be found in Snyder, *The Radical Wesley and Patterns for Church Renewal*" 54.

This book will show that Wesley's ecclesiology relied on Methodism being held in tension with the Anglican Church. This created a particular *partial* ecclesiology of being church. By this I mean that every need of Christian life could be met within the society, except the sacraments and the Occasional Offices, (baptism, marriage and death).[16] This was a discipline of belonging to the Wesleyans, certainly in the earliest years, and was held to be important by Wesley to his death.

A number of Church Methodists survived after Wesley's death. Kent holds that those who did remain "melted back into the Establishment, because they wanted to receive holy communion from an Anglican parson, not from the itinerants."[17] This view is not shared by Goldhawk, who pointed out the number of arrangements made for Methodists in relation to the administration of communion over a period of thirty years from the 1795 Plan of Pacification to support itinerants, and societies who desired the sacrament from Anglican rather than Methodist hands.[18]

Baker[19] and Bowmer,[20] in their discussions on sacraments in Methodism, asserted that the issue of Church as against society administration had been on Conference and circuit agendas for some years prior to Wesley's death. In 1773, Thomas Taylor discovered to his cost that suggesting the possibility of Methodist administration in future years was unpopular: "The very intimation of any such thing was as bad as high treason, and I soon found myself in hot water."[21] Taylor noticed that many of his society did not attend the parish church or receive the sacrament. Taylor felt the Methodists of the society were unaware of the dominical command.[22] His comment, however, foreshadowed a later decision. Once Wesley died, the discussion continued as Methodism sought its way without the leader who had held the argument in tension.

---

16. It is correct to state that London was an exception to the sacramental rule, as the leasing of West Street Chapel, and other episcopally blessed meeting houses, mean that the Wesley's or their ordained assistants could provide a sacramental ministry, away from the parish church.

17. Kent, *Wesley and the Wesleyans Religion in Eighteenth Century Britain*, 205.

18. Goldhawk, "Early Victorian Age: Spirituality and Worship," 134–7.

19. Baker, *John Wesley and the Church of England*, 288–303.

20. Bowmer, *The Sacrament of the Lord's Supper in Early Methodism*, 187–205.

21. Taylor, "The Life of Thomas Taylor," 62.

22. Taylor, "The Life of Thomas Taylor," 62.

There was no period of respectful mourning for John Wesley before dispute arose regarding separation from the Church of England, with the Hull Declaration of the 4th May 1791 urging the Wesleyans to remain loyal to the Church and her sacraments, followed by a strong rebuff from Wesleyans in Birmingham and Hull. Conference did little to help resolve the matter, adopting a decision by lot in 1792 not to administer the sacraments, nor ordain without permission of Conference. Prevarication continued until the Plan of Pacification was agreed in 1795.[23]

From Wesley's death, pamphlets, and books written by leading Methodists urged class leaders and members to continue meeting in class, and offered catechetical material for use within the class. Other publications added to the debate surrounding continuing compulsory class attendance. A literature search of the Methodist Archive at the John Rylands Library produced 31 separate documents published from 1797 onwards.[24]

The word "organization" will be used to distinguish Wesleyanism post 1749, when the circuit system was fully established as a contrast to the word "movement" prior to 1749, when Wesleyanism was developing. It is accepted that the ordination of preachers[25] for the itinerant work took place after this date, but to all intents and purposes Wesleyan Methodism had emerged by 1749.

The Oxford English Dictionary defines "organization" as the "condition of being organized; the mode in which something is organized; co-ordination of parts or elements in an organic whole; systematic arrangement for a definite purpose."[26] This contrasts with "movement" which can be properly used in the earliest years of Wesleyanism, when structures were still being created. The fluidity of early Wesleyanism can

---

23. See Smith, *History of Wesleyan Methodism*. 12–34. See also Turner, *Conflict and Reconciliation*, 66–78.

24. The earliest document at the John Rylands on this subject is *An Address to the Heads of Families on the Necessity of Family Religion: Also an Interesting Discourse on Weekly Class Meetings* (Leeds: A. Newsom. 1797) The author is simply described as "Author of the last Century" MAW Pa 1797.3.

25. Wesley ordained Richard Whatcoat and Thomas Vasey as elders, and Thomas Coke (already an Anglican Minister) as Superintendent for the work in America in 1784, he ordained John Pawson, Joseph Taylor and Thomas Hanby for Scotland in 1785, and Alexander Mather as an elder for the English work in 1788, following this in 1789 with Thomas Rankin and Henry Moore.

26. *Oxford English Dictionary*, Volume X, 923. The definition quoted above is found at section 2b.

be seen from the definition of "movement" as a "course or series of actions and endeavours on the part of a body of persons, moving or tending more or less continuously toward some special end."[27]

This book is separated into three sections. In the first part I examine the antecedents to the class meeting in the context of an associational age. The changing religious context is set alongside social developments. In the main, the religious milieu under examination is English. The development and purpose of the Religious Society has not been considered in detail since Portus' *Caritas Anglicana* and Bullock's *Voluntary Religious Societies 1520–1799*. Most recently Clark primarily reviewed secular associations in *British Clubs and Societies 1580–1800: The Origins of an Associational Age*, but did not address the development of the Unitary societies. In *The Moravian Church in England 1728–1760*, Podmore deals specifically with the founding of the Fetter Lane Society, and does not review the earlier associations from which the English founders had come. This book reviews the distinct associations of the late seventeenth and eighteenth century, encompassing elements from all these authors, and drawing a broad picture of the setting into which John and Charles Wesley were born, educated, and worked.

The distinctive aspects of Unitary and Fetter Lane's communal life are drawn out in this section. These distinctives illustrate how the priorities of societal life developed from 1678. Each model of societal life added new distinctive features from its own milieu into the larger societal "picture." These were then subsumed into the societal model which followed. This original approach enables section two to show how the class drew upon these established patterns and expectations and furthered them in the early years of class life.

I will argue that the class meeting, as every aspect of Wesleyan organization, owes much to others. The Wesleyan movement owed everything of its life and vigor, not to the originality of Wesley, but to his ability to assimilate the doctrine, spirituality, teaching, and structures of others into a single schema, which became Wesleyanism.

The resulting model of Wesleyanism consisted of practical or social piety, inherited from Halle and the Holy Club of Oxford; Tory Anglicanism in the insistence of the place of the established Church in the life of the Christian; Non-Juring Anglicanism through the emphasis

---

27. *Oxford English Dictionary*, Volume X, 35. The definition above is from section 6a of the definition of "movement" which begins on p. 34.

of ancient or primitive Christianity; Moravianism through the adoption of the Moravian model of religious organization; Puritanism with its teaching on degrees of faith, which led to the rigorous keeping of spiritual journals, and later the inclusion of reason as a tool to assist in the life of faith; Roman Catholicism, in the model of class adopted by the Marquis de Renty, and the importance of perfection as a goal of the Christian life (a goal also found in the mystics and the Puritan tradition).

In the second part of the book I will show how the class meeting was the vital center of early Methodism. An understanding of the eighteenth century social and religious milieu adds depth to the sophistication of the class's purpose as a body of individuals meeting for a mutual purpose. The originality of the approach I have used is shown in the subdivisions of the chapter, highlighting specific elements of the purpose of the class. Within the chapter, I refer back to part one to emphasize how Wesley's previous experience, and his theology drew upon antecedents which he had personally experienced or had read of.

Wesley scholars contend that the class was the primary subdivision of the society. Henry Rack for example states:

> Each society contained smaller groups. All full members were placed in "classes" of about a dozen members under a leader which met weekly for spiritual conversation and guidance. Membership of the Connexion was defined by membership of a class.[28]

J. S. Simon asserted that Wesley, after meeting the leaders of the London Societies, agreed to "divide the Society into classes like those at Bristol, and place them under the supervision of leaders in whom Wesley could most confide."[29] Heitzenrater also makes this distinction, "The whole Society was divided into classes (from the Latin classis, or "division"), neighborhood subdivisions of about twelve persons, each having an assigned leader."[30]

Earlier subdivisions were the band, the select band and the penitential band. These were the means by which men, women, and children experienced at firsthand the closest accountability of Wesleyan discipleship. The oldest subdivision was the band, carried into Wesleyanism from

---

28. Rack, *Reasonable Enthusiast: John Wesley and the Rise of Methodism*, 238–9.

29. Simon, *John Wesley and the Methodist Societies*, 64.

30. Heitzenrater, *Wesley and the People Called Methodist*, 118. See also Howdle, "Class Meeting," 69–70.

the Fetter Lane Society. Heitzenrater suggests that not every Wesleyan belonged to a band prior to the introduction of the class meeting, "one gap in the society structure was that persons who were not in a band had no small group in which to seek encouragement and guidance."[31] This may not be so. In Bristol from 1739, Wesley, at the suggestion of George Whitefield[32] did place society members into bands. The same process occurred in London from 1740.

After 1742 the emphasis of the band meeting changed as Wesley used the class as the entry point into the society. Previously, the period "on trial" was spent within the larger society, and band membership was granted once an individual was a member of the society. Band membership was also predicated on segregation by age, sex or marital status. The class meeting was not segregated.

I will assert that the band, select band and penitential band were subdivisions of the class meeting from 1742, but that the class meeting was not a subdivision of the society; rather the classes were the society meeting in small groups, and the society was the classes meeting together. Effectively an "organic" union existed between class meetings and society meetings. This can be seen from the distinction between the preaching service, which was open to all, and the society meeting, at which only class members were admitted.

The account of Thomas Olivers makes this distinction between class members (by default society members) and hearers clear:

> As to the people of God in this place (Bradford Upon Avon), I loved them as dearly as those I had left in Bristol; and longed to be united with them in Christian fellowship, but knew not how. When the public preaching was over on a Sunday evening, and I, along with the multitude, was shut out from the Society, I used to go into the field at the back of the preaching-house, and listen while they sang the praises of God. I would then weep bitterly at the thought, that God's people were there, praising his name together, while I, a poor and wretched fugitive, was not permitted to be among them.[33]

---

31. Heitzenrater, *Wesley and the People Called Methodist*, 118.

32. Wesley *Works [BE,]* Vol. 25, 611–12. In a letter to John Wesley dated March 22nd 1738/39, Whitefield invited Wesley to continue his work in Bristol. In the letter he suggests that "many are ripe for bands."

33. Olivers, "The Life of Thomas Olivers," 85. (Words in brackets mine.)

From 1742, the smaller group meetings, band, select band and penitential band became subservient to the class meeting, as they were subdivisions of the class rather than the society. Any class member might become a member of a more intimate group, but it was not possible for a member of a smaller group to belong to the society without belonging first to a class. Thomas Rankin describes a further small meeting, the body band, in his autobiography. This is mentioned nowhere else as a Methodist group, but Rankin suggested this was part of the Methodist pattern,

> I now saw the whole economy of Methodism in the most favourable light, - the class and band meetings, meeting of the society, body-bands, lovefeasts &c.[34]

If, as Rack suggests, the ticket of membership was given to class members, and this ticket admitted the individual to connexional membership,[35] the ticket brought admission to membership of the local society too, and to gain entry to the society meeting, the ticket had to be produced. When classes met as a society, it was not that the small groups of the society were meeting, but that the classes were meeting as the society. This contention will be expanded in the book.

The reasons for holding this view of the close relationship of class to society can be summed up briefly thus: one, the close accountability of the class meeting offering a communal, deep, mutual trust and honesty was not possible in the society meeting; two, every society after 1742 began life as a class, and the growth of a society was as a group of classes; three, in the class it was easier to be aware of an individual's Christian life, and disciplinary issues might be more easily dealt with (on the model of Matthew 18);[36] four, the class allowed Wesleyans living in a locality to recognize and know each other; five, the class could also be used as a place for instruction and catechism. Heitzenrater is therefore correct in his statement relating the class to "neighborhood" meetings.

The success of the class meeting rested upon class members undergoing a similar, if not identical process of awakening, justification, and

---

34. Rankin, "The Life of Mr Thomas Rankin," 159.

35. Rack, *Reasonable Enthusiast*, 239.

36. See Appendix 9, Wesley *Works [BE]*, Vol. 9, 73. Rule 7 of the *General Rules of the United Societies* appears to have as a base the warrant from Matthew 18 regarding private and public admonishing of individuals. The discipline of Wesleyans was for salvific purposes.

sanctification. The process of conversion and discipleship, which these three separate elements might be said to represent, required a highly experiential and sometimes dramatic course. Fits and fainting, visions, and dreams are frequently recounted in personal testimonies.

A note of caution has to be inserted in relation to the extant records of class (and band) meetings; there are very few surviving accounts of class proceedings. Within Methodism today an archaic phrase "in band" exists to distinguish a discussion that is to be secret. This little used term highlights the nature of band and class meetings; that any open conversation was held as a confidence by fellow members to enable a spirit of openness and honesty to be engendered. This confidential trust was vital to the initial success of the class. Any records or references to both class and band conversation are therefore rare. They provide lively and vital interest to the class both as the crown, and as a cross to Methodism. The testimonial, diary and journal material I have gathered in this book has not previously been brought together with the purpose of illustrating how the class meeting functioned experientially, yet also failed as the desire for experience waned.

In each class meeting there was pressure for each member to conform to a stereotypical awakening/justifying experience. This occurred because Wesleyans who had undergone that experience, recounted the same to newer members, and having no other reference point for conversion *per se* they believed that this was the mode for becoming a Christian in the Wesleyan manner. This could then be recounted to the next generation of Wesleyans. However, the experience cannot be recreated. A single generation alone feels the full experiential nature of the class and later Methodists did not identify with this.

A brief examination of the place of Charles Wesley's spiritual poetry, frequently turned into hymns, will also feature as one of the elements of success within the class meeting. Testimonies will show how important the hymn was in Weslyanism as a tool for awakening, justification, and sanctification. Charles Wesley's hymnody was a unique feature of Wesleyanism.

Within classes of around twelve people, the whole of Wesley's doctrine and teaching could be found. This small group, more than any other Methodist meeting, embodied everything that Wesley had discovered during his lifetime and allowed men and women (and children) to discover for themselves; a distinctive amalgamation of disparate theologies and teachings.

In some respects the class was the very zenith of Methodist organization, and when placed into the context of the other Methodist meetings and eighteenth century society, John Wesley discovered, perhaps by accident, the one meeting which gave a coherent and achievable structure of discipline and discipleship for previously unchurched or "church-disconnected" people.

In the class, personal and spiritual life could be discussed, problems shared, sin, and temptation made plain to a sympathetic and understanding group, and admonition or congratulation offered by the class leader. This took place during the course of a meeting that prayed, sang, and shared open testimonial conversation.

However, much more than that was taking place within the class meeting. Meeting in a class meant far more than living an introverted spirituality. As a simple example, the Methodist people were called to live their lives amongst their community and practice within it acts of piety, giving money for the poor or visiting the sick. These same Methodists were encouraged to see their adherence to the Methodist movement *within* the parish system, so the parish church became a focus for sacramental life and worship.

Perhaps it is right to say that in the class system Wesley discovered the primitive Christianity he had left England to discover in 1735. In this small group members spoke openly and experienced their faith together, learning, and growing in the Christian faith as the earliest Christians did. That which Wesley had sought to rediscover or recreate in the New World amongst the settlers and Native Americans was before him amongst the class members who sought to join his movement.

In the third part, I use themes from the social sciences to examine reasons for the class's decline within a relatively short period of time. This approach is original in that each strand of social science: totemism, routinization and mystical/sect model of church, when taken together adds weight to the argument I pose that the decline of the class meeting was inexorable, and beyond the control of Wesley, who as I will show, was concerned once he was unable personally to oversee the local societies that class attendance was maintained.

I use *totem* as a theme in the same way as Emile Durkheim who coined this word in his *Elementary Forms of the Religious Life*. Durkheim separated that which is accorded a sacred status (the totem) from that which is profane, or worldly. Durkheim studied primitive Aboriginal Australian belief. Totemism,[37] or the use of symbol in Aboriginal society imbues the object, painted or crafted with a sacred significance, separating it from the worldly. The totem "is sacred; it cannot be approached, it is held in respect."[38] But it is more than mere symbol because it is recognized by the society and reflects "that group in the religion it creates."[39]

In some way then the class meeting has been instilled with a religious significance that it was never originally intended to have, and amongst Methodists and cell church teachers and writers, is afforded a reverence which calcifies the class meeting in its eighteenth century context and yet suggests that a rediscovery or reintroduction of the class meeting would act as a panacea for all ills within the organized Church in terms of a point of entry into Church, a means of personal regulation in a supportive community, and as a method, or model for Church growth.

Another reason for the decline of the class as an effective element of Wesleyan organization is the place, purpose, and role of the class itself once Wesleyanism became carefully structured and organized. When organization replaced movement, *routinization of charisma* occurred as outlined and developed by Max Weber. Weber was a leading early exponent of the sociology of religion and with "his friends Ernst Troeltsch and Werner Sombart, actually created the discipline of the sociology of religion."[40]

The nature of Wesleyanism changed after Wesley admitted itinerant Preachers and created circuits. Increasingly, toward the end of John Wesley's life, the leaders of Wesleyanism wrangled fiercely over whether or not to separate from the Church of England entirely, an act which in many respects had taken place *de facto*, with ordination, and assistants baptising and administering the sacraments. Wesleyanism had changed from the revivalist group that emerged from Fetter Lane and was spreading its ecclesiastical wings as a fledgling Church.

---

37. For a discussion of the significance of totem see Giddens, *Durkheim*, 88–95.
38. Pickering, *Durkheim on Religion*, 178.
39. Bierstedt, e[acute over e]mile Durkheim, 201.
40. The above quotation is from the translator's preface to Weber, *The Sociology of Religion*, x.

The class meeting lost its organic association with the society which was vital to its effectiveness as Preaching Houses were registered as Dissenting places of worship, and Wesleyan societies came to be seen as "churches" in their own right. The collegial, pastoral, and disciplinary roles that class members held in common were subsumed into the itinerant preacher's role. I will show how the tacit removal of collegial responsibility, (not only pastoral and disciplinary responsibility, but also the collegial sacramental responsibility of attendance at the parish church) to the itinerant preacher, meant the class meeting's primary functions were removed.

I will also discuss the class meeting's life as "one generational." By this I mean that the class had a short effective life in the manner which Wesley envisaged it; a small group for close mutual accountability, sacramental observance, and discipline. Second or later generations of class members desired respectability, routine, and the opportunities of leadership rather than the experiential and accountable fellowship of the class's early period.

In summary this book traces the developments in religious understanding that gave rise to the class meeting. While these are primarily studied from an English background, continental Pietism is considered. I will show the desire to associate in religious meetings that grew out of a Pietist understanding of faith and life, and how this, together with other influences on Wesley, led to the creation of the class meeting.

The book will also indicate that the class was a unique development of itself, moving the nature of Pietist association to an experiential, mutually accountable, disciplinary and discipling meeting. This second section, which considers the class as the "crown" of Methodism has detailed original material brought together for this purpose.

Through the writings of three social scientists, I will show that the class meeting became a "cross" to the Methodist people. I contend that the class declined during Wesley's lifetime, as the Wesleyan organization moved toward an independent existence away from the Church of England and the Wesleyan class became routinized, "totemised," and a one generational meeting. In the conclusion the class meeting will be evaluated and its value and purpose appraised.

(1896–2005).

Part One

Introductory Comments

In this section, the antecedents of the Methodist class meeting are examined. The Unitary societies of the Anglican Church and the Fetter Lane Society are both models of association that predated Wesley's movement.

Prior to the chronological and analytical studies of these society types, I will outline the developments in religion; both continental and English, and society from the late sixteenth century. This outline is contained in chapter 1. It is included to assist in the full understanding of the foundation of the Unitary societies, which began to meet a desire for piety and association which developed after the Restoration.

Chapter 2, which details the Wesleyan heritage, offers a comprehensive scrutiny of the Wesley family. This chapter highlights the important developments in John Wesley's self-understanding, and his model of appropriation of doctrine. Chapter 1 is vital to the consideration of Wesley's dogma, which will be seen to be a hybrid of theological models.

The following chapters, 3 and 4, chart the rise of the Unitary societies, and Fetter Lane, and analyze the model of faith development which each type of meeting offered a seeking populace. The chronological study of each society type, followed by analysis is an original approach to the background of Wesley's Methodism. In Part Two, I will follow the same pattern when discussing the Methodist class meeting as the "crown" of Methodism.

1

Religion and Society at the Turn of the Eighteenth Century

JOHN WESLEY'S "TURN TO seriousness" of 1725 marked the beginning of a spiritual journey that would reach a climax on May 24th 1738. From 1725, Wesley sought a vital and engaging faith. This chapter will trace the background to Wesley's schema of faith and spirituality. I will examine Pietist and Puritan developments, together with the social developments in England and Europe, all of which came to affect Wesley's life, practice, and understanding, and ultimately the Methodists themselves. Wesley's mind was ever receptive to other Christian traditions, and he synthesized the elements he found useful into the Methodist movement. No one tradition could claim Wesley for its own, least of all the Church of England.

CONTEXT

Pietism and later seventeenth century religious developments grew in a milieu of paradigm shifts; that is that a new way of thinking superseded that which previously held sway. This milieu is evidenced by David Bosch,[1] for whom the work of Spener marks a new mode within the paradigm:

> Published in 1693, Philipp Jakob Spener broke radically with the melancholic view of history that had characterised late orthodoxy... In the words of H. Frick (quoted in Gensichen 1961:16): for orthodoxy the proclamations of the gospel to all nations was, at best only a Wunschziel ("desired aim"); for Pietism it became a Willensziel ("aim of the will"). The new movement combined

---

1. Bosch, *Transforming Mission; Paradigm Shifts in the Theology of Mission*.

the joy of a personal experience of salvation with an eagerness to proclaim the gospel of redemption to all.²

This mode resulted in a desire to convert others, the need for inward struggle; an understanding that individuals rather than communities come to faith and the development of *ecclesiola in ecclesia*.

The enlightenment, the paradigm shift in which Pietism developed, allowed a worldview to develop offering individuals expression for the first time. Of this paradigm shift, Bosch wrote that "the *church* was gradually eliminated as a factor for validating the structure of society."³ This enlightened view allowed philosophy and science to be taken seriously as offering a reasonable rationale for the way the world was.

Progress was possible beyond the church and her structures, and individuals were considered autonomous beings. Again, Bosch provides a forceful critique of the Church's position in respect of the enlightenment, "even though the Christian faith continued to be practiced after the Enlightenment, it had lost its quiet self-evidence; it became strained and tended to overemphasize itself, for it felt itself to be operating in an alien and hostile world."⁴ This meant that men and women not only looked to themselves, or science, rather than the institutional Church for answers, but if they were people of faith, such faith was a private issue. It will be noticed from the religious developments in Europe and England outlined below that the enlightenment gave impetus to the personalized religious experience characterized by Pietism and Puritanism.

CONTINENTAL PIETISM

"The Pietist movement was a call to action; a call to vigorous Christian experience out-feeling the passive acceptance of creed and conformity."⁵ Lewis' statement somewhat oversimplifies the growth of religious movements in the seventeenth and eighteenth centuries, Pietism was as much a throwing off of "old Catholicism" in former Catholic states as it was a reaction against the formalized Lutheran theology and Christian practice in Protestant European nations. Lewis does capture a sense of the urgency that Pietism spread across Europe and into England.

2. Ibid., 252.
3. Ibid., 263.
4. Ibid., 268. See also the remainder of the second major paragraph.
5. Lewis, *Zinzendorf the Ecumenical Pioneer*, 22.

It is generally recognized that Philip Jakob Spener was "the man chiefly responsible for the rise of pietism."[6] While Ted Campbell agrees with this view, stating that through Spener "Arndtian spirituality was combined with reformed pietism,"[7] W. R Ward contests Spener's importance, and Pietism's origins:

> Pietism has constituted one of the most relentlessly contested battlefields of modern historiography, disagreement about when it began being so well balanced by its obscurity as a concept, and the whole so confused by the application of often arbitrary theological preferences or varying degrees of national self-isolation.[8]

Spener, a Lutheran, wanted to improve clergy training, and recover preaching. His *Pia Desideria* was primarily a reprinting of the Lutheran sermons of Johann Arndt, to which he added an introduction. The heart of Spener's teaching was the New Birth, which was "a Pietist party badge not because it was peculiar to them, but because of the prominence they gave it."[9]

Ward suggests that Luther's Preface to Romans, as a sign of conversion was as significant as the New Birth. "He (Spener) absorbed the message of Luther's Preface to Romans, which became almost obligatory for approved conversion in the later Pietist movement."[10] John Wesley's 1738 experience was "triggered" by a reading from that volume.[11]

Spener sought to relate the doctrine of the priesthood of all believers to experience, and he did this in the *Collegia Pietatis*. In these meetings, members would "teach, warn, convert and edify each other; in a word, they should practise the general (or spiritual) priesthood."[12]

This meeting was an attempt to move away from formality, and toward a more experiential faith:

> They (Spener and Francke) reacted against the official stress on formal theological correctness and merely conventional church-going and what they felt to be the impoverished state of spiritual

---

6. Cragg, *The Church & the Age of Reason, 1648-1789*, 101.

7. Campbell, *The Religion of the Heart A Study of European Religious Life in the Seventeenth and Eighteenth Centuries*, 82.

8. Ward, *The Protestant Evangelical Awakening*, 57.

9. Ibid., 57.

10. Ward, *Christianity under the Ancien Régime, 1648-1789*, 74.

11. See Wesley, *Works [BE]*, Vol. 18, 249-50.

12. Ward, *The Protestant Evangelical Awakening*, 57.

life. Instead, they wished to create a more personalized and inward type of piety and stressed the importance of good works.[13]

Spener did not seek to divide the Church, separating those who sought "experience" from those who held to "form." Wesley would later stand firm to Spener's principle, indicating Methodism was an *ecclesiola in ecclesia*. Watson states that Wesley drew on Spener's thinking: "This concept is usually attributed to the collegia pietatis of Philipp Jakob Spener."[14]

Spener's *Collegium*[15] were intended to renew Lutheranism. Ward writes: "If every Christian exercised his spiritual obligation to warn and comfort his fellow believers instead of leaving everything to the clergy, church renewal would begin in earnest."[16]

Spener's Frankfurt[17] meeting was elitist, but "it was soon joined by artisans and servants of both sexes who surprised him with their knowledge."[18] Johann Schutz took Spener's idea to an extreme, separated from him and moved to Penn's Quaker group in the American colonies.

Johann Benedict Carpzov argued that Pietism replaced faith for Spener and his friends, and he led the groundswell of criticism against Spener. However Carpzov encouraged the formation of "Bible Colleges" (*Collegia Philobiblica*) in 1686 to assist poor students in their Bible knowledge. The colleges comprised groups of students under the leadership of a senior student. The success of these colleges was far greater than anyone thought possible. Ward states:

> Students without any degrees began their own collegia to study Paul, and, worse again, citizens of the very unchurched city of Leipzig, where two parish churches had to suffice for a population of 20,000, joined the student exercises, and even opened conventicles. The spreading of the general priesthood to lay people was

---

13. Rack, *Reasonable Enthusiast*, 162.
14. Watson, *The Early Methodist Class Meeting*, 154. See note 22.
15. See Ward, *Christianity under the Ancien Régime*, 75. According to Ward these groups became Bible classes by 1674.
16. Ibid., 75.
17. Spener was a Lutheran pastor in Frankfurt.
18. Ward, *The Protestant Evangelical Awakening*, 57.

happening much faster than Spener intended or authority was prepared to tolerate.[19]

Spener became court chaplain to the Elector of Saxony in 1686, and in 1691 he came under the protection of Frederick III Elector of Brandenburg (Frederick I of Prussia from 1715). In 1694 the University of Halle was founded. August Herman Franke,[20] Spener's successor, staffed the theology faculty. Halle's importance to Pietism cannot be overestimated and "At the height of its fame, 1,200 students passed through its theological faculty each year."[21]

The university's work was not purely academic; there was an orphanage, Bible school, and secular schools; each an integral part of the Halle Pietist movement, which "stood for a theology less sunk in apathy and less contaminated in worldliness, a Christian fellowship more deeply conversant with the Bible and more actively participating in every kind of philanthropic enterprise."[22]

Spener's patronage gave an unrivaled position from which to spread Pietism. Ward suggests the University was the right place to draw those sympathetic to Spener to teach Pietist doctrine. "Halle became the beacon on the hill for the Pietists of the next generation."[23]

The teaching of Spener and Franke, and their ideal for scriptural and practical religion, was not unique. Jean de Labadie, a French "nobleman,"[24] raised a group around himself, who sought to achieve the pure church. This elitist group fared badly, refusing to heed advice from local people where the "Labadists" moved to form their settlement. By the time of the Wesleyan revival, the Labadists had died out.

Ward described Labadie as a "rather unsympathetic character."[25] In short, Labadie touched among the social elite a desire to escape from the orthodoxy offered by the church, yet he had no solution to offer. Labadie affected preaching in the Rhineland and Netherlands, with emphasis

19. Ibid., 77.

20. For brief biography of Franke, and of his achievements at Halle see Campbell, *The Religion of the Heart*, 87–88.

21. Cragg, *The Church & the Age of Reason*, 102.

22. Ibid., 102.

23. Ward, *Christianity under the Ancien Régime*, 78.

24. Ibid., 83. It was thought that Labadie was an illegitimate child of Henry IV of France

25. Ward, *The Protestant Evangelical Awakening*, 205.

between the "converted and unconverted, between the regenerate and unregenerate."[26] This difference was clearly part of the Wesleyan revival some 60 years later, and is an emphasis within any theology of Christian perfection.

Labadism gave rise to a revival under the name of *Resurrectio* (a Jansenist name). These less elitist settlements were more successful than Labadie's. They too used class meetings, or conventicles. Zinzendorf and the Moravians were influenced by the resurrectio settlements.

A study of Pietism is incomplete without reference to the Moravians whose history is bound up with Zinzendorf, an aristocrat, who owned the Hernhutt estate on which a religious community was founded, offering a safe haven during religious turmoil in Europe. The Moravians, or *Renewed Unity of the Brethren*, grew from the union of Protestant groups from Bohemia and Moravia. The earliest members of the *Unitas Fratrum* had roots in the followers of John Hus, who was executed as a "heretic" in 1415. Hus united diverse Protestant groups within Bohemia, which fragmented after his death. The *Unitas Fratrum* held their first synod in 1467, and continued to grow despite persecution.

The Renewed Brethren coupled the Protestantism developed from the teachings of Hus with the German Pietism of Lutherans like Spener. The Brethren who settled at Herrnhut readily accepted Spener's small groups and other social aspects of Pietism.

As a "persecuted group," they attracted other disenfranchised Christians from continental Europe. However, the Moravians were not popular. According to Ward, they were the subjects of a great deal of polemical writing by the 1740s, because the nature of Moravianism as a community and ecclesiastical body, was not easily definable:

> There being some solid evidence for all the views of a movement of heterogeneous origin: for the view of some, though not all, of its original adherents that it was a rebirth of the old Unity of the Brethren, a body which had succumbed to the violent pressure of the Counter-Reformation in its old heartlands of Bohemia and Moravia; for the views of its Orthodox opponents that it was either a new sect with no right to toleration in the empire, or indifferent, that is, denying the ultimate importance of confessional loyalty on the way to salvation.[27]

26. Ibid., 122.
27. Ibid., 119.

Although Zinzendorf is best remembered for his leadership of the Moravians, Christian David was responsible for their settling at Herrnhut. David, born in 1690 in Moravia to Catholic parents, later recalled: "his heart burned like a stove with religious devotion."[28] David was influenced by a Pietist evangelical carpentry apprentice master, and after his conversion in 1717, he became a lay preacher, meeting persecuted Christians. In 1722 David met Zinzendorf, after which David directed persecuted Christians to Herrnhut.

Zinzendorf, born in 1700, was fatherless after less than two months. After his mother remarried he was raised by his Pietist grandmother. At 10, he went to Halle and was influenced by Franke. At Halle, Zinzendorf began his first movement, the "Order of the Grain of Mustard Seed." The group's purpose was "a Christian fraternity committed to loving "the whole human family" and to spreading the gospel."[29] Zinzendorf was reluctant to enter court service preferring to serve the Christian Church. After purchasing from his grandmother the Berthelsdorf estate, which he renamed Herrnhut,[30] he opened his estate to Christian refugees.

Herrnhut's population grew rapidly, but the diversity of the new tenants caused problems. Zinzendorf moved to Herrnhut to control them, imposing a religious and village constitution. The latter included the formation of bands for the sharing of religious experience, and the creation of the office of elder.

In 1727, a major religious revival occurred. In the early part of the year, Herrnhut was regulated as a civic and spiritual community, establishing Moravian and Lutheran communities.[31] The rule of the community was mutual fellowship as shown by the bands organized in July 1727.[32] While Zinzendorf was in Silesia, he read Comenius' *Ratio Disciplinae*. Returning with these rules to Herrnhut, a relationship between the recently agreed Herrnhut rules and the "ancient Discipline"[33] was noticed, leading to an expectation of God's grace being poured out. On the 13th August, following the experience of eleven-year-old Susanne

---

28. Tucker, *From Jerusalem to Irian Jaya*, 74.
29. Ibid., 70.
30. Herrnhut means "The Lord's Watch."
31. Lewis, *Zinzendorf the Ecumenical Pioneer*, 54. Lewis states that the 12 elders were all from the artisan classes.
32. Ibid., 55.
33. Ibid., 56.

Kühnel [34] whose mother had died, the expectation was fulfilled. After three days and nights of prayer, Susanne and two other girls were converted. Fervor spread throughout the settlement and at a Confirmation and communion service the community sensed its own pentecostal experience:

> Several brethren prayed with great power and fervour. They prayed not only for themselves, but for their brethren still living under persecution; they prayed for those who taking the name of Christian were yet separated from one another.[35]

As a result doctrinal differences were set aside to concentrate upon unity and dependence upon God. Mission was the practical outworking of the experience, and Christian David became the first Moravian missionary.

As news of this night spread across Silesia, Herrnhut grew. In 1727, Herrnhut had 300 residents; by 1734 this had risen to 600. Conversation began to center on the signs of "old time" revival: Christian David began a men's Bible class, prayer meetings lasted all night, and there was a spirit of prayer amongst the community's children.

Zinzendorf's correspondence reflects this new unity: "Little as I desire that born Lutherans should go over to other sects, I cannot conceive that Catholics, Reformed and separatists who have united with us in love must become Lutheran."[36]

Credit must be given to Zinzendorf for holding the community together in the summer of 1727, when he afforded the Moravians the status of *ecclesiolae in ecclesia*. At this time, the community members who so wished could join an inner fellowship or "Gemeine." It was here that the class system was formed. David Lowes Watson describes them:

> The members were divided into groups, or classes, according to age, sex and marital status, each with a director chosen by the members themselves. Within these classes there was a mutual oversight for the furtherance of spiritual growth, each member being visited daily . . . Spiritual growth was to be assessed, and members identified as "dead," "awaked," "ignorant," "willing dis-

---

34. Ward, *Christianity under the Ancien Régime*, 115.
35. Lewis, *Zinzendorf the Ecumenical Pioneer*, 58.
36. Ward, *The Protestant Evangelical Awakening*, 122.

ciples" or "disciples that have made a progress." Similar language appears on early Methodist class papers.[37]

The classes were termed "choirs" and sub divided into "bands."[38] The bands were small, numbering perhaps three people who shared a spiritual affinity. Every band was accountable to Zinzendorf personally, and he believed they were important to community life. "I believe without such an institution, the church would never have become what it is now."[39] This close religious experience and accountability seems to have enabled the community with all its tensions to live together.

Difficulties however, could not be permanently overcome, especially as Watson recounts, the bands became "compulsory" and the community adopted the Lutheran parish system. Many of those who became elders were aristocrats like Zinzendorf, who were over-represented amongst the community. The Moravians separated in 1735 when David Nitschmann was ordained bishop. Zinzendorf was ordained bishop in 1737. The Wesleys encountered the Moravians under David Nitschmann's leadership on board the *Simmonds*[40] en route for Georgia in 1735. This meeting had a lasting effect for two reasons: piety (especially in times of crisis) and church order.

Pietism spread through a Europe free from Papal authority in a weakened Holy Roman Empire. As monarchs sought religious self-determination, Christian leaders began to seek out fresh ways in which to exercise faith. Piety was one means to combine an understanding of belief with a practical application toward the poor, the sick, and the uneducated.

ENGLISH PURITANISM AND PIETY

Stoeffler comments that no reformation church was free of the experiential nature that Pietism embodies, and because of this:

> Whether it occurs in England, in Scotland, in Wales, in the Netherlands, in Germany, in Switzerland, in Denmark, Norway,

---

37. Watson, *The Early Methodist Class Meeting*, 77.

38. Bands first began in 1727. They were small, and members met to talk about their spiritual state openly. See Lewis, *Zinzendorf the Ecumenical Pioneer*, 55.

39. Watson, *The Early Methodist Class Meeting*, 78. Watson is citing from Towlson, *Moravian and Methodist*.

40. See Wesley, "Works [BE], Vol. 18," 312–13.

Sweden, Russia or North America, whether it is linked with a Calvinistic, Lutheran, or Arminian theology its main features are always the same.[41]

The English Pietist tradition developed through the Puritans who aspired to remove the remnants of Catholic practice from the Church in the mid sixteenth century. This widened to include every aspect of church discipline and ultimately forced a retrenchment from established religion. Beginning during the reign of Elizabeth I[42] the Puritans developed a tradition of personal "preciseness," away from quasi-political debate surrounding the nature of Puritanism itself.[43]

Stoeffler's statement above is partially explained by the exile of Puritans under the reign of Mary (1553–1558). The Puritans who left England traveled to Switzerland and Germany, and were influenced by continental reformed teaching, returning on the accession of Elizabeth I, bringing the influence of their continental teachers, and aiming to remodel the church along continental Protestant lines.

Some Puritans were aware of continental piety before any "mainstream" exile occurred. John Hooper spent many years in Paris, Strasbourg, and Zurich, writing about Puritanism. He returned to England during the reign of Edward VI, and became Bishop of Gloucester and Worcester. He was executed in 1555. While in prison, Hooper wrote on predestination to the Kentish conventiclers, in an attempt to persuade them of that doctrine. Though not perhaps strictly in the later Puritan tradition, Hooper took the need for conversion, repentance, and pietistic living from his continental influences.

Moving into the period of Mary Tudor, John Bradford stood as a "link between the continental Reformation and Pietistic Puritanism."[44] Bradford held to the authority of the Word, justification by grace through faith and the doctrine of double predestination.[45] Piety figured

---

41. Stoeffler, *The Rise of Evangelical Pietism*, 7.

42. See Campbell, *The Religion of the Heart*, 45.

43. Stoeffler, *The Rise of Evangelical Pietism*, 27–28. Stoeffler has a brief but informative introduction to Puritan development.

44. Ibid., 42–43.

45. See Watts, *The Dissenters From the Reformation to the French Revolution*, 11. The Kentish conventiclers rejected the doctrines of original sin and predestination. See also Marshall and Ryrie, *The Beginnings of English Protestantism*, 134–37. Bradford also wrote defending predestination against his opponents "the freewillers," many of whom were also in prison.

in Bradford's writing, although as with Hooper this was a personal, rather than "societal" piety.

Calvinism was assimilated into Puritan piety through the return of exiles. Calvin's *Institutes* were translated into English in 1561 and his catechism was imposed by law upon the universities in 1587. William Perkins drew upon Calvin's *Institutes* and set the theory into practice in the form of piety. Again, there was emphasis upon repentance, which for Perkins meant "the whole process through which the individual proceeds from the natural state to the state of grace."[46] Such a reliance upon process emerged through his dependence on covenant theology, the covenant which humankind had to maintain. Perkins however also held that doubt was a requirement for the elect. Indeed, he believed that without perpetual doubts, an individual was damned.[47] William Ames, a student of Perkins, developed his teachers thinking, and worked during the period that Jakob Harmenson, or Arminius, wrote against the election theology of Calvinism.[48]

Perkins and Ames stressed the degrees of faith; effectively the order of salvation itself. These emphases encouraged men and women rigorously to maintain journals and diaries outlining personal journeys of faith, detailing, from conversion onwards, the Christian struggle. This affective[49] passage "served as a means of making clear the affections experienced by particular women and men as they traversed the order of salvation."[50] The ultimate degree was that of assurance.[51] Wesley turned the Puritan emphasis on assurance as the final degree on its head. For him assurance was a first step in Christian experience.

---

46. Stoeffler, *The Rise of Evangelical Pietism*, 56.

47. Watts, *The Dissenters*, 173–74. See also 177–78. Others taught and led their congregations to follow this understanding of the Christian life, but for a pastor it posed significant problems.

48. See Campbell, *The Religion of the Heart*, 46.

49. Campbell defines "affective" as "heartfelt." See Campbell, *The Religion of the Heart*, 2–3.

50. Campbell, *The Religion of the Heart*, 48.

51. Ibid. See also Watts, *The Dissenters*, 432.

At this time, a reliance on law began to surface, which led to:

> An ethical code . . . which purported to delineate through careful exposition of Scripture and logical deduction God's sovereign will for every conceivable condition of the Christian's life.[52]

Alongside law, reason became a tool for the Puritans. The ensuing piety became known as "godliness," offering a life regulated by habit and practice. Richard Rogers systematized this lifestyle in his *Seven Treatises*, offering a closely organized arrangement of personal living, which would surface in a communal form through the Anglican societies of Horneck and Woodward at the end of the seventeenth century. These societies will be considered in chapter 2.

A piety based on law and reason drove writers like Richard Sibbes and William Ames to use reason, logic, and analysis in sermons and books.[53] The *Cambridge Platonists* developed the use and place of reason in the experience of the Christian, and sought religious toleration, a hope that was in part enshrined in the *Act of Toleration* of 1689. Campbell asserts: "'Puritanism,' as the hope of 'purifying' the national church, was dead; but the spiritual impetus of Puritan piety was carried on by both Anglicans and Dissenters in the ensuing decades."[54]

The reliance of godliness on daily exercises for spiritual growth led to an increased observance of the sabbath. For Richard Greenham, the fourth commandment required adherence so that personal works of piety might have priority over personal recreation or wastefulness. Greenham emphasized the need for assurance based not on personal feeling, but on the work of God. Using the analogy of a swimmer he wrote:

> Though you swim in deep seas of dangerous temptation, yet are you sure and secure because Christ Jesus your head is still above all your troubles; and therefore able to draw you (his members) to the shoare of salvation without all peril of perishing.[55]

Greenham's piety would be adopted into the Holy Club's pattern. While usually linked with the piety of Halle, it can be seen there was also an English tradition for active engagement in social effort.[56]

---

52. Stoeffler, *The Rise of Evangelical Pietism*, 58.
53. Miller and Johnson, *The Puritans*, 66.
54. Campbell, *The Religion of the Heart*, 65.
55. Wakefield, *Puritan Devotion*, 125.
56. Stoeffler, *The Rise of Evangelical Pietism*, 64.

Puritan piety developed further with the pursuit of holiness as the goal of the Christian life. This meant that whereas godliness required the Christian *to do*, holiness required the Christian *to be*. In essence a change of state was envisaged by *becoming* holy. This moved from a piety "centered in law to a piety centered in an immediate relationship to God."[57] Prayer, meditation, and the means of grace were important in this process, and over time, these were incorporated as holy exercises, and stood alongside the practice of piety itself.

Holiness brought the Puritan Pietist into a search for an inward awareness of God's love; Monk states, "The love of God permeating all the interests, affections, and "tempers" of the person is regarded as inward holiness."[58] Richard Sibbes and Joseph Alleine's writing on holiness urged readers to seek the image or nature of Christ within.

Because the pursuit of holiness was primarily subjective, mysticism crept into Puritan understanding. Paul Baynes and Richard Sibbes led this development, moving Puritanism toward devotion to the love of God, leading to inner peace and union with God. Ultimately for Sibbes the "end of a Christian's striving was communion with God, the means was prayer, the result was fervent affection for God and man."[59] R. H. Coats offers a flowery but appropriate summation: "Mysticism as a form of piety, is the passion and hunger of the soul for immediacy of access to the Father, and the all-satisfying vision of his eternal glory."[60]

The bedrock of English Puritan mysticism lay in the study of earlier mystical traditions.[61] Joseph Hall[62] referred to Origen, St. Augustine, and Gerson (amongst others). Francis Rous[63] looked toward the Eastern

---

57. Ibid., 79.

58. Monk, *John Wesley His Puritan Heritage*, 154.

59. Stoeffler, *The Rise of Evangelical Pietism*, 83.

60. Coats, *Types of English Piety*, 156.

61. Brauer, "Puritan Mysticism and the Development of Liberalism," 152. See also Mursell, *English Spirituality from the Earliest Times to 1700*, 356–80. Mursell, in his helpful discussion of Puritan Spirituality does not refer to the English mystics.

62. See McCabe, "Joseph Hall," 633–37. Hall (1574–1656) was Bishop of Exeter and Norwich. He was a Calvinist, but sought an "ideal mean between radical Non-Conformity and Roman Catholicism." 635.

63. See Rigg, "Francis Rous." Rigg was an M.P. and also Provost of Eton. He was interested in a subjective piety, and wrote "Mystical Marriage," describing the marriage of the soul to Christ. See also Brauer, "Puritan Mysticism and the Development of Liberalism,"152. Brauer asserted that Rous was the "first Puritan mystic."

mystics; Dionysius the Areopagite and Clement of Alexandria, as well as mystics of the later middle ages, among them Thomas à Kempis.[64] Gordon Wakefield asserted that there was "a school of English mysticism derived from Jacob Boehme."[65] However, Boehme's mysticism was drawn from a German, Lutheran milieu, rather than the medieval English mystics. Boehme was rejected by the Lutherans for his views. Among the Puritans, John Pordage was best known for his study of Boehme.[66]

Surprisingly, the Puritans who accepted mysticism did not look back to the English mystics, such as Margery Kempe,[67] Richard Rolle,[68] Julian of Norwich,[69] Walter Hilton,[70] and *The Cloud of Unknowing*.[71] In email correspondence[72] Professor Diarmaid MacCulloch[73] suggested that this may have been because their work was not available to be read. Equally, mysticism was viewed with suspicion, as Boehme discovered through his own mystical writings, with the term "Behemist"[74] being applied to those who sought to follow a similar path of mysticism.

---

64. See Stoeffler, *The Rise of Evangelical Pietism*, 84–86.

65. Wakefield, *Puritan Devotion*, 102. See also Cross and Livingstone, "Boehme, Jakob," 182–83.

66. See. Brod, "A Radical Network in the English Revolution: John Pordage and His Circle, 1646–54," 1231.

67. See Riddy, "Kempe [nee Brunham], Margery," 188–89. Kempe's autobiography, her *Book* is the earliest surving autobiography in English. She was born in Kings Lynn, Norfolk in around 1373 and died in or after 1438.

68. See Hughes, "Rolle, Richard," 619–22. Rolle was a hermit, whose main work was *Super Canticum Canticorum*. He was born in Thornton Dale, Yorkshire in 1305–10 and died in 1349.

69. See. Bhattacharji, "Julian of Norwich," 819–20. Julian may have taken her name from the parish church of St. Julian at Conisford, where she had her cell. She is known for *Revelations of Divine Love*, written after 16 visions of the crucified Christ. Julian was visited by Margery Kempe in 1413. She was born in 1342, and died around 1416.

70. See Clark, "Hilton, Walter," 250–51. Hilton is best known for *Scale of Perfection*, and he joined a Priory of Augustinian Canons in Thurgarton, Nottinghamshire in around 1386. He was born in 1343, and died in 1396.

71. See Russell, "Cloud of Unknowing, The," 89–91.

72. Email correspondence between the writer and Professor Diarmid MacCulloch, 11th December 2006.

73. Professor Diarmaid MacCulloch is Professor of the History of the Church at St. Cross College, Oxford.

74. Cross and Livingstone, "Boehme, Jakob," 183. The Behemists later amalgamated with the Quakers.

As I shall show later in this book, Wesley drew on the Puritans while creating his own schema of belief. Wesley's reading and publications may offer further insight into the absence of English mysticism from the Puritans of a previous generation, and suggests that Dr. MacCulloch's comment is correct. V. H. H. Green's appendix to *The Young Mr Wesley*[75] lists Wesley's reading between 1725 and 1734. In his reading of classics, plays, general reading, and religion, there are no English mystics noted. Bullock recorded In *Evangelical Conversion in Great Britain 1516-1695*, that the *Christian Library* which Wesley began publishing in 1749 contained a wide range of spiritual biographies, and abridged writings. Among the authors published for a Methodist readership were conversion accounts of "Bilney, Frith, Latimer, Hamilton, Straiton, Welsh, Blackerby, Bolton, Winter, Mather, Hale and Fraser."[76] Wesley's abridgments contained works by "Baxter, Bolton, Goodwin, Ambrose and Alleine, also by John Ardnt, Blaise Pascal, Hugh Binning, Henry More, Bishop Edward Reynolds and Jonathan Edwards."[77] Wakefield notes the omissions in *Fire of Love*. "The omissions are important: no medieval mystics, no Carmelites, no great reformers, no St Anthony, St Augustine, St Anselm, St Bernard, St Thomas (except indirectly through the Puritans); no one indeed whom the Catholic Church has canonised."[78]

Wesley's later pattern offers an insight, but not conclusive evidence as to why the English mystics may have been overlooked by the Puritans. If their Catholic heritage meant that these mystics were anathema to the Puritans, then Wesley, drawing on their reading was following a pattern set by his religious forebears. Wakefield suggested that Wesley's omission was due to "the prejudices of the age."[79] If this was so, then he was doing nothing more than the Puritans had largely done before him. Equally, if their work was not available, it is not merely an omission because of religious background, but an understandable omission, as their writings were little known.

In contrast to his contemporaries, Richard Baxter, though a Puritan and Pietist, maintained a broadly Arminian theology.[80] He sought to

75. Green, *The Young Mr Wesley*, 305-19.
76. Bullock, *Evangelical Conversion*, 110-11.
77. Ibid., 111.
78. Wakefield, *Fire of Love the Spirituality of John Wesley*, 20.
79. Ibid., 20-21.
80. Baxter did not accept universal salvation (Arminianism), but equally would not

unite the various strands of Piety. Baxter wanted to ensure that the reliance on law, that is, God's sovereign will, stood alongside the gospel, that is, God's grace. Here he sought to bring together an understanding of God's glory, with the happiness of humankind. Baxter was at the forefront of the creation of a "reasonable and tolerant piety."[81]

Baxter began two small weekly groups, one to discuss the previous Sunday's sermon, pray, and occasionally to sing a psalm, and another of younger people to pray. A third group met on a Saturday, to discuss the previous week's sermon and prepare themselves for the following day. Overtones of the later Unitary societies are apparent, but Baxter allowed extempore and a freer style, which was forbidden in these societies. Baxter and his assistant also met families for catechising and discussion.[82]

Many groups or sects sprang up in the the seventeenth century. Most were short-lived, and relied on the prophetic visions of the leader. Muggletonians, Levellers, and Soul Sleepers added a new dimension to Puritan piety. In the main, these groups were "enthusiasts" who in following their teacher often relied only marginally on the authority of Scripture and more on the teaching of their leader, with little time for the structures of church or state. It is unsurprising that the term "enthusiast" should be so negative when applied to the Methodists in the eighteenth century. John Wesley was swift to distance himself from any charge of enthusiasm and from people he thought to be enthusiasts.[83]

Jeremy Taylor, (who stands outside Puritan Pietism) deserves reference. His two major works, *The Rule and Exercises for Holy Living*[84] and *The Rule and Exercises for Holy Dying*,[85] synthesized the traditional

---

allow the harshness of Calvin's election theory. He therefore mellowed both doctrines. See Campbell, *The Religion of the Heart*, 65–67.

81. Campbell, *The Religion of the Heart*, 69.

82. Stoeffler, *The Rise of Evangelical Pietism*, 89–90.

83. For example see Wesley, "Works [BE], Vol 19," 31. The men he "charges" with enthusiasm are Mr. Hollis and William Seward.

84. Taylor, *The Rule and Exercises for Holy Living in which are described The Meanes and Instruments of obtaining every Vertue; and the Remedies against every Vice, and Considerations serving the resisting all temptations. Together with Prayers containing the whole duty of Christians, and the parts of Devotion fitted to all occasions and furnish'd for all Neccessities.*

85. Taylor, *The Rules and Exercises of Holy Dying, in which are described The Means and Instruments of preparing ourselves, and others respectively for a blessed death: and the remedies against the evils and temptations proper to the state of sicknesse. Together with*

teachings of Puritan Pietists outlined above with the Arminian teaching of Lancelot Andrewes, a High Church Anglican. There was a year's gap between publications.[86]

Taylor's understanding of the Christian life was "sweetness, reasonableness, and implicit trust in a good God of whom all creation speaks to the devout spirit."[87] Holiness, motivated by the love of God shown through practical piety was the way toward God. Alongside this journey was the necessity of proper preparation, and in the High Church tradition, he believed the means of grace necessary to the life of the Christian. Taylor also believed the monarch's role in the order of state to be sacrosanct, acknowledging Charles II as king, by divine right during the Commonwealth. Wesley's reading of *Holy Living* and *Holy Dying* influenced his spiritual practice, as much as the teaching of more traditional Puritans.

Taylor wrote during the Commonwealth, when the Anglican Church had seemingly lost its place in English life and the need to write *Holy Living* and *Holy Dying* was urgent. His writing, according to Askey, was "not a supplement to a church-goer's devotional literature, but . . . the whole of Christian life for the unchurched English parishioner in the middle of the seventeenth century."[88] *Holy Living* then is intended to assist daily devotional life in the absence of Anglican clergy to support the process. Living a holy life was important; Taylor had no place for deathbed conversions. The whole of life was bound up with living for God, and denial of that through life was not overcome at death.[89] Wesley's own early repugnance for deathbed conversions[90] was similar to Taylor's.

Prayers and acts of Vertue to be used by sick and dying persons, or by others standing in their attendance. To which are added Rules for the visitiation of the sick, and offices proper for that Ministry.

86. Stranks, *The Life and Writings of Jeremy Taylor*, 104.
87. Stoeffler, *The Rise of Evangelical Pietism*, 107.
88. Askey, *Muskets and Altars: Jeremy Taylor and the Last of the Anglicans*, 2.
89. Stranks, *The Life and Writings of Jeremy Taylor*, 106.
90. Wesley, "Works [BE], Vol. 18," 228. See the entry for the 6th March 1738. Bohler had invited Wesley to speak with a condemned prisoner called Clifford on several occasions. Wesley wrote "I could not prevail on myself so to do, being still (as I had been many years) a zealous asserter of *the impossibility of a death.bed repentance*."

Holy Dying[91] was equally devotional, intended to aid the Christian through the process of death. As the holy life, so the holy death was found in the practice of the individual during life. If there was no priest to visit and perform an office for the dying, the book was to fill that place:

> *Holy Dying* is not a handbook for the clergy. It is a self-help manual for those especially in the dismantled Church who have no priest. It is for those who need instructing about the danger they are in . . . What *Holy Dying* aimed at was to convince the reader, in the absence of the Church of England and its ministry, of the divine mercy in pardoning sinners, and not to despair.[92]

Holy Dying was not to be read by the dying: it is a book for those who live, yet wish to die a "good death." It is intended to assist the process of death when it comes, not comfort those who are in a final illness.[93]

Piety was a constantly developing spirituality both in continental Europe and England throughout the sixteenth and into the seventeenth century. Developed as a means of expressing faith through life, and ranging from the completion of spiritual exercises to the introverted journeying of the mystics, to the communal life of the Herrnhutters or the small groups of Richard Baxter, Pietsm in all its forms sought to move the individual through life toward an understanding and experience of faith that was not cold, or intellectual, but *affective*[94] to the emotions and experience.

In Wesley both continental and English piety can be discerned through his lifestyle, reading, and organization, and I will evidence this in later chapters. Wesleyan piety was a distillation of Pietist and Puritan attitudes and practices with which John Wesley could agree, or more importantly could say were experientially true. Chapter 2's discussion of the Wesleyan inheritance will show further influences on Wesley.

---

91. *The Rule and Exercises for Holy Dying* was written following the death of his wife, Phoebe. See Askey, *Muskets and Altars*, 144–45.

92. Askey, *Muskets and Altars*, 147.

93. Stranks, *The Life and Writings of Jeremy Taylor*, 114.

94. Campbell, *The Religion of the Heart*, 2–3.

SOCIAL DEVELOPMENTS

A. M. Allchin asserts that the "seventeenth century both in Britain and in Europe had been a period of great religious fervour and theological creativity."[95] This fervor and creativity followed the emancipation of European Catholic states, and an England gradually emerging from her own religious change. Such change was paralleled by social and political changes.

With the emergence of enlightened thought, philosophy began to view the nature of being human differently from that previously taught within the Roman Catholic Church. "Reason" became the byword for philosophers. Science also began to surface as a means of understanding how the world functioned. Gerald Cragg writes:

> Bacon had pointed to the scientific method which would rule the future, and Descartes had unfolded *The Principles* of thought which inaugurated the new age in philosophy. Men's minds would no longer be governed by assumptions which were an inheritance from medieval and classical times.[96]

This placed philosophy on a collision course with the entrenched views of Catholicism. That is not to say that philosophy had no place for religion, rather it viewed the world from an alternative perspective. Cragg also asserts that travel was broadening the horizon beyond Europe and opening inquiring minds to other philosophies.[97] Travel led to a greater awareness of alternative thinking, behaving, and understanding. Allied to the associational age which will be considered later, the flowing exchange of ideas gave rise to an age of inquiry.

Maximin Piette holds a starker view, stating that the dawn of the Age of Reason occurred with the breakdown of the authority of religion through nationalism. In the new age, reason sought to influence every area of life and each country "made its own philosophy and followed its own masters. France looked to Descartes, England to Hobbes, Locke, Berkley, and Hume. Germany went to school to Leibnitz and his follower Wolff."[98] As Allchin states:

---

95. Allchin, *Participation in God: A Forgotten Strand in Anglican Tradition*, 25.
96. Cragg, *The Church & the Age of Reason*, 37.
97. Ibid., 46.
98. Piette, *John Wesley in the Evolution of Protestantism*, 98.

> The eighteenth century emerged as an age of rationalism, moralism and scepticism, an age which saw the beginning of the modern rejection of the classical Christian tradition.[99]

In England Deism emerged, shunning revelation, and the surety of a knowledge of God. Deists denied original sin and praised humankind's innate goodness, doing away with any need for atonement.[100] Deism also influenced continental Europe.[101]

In 1648 at the end of the Thirty Years War, nation states began to emerge across Europe from a weakened Holy Roman Empire previously gripped by the Hapsburg dynasty.[102] Small electoral states, which elected the Holy Roman Emperor, had always owed allegiance to Rome. Once the power of the Holy Roman Emperor diminished as a unifying force for Rome, rulers were swayed by the force of other dogma creating confessional states. That did not mean that the new Protestant states were havens for all, but neither were the "old" states. Catholic France enacted the Edit of Nantes in 1598, granting religious toleration to Protestant Huguenots. In 1685, after whittling at the heart of the Edict,[103] Louis XIV revoked it. This sanctioned the persecution of Huguenot ministers and people and led to an exodus to England, Europe, and the new American colonies, taking not only skilled artisan trades, but Huguenot piety beyond its traditional boundaries.

The Treaty of Westphalia altered the nature of nationhood forever. Europe in 1648 was defined outside the Holy Roman Empire. P. K. Monod is clear that the negotiators of the Treaty of Westphalia believed that they could rationally create borders and nations: "they defined the autonomy of new states, and confirmed the sovereignty of old ones, by recognizing the balance of military power. Their work was supposed to

---

99. Allchin, *Participation in God*, 25.

100. See Rack, *Reasonable Enthusiast*, 30–31. Rack helpfully sets out the basic viewpoint of deist thought.

101. See Piette, *John Wesley*, 99–100.

102. The Hapsburg's were Kings of Spain and the Austro-Hungarian Empire. Their Catholic faith ensured European allegiance to Rome through their political power.

103. Cragg, *The Church & the Age of Reason*, 18–21. Cragg usefully sums up the manner in which Louis XIV gradually whittled the toleration granted under the Edict until it was revoked.

provide a permanent territorial settlement for the Empire."[104] This treaty enshrined religious toleration.

In England, a similar situation brought about by the break from Rome under Henry VIII, and the subsequent turbulence around the faith of the monarch was finally put to rest with the Act of Settlement in 1701. The English and Scottish[105] crowns were abolished in 1649 with the execution of Charles I and were only restored after Richard Cromwell, Lord Protector in succession to Oliver Cromwell, resigned in 1660. Charles II ascended the throne and reigned until 1685.

James II, Charles' brother, was deposed in the "Glorious Revolution" of 1688. This led to the invitation to William of Orange (William III) and Queen Mary II to ascend to the throne. From the accession of Charles I onwards the monarch had been Catholic. At the Restoration in 1660, Charles II distanced himself from the advancement of the Catholic cause. James II, however, intended to return England (and Scotland) to Rome. Both William and Mary were Protestants, and with their accession, Parliament made the choice not only of monarch, but also of "state religion."

The Act of Settlement linked the crown to the Established Church and forbade the monarch, or heir to the throne from marrying a Catholic:

> every person and persons that then were, or afterwards should be reconciled to, or shall hold communion with the see or Church of Rome, or should profess the popish religion, or marry a papist, should be excluded, and are by that Act made for ever incapable to inherit, possess, or enjoy the Crown and government of this realm, and Ireland, and the dominions thereunto.[106]

Parliament enacted the Protestant succession to allow "for the happiness of the nation, and the security of our religion; and it being absolutely necessary for the safety, peace, and quiet of this realm."[107]

In England (Britain after the Act of Union of 1701), the monarchy was considerably weaker than in any European country. After the death of Queen Anne in 1714, the throne was passed to the Hanoverians. George I spoke no English and showed little interest in Britain; Parliament's as-

---

104. Monod, *The Power of Kings Monarchy and Religion in Europe, 1589–1715*, 155.

105. The thrones of England and Scotland were brought under one monarch with James I, although they remained distinct nations.

106. *The Act of Settlement*, 1701.

107. *The Act of Settlement*, 1701.

cendancy was assured. Under Charles I, the Covenanters in Scotland and the "Root and Branch" petitioners of England had been concerned to restore national fortunes by a decisive swing away from Catholicism. The king was considered "uncounselled" in Scotland, because he relied on bishops (among others) for advice.

P. K. Monod comments that Charles' coronation in Scotland in 1633 with its "perceived attachment to 'popish' ceremony"[108] caused criticism. In England, the Presbyterian signatories to the "Root and Branch" petition sought the removal of episcopacy as bishops were thought to be the cause of unrest. Monod makes plain that the movement was not merely a religious reformation, with the desire to impose a presbytery. The movement literally sought "root and branch" to reform English society. Monod writes:

> It delineated the outlines of a "government according to God's word," a godly English polity incorporating public moral regeneration along with personal discipline and just commercial values. It called for reform of everything . . . In the new English Israel, the holy was to be completely separated from the unholy.[109]

The Covenanters and "Root and Branch" petitioners were not seeking the removal of the king. Indeed, as monarch he embodied the mystical nature of the state. They wanted the nation to amend its ways, both socially and spiritually, and many Presbyterians in Parliament were looking for the king to share power with them. However, the English Civil War countenanced the unthinkable, that the king had no place in government. The Levellers who were at the forefront of this thinking, were represented in the army and looked away from Presbyterian and Anglican teaching to "sectarian" Independent preachers, often regimental preachers. The Levellers were offered hearings by Cromwell and other generals; hearings that more moderate Presbyterians were not offered. Monod is clear these conversations were by no means the only reason for the trial and execution of the king.

These were Dissenters, and Parliament's later ascendancy ensured that only Anglicans held positions of authority, and Dissenters were disadvantaged. The Act of Uniformity,[110] which placed the Prayer Book as

---

108. Monod, *The Power of Kings*, 155.

109. Ibid., 157.

110. The Act of Uniformity 1559. *1 Elizabeth, Cap 2.*

the single volume for public worship, stood beside the Test Act of 1673 which excluded Non-Juring priests from pulpits and laymen from holding office. The invitation to William and Mary in 1689 ushered in an age of religious toleration. While disadvantage remained, the earlier hunt for Catholics ended.

At the same time, the agrarian revolution changed the settled way of life for many in a rural society. The Enclosure Acts had ended generations of tenant farming. The agrarian revolution, which would fuel by labor, the industrial revolution, meant that crops and livestock were now farmed to feed a growing population which had no dependence upon the land. The small-holders who had lost their land through enclosures became waged laborers and some of them would become the personnel who would move into the developing towns, and into artisan trades. Clark asserts that amongst those joining the earliest Unitary societies were young male apprentices, displaced from rural communities and living in the emerging towns and cities.[111]

By 1715, the population of Europe stood at around 118 million. In England there were around "5.1 million in 1701, 5.8 million in 1751 and 8.7 million in 1801."[112] Population growth increased the pressure on outdated agricultural methods, and in England the new farming methods of the agrarian revolution provided sufficient food, although many were no longer working the land.

In the period to the rise of the Evangelical Revival, the religious leaders discussed earlier in this chapter were known by later generations through spiritual autobiography, and their writings on divinity. These set out Puritan Pietistic models for the conversion experience, and in the seventeenth and early eighteenth centuries, were read, according to Hindmarsh, by Dissenters and early evangelicals alike. Perkins work particularly affected later writers and readers, "the theology of conversion expounded by Perkins in the late sixteenth century had by the late seventeenth century spawned a whole literature, which was widely read by English Nonconformists well into the eighteenth century."[113] The resulting desire amongst the people was for the same or similar experience. This book will show that from the rise of the Anglican Unitary society,

---

111. Clark, *British Clubs and Societies*, 55.

112. Rack. *Reasonable Enthusiast*, 1.

113. Hindmarsh, *The Evangelical Conversion Narrative. Spiritual Autobiography in Early Modern England*, 50.

into the period of Fetter Lane and Methodism, Anglicans, Dissenters, and the "unchurched" sought out spiritual purpose to their lives.

It is therefore important to note that the rising "artisan" classes, those who were moving into the new towns, forming part of the societal change in early modern England, were not without religious or spiritual longings. The desire for seriousness, awakened by reading, was not fed by the parish system which was failing to meet growing communities, or which was unable to answer the questions raised by such reading. Hindmarsh evidences the desire for individual and communal spirituality in a study of the earliest Methodist testimonies.[114] This desire formed the bedrock on which Methodism grew. Added to the individuality which Methodism offered, was the new sense of community that membership of a society brought. "For many of the Methodists who were dislocated through employment or domestic troubles, Methodism offered the family that they missed or never had. Notwithstanding the intensely individual language in these narratives, conversion was not experienced in isolation."[115]

I have shown in this chapter how the creation of small groups as vehicles for faith development and ecclesiastical renewal spread across Europe and into Britain in the seventeenth century. Bullock traced religious societies in England to around 1678. Writing of the development of religious societies from Luther onwards, Bullock states of the English scene:

> This expectation (to find religious societies) is amply fulfilled from 1678 onwards, but before that date there is not much expression in England of the idea of an inner circle, loyal to the main body, but trying also to stimulate it to fresh life and quickened enthusiasm.[116]

The emergence of religious societies was perhaps a response to the growing number of secular societies. Clark indicates that in 1661 clubs and societies, met in both alehouses and coffee houses.[117] Their rise was encouraged as Commonwealth censorship had ceased, and society had pluralised. For Clark, the beginning of the eighteenth century saw a

---

114. Ibid., 142–56.

115. Ibid., 151.

116. Bullock, *Voluntary Religious Societies 1520–1799*, 109. (Words in brackets mine.)

117. Clark, *British Clubs and Societies 1580–1800*, 26.

marked change in societal behavior, which had previously focused on the home. As an instance he cites the emergence of Mothering Sunday, which began as a family meal on "mid Lent Sunday" and in the seventeenth century developed into Mothering Sunday.[118] Bullock contends that there was no single catalyst for the religious societies which will be discussed in detail in the next chapter, but suggests that "the root cause was the general decay of religion and the corruption of morals."[119]

Clark challenges Bullock's assumption suggesting that the rise of Catholicism, and Protestant Dissent in Britain set in process the rise of Anglican societies. Clark accepts their primary function was religious, but indicates that there was also an element of personal advancement attached to membership:

> Most of those joining were young men and apprentices for whom the attraction of the meetings was not just spiritual: according to the Scot Robert Kirk, discussions included "advice for advancing [in] trade, getting a maintenance, [and] helping the sick of their society."[120]

Young men, recently out of apprenticeship may have looked to a society such as that at the Savoy Chapel to advance their careers.[121]

In an interview the Reverend Dr. Henry Rack described the eighteenth century as a period of "clubability."[122] Peter Clark offers a detailed critique of the many clubs and societies formed between 1580 and 1800. The new "associational"[123] nature of society arose from individualization, and the emergence of clubs and societies was intended to counter this, and offer a form of religion which was not as dry as organized religion, and offered more than familial piety.

According to Clark, associations expanded because "living standards improved among the upper and middling groups of society."[124] Bullock clearly indicates that there were a large number of organizations seeking to meet felt religious needs. There were also secular clubs

---

118. Ibid., 28.
119. Bullock, *Voluntary Religious Societies*, 127.
120. Clark, *British Clubs and Societies*, 55.
121. See Appendix 1: Rule 14.
122. Interview with the Reverend Dr. Henry Rack on the 15th June 2000.
123. Clark, *British Clubs and Societies*. Clark's subtitle for the book is "*The Origins of an Associational World.*"
124. Ibid., 75–76.

and coffee houses. Some clubs began to pursue political aims; the mug-house clubs,[125] to which Whigs brought their own mugs out of which loyal toasts were drunk, and The Cocoa Tree Coffee House[126] for Tories. Clubs were not always founded for political, educational or religious aims, members of the "Ugly Face Clubs"[127] prided themselves on an ability to drink heavily and have facial oddness!

CHAPTER SUMMARY

In a rapidly changing social, political, and economic scene which had been tested by revolution and the emergence of nation states, renewal in religion, represented by the religious leaders discussed in this chapter, was a far cry from the old order existing prior to the Treaty of Westphalia of 1648, or to the death of Charles I. As theological consideration enabled religious development, men and women, liberated to think and practice religion beyond Catholicism, sought out those leaders who could assist their growth in faith.

This overview was necessary to place John and Charles Wesley into their religious, cultural, and social milieu, and their background and heritage will be reviewed in the following chapter. In the subsequent chapters of this section the emergence of Unitary societies and Fetter Lane will be charted against the backdrop of this chapter.

In the Evangelical Revolution of the eighteenth century, the associational desires of men and women were met by those religious leaders influenced by the developments of the past, who looked away from the Catholic Church toward the warm hearted, socially engaging religion of Protestantism. The Wesleyan mission evolved from this milieu, and met the needs of those who were seeking an associational life beyond their home, work, and social life.

---

125. Ibid., 73.
126. Ibid., 73.
127. Ibid., 71.

2

The Heritage of John and Charles Wesley

CONTEXT

THIS CHAPTER WILL REVIEW the life of John, and less extensively Charles Wesley, to May 1738, evaluating their inheritance within the broader framework outlined in chapter 1 and offering insight into the Wesleys' life detailed in the following chapters.

As might be expected John Wesley's family were affected by religious fractiousness in the seventeenth century. At Oxford University, John Wesley turned toward living a serious life. In his 1738 retrospective, Wesley accounts of the period from 1725,

> I executed a resolution which I was before convinced was of the utmost importance, shaking off at once all my trifling acquaintance. I began to see more and more the value of time. I applied myself closer to study. I watched more carefully against actual sins; I advised others to be religious, according to that scheme of religion by which I modelled my own life.[1]

Wesley's personal life was marked by exactitude, his reading centered on authors with whom he could only partially agree, and who did not bring him a sense of peace. The more he read and searched, the more he longed for the unattainable: Primitive Christianity. In part, this search took him to America, yet was to prove futile. Primitive Christianity was not found among the settlers of Georgia, or among the Native Americans. Finally, returning home a fugitive, he searched out Peter Böhler, became active in the fledgling Fetter Lane Society, and preached in several Unitary societies. On the 24th May 1738 in the heated surroundings of Aldersgate Street, Wesley received a sense of assurance,

---

1. Wesley, *Works [BE]*, Vol. 18, 244.

while listening to Luther's Preface to Romans, which W. R. Ward asserts "became almost obligatory for approved conversion in the later Pietist movement."[2]

In what sense this was Wesley "coming home" from a long journey of 13 years cannot be assessed without an understanding of the journey to 1738.

THE FAMILY HOME LIFE

Samuel and Susanna Wesley, in their adult lives Anglican high Tories, came from Dissenting families. Samuel's father, the Reverend John Westley[3] had been ejected from his living in 1662 as he refused to accept the Act of Uniformity. He died in 1670 while minister "of a 'gathered church' in Poole".[4] Susanna's father, Samuel Annesley was a Presbyterian minister in Spitalfields London until his death in 1696. Robert Monk states Dr. Annesley was, "one of the most eminent of the later Puritan Nonconformists."[5]

Samuel Wesley was educated in two Dissenting Academies, although he later wrote a scathing attack on them in his *Letter from a Country Divine* in 1703. He received the living of Epworth (a Crown living) through the offices of his patron, the Marquis of Normanby, later the Duke of Buckingham. This patronage would exist until his death in 1735 as the Dowager Duchess of Buckingham appointed Samuel her chaplain in 1721.[6] This previously unknown appointment was discovered at the Lambeth Palace Archives. For Samuel Wesley patronage did not bring further advancement,[7] neither did it prevent near penury in the Wesley Rectory.[8]

---

2. Ward, *Christianity under the Ancien Régime 1648–1789*, 74.
3. See Lee, "John Westley," 314–17.
4. Monk, *John Wesley: His Puritan Inheritance*, 20.
5. Ibid., 20. For a fuller account of Dr. Annesley's life and ministry see 20–21. See also Stephen, "Samuel Annesley," 7–9.
6. Lambeth Palace Library. *Noblemen's Chaplain's*. Catharine, Dowager Duchess was the third wife of the Duke who died in 1721.
7. He had been suggested to the Archbishop of Canterbury for an Irish bishopric in 1694, but this was not furthered.
8. Samuel Wesley was jailed for debt in 1705 See Rack, *Reasonable Enthusiast*, 46. See also 49.

This Puritan heritage offered to these converts to high Tory Anglicanism a background of Pietst teaching and influence. Monk and Ward, while cautious of this influence, accept that to be educated within a Dissenting Academy, or to be raised in a Puritan household, will leave certain "marks." Rack cites that Susanna's piety in particular was significant for the upbringing of her children, and that Samuel Wesley's dying words as to the "inward witness" are signs of that heritage breaking through.

Samuel and Susanna raised between 17 and 19 children, of whom Samuel Jr. was the eldest (10th February 1690) John was the second (17th June 1703),[9] and Charles (18th December 1707)[10] the third surviving sons.[11] It is almost folklore that John Wesley was born as the result of a reunion between Samuel and Susanna Wesley following the death of William III and accession of Queen Anne.[12] The cause of the Wesleys' separation was the refusal of Susanna to say "amen" after the prayer for the King, William III of the House of Orange.

Susanna took responsibility for the family's education, and her thoughts upon raising children are contained in a letter written to John in 1732. Charles Wallace comments:

> Dealing with the household regimen and the early education of her ten children who survived infancy, it has become something of a classic statement of evangelical child-rearing practices.[13]

Wallace notes that Susanna, like many Puritan and Anglican parents, educated her children. What are perhaps extraordinary are the clear references and "resonances"[14] through her writings to the works of the philosopher John Locke.[15] Wallace concludes that this mixture of ideas

---

9. Old style

10. Old style. See Baker, "The Birth of Charles Wesley," 25–26. Baker's article put to rest any question about the date of Charles' birth. However, Charles' birth continues to be reported as a mystery: See Gill, *Charles Wesley The First Methodist*, 17. See also Wiseman, *Charles Wesley Evangelist and Poet*, 17.

11. See Wesley, *Susanna Wesley. The Complete Writings*, 8. Wallace reproduces a table of the Wesley family completed by Frank Baker.

12. See Rack, *Reasonable Enthusiast*, 48–49.

13. Wesley, *Susanna Wesley*, 367. Introductory comments to "On Educating my Family."

14. Ibid., 368. Introductory comments to "On Educating my Family."

15. Locke wrote *Essay Concerning Human Understanding* and *Some Thoughts Concerning Education*

and ideals led to "the remarkable children of the Epworth rectory and that illustrates the zeal with which Susanna Wesley pursued an educational vocation within the bounds of contemporary social constraints."[16] The hallmarks of Susanna's educational style might be summed up as: fearing the rod and crying softly; regular and disciplined hours; conquering the will; learning the Lord's Prayer and other catechisms; learning to read from five years; beatings only when required.[17]

Three major events stood out in the Wesleys' upbringing, the Epworth religious society discussed in the next chapter; the fire in the rectory in 1709, and the Evening Prayers Controversy.

Susanna Wesley's account of the Epworth fire states that the reason for it was unknown, although John Wesley attributed the cause to wicked parishioners. Samuel escaped the fire through the front of the rectory, Susanna through the back. John was in the house in an upstairs bedroom. As fire swept through the house, Samuel began to pray, as there seemed no escape for his son. Villagers rescued John from the window just before the roof fell in.[18] The family lost all their possessions.[19]

John's parents considered his rescue providential, and Susanna noted she would be "more particularly careful of the soul of this child that thou hast so mercifully provided for, than I have ever been, that I may do my endeavours to instil into his mind the disciplines of thy religion and virtue."[20]

Rack[21] and Heitzenrater[22] assert that around 1737 Wesley took for himself the term "a brand plucked from the burning," resonant of the providence of God in his life. He certainly used phrases reminiscent of

---

16. Wesley, *Susanna Wesley*, 368. Introductory comments to "On Educating my Family."

17. Ibid., 369–73. Susanna sets out what might be termed a rigorous, yet comprehensive education system for all her children.

18. Wesley, *Susanna Wesley*, 65–66. Susanna recounted the events of the night to Samuel, her eldest son at school in Westminster. Letter dated 14th February 1708/09. See also the letter to the Reverend Joseph Hoole, vicar of Haxey, 66–68. Letter dated 24th August 1709.

19. Wallace, *Susanna Wesley*, 11–12. See Charles Wallace's "Introduction" to the volume.

20. Rack, *Reasonable Enthusiast*, 57. Rack is quoting an entry from a meditation written by Susanna Wesley in 1711

21. See Rack, *Reasonable Enthusiast*, 57.

22. Heitzenrater, *The Elusive Mr. Wesley*, 44.

this term, if not exact in wording.[23] The exact phrase was used by Wesley in his epitaph, published following an illness in 1753.[24] Others used this same term of their salvation, as I will show in other parts of this study.[25] Henry Rack believes this was used to effect by John Wesley in his *Journal* and other writings:

> Like many evangelicals he could see the finger of God acting in apparent accidents to preserve them to the day of conversion, though this is not the same as a sense of calling to a particular work.[26]

Richard Heitzenrater has a stronger opinion of the effect of the fire on John Wesley. In *The Elusive Mr. Wesley*, Heitzenrater reproduces a 1742 engraving of Wesley containing a vignette drawing of the Epworth fire. The notes to the engraving are telling, "The embellishments on this 1742 engraving . . . include a vignette . . . an image that became fixed in Wesley's self-consciousness."[27]

During Samuel Wesley's absence at Convocation in London, in the winter of 1711–1712, Susanna began a Sunday meeting, immortalized as "The Evening Prayers Controversy." While Samuel was away, a curate, the Reverend Mr. Inman was employed to take the parish services. Inman was unpopular, evidenced by poor Church attendance. Susanna wrote to Samuel, "We used not to have above twenty or twenty five at evening service."[28] Susanna's meeting attracted substantially more, "we

---

23. See Wesley, *Works [BE]*, Vol. 18, 482. "So I was once more 'snatched as a brand out of the fire.' " (Entry for 7th March 1737.) See also Wesley, *Works [BE]*, Vol 18, 213. "May I praise him who hath snatched me out of this fire likewise, by warning all others that is set on fire of hell." (Entry for Jan 25th 1738.)

24. See Wesley, *Works [BE]*, Vol. 20, 482. "Here lieth the Body of John Wesley. A Brand Plucked out of the burning." (Entry for 26th November 1753.)

25. Margaret Austin, in *Early Methodist Volume*, 19th May 1740, 1. Catherine Gilbert, in *Early Methodist Volume*, 1740, 6. See also Olivers, "The Life of Thomas Olivers," 55–56. Olivers was converted after hearing George Whitefield preach on the text "Is this not a brand plucked out of the fire?" 55. See also Valton, "The Life of John Valton," 30. This entry dated the 1st January 1765 is a review of his spiritual life over the previous twelve months.

26. Rack, *Reasonable Enthusiast*, 57.

27. Heitzenrater, *The Elusive Mr. Wesley: John Wesley His Own Biographer. Volume I*, 41.

28. Wesley, *Susanna Wesley*, 82. Letter to Samuel Wesley Sr., 25th February 1711/12.

have between two and three hundred, which is more than ever came to hear Inman in the morning."²⁹

The reading of family prayers on Sunday evenings, supplemented the time Susanna spent with each of her children during the week. Wallace comments, "Such a practice, which involved reading prayers and a sermon and discussing devotional topics, would not have been exceptional had it remained within the family."³⁰ When these evening prayers became popular amongst Epworth residents, Inman wrote to Samuel Wesley, and Samuel to Susanna.

Initially Susanna deals with Samuel's concerns that she is creating a "particular" group, that she is a woman, and that she is leading prayers not only with her children, but also with neighbors. Her response to the charge that she was a woman is unique. Rack writes: "Though she had some qualms about leading, being a mere woman, she really did not care if people thought it scandalous, for 'I have long since shook hands with the world.'"³¹ Susanna took her role seriously:

> With those few neighbours who then came to me I discoursed more freely and affectionately than before. I chose the best and most awakening sermons we had and I spent more time with them in such exercises. Since this our company has increased every night, for I dare deny none that asks admittance. Last Sunday I believe we had above two hundred.³²

Susanna was accused of creating a Conventicle. Her response is determined, a foretaste of her son's later defiance:

> Do you think that what they say is sufficient reason for forbearing a thing that hath already done much, and by God's blessing may do more good? . . . 'tis plain fact that this one thing has brought more people to church than ever anything did in so short a time.³³

Susanna refused to dissolve the meeting without Samuel's instruction: "Send me your positive command in such full express terms as may

---

29. Ibid., 82. Letter to Samuel Wesley Sr., 25th February 1711/12.

30. Ibid., 78. Charles Wallace's introductory comments to "The Evening Prayers Controversy."

31. Rack, *Reasonable Enthusiast*, 54.

32. Wesley, *Susanna Wesley*, 80. Letter to Samuel Wesley Sr., 6th February 1711/12.

33. Ibid., 82. Letter to Samuel Wesley Sr., 25th February 1711/12.

absolve me from all guilt and punishment for neglecting the opportunity to doing good to souls."[34]

Rack comments that Susanna, like John later, experimented with a structure beyond the accepted norm and continued with it if people were positively influenced: "Societary experiments identified a class of pious people not touched by the ordinary church routine, and Susanna, like her son later, showed that she had few inhibitions about formal restrictions if she thought souls were at stake."[35]

FROM THE FAMILY HOME TO OXFORD

John attended Charterhouse school from 1714 and went up to Christ Church, Oxford in 1720. He received his Bachelor of Arts degree in 1724 and in 1725 began studying for the priesthood, the point at which he was drawn toward expressing his faith in practical piety:

> Wesley's search during this period (*University*) for a meaningful understanding of the demands of Christian living eventually led him to tie together the perfectionism of the Pietists, the moralism of the Puritans, and the emotionalism of the mystics, which he felt could operate within the structure and doctrine of the Church of England.[36]

Holy living was not easy for John Wesley. Reminiscing in his *Journal* on the 24th May 1738, he reflected that even though he was from a devout family, he had no personal sense of faith:

> Being removed to the University for five years, I still said my prayers, both in public and in private, and read, with the Scriptures, several other books of religion, especially comments on the New Testament. Yet I had not all this while so much as a notion of inward holiness.[37]

As Wesley began formal ordination studies, his personal practice began to change. He was encouraged in 1725 to read Thomas à Kempis' *Christian Pattern* by Sally Kirkham known in correspondence as *Varanese*. While Wesley considered à Kempis "too strict"[38] he under-

---

34. Ibid., 82. Letter to Samuel Wesley Sr., 25th February 1711/12.
35. Rack, *Reasonable Enthusiast*, 54.
36. Heitzenrater, *Wesley and the People Called Methodists*, 31. (Word in italics mine.)
37. Wesley, *Works [BE]*, Vol. 18, 243.
38. Ibid.

stood religion was a state of being, as well as an exercise of living. Wesley wrote to his mother: "I think he must have been a person of great piety and devotion, but it is my misfortune to differ from him in some of his main points."[39] Wesley began to change his lifestyle:

> I began to alter the whole form of my conversation, and to set in earnest upon *a new life*. I set apart an hour or two a day for religious retirement. I communicated every week. I watched against all sin, whether in word or deed. I began to aim at, and pray for, inward holiness. So that *now doing so much, and living a good life* I doubted not but I was a good Christian.[40]

According to Bob Tuttle's[41] "quasi autobiography" of Wesley, Sally Kirkham also suggested Bishop Jeremy Taylor's *Holy Living* and *Holy Dying*: "I have heard one I take to be a person of good judgement say that she would advise no one very young to read Dr. Taylor *Of Living and Dying*: She added that he almost put her out of her senses when she was fifteen or sixteen year old."[42] Taylor led Wesley to begin a spiritual *Diary*, a practice from the Puritan exercise of godliness:

> It was in pursuance of an advice given by Bp. *Taylor*, in his *Rules for Holy Living and Dying*, that about fifteen years ago, I began to take a more exact account that I had done before, of the manner wherein I spent my time, writing down how I had employed every hour.[43]

Writing to John Newton in 1765 on the issue of perfection Wesley said, "In 1725, I met with Bishop Taylor's *Rules of Holy Living and Dying*. I was struck particularly with the chapter upon *intention*, and felt a fixed intention "to give myself up to God." In this I was much confirmed soon after by the *Christian Pattern (à Kempis)*, and longed to *give God all my heart*.[44]" He also refers to William Law whose *Christian Perfection* and *A Serious Call to a Devout and Holy Life* he read in 1727. As a result he decided to be, "more explicitly resolved to be *all devoted to God*, in

---

39. Ibid., 16.
40. Ibid., 244.
41. Tuttle, *John Wesley His Life and Theology*.
42. Wesley, *Letters [SE]*, Vol. I, 19.
43. Wesley, *Works [BE]*, Vol. 18, 121.
44. Wesley, *Letters [SE]*, Vol. IV, 298–99. (Name italicised in brackets mine.)

body, soul, and spirit."⁴⁵ Bebbington suggests that the foundations which Taylor laid for Wesley were anything but secure: "Sincerity, good works and the contempt of the world remained the rather sandy foundations for his hope of salvation."⁴⁶ This is insightful, as Wesley remained constantly unsure of his salvation prior to May 1738.

In *A Plain Account of Christian Perfection* of 1766, Wesley suggests that he was reading William Law before 1730: "A year or two after (*1726*), Mr Law's *Christian Perfection* and *Serious Call* were put into my hands,"⁴⁷ but Rack urges caution in accepting Wesley's recollection:

> The reading of William Law came after these (*Taylor and à Kempis*), and much later than Wesley implied in his later accounts. He probably began reading the *Serious Call* at the end of 1730 and *Christian Perfection* after meeting Law himself in 1732.⁴⁸

From his father, John Wesley was aware of the Catholic mystic Marquis de Renty, whose biography had been written by Saint-Jure. Wesley began to abridge de Renty's *Life* on the journey home from Georgia in 1738. Orcibal comments that Wesley refers to no other person with such regularity: "His letters are constantly filled with allusions to the noble simplicity of his actions and the extraordinary intimacy of the union with God which this layman enjoyed."⁴⁹

Wesley's reading opened to him a "pietist mysticism" which encouraged him to lead a serious life by recording his every action and feeling. His regard for mystical teaching was expressed in his quest for spiritual experience and perfection. In this, Wesley was reaching back into the experience of the Puritans discussed in chapter 1, who in search of holiness, came to an inward, even introverted, spiritual journey.

Wesley scholars have placed great emphasis on Wesley's formative reading, but Rack believes Wesley assimilated the detail which affected him, and in his own abridgments left out that with which he disagreed: "His selection was conditioned and his interpretations coloured by his own needs and experiences, and those of his followers. They become

---

45. Ibid., 299.

46. Bebbington, *Evangelicalism in Modern Britain. A history from the 1730s to the 1980s*, 49.

47. Wesley, *A Plain Account of Christian Perfection*, 6. (Date in italics mine.)

48. Rack, *Reasonable Enthusiast*, 73.

49. Orcibal, "The Theological Originality of John Wesley and Continental Spirituality," 90.

part of his own synthesis of piety and are very much eighteenth-century documents."⁵⁰

Wesley's assimilation is seen in a letter to his mother: "Two things in Bishop Taylor I have been often thinking of since I writ last; one of which I like exceedingly, and the other not."⁵¹ Wesley expurgated from his reading any theology, doctrine or comment with which he did not agree. Wesley's behavior was reminiscent of Pietists and Puritans of the seventeenth century. Like them, he was creating his own synthesized doctrine, suitable to his temperament and spiritual journey.

In *A Plain Account* Wesley refers to his 1733 sermon, *the Circumcision of the Heart* as the place where his understanding of Christian living was first published. In the sermon, he gave an account of the circumcision thus:

> It is that habitual disposition of soul, which in the sacred writings is termed holiness, and which directly implies the being cleansed from sin; from all filthiness both of flesh and spirit; and, by consequence, the being endued with those virtues which were in Christ Jesus; the being so "renewed in the image of our mind" as to be "perfect as our Father in heaven is perfect."⁵²

Once again, Rack urges caution: "If this is a true account of Wesley's ideals at the time . . . contemporary evidence shows considerable uncertainties about the means of achieving it."⁵³ Heitzenrater believes the sermon "was a pivotal document in the development of the Wesleyan movement."⁵⁴ He writes that the sermon outlines the basis upon which Wesley was attempting to create a Christian lifestyle. It is interesting that Heitzenrater writes:

> Contrary to the impression carried by many of his contemporaries and perpetuated by subsequent analysts, Wesley's life style . . . was neither circumscribed by negative injunctions nor impelled primarily by a set of prescriptive rules. Lists of questions for self-examination guided their actions.⁵⁵

---

50. Rack, *Reasonable Enthusiast*, 97–98.
51. Wesley, *Works [BE]*, Vol. 25, 244.
52. Wesley, *A Plain Account*, 7.
53. Rack, *Reasonable Enthusiast*, 96.
54. Heitzenrater, *Wesley and the People Called Methodists*, 47.
55. Ibid.

Neither Rack nor Heitzenrater is wholly correct. Rack cites Wesley's use of increasingly complex lists and scales to assist his argument that Wesley was not privy to the state of perfection about which he preached: "His private discipline gradually became more complex, intense and obsessive."[56] Heitzenrater notes that the Christian perfection explained in the sermon would become "the distinctive hallmark of Methodist theology in the eighteenth century, but also act as a compass for his own lifelong spiritual pilgrimage."[57]

Wesley was at best uncertain of his salvation, and the means to work it out. Written with hindsight, it is much easier to express memories positively. Both opinions, taken together, offer a fuller picture. Wesley had not, in 1733, fully worked through the "Methodist" interpretation of perfection, but he was seeking perfection for himself. He was racked with self-doubt about his own state, yet nonetheless preached perfection. By 1733 he had come to understand a doctrine of Christian perfection that was to remain with him through his life, and which was to influence the classes and bands. In 1746, when the sermon was first published, Wesley inserted a paragraph relating the vitality of the relationship between the Christian and Christ, brought about by the Holy Spirit in the process of conversion. This addition, inserted after Wesley's 1738 heart-warming moment, details theologically a relationship Wesley could by then write about from personal experience.[58] It was this relationship that was the driving force behind the quest for perfection that Wesley had preached about in 1733.

From 1732 Wesley was influenced by the mystics, introduced to him by John Clayton[59] and William Law. The mystics stressed the need for an inward communion with God. Already aware of de Renty, Wesley was introduced to Tauler, Molinos, the *Theologia Germanica*, Madame Guyon, Antoinette Bourignon, and Fénelon. Wesley immersed himself in their writings and shared their "concern for holy living."[60]

The result of this reading was an even more exact *Diary* that detailed every moment of the day. Reviewing the *Diary* served to wipe away

---

56. Rack, *Reasonable Enthusiast*, 95.

57. Heitzenrater, *Wesley and the People Called Methodists*, 48.

58. See Wesley, *Forty-Four Sermons*, 155.

59. John Clayton was an ordained Anglican and Non-Juror. See Vickers, "Clayton, Rev. John," 70.

60. Heitzenrater, *Wesley and the People Called Methodists*, 52.

the little assurance that Wesley had. He later charged the mystics with almost causing him to lose his faith.[61] Bob Tuttle, in his paraphrase of Wesley's *Journal* suggests that mysticism affected the young Methodists: "Our entire "company" developed an interest in the ascetical aloofness of mysticism."[62] Tuttle refers to Wesley's letter to Mary Bishop of 1774 to assist his assertion. In the letter Wesley wrote: "Most of our little flock at Oxford were tried with this, my brother and I in particular."[63] The combination of mysticism, which urged separation from the world, and practical piety that engaged with those in need, must have caused confusion in Wesley's mind, life and practice. However, the Holy Club, with the variety of personalities and Christian understanding that it contained may well have prevented Wesley from complete introversion.

Although Rack urges caution in accepting Wesley's recollection, there is no doubt that this period was significant to Wesley's spiritual development. Maldwyn Edwards comments: "All these writers created a want they could not satisfy. Strongly as Maximin Piette may speak of Wesley's moral conversion in 1725, it could not and did not supply the dynamic which came through his evangelical conversion of 1738."[64] Similarly, Orcibal notes the change. "Until 1725 he was only lukewarm, but then he realized the impossibility of being "half a Christian" and the necessity—in the world just as much as in the monastery—of consecrating "one's whole heart and one's whole life to God."[65]

Both Edwards and Orcibal refer to 1725 as Wesley's "first conversion," and while this did not lead him to the fields to preach, it did bring sharply into focus his need for a change of lifestyle. The authors he read, and his reflection on them, provided him with the first stages of the theology and practice he was to hold and teach after his conversion. From 1725 Pietsm, perfection, and personal experience marked a succession of changes in Wesley's religious life and understanding. Heitzenrater notes that during this period of Wesley's life "the demands of Christian

---

61. Wesley, *Works [BE]*, Vol. 25, 487. In a letter to his elder brother Wesley wrote, "I think the rock on which I had the nearest made shipwreck of the faith was in the writings of the mystics"

62. Tuttle Jr., *John Wesley*, 122.

63. Wesley, *Letters [SE]*, 128.

64. Edwards, "John Wesley," 43.

65. Orcibal, "The Theological Originality of John Wesley and Continental Spirituality," 89.

living eventually led him to tie together the perfectionism of the Pietsts, the moralism of the Puritans, and the devotionalism of the mystics in a pragmatic approach that he felt he could operate within the structure and doctrine of the Church of England."[66]

The first "Methodist" group was formed in Oxford, but it was Charles, who had gone up to Oxford in 1726, who began the Holy Club. By that time, John, ordained deacon and Master of Arts and Fellow of Lincoln College, had become curate to his father at Wroot near Epworth.

In 1729 Charles asked his brother how he might be serious in religion: "If you would direct me to the same, or a like method with your own, I would gladly follow it."[67] Charles Wesley was already meeting with a colleague for study and weekly church attendance when John returned to Oxford. From the middle of June 1729, Charles met with John, William Morgan and occasionally Robert Kirkham. Heitzenrater comments, "The little band of friends, encouraged by the presence of John, occasionally met together for study, prayer, and religious conversation, attended the sacrament regularly, and kept track of their lives by daily notations in a *Diary*."[68]

In reality, while the group first met in the summer of 1729, it was not until the winter, when John took up his fellowship at Lincoln College as tutor to eleven paying students that the Holy Club met regularly. John's *Diary* records the rooms in which the group met through the week, and study included classics on weekdays and divinity on Sundays. The group observed the fasts of the early Church, confession, penance, and mortification, and attended to the means of grace: prayer, Bible study, communion, and fellowship. Wesley received communion at every opportunity;

> He communed every week if possible (a rarity in his day), and often communed daily in the octave of Easter and the twelve festival days of Christmas. As a result he averaged communing about once every five days through his adult life.[69]

During the early part of 1730 this small group was merely one of a number of groups in Oxford, and although the Holy Club remained a

---

66. Heitzenrater, *Wesley and the People Called Methodists*, 31.
67. Ibid., 38.
68. Ibid.
69. Maddox, *Responsible Grace. John Wesley's Practical Theology*, 202.

small gathering throughout its five-year life, it was the events of August 1730, when the Holy Club took up practical piety that set Wesley and his friends apart from any other group. Wesley may have rejected the label "pietist" but his understanding and social action reflected Pietst intentions. If he was not then aware of the social Pietsm of Halle, his actions belied that lack of knowledge. Through the influence of William Morgan, Wesley began work amongst groups singled out by Pietsts as needful: prisoners, the poor, the uneducated, and the sick.

Around the time Morgan took Wesley to the prisons of Oxford, he resolved to hold the Bible as his rule for living. In 1765 he reminisced that in 1730,

> I began to be *homo unius libri*; to study (comparatively) no book but the Bible. I then saw in a stronger light than ever before, that only one thing is needful, even faith that worketh by the love of God and man, all inward and outward holiness; and I groaned to love God with all my heart, and to serve Him with all my strength.[70]

Heitzenrater and Rack make nothing of this statement, yet surely this has to be an important milestone in Wesley's life? If he did place himself entirely under the authority of the Bible then his whole life came to be scrutinized in relation to Scripture itself. Gregory Clapper does pick up on this statement and aims to show that Wesley's understanding of Scripture was grounded in his parents' Dissenting background, but arose too from his regard of it.[71]

Clapper evidences his point by considering Wesley's abridgments of Jonathan Edwards' *Treatise on Religious Affairs*. Clapper agrees with Baker that Wesley's method of dealing with a "dangerous" book "was by publishing an expurgated version of it."[72] But that is not the whole picture. Wesley did not disagree entirely with Edwards. Rather, those elements that Wesley did not hold to be true to Scripture, especially Edwards' Calvinism, he expunged from the abridgment. Although Wesley was opposed to Calvinism,[73] he found aspects of Edwards' work which, in the light of his understanding of Scripture, were worthy of publication.

---

70. Wesley, *Letters [SE]*, Vol. IV, 299.
71. Clapper, *John Wesley on Religious Affections*.
72. Ibid., 139.
73. Ibid., 142.

In the sermon *On God's Vineyard*,[74] Wesley offers an apologia for the Holy Club's turn to Scripture as the sole source of authority, setting out the manner in which Scripture was used. "They had one, and only one, rule of judgement with regard to all their tempers, words, and actions; namely the oracles of God."[75] The decision made individually by Wesley, and corporately by the Holy Club led to derision.[76] Further, the sermon sets out how Scripture was the driving force behind the Methodist people, and the organization of Methodism itself. Here as elsewhere the primary source for this change is Wesley's own memory, but this sermon, and the letter of 1765 adduces evidence for accepting that the Bible became his primary authority. In Wesley's later life, as will be seen by his use of Scripture after speaking with Böhler about assurance in 1738, all matters were subject to the rule of Scripture, and there is no reason to doubt that in 1730, Wesley made another important decision as to the government and rule of his life and practice.

Wesley and his companions first visited the Castle prison for debtors and condemned prisoners, at William Morgan's request on the 24th August 1730. They also took up Morgan's practice of visiting the poor and elderly. Later the same year, visits to the prison at the North Gate of the city began, and the children of poor families were brought together for education.

Maldwyn Edwards succinctly captures the work of these eager men:

> In its five-years of active life the Oxford Methodists observed a remarkably disciplined personal life, and at the same time they visited the prisoners in the castle jail and the debtors in the Bocardo. Under John Wesley's direct guidance they strove to maintain a school for children, and organized visiting and relief of the poor. Food, clothes and physic were found for the poor both in St Thomas's workhouse and in the city.[77]

---

74. Wesley, *Works [BE]*, Vol. 1, 502–17. See also Wesley, *Works [BE]*, Vol. 1, 105. In the introduction to the 1746 edition of the *Sermons*, Wesley wrote, "God himself has condescended to teach the way; for this very end he came from heaven. He hath written it down in a book. O give me that book! At any price give me the book of God! I have it. Here is knowledge enough for me. Let me be *Homo Unius Libri*."

75. Wesley, *Works [BE]*, Vol. 1, 504.

76. Ibid., 505.

77. Edwards, "John Wesley," in *A History of the Methodist Church in Great Britain*, Vol. 1, 44.

While Wesley's organizational ability was responsible for a great deal of the Oxford work after August 1730, William Morgan was engaged in social action before then, and he encouraged the Holy Club to join him. Wesley attributed the first stirrings of this social enterprise to William Morgan and Samuel Wesley wanted to "adopt" William Morgan for introducing his sons to the work, "I think I must adopt Mr. Morgan to be my son, together with you and your brother Charles."[78]

To assist their work, it appears that sympathetic supporters were encouraged to help financially. "Several we met with who increased our little stock of money for the prisoners and the poor by subscribing something quarterly to it."[79] Edwards adds that social action amongst the prisoners and needy of Oxford prevented introversion. Although almost persuaded to refrain from "practical holiness," Wesley's natural eagerness and his father's encouragement meant he continued the work. Edwards comments, "The Holy Club therefore preserved Wesley from the worst effects of a too-introverted mysticism. It encouraged the practice of the Christian ordinances as well as the expression of Christian doctrine in social action."[80] Edwards concludes, "What was then joined together he never afterwards put asunder."[81]

At Oxford much of Wesley's doctrine was formulated and refined. Eventually, he moved away from the mystics but never wholly abandoned their spirituality. Wesley mixed his understanding of perfection and scriptural holiness, and the personal and practical out workings of piety, with the use of the means of grace and social action to live and expresss his faith.

Heitzenrater considers Wesley to be close to the momentous event of Aldersgate Street, even as a working Fellow of Lincoln College, but needed, "to go through the Oxford experiment."[82] Rack contends that the experience of Oxford was deeper than Heitzenrater allows. Oxford was necessary for Wesley's future direction. Much that Wesley accepted and came to teach could only have been formulated from the opportunity Oxford afforded to read and engage in social outreach.

---

78. Wesley, *Works [BE]*, Vol. 18, 125.
79. Ibid., 129.
80. Edwards, "John Wesley," 46.
81. Ibid.
82. Rack, *Reasonable Enthusiast*, 104.

1725 and beyond was part of Wesley's process of Christian conversion. Instantaneous conversion is possible and while Wesley would meet many who professed this, for the majority of people conversion is a process. John Finney's study on the way people come to faith shows that it is frequently a gradual process:

> On average 31% said their experience was "dateable," and 69% said it was gradual. Even among the New Churches sudden conversions rose to only just over a half of their new members . . . The gradual experience was said to take anything from one day to 42 years, though many people saw it as an ongoing process which had not yet finished.[83]

Wesley experienced nothing more or less unusual than others experience. His decision of 1725 to live a more devout life cannot be set aside in favor of the single moment in 1738. In the cloistered environment of an Oxford college, Wesley was able to work out spiritually and practically many of the issues which he faced in his quest for salvation and assurance.

The experience of the Holy Club, Wesley's first taste of leadership, would not have been available in a parish. Likewise, for many in the Methodist classes of the eighteenth century, the first experience of being in a position of authority is a benefit that cannot be overestimated. Graham Dale's biographical studies of early labor leaders evinces how they first learned to articulate thought and plan activities through the leading of small groups.[84]

At Oxford, as student and don, Wesley searched for a personal experience of Christ, which he attempted to fathom for himself through a variety of spiritualities expressed in personal piety and its social outworking, regular attendance at the ordinances and use of the means of grace.

MISSIONARY TO GEORGIA

John Wesley's decision to travel to Georgia under the patronage of the *Society for the Propagation of the Gospel* (SPG) was twofold. First, it cleared away any remaining pressure to take the Epworth living and fulfilled an ambition that Samuel Wesley had expressed to serve in the colo-

---

83. Finney, *Finding Faith Today*, 24.
84. Dale, *God's Politicians*.

nies. Second, Wesley embarked on another stage of his spiritual quest for inward holiness and perfection, searching for primitive Christianity.

Before his father's death, pressure was brought on John Wesley by his elder brother Samuel and his father to take the Epworth living. In 1733, he declined, writing: "You observed when I was with you that I was very indifferent as to having or not having Epworth living. I was, indeed, utterly unable to determine either way."[85] In December 1734, Wesley wrote to his father, outlining in 26 numbered paragraphs arguments for and against taking the living. The letter is a mixture of argument and theological treatise. Wesley even argued against the living because he might not be loved: "If you say "the love of the people of Epworth to me may balance all these advantages," I ask, How long will it last?"[86]

Samuel Jr. refused the living, but tried to get his younger brother to accept the appointment. Telford states: "Samuel Wesley's strength was failing, and he was anxious about his family and his parish. He wanted his eldest son to succeed him; but he declined to leave his schoolmaster's life."[87] Samuel Jr. had argued that the very nature of his brother's ordination obliged him to accept a parish. "The continuing exchange of letters led John to note in his *Diary* at the end of February 1735, "almost convinced to go to Epworth.""[88]

John's somewhat ill-tempered replies to Samuel ended after Bishop Potter confirmed Wesley's view that parish life was not compulsory. Wesley quoted the bishop to his brother:

> REVD. SIR–It doth not seem to me that at your ordination you engaged yourself to undertake the cure of any parish, provided you can, as a clergyman, better serve God and His Church in your present or some other station.[89]

Wesley ends triumphantly: "Now, that I can as a clergyman better serve God and His Church in my present station I have all reasonable evidence."[90] As his father lay dying Wesley finally agreed to see whether he could assume the living. He engaged Sir John Phillips, who knew

---

85. Wesley, *Works [BE]*, Vol. 25, 348.
86. Wesley, *Letters [SE]*, Vol. I, 174. See also Wesley, *Works [BE]*, Vol. 19, 43.
87. Ibid., 133.
88. Heitzenrater, *Wesley and the People Called Methodists*, 55.
89. Wesley, *Works [BE]*, Vol. 25, 421.
90. Ibid.

the Bishop of London. Sir John declined to interfere and the matter was settled.

Once Epworth was closed to Wesley, he was free to continue his life as an Oxford Fellow. However, having refused his father's wish, the alternative to parochial life was that of a missionary, and Samuel Wesley had indicated that he would have been willing to become a missionary in a letter written to General James Oglethorpe in the autumn prior to Samuel's death.[91]

Heitzenrater captures the events that led to Wesley's offer of working in Georgia well:

> While in London to assist Charles Rivington in the final stages of publication (*his father's book on Job*), Wesley was contacted by John Burton about the possibility of him and his friends going to Georgia, the new colony about which Samuel Wesley had written Oglethorpe the previous fall, "had it been but ten years ago, I would gladly have devoted the remainder of my life and labours to that place" (Memorials, 142). Here then was an alternative to the Epworth living that would still provide a chance for Wesley to fulfill his father's dreams.[92]

Susanna Wesley responded favorably to her son's suggestion to travel to Georgia: "Had I twenty sons, I should rejoice that they were all so employed, though I should never see them more."[93]

Wesley's decision to travel was fuelled by his continuing spiritual quest. Rack remarks that as Wesley's spiritual life at Oxford was not progressing as it might, Georgia seemed an appropriate place to begin again: "In an idealized wilderness he would revert to a spiritual state of nature and start primitive Christianity all over again."[94]

Wesley was deeply influenced by the Non-Jurors and High Church ideals of John Clayton and Thomas Deacon, who proposed that apostolic and patristic patterns of worship, from the first five centuries, were "authentic Christianity." These patterns included instructions for devotions and discipline. Allied to his reading of the mystics, Wesley struggled

---

91. Stevenson, *Memorials of the Wesley Family*, 142.

92. Heitzenrater, *Wesley and the People Called Methodists*, 56. (Words in italics mine.)

93. Ibid., 57. Heitzenrater takes this quote from Volume 1 of Henry Moore's *The Life of the Rev. John Wesley*, in 2 Volumes published by John Kershaw in 1824.

94. Rack, *Reasonable Enthusiast*, 111.

with his spiritual life and Georgia might have seemed the place where any tensions could resolve themselves. Georgia became:

> an experiment in "primitive Christianity," and that in more than one sense. It was a way of starting all over again in a virgin land with the prospect also of creating Christians from scratch so far as the Indians were concerned.[95]

It was in Methodism, still some five years away from 1735, that Wesley considered he had "found" primitive Christianity. Forty-two years later, at the laying of the foundation for City Road Chapel in 1777, he declared: "Methodism, so called, is the old religion, the religion of the Bible, the religion of the primitive church, the religion of the Church of England."[96]

In correspondence with John Burton,[97] Wesley wrote: "My chief motive, to which all the rest are subordinate, is the hope of saving my own soul."[98] This reversed Burton's perception of Wesley's purpose for traveling to Georgia. He understood Wesley was traveling for "the desire of doing good to the souls of others, and in consequence of that, to your own."[99] The full text of the letter to Burton shows Wesley hoping to escape England, find faith, and employ that for the benefit of others: "A right faith, will I trust, by the mercy of God, open the way for a right practice; especially when most of those temptations are removed which here so easily beset me."[100]

Henry Rack disapproves of Wesley's air of superiority toward Burton, and holds that he should have been more accepting of Burton's advice: "It was in response to this moderating advice that Wesley adopted his high apostolic tone. Burton clearly knew his man, and Wesley might have avoided much grief if he had taken his advice."[101]

---

95. Ibid., 114.

96. Wesley, *Works [BE]*, Vol. 3, 585. Sermon 112, *On laying the Foundation Stone for the New Chapel*. See also the essay by Carveley, "From Glory to Glory: The Renewal of All Things in Christ. Maximus the Confessor and John Wesley," 173–88. Kenneth Carvely quotes this passage from Wesley's sermon in his essay.

97. John Burton was a tutor at Corpus Christi College, and he also became a Fellow of Eton College. Burton knew General Oglethorpe as they had both studied at Corpus Christi. See Wesley, *Letters [SE]*, 187–88.

98. Wesley, *Letters [SE]*, Vol. I, 188.

99. Heitzenrater, *Wesley and the People Called Methodists*, 58.

100. Wesley, *Letters [SE]*, Vol. I, 188–89.

101. Rack, *Reasonable Enthusiast*, 112.

Wesley set sail for Georgia on board the *Simmonds* in October 1735. Georgia was a new colony, the first 116 colonists arriving in 1733. By 1737 there were 518 people, of whom 149 were under sixteen and about 180 nominal Anglicans. In the fleet with Wesley's ship were Salzburgers and Moravians. Wesley was joined by his brother, Charles, who had been ordained deacon and priest on successive days, and who was to be secretary to General Oglethorpe; Benjamin Ingham, of Queen's College; and Charles Delamotte.

On board, the Holy Club continued: "At twelve we met to give an account to one another what we had done since our last meeting, and what we designed to do before our next."[102] The primitive writers remained part of Wesley's reading at that time:

> From five to seven we read the Bible together, carefully comparing it (that we might not lean to our own understandings) with the writings of the earliest ages.[103]

The group continued their ministry to others, especially the sick. To one woman Wesley lent a copy of Law's *Treatise on Christian Perfection*. Wesley read August Franke's book A *Treatise on the Fear of Man*[104] or *Nicodemus* on the journey to Savannah. He was so impressed with Franke's work, that on a visit to Halle in July 1738, he described his name as "Precious ointment."[105]

During a violent storm, Wesley's cerebral understanding of German Pietism became personal experience. While many passengers were terrified, the Moravian travelers remained calm and continued with the evening service he was attending. Wesley's *Journal* reads:

> At seven I went to the Germans. I had long before observed the great seriousness of their behaviour . . . In the midst of the psalm wherewith their service began, [wherein we were mentioning the power of God,] the sea broke over, split the main-sail in pieces, covered the ship, and poured in between the decks, as if the great deep had already swallowed us up. A terrible screaming began among the English. The Germans [looked up and without intermission] calmly sang on. I asked one of them afterwards, "Was you not afraid?" He answered, "I thank God, no." I asked "But

---

102. Wesley, *Works [BE]*, Vol. 18, 138.
103. Ibid.
104. Wesley, *Letters [SE]*, Vol. I, 183. (Footnote 1.)
105. Wesley, *Works [BE]*, Vol. 18, 264.

were not your women and children afraid?" He replied mildly, "No; our women and children are not afraid to die." . . . This was the most glorious day which I have hitherto seen.[106]

Wesley's witness of the Moravians' behavior during the storm led him to seek out their leaders. The Moravians under Spangenberg were not, as would previously have been the case, merely cast aside by Wesley as Dissenters but met with an open ear and an inquiring mind.

The *Simmonds* anchored on February 5th 1736 in the Savannah River. Two days after landing, Wesley met August Spangenberg who inquired whether Wesley had the assurance of the Holy Spirit and knew Jesus Christ. Wesley felt his answers were less than convincing, and his *Journal* entry is revealing: "I fear they were vain words."[107] However, Spangenberg was not unimpressed with Wesley's responses, writing in his *Journal*: "I observe that grace really dwells and reigns in him."[108]

Spangenberg also introduced Wesley to the differences between the Lutheran Salzburgers, who had settled at New Ebenezer, and who followed Franke and Urlsperger, and the Moravians in Savannah, who followed Zinzendorf and Spangenberg himself. Wesley thought the Moravians manifested many signs of primitive Christianity. By this, Wesley meant the Moravian lifestyle was closer to the apostolic period than any other, sharing possessions and living communally. The Moravians under Spangenberg's direction mixed mysticism (primarily stillness), with a need for the sense of assurance of faith.

Tuttle argues that Spangenberg held a "synthesis between mystical piety on the one hand and the theology of the continental reformers on the other."[109] Further, he comments that the time spent in America was nothing more than a mystical experiment. In the early period in Georgia, Wesley was reading and discussing the mystics with Spangenberg, and indeed recommending them to others, but he continued his use of the means of grace and maintained his work as parish priest amongst the colonists, and, albeit abortively, amongst the indigenous Indians and the slave colony.

Jean Orcibal suggests Georgia was a mystical crisis for Wesley, dating his change of opinion about the mystics to October 1736 and

106. Ibid., 142–43.
107. Ibid., 146.
108. Heitzenrater, *Wesley and the People Called Methodists*, 60.
109. Tuttle, *John Wesley*, 151.

arguing that Wesley "confused mysticism with a love of solitude."[110] His experiences of feverish activity in Georgia, and Spangenberg's influence of a settled assured faith, were a part of the process of rejection. Orcibal adds that Wesley found the mystics condemned the Christian to a melancholic existence, devoid of any form of spiritual comfort. Wesley would add Pelagianism to his charges against the mystics.[111]

Wesley faced a crisis and he poured out his feelings about the mystics in a letter to his brother Samuel. Wesley included anyone who belittled the means of grace under the term "mystic."[112] Primarily, he disliked their use of the means of grace only when they seemed personally useful, or when it would offend others not to use them. The letter offers a developing Wesleyan theology. Wesley would not renounce, as the mystics had, the use of reason in the Christian life. In writing to his brother, Wesley claimed the mystic "renounced reason and understanding,"[113] as these prevented guidance by "divine light."[114] Wesley turned away from the spiritual introversion promoted by the mystics, because the means of grace and works of piety were subordinated to personal "conversion" found in self-examination.

He did, however, absorb the mystical understanding of perfection; the need for every Christian to pursue "inward holiness or a union of the soul with God."[115] Rack observes that perfection, especially as outlined by Scupoli, whom Susannah Wesley had also read, "appealed to them by its concentration on will and intelligence rather than feeling."[116]

Wesley wanted a wider ministry than that of parish priest. He hoped to work with the Native Americans. Despite meeting with both

110. Orcibal, "The Theological Originality of John Wesley and Continental Spirituality," 91.

111. Ibid.

112. Wesley, *Works [BE]*, Vol. 25, 487–90.

113. Ibid., 488.

114. Ibid. See also Wesley, *Works [BE]*, Vol. 25, 540–50. For correspondence with William Law about the reading of mystical works. Wesley is sharp in writing, while Law remains courteous in reply. These letters give insight into Wesley's understanding, and acceptance of the writings of others.

115. Rack, *Reasonable Enthusiast*, 96. Rack writes of Wesley's May 1738 review. He notes from paragraph 11 of the review that Wesley met "a contemplative man" (William Law) who encouraged the pursuit of inner holiness. The review, written after conversion, shows how Wesley had come to understand perfection in the light of justification by grace.

116. Ibid., 101.

the Choctaws and the Chickasaws, he was unsuccessful. He met with slaves, instructing a young girl and boy and became involved with the school in Savannah.

In May 1736 Wesley created groups in Savannah and Frederica. Rack notes this has "always been seen as foreshadowing the future Methodism."[117] Wesley gathered together the serious members of his congregation and met with them once or twice a week. Their purpose in meeting was "to reprove, instruct, and exhort one another."[118] From this group, a smaller, more intimate number were selected, for personal instruction and group conversation. Wesley writes of their first meeting:

> This evening we had only Mark Hird. But on Sunday Mr Hird and two more desired to be admitted. After a psalm and a little conversation, I read Mr Law's *Christian Perfection*, and concluded with another psalm.[119]

Heitzenrater adds the names of the members who joined Mark Hird at the second meeting; Betty Hassel, Phoebe Hird, and Mrs. Hird (not Mr. Hird as the *Journal* recounts). Mark, Betty, and Phoebe were 21, 18, and 17. Like the Oxford Methodists, this group was by and large young.

Nehemiah Curnock, editor of the 1909 edition of the *Journals*, footnoted that this was the first attempt at the classes and bands.[120] Rack cautions that these meetings were simply attempts to meet a particular need. They were for personal and group spiritual devotion, and had neither the earlier charitable or educational elements of Oxford. Wesley timed the meetings according to many of the primitive methods of the Church, notably fast days. If anything, they owed more to the Anglican Unitary societies, but in a small colony divisions by age or sex were impractical, hence the groups unusual make up.

Wesley's adherence to a strictly disciplined life for himself and his fellow Anglicans led to his leaving Georgia under a cloud. By banning Sophy Williamson (née Hopkey) from communion, he was charged to appear before a grand jury. Sophy had married William Williamson in South Carolina without waiting for banns to be read. As her suitor himself, Wesley was no doubt upset. Treating her behavior as improper, he refused

---

117. Ibid., 119.
118. Wesley, *Works [BE]*, Vol. 18, 157.
119. Ibid., 60.
120. Wesley, *Journal [SE]*, Vol. 1, 198.

her communion. Her guardian, Thomas Causton, Chief Magistrate for Savannah, called a grand jury to hear the charges. Wesley chose to leave America and slipped away from Georgia in December 1737.

Despite the apparent failure of Wesley's parish ministry and mission, it is evident that he left America far more ready for the events of Aldersgate than he had been when he arrived. Conscious of what was to come, Wesley's account of the return journey is that of an unsettled individual:

> By the most infallible of proofs, inward feeling, I am convinced,
> 1 Of unbelief; having no such faith in Christ as will prevent my heart from being troubled; which it could not be, if I believed in God, and rightly believed in him.[121]

This contemporaneous account, written on board the *Samuel* while returning to England, and published retrospectively shows a troubled spirit. Rack notes the clear Moravian influence on Wesley who portrayed faith not as intellectual belief, but as a personal, inward assurance, which he felt he lacked.

THE JOURNEY TO FAITH

Once home, Wesley considered his future. The duties of a Fellow of Lincoln College, his only formal and paying appointment, were possible. This would have allowed him to resume leadership of the Oxford Methodists. Returning to Georgia was impossible,[122] and though he eventually chose to visit the Moravians in Herrnhut, he did not do this until later in 1738.

Significant to Wesley's future was his meeting with Peter Böhler at the home of the Reverend and Mrs. John Hutton, a Non-Juring Anglican family. Under Böhler's influence, Wesley's preaching included "justification, faith and the new birth."[123] Characteristically, as Wesley reflected upon his meeting with Böhler, he used providential language in his *Journal*:

> When Peter Böhler, whom God prepared for me as soon as I came to London, affirmed of true faith in Christ (which is but one) that it had those two fruits inseparably attending it, "domin-

---

121. Wesley, *Works [BE]*, Vol. 18, 208.
122. See Schmidt, *John Wesley A Theological Biography, volume I*.
123. Rack, *Reasonable Enthusiast*, 139.

ion over sin, and constant peace from a sense of forgiveness," I was quite amazed, and looked upon it as a new gospel. If this was so, it was clear I had not faith.[124]

As with Wesley's first meeting with the Moravians under Spangenberg, experience was seminal to his continuing quest for assurance. Wesley rejected Böhler's belief in the felt assurance of forgiveness. His contention was simple. If Böhler was right, he did not have faith. Wesley read the Scriptures and found ample points in support of Böhler's position. However, he was certain experience would prove him right, and that no one could state this position as a personal experience of assurance. Böhler held the trump card, and introduced Wesley to three people who could so testify:

> He came again with three others, all of whom testified, of their own personal experience, that a true and living faith in Christ is inseparable from a sense of pardon for all past and freedom from all present sins. They added with one mouth that this faith was the gift, the free gift of God; and that He would surely bestow it upon every soul who earnestly and perseveringly sought it. I was now thoroughly convinced; and, by the grace of God, I resolved to seek it unto the end.[125]

Böhler also advised Wesley to continue preaching, despite Wesley's misgivings while he felt he sorely lacked assurance himself. Wesley wanted to stop preaching altogether, and asked Böhler whether he should carry on. When Böhler replied he should, Wesley asked, "what can I preach?"[126] Böhler's famous advice was, "Preach faith *till* you have it; and then, *because* you have it you *will* preach faith."[127] In this response, Böhler was advising Wesley that preaching the reality of the new birth (faith) to others would enable Wesley to experience the forgiveness and assurance about which he preached.[128]

From Böhler's own testimony, and the testimonies of those Böhler brought to meet Wesley, he was becoming convinced that there could be degrees of faith. For this reason, despite that his "soul started back

---

124. Wesley, *Works [BE]*, Vol.18, 247–48.
125. Ibid., 248.
126. Ibid., 228.
127. Ibid., 228.
128. See McGonigle, *Sufficient Saving Grace John Wesley's Evangelical Arminianism*, 108.

from the work,"¹²⁹ he began to preach justification without a personal sense of assurance.

Peter Böhler also insisted that faith could be instantaneous, another obstacle for Wesley. Once again, Wesley resorted to Scripture, and wrote in his *Journal*, "I searched the Scriptures again touching this very thing, particularly the Acts of the Apostles: but to my utter astonishment, found scarce any instances there of other than *instantaneous* conversions."¹³⁰ Wesley argued this was the pattern described in Scripture of the early Church, but denied that God still worked in such a manner. Again, through personal testimony Böhler proved that such conversion was a reality. Wesley records his reaction, "Here ended my disputing. I could now only cry out, 'Lord, help Thou my unbelief!' "¹³¹ Böhler, noted:

> I took . . . four of my English brethren to John Wesley. They told, one after another, what had been wrought in them. Wesley and those that were with him were as if thunderstruck at these narratives. I asked John Wesley what he then believed. He said four examples were not enough. I replied I would bring eight more here in London. After a short time he stood up and said, "We will sing that hymn. . ." During the singing of the Moravian version he often wiped his eyes.¹³²

It would be a month before the events of Aldersgate would turn acceptance into experience. Before that, Wesley would play a part in the beginning of a society in Fetter Lane. The society, which initially met as a band on the 1st May, was termed "our little society"¹³³ by Wesley. Colin Podmore evidenced this society to be neither Anglican nor Moravian.¹³⁴

Membership of Fetter Lane was open, with clear nuances of the later Methodist movement. Admission to a Methodist class was based upon a "desire to flee from the wrath to come."¹³⁵ Wesley would later

---

129. Wesley, *Works [BE]*, Vol. 18, 228.

130. Ibid., 234.

131. Ibid.

132. Wesley, *Journal [SE]*, Vol. I, 455. The hymn was, *My soul before thee prostrate lies*. Wesley had translated this hymn from the German. (Footnote 1.)

133. Wesley, *Works [BE]*, Vol. 18, 236.

134. Podmore, *The Moravian Church in England 1728–1760*, 39.

135. Wesley, *Works [BE]*, Vol. 9, 69–75. The specific entry requirement is found on page 70 at paragraph 4. Wesley used this term of his own spiritual search for faith.

write of his own quest for salvation that he "found an earnest desire to live according to those rules (*Holy Living and Holy Dying*), and to flee from the wrath to come."[136] The requirement that he placed on others he had expected of himself.

THE CONVERSION OF THE WESLEYS

At the foundation of the Fetter Lane Band on the 1st May, Charles Wesley was ill, and staying at the Huttons. John Wesley was present only because he had returned to London to see his brother. Podmore stresses that the society was Moravian in its foundation. William Addison described the Fetter Lane Society as a "fusion of law and grace."[137] This is a good description of a society, which looked neither to the Church of England nor to the Moravian Church for oversight.

Just three days after the Fetter Lane Society began, Böhler left for America. In early May 1738 Charles Wesley, like his brother, was convinced of his sinfulness and lack of faith: "Mr Piers called to see me. I exhorted him to labour after that faith which he thinks I have, and know I have not."[138]

Charles' meetings with Böhler, whom he clearly admired, describing him as a "man of God,"[139] led to a crisis of faith. He, too, had been convinced of the doctrine of salvation by grace through faith,[140] and eagerly desired it. On the 17th May, Charles wrote in his *Journal* that he had read for the first time (with Mr. Holland) Luther's commentary on the Letter to the Galatians. As a result he wrote:

> Who would believe our Church had been founded on this important article of justification by faith alone? I am astonished I should ever think this a new doctrine; especially while our Articles and Homilies stand unrepealed, and the key of knowledge is not taken away.[141]

---

136. Wesley, *Works [BE]*, Vol. 3, 581. Sermon 112, *On laying the Foundation Stone for the New Chapel*. Words in brackets mine. Ibid.,

137. Addison, *The Renewed Church of the United Brethren 1722-1930*, 84.

138. Wesley, *Journal*, Vol. I, 85.

139. Ibid., 84.

140. Wesley, *Works [BE]*, Vol. 18, 237.

141. Wesley, *Journal*, Vol. I, 88.

Arnold Dallimore, quoting William Holland's *Narrative*, shows how Holland, in an autobiographical note on that evening's events, received assurance there and then.[142] Luther's doctrines were virtually obligatory for those wanting to claim Pietst credentials.[143] Bebbington writes, "The decisive impulse to the brothers Wesley came from Luther: Charles was reading his commentary on Galatians and John was listening to his preface on the letter to the Romans when they first came to vital faith."[144]

I indicated in chapter 1 that Spener first drew attention to Luther's work, especially the Preface to Romans, and "made the connection between conversion and the New Birth."[145] This doctrine became central within the Wesleyan movement born from the brothers' May 1738 experience. Alongside the doctrine of justification, stood New Birth, which Wesley held was a process from the moment of salvation to holiness.[146]

Charles recorded his spiritual state as: "hungry and thirsty after God."[147] He wrote that he was tempted, and called out to Christ. Although he was ill with pleurisy, on the 11th May Charles moved lodgings as the Wesleys' acceptance of justification had led to disagreement with James Hutton's parents. Jackson's *Memoirs* quaintly states "their host and hostess (the Huttons) were exceedingly averse to those evangelical views of conversion, justification and the new birth, which the brothers entertained."[148] Charles met Mr. Bray,[149] a fellow member of the fledgling Fetter Lane Society, and lodged with him. At that point, he still lacked

---

142. Dallimore, *A Heart Set Free – The Life of Charles Wesley*, 60. For a fuller account of William Holland's record of this event see Ward, *The Protestant Evangelical Awakening*, 340–42.

143. Ward, *Christianity under the Ancien Régime*, 74.

144. Bebbington, *Evangelicalism*, 38.

145. Ward, *Christianity under the Ancien Régime*, 74.

146. See Rack, *Reasonable Enthusiast*, 394. Rack contends that "New Birth" is a slippery term. For Wesley the New Birth was more than an instantaneous event, it was a process of transformation from sin to holiness. See also Wesley, *John Wesley's Forty-Four Sermons*, 514–25. This is the sermon on *The New Birth*. (Sermon XXXIX.)

147. Wesley, *Journal*, Vol. I, 87.

148. Jackson, *The Memoirs of the Rev Charles Wesley MA*, 59. (Words in brackets mine.)

149. See Wesley, *Journal*, Vol. I, 86. Charles described Mr. Bray as "a poor ignorant mechanic, who knows nothing but Christ." Charles also considered his meeting with Mr. Bray to be providential.

faith. A *Journal* entry for the same date reads "*I have not now the faith of the Gospel.*"[150]

Charles' *Journal* records his debilitating illness and his anxiety about his spiritual state. On the 19th May, Wesley, confined to bed, met Mrs. Turner (Mr. Bray's sister), and his conversation with her led him to seek faith more eagerly:

> At seven Mrs Turner came, and told me, I should not rise from that bed till I believed. I believed her saying, and asked, "Has God then bestowed faith upon you?" "Yes he has." "Why, have you peace with God?" "Yes, perfect peace." "And do you love Christ above all things?" "I do, above all things incomparably." . . . Her answers were so full to these and the most searching questions I could ask, that I had no doubt of her having received atonement; and waited for it myself with a more assured hope.[151]

Following his reading of Luther's second chapter on the Galatians (17th May)[152] Charles was assured from Scripture that "he (*Christ*) would come, and would not tarry."[153] Indeed, he actively sought Christ's appearance.

Mrs. Turner was seminal to Charles' experience of the 21st May. As Charles rested, preparing to sleep, he thought Mrs. Musgrave[154] had come into his room and said: "In the name of Jesus of Nazareth, arise, and believe, and thou shalt be healed of all thy infirmities."[155]

After questioning Mrs. Turner whether she had spoken, he wondered whether Jesus himself had spoken, as he had been praying and waiting for Christ: "I hoped it might be Christ indeed."[156] As further inquiries were made, Charles Wesley came to a personal assurance of faith: "I said, yet

---

150. Wesley, *Journal*, Vol. I, 86. (Original italics.)

151. Ibid., 89.

152. Wesley, *Journal [SE]*, Vol. I, 475–76. Footnote 2 details an account of how William Holland understood the events of 17th May. Holland was present that day, and indeed brought Luther's Commentary to Charles.

153. Ibid., 88. (Word in italics mine.)

154. Mrs. Musgrave was sister to Mrs. Turner and Mr. Bray. Charles Wesley mistook her voice for that of Mrs. Turner. It was only after Charles had been told that Mrs. Musgrave had not been in Bray's house that Mrs. Turner stated she had spoken. See Wesley, *Journal*, Vol. I, 91.

155. Wesley, *Journal*, Vol. I, 90.

156. Ibid., 91.

feared to say, 'I believe, I believe!'"[157] Finally, Mrs. Turner admitted she had spoken those words, following a dream in which Christ appeared to her.[158] Charles sent for Mr. Bray and asked him whether he had indeed received faith. Mr. Bray did not doubt that he had. Eventually Wesley recorded, "I found myself convinced, I knew not how, nor when, and immediately fell into intercession."[159] John Wesley commented on his brother's experience: "I received the surprising news that my brother had found rest to his soul. His bodily strength returned also from that hour."[160]

Charles Wesley's conversion occurred after three factors had come into play: First, through Peter Böhler, he was not only receptive to the Moravian doctrines of justification by grace through faith, New Birth, and assurance, but had accepted these to be hallmarks of salvation which he could not evidence in his own life. Second, being unwell, he was confined to his room, and this gave opportunity for soul searching, and introspection: "I seemed deeply sensible of my misery."[161] Within his room, Wesley had ample time to reflect on that of which he had heard Böhler speak. By the same token his meeting with Mr. Bray, William Holland and others left him in no doubt that assurance was a real experience.

Third, it may be that Charles Wesley's openness to supernatural events led him to place greater emphasis upon Mrs. Turner's statement to him than his brother might have done. From the *Journal* there is no doubt that once he had heard the full story of how Mrs. Turner came to speak to him on the morning of the 21st May, he believed Christ had spoken through her. This was confirmed by Bray's assertion that as Mrs. Turner was speaking, Christ was indeed present.[162]

This does not diminish the importance of the event for Charles Wesley. As for John on the 24th May, the events of the 21st May were a "heart experience," rather than a "head decision." Charles had made the decision in his head to be a Christian but until the 21st May 1738 had not made the "personal invitation" to Christ.

---

157. Ibid.
158. See Wesley, *Journal*, Vol. 1, 91–92.
159. Ibid., 91.
160. Wesley, *Works [BE]*, Vol. 18, 241.
161. Ibid., 88.
162. Wesley, *Journal*, Vol. I, 92. See also Wesley, *Journal*, Vol. I, 95. Charles recorded a conversation with Mrs. Pratt in which Christ appeared to her in a dream.

W. R. Ward, commenting on William Holland's journey from Anglicanism into Moravianism, could be speaking of the Wesleys: "In one man's [Holland's] experience was a religious pilgrimage diverted from the Church of England (temporarily) into Moravianism by a liberating conversion experience without any sense of institutional discontinuity."[163] Neither Charles nor John would believe or accept that they had wavered from the Church of England through their encounter with Moravianism: a meeting that led both to experience a personal, decisive moment of assurance. As with William Holland, the foray into Moravianism did not persuade Charles or John that they had in any way broken with the past. "What occurred on *Wednesday* the 24th, I think it best to relate at large, after premising what may make it the better understood."[164] So began the entry for the day upon which John Wesley was to experience a sense of personal assurance and salvation.

In the days before the 24th May, John described his spiritual state as "continual sorrow and heaviness" in my "heart"[165] writing to an unnamed friend that he was nothing more than a sinner.[166] The temper of this letter indicates clearly the sense Wesley had of his own spiritual state, and his desire to experience the same assurance that Böhler and others whom he had met since returning from Georgia had themselves experienced.

Wesley included the letter as a form of propaganda in the *Journal* to display the drama of the 24th May, but it is useful to notice that in a contemporaneous letter, as opposed to the reflection of the *Journal*, Wesley is in turmoil. Rack writes "On 24 May he was certainly in a highly wrought frame of mind, and a letter to a friend that day (probably Gambold) shows in a mixture of scriptural and personal epithets how conscious he was of sin, of the need for personal fruits of faith and of his lack of them."[167]

Wesley attended the meeting in Aldersgate Street reluctantly, yet it was here that he was to find the assurance that he had been seeking:

> In the evening, I went very unwillingly to a society in Aldersgate Street, where one was reading Luther's preface to the Epistle to the Romans. About a quarter before nine, while he was describing

163. W.R. Ward, *The Protestant Evangelical Awakening*, 342.
164. J. Wesley, *Works [BE]*, Vol. 18, 242.
165. Ibid., 241.
166. Wesley, *Works [BE]*, Vol. 18, 242. See also Wesley, *Letters [SE]*, Vol. I, 245.
167. Rack, *Reasonable Enthusiast*, 144.

the change which God works in the heart through faith in Christ, I felt my heart strangely warmed. I felt I did trust in Christ, Christ alone for salvation; and an assurance was given me that He had taken away my sins, even mine, and saved me from the law of sin and death.[168]

Wesley testified publicly to his experience in the meeting. Charles' *Journal* entry adds another dimension to the evening. At around ten o'clock, John was brought in a state of great excitement to Mr. Bray's where Charles was staying. "My brother was brought in triumph by a troop of our friends, and declared, 'I believe.' We sang the hymn with great joy and parted with prayer."[169] The evening of the 24th May had brought John, like Charles, to declare that he was saved "from the law of sin and death." Not by works of righteousness, but simply by faith. The hymn that was sung is likely to have been "Where shall my wondering soul begin?" composed by Charles as a "hymn upon my conversion."[170]

JOHN WESLEY'S CONVERSION REVIEWED

What occurred in May 1738 that differed from 1725? In 1725 Wesley made a "head" decision to seek faith and turned to seriousness. He sought out writers who would enlighten and influence him. He read and discarded the writings of the mystics (with the exception of de Renty). Yet he did not find a personal faith. Bebbington's assertion that Jeremy Taylor's writings proved to be a "sandy foundation" appears true. Between 1725 and 1738, in the process of the journey, Wesley used the means of grace and from late 1729, met the Holy Club to discuss faith and share mutual concerns. In 1730 he turned to social action at the suggestion of William Morgan.

In 1738 Wesley's heart was strangely warmed in a meeting room in Aldersgate Street.[171] Without Aldersgate, Wesley might have remained an Oxford don seeking a personal faith, but without 1725 the warmed

---

168. Wesley, *Works [BE]*, Vol. 18, 249–50.
169. Ibid., 95.
170. Wesley, *Journal*, Vol. I, 95.
171. For a fuller account of the 1725 turn to seriousness and the 1738 conversion see Rack, *Reasonable Enthusiast*, 145. Rack asserts that a Catholic (and Anglican) view may be taken of Wesley's 1725 change, and he refers to Green, *The Young Mr Wesley*, 258–74. An evangelical view may also be taken of the event of May 1738 and he refers to Schmidt, *John Wesley, A Theological Biography*. Volume 1, 213–310.

heart could not have been put into context of a broad, welcoming and evangelical theology that by 1738 encompassed many types of theological understanding.

As a demonstration of this, Wesley later urged his followers to use the means of grace, a distinct Anglican practice, and at the same time, meet for mutual confession and absolution, a Moravian practice. I will show in chapter 4 how, when the issue of stillness arose at Fetter Lane, discarding the means of grace for "waiting on the Lord," he was prepared to separate from the Fetter Lane Society.[172] Wesley would not afford preeminence to one doctrine. For Wesley, the issue was not that stillness was wrong, but that to abandon all other practices in its favor was.[173] Wesley's faith was a mixture of practice and teaching that set him apart from other church leaders. Thomas Langford, quoting Gordon Rupp, evidences this:

> Here, then, are some of the reasons why the Methodists became distinct from the other evangelicals: the Arminianism of the Wesleys, their High Church, Non-Juring associations, their many-sided spiritual inheritance, Protestant and Catholic, and the influence upon them of the Pietists and the Moravians.[174]

It would be wrong to ignore the 24th May experience. Not only did Wesley *feel* forgiven (new birth), but he also received assurance that he *was* forgiven (the Witness of the Spirit). Many of Wesley's letters and *Journal* entries prior to May 24th show a longing to experience what he knew in his mind to be true. The letter to his friend on the day of his conversion is an indication of what he felt personally—sinfulness[175] and what he longed to experience—peace and joy.[176]

J. Ernest Rattenbury[177] drew upon Charles Wesley's hymnody as a source for understanding the Wesleys' life-changing experience. He

---

172. See also Podmore, *The Moravian Church*, 59–66. Podmore asserts that Spangenberg had also taught the doctrine of stillness at Fetter lane.

173. Wesley *Works [BE]*, Vol. 19, 122. The *Journal* entry for Monday 19th November 1739 shows that Wesley preached to the Bristol Society from the Psalms and urged the members to "wait upon God in *all* his ordinances." (Italics mine.) Stillness was acceptable, but not to the exclusion of other practices.

174. Rupp, "Introductory Essay," quoted in Langford, *Methodist Theology*, 5.

175. Wesley, *Works [BE]*, Vol. 18, 242.

176. Wesley, *Works [BE]*, Vol. 18, 242.

177. Rattenbury, *The Conversion of the Wesley's*, 95–100.

argued that the reprinting of his brother's hymns was an acceptance by John of their doctrines and the experiences they related. Using the hymns "Where shall my wondering soul begin?," "And can it be that I should gain?" and "Come, O thou traveller unknown," Rattenbury argued the moment of conversion was not merely an academic acceptance of faith, but an experiential moment. He asserted the hymn "Come, O thou traveller" to be "the great classic of evangelical conversion."[178] Of this hymn Rattenbury wrote that the recognition of divine love came in the verse containing the words:

> Assurance comes, and adoption, and then the victorious wrestler declare his message to the world; he generalises his experience.
>   The morning breaks, the shadows flee,
>   Pure UNIVERSAL LOVE THOU ART.[179]

Rattenbury concluded that once this divine love was recognized and received, "faith is born and faith penetrates into the mystery of God."[180] In the 1780 edition of *A Collection of Hymns for the Use of the People Called Methodists*, John Wesley placed this hymn in the section "For Mourners Brought to the Birth."[181] The hymn was written in 1742, and first appeared in the collection *Hymns and Sacred Psalms*.[182]

For both John and Charles Wesley, the experience of faith received in the moment of assurance was to be a guiding principle amongst the people called Methodist. From this life-enhancing moment of justification by grace through faith, the Wesleys would become leaders of a movement that would seek to spread "Scriptural Holiness," built upon a personal assurance of faith and a desire to be discipled as a Christian by peers and leaders alike. The classes and bands of the movement would become the primary meeting places where that holiness could be discovered, experienced, and practiced.

THE WESLEYAN INHERITANCE

So far, I have shown that the Wesleyan inheritance is a broad schema. John Wesley embraced the piety of the English Puritans, and the conti-

---

178. Ibid., 99.
179. Ibid., 100.
180. Rattenbury, *The Evangelical Doctrines of Charles Wesley's Hymns*, 98–99.
181. Wesley, *Works [BE]*, Vol. 7, 250–52.
182. See Wesley, *Works [BE]*, Vol. 7, 250. Footnote to hymn 136.

nental Pietsts, and created a routine of Pietstic fervor. Wesley was influenced by mystics, and Non-Jurors under whom he sought a primitive Christianity, primarily in Georgia, and he was a clergyman for whom the articles and practice of the Church were of utmost importance, even though he held lightly to these on more than one occasion.

In all, the Wesleyan heritage is not a neat package of doctrine but an eclectic collection of influences and ideals which became embedded in John Wesley's psyche. This model of faith and practice, when allied to his organizational skill, created at first a movement, and later an organization for men and women who did not, or were not able to, engage with the established Church. Methodism received the legacy of John Wesley, codified it, and perhaps fossilized it, so that as will be discussed later, the class meeting, the group that embodied the bulk of the Wesleyan inheritance, petrified too.

A note of caution must be raised about the depth of the Puritan influence on John Wesley.

> It is possible that not only did Wesley inherit his High Church and anti-Dissenting prejudices from his parents, but they kept him in ignorance of his strong Puritan ancestry.[183]

This view is shared by Frank Baker,[184] who remarks that Wesley only became aware of his grandfather's ejection after reading Edmund Calamy's *Continuation* in 1765.[185] Not only did Calamy give a full account of the appearance before the Bishop of Bristol and subsequent trial of John Westley,[186] Wesley's grandfather, but he also notes the ejection of his great grandfather, Benjamin Westley.[187] Bearing in mind this caution,

---

183. Rack, *Reasonable Enthusiast*, 306.

184. Baker, *John Wesley and the Church of England*, 237.

185. See Calamy, *A Continuation of the Account of the Minsters, Lecturers . . . who were ejected and slenced after the Restoration in 1660, by or before the Act for Uniformity. To which is added the Church and Dissenters compar'd as to persecution, in some remarks on Dr. Walkers attempt to recover the names and sufferings of the clergy that were sequestered, &c Between 1640 and 1660, And also some free remarks on the twenty-eighth of Dr. E. Bennets Essay on the 39 Articles of Religion.*

186. Calamy, *Continuation*, 437–52. An account of the conversation between John Wesley's grandfather, John Westley, and the Bishop of Bristol is recorded in Wesley, *Works [BE]*, Vol 21, 513–18. John Westley was minister of a gathered church in Dorset.

187. Calamy, *Continuation*, 429. Bartholemew Westley was ejected from his living in Arlington, Dorset.

I will argue that through his reading, and his background, Puritan teachings were an influence on the developing Wesley.

In 1725 as Wesley began to amend his personal practice, he read English Puritan and mystic writers, evincing a move toward godliness in the tradition of Richard Rogers. For those who sought to be godly, the final state to be achieved was assurance, and as I mentioned in chapter 1, Wesley would ultimately accept a Pietst understanding of assurance as a first step of faith, thereby overturning the Puritan teaching. Godliness developed into a search for holiness, which took piety "centered in law to a piety centered in an immediate relationship to God."[188]

As Wesley began, in the pursuit of godliness, to write exact diaries of his spiritual state, so with the pursuit of holiness he longed for a relationship with God that seemed lacking. This is evidenced in correspondence with Burton:

> But you will perhaps ask: "Can't you save your own soul in England as well as in Georgia?" I answer, No; neither can I hope to attain the same degree of holiness here which I may there; neither, if I stay here knowing this, can I reasonably hope to attain any degree of holiness at all.[189]

Godliness failed to impart any sense of assurance. Once the godly life was linked to the Puritanism of Richard Greenham, who urged Christians to use time wisely in Pietstic acts, and Wesley adopted these into his way of life in the Holy Club, he needed to receive a sense of assurance that his work was pleasing to God. This was not forthcoming.

Through his turn to seriousness Wesley was exhibiting classic Puritan behavior by way of exact diarying and living. The use of reason within Puritanism was not simply to know that God had given a means of ascertaining his will ("what to do") as was the case for the Anglicans, but to use reason as a tool for daily living ("how to be"). From 1725, Wesley used reason in the classic High Church manner, but his later meetings with Dissenters, while maintaining the correctness of Anglican order and practice, allowed a generosity of intellectual spirit which meant that he saw reason in another tradition and could assimilate it into his own faith pattern.

---

188. Stoeffler, *The Rise of Evangelical Pietism*, 79.
189. Wesley, *Works [BE]*, Vol. 25, 441.

Wesley's accommodation of mysticism into his schema of Christian living did nothing to help his searching soul. Puritanism encountered mysticism through the pursuit of holiness, the state of being which drew a Christian into union with God. The writings of Thomas à Kempis, and the Marquis de Renty, dogged Wesley's pursuit of holiness through their mystical devotion to God. Through his life, Wesley adhered to the means of grace and other models of spiritual development, and he drew his use and reliance on the means from the High Anglican tradition as much from the Puritans.

The most striking element of Wesley's theology was his Arminianism, which came through his parents. Herbert McGonigle illustrates the depth of Wesley's familial inheritance in *Sufficient Saving Grace*.[190] However, McGonigle also shows how Wesley inculated a personal Arminianism through his reading from 1725 onwards.

Arminianism had been the Court party line under Charles I, with Parliament taking a Calvinist line. Martin writes:

> The courtiers damned the predestinarians, while the mob jeered at the Arminians. The King, Laud and Buckingham were for free will: Parliament was for predestination.[191]

The doctrine of Arminianism cannot be nailed to the Puritan, or the High Church tree; although Calvinism was predominant amongst Puritans, it was not the only teaching on salvation and the efficacy of the atonement.

The Arminian versus Calvinist debate spilled beyond academic argument into the life of society. Peter Lake, in his study of pamphleteering and the stage in the sixteenth and seventeenth centuries, draws out the doctrinal views of the pamphleteers who were anxious to show the death of offenders as good or bad, depending on their background and the author's own doctrinal stance. As an example, Lake shows how Peter Studley, "an Arminian in theology and as a rabid anti-Puritan"[192] took the

---

190. McGonigle, *Sufficient Saving Grace*, 73–106. See also 124–28. Susanna Wesley published a response to Whitefield's anti-Arminian pamphlet *A Letter to the Rev Mr John Wesley*, itself a reply to Wesley's sermon on *Free Grace*. McGonigle asserts this response represented the Wesley familys' Arminianism. The sermon *Free Grace* can be found in Wesley, *Works [BE]*, Vol. 3, 542–63.

191. Martin, *Puritanism and Richard Baxter*, 124.

192. Lake with Questier, *The Antichrist's Lewd Hat Protestants, Papists and Players in Post-Reformation England*, 171.

case of Enoch ap Evans, a Puritan convicted of murder, and attempted to show how Evans' Puritan Calvinist brethren had depicted him as mad, rather than encourage Evans to accept his fate and own a good death. The Puritans wanted Evans to eschew his Puritanism. Effectively, they tried "to persuade ap Evans himself to suppress all mention of his Puritanism in his account of the crime."[193] As an Arminian chaplain, Studley sought to prove from conversation that he had attempted to show ap Evans the error of his ways and bring him to an Arminian view.

Wesley inherited his Arminianism from parents who reached back to the Stuart inheritance. Susanna's Arminian credentials can be seen in an undated *Journal* entry:

> I so long labour under such and so many difficulties in my way to heaven as makes me so often upon the point of despairing ever to arrive there. I cannot without renouncing my reason as well as faith question or doubt of thy being willing all men should be saved.[194]

Christopher Hill alludes to why this might be so. He suggests that under Archbishop Laud, there was an attempt, through Arminianism, to restore to the priesthood a position of honor and reinvigorate the sacraments and ceremonies. In other words, to establish free will within the constructs of a State Church. This contrasted with the Puritan Arminianism of people like Milton, who espoused individualism.[195]

For John Wesley, Arminianism arose from the safety of an Established Church of England, rather than from the individualistic sects who devised their own understanding of free will. This view is strengthened by Hill. He suggests that under James I, Arminianism was ascendant in the Church of England, with the Arminians holding "all the best bishoprics and deaneries in England, the restriction by rank was in effect a party restriction."[196] This makes the ascendancy of Calvinism under Parliament all the more understandable, and the resulting Church, post-Restoration, was predominantly Calvinist. John Wesley's inheritance of Arminus' teaching came through his parents, his personal regard for the Church of pre-Commonwealth England and his exhaus-

---

193. Lake with Questier, *The Antichrist's Lewd Hat*, 171.

194. Wesley, *Susanna Wesley*, 306. This is from an undated sabbath meditation. See also 465–79. In this response to a letter from George Whitefield to John Wesley, Susanna is defending her sons preaching and teaching of Arminian doctrine.

195. See Hill, *Society and Puritanism in Pre-Revolutionary England*, 495.

196. Hill, *Society and Puritanism*, 37.

tive anti-Calvinist reading. Whether Wesley read Arminius firsthand is debatable, as McGonigle states, "Among scholars who have researched John 'Wesley's 'Arminianism' there has been uncertainty as to whether or not he had read the Dutch theologian."[197]

Wesley was also influenced by the non-jurors,[198] meeting John Clayton in 1732, when he began to attend the Holy Club. Rack believes Clayton has been underestimated: "Clayton was a more important influence on the Oxford Methodists and Wesley himself than has perhaps always been recognized."[199] Wesley's own quest for primitive Christianity in Georgia was fuelled by Clayton and others of his circle. Clayton introduced Wesley to Thomas Deacon, a Manchester Non-Juror, and they led Wesley to practice (along with the Holy Club) the fasts of the Church, and look to the apostolic period for the most authentic or primitive form of the Christian life. It was this which Wesley sought in Georgia.

After reading the *Apostolic Constitutions* Wesley's life was guided by its principles, and by the influence of Clayton and Deacon. He observed the fasts, baptized by immersion, and used communion observances (adding water to the wine) that were not regularly practiced.

Wesley's first baptism in Georgia was by immersion; "Mary Welch, aged eleven days, was baptized according to the custom of the first church and the rule of the Church of England, by immersion. The child was ill then, but recovered from that hour."[200] Wesley refused to baptize the child of Henry Parker whose parents declined immersion, and would not certify the child as sick to salve Wesley's conscience sufficiently to allow sprinkling.[201] Although this view was tempered, he maintained his view of the need for an episcopally ordained minister to perform a baptism. He refused communion to John Martin Boltzius because of this scruple, an occasion he reflected upon after he received a letter from Boltzius in 1749, "I did refuse to admit (Boltzius) to the Lord's Table,

---

197. McGonigle, *Sufficient Saving Grace*, 100.

198. The Non-Jurors were those who supported the Stuart monarchy which had been expelled in 1688. Unable to assent to the Act of Supremacy, and the accession of King William III and Queen Anne, ordained ministers lost their livings. Non-Jurors also looked to the first five centuries of the church for "primitive" teaching and practice.

199. Rack, *Reasonable Enthusiast*, 90.

200. Wesley, *Works [BE]*, Vol. 18, 150. The diary entry for the following day states Wesley baptized Mary Welch "by trine immersion." See 360.

201. Wesley, *Works [BE]*, Vol. 18, 157.

because he was *not baptized*—that is, not baptized by a minister who had been *episcopally ordained!*"²⁰²

Wesley's Non-Juring credentials were bolstered by his observance of the Prayer Book of Edward VI (1549), believing it to have greater authority than the authorized 1662 Prayer Book. The Manchester Non-Jurors also introduced Wesley to the poor of the workhouse, and to discriminate between "idle and worthy beggars."²⁰³ They were concerned for education, and Rack suggests this may have led to Wesley's request to his mother for her views on childhood education.²⁰⁴

Wesley's Pietst influences are clearly seen in the period of Fetter Lane membership, but it is important to reach back to the journey to Georgia. Wesley was clearly predisposed toward Spangenberg's Moravian group and the Lutheran Pietsts in New Ebeneezer. While the firsthand witness of the Moravians' behavior during a storm deeply unsettled Wesley's personal spiritual state, he was drawn toward the practical piety of the Pietsts who followed Franke and Urlsperger.

Wesley considered Moravian practice and lifestyle close to ancient Christianity, yet he maintained a healthy skepticism toward their leader Zinzendorf, especially after meeting the Lutherans. As Rupp noted, "From what he learned from the Ebeneezer Lutherans, from correspondence, and from his own later first-hand knowledge, he had reservations about Count Zinzendorf."²⁰⁵ In Wesley's opinion, Zinzendorf exercised undue authority over the Moravians, allowed his followers to use guile in order to achieve an aim, maintained secrecy over matters of importance²⁰⁶ and undervalued good works. In Wesley's conversation with Zinzendorf on the 3ʳᵈ September 1741,²⁰⁷ Wesley raised a further

---

202. Wesley, *Works [BE]*, Vol. 20, 305. (word in brackets mine) See also Wesley, *Works [BE]*, Vol. 18, 528. Wesley's *Journal* and *Diary* show that he spoke with Boltzius on the 17th July 1737 and this was the day on which he refused him communion

203. Rack, *Reasonable Enthusiast*, 91.

204. See Wesley, *Susanna Wesley*, 369–73. Here, Susanna expresses her views.

205. Rupp, "Introductory Essay," pxxxiii.

206. Wesley, "Minutes of the Methodist Conferences from the First, Held in London, by the Late Rev. John Wesley, A.M., in the Year 1744," Volume I, 60. In the *Minutes* the question is asked "Q. What power is this, which you exercise over both the Preachers and the Societies?" The response is, "Count *Zinzendorf* loved to keep all things close."

207. See Wesley, *Works [BE]*, Vol. 21, 211–15. Wesley raised the issue of Zinzendrof's understanding of imputed perfection; that is perfection comes only in Christ. In Wesley's view a believer grew in holiness towards becoming perfect.

reservation; that Zinzendorf accepted imputed perfection, while Wesley allowed that perfection was inherent. Wesley was aware of continental piety before meeting with them in the New World, having read Franke on the *Simmonds*. The life of the Holy Club owed much to the practice of the Halle Pietsts through William Morgan's influence.

In Georgia, Wesley established two small pietist societies, in Savannah and Frederica, and from them smaller groups.[208] Their purpose was to "reprove, instruct and exhort one another." It is noteworthy that Wesley saw firsthand the Moravian's organization into groups for instruction and devotion. He chose to allow some laxity in membership, admitting females into the society, eschewing the strict segregation of the Moravians.

The return to London in 1738 brought Wesley into contact with the Unitary societies detailed in chapter 3, at which he became a frequent preacher, if not leader. There is no evidence to suggest that Wesley had any involvement with Anglican societies prior to sailing for Georgia, and this may well have been due to his work with the Holy Club.

From May 1738 to April 1739, Wesley's time was predominantly spent in the company and organization of the Fetter Lane Society, a Moravian-inspired, but Anglican-led society which advanced the form of societary life. After April 1739, Wesley was increasingly absent in Bristol. However, his association continued until the separation of 20th July 1740. Through Fetter Lane Wesley found a model of organization, which with a few important amendments would become the structure of Methodism. Equally Wesley appears to have shed his scruples toward lay leadership, female leadership, and Dissenters. All were a part of the life at Fetter Lane discussed in chapter 4.

Wesley continued to rebaptize Dissenters, even as members of Fetter Lane, and his own societies, and evidence will be adduced to show Wesley's determination to ensure Methodists were Anglicans too. Wesley's baptismal views were not swayed, even after Georgia and Fetter Lane. Essentially, Wesley "retained his rubrical scruples and punctilios as to the necessity of Episcopalian baptism, and even went so far, on at least one occasion . . . to rebaptise Dissenters."[209]

In the Fetter Lane period the administration of communion in societies and private homes was a point of difficulty for Wesley; sacra-

---

208. See Wesley, *Works [BE]*, Vol. 18, 157.

209. Holland, *Baptism in Early Methodism*, 6.

mental observance was properly limited to the parish church. Wesley's High Church principles were tested by his presidency at communion in private homes. John Wesley argued he administered home communion to the sick and to those who were "Methodist friends, claiming that this was not the sort of "private administration" that was prohibited by the Church."[210] The numbers mentioned in the *Journal* and the regularity with which he administered at specific homes indicates his practice was to preside at a private service.[211] Between April and October 1739 he communicated a minimum of 9 and a maximum of 56 people at any given time.

Wesley exercised a distinctive ministry beyond the unorthodox organization of the Fetter Lane Society. In some ways he delved into the Pietst Anglican inheritance of the late seventeenth and early eighteenth century, detailed in chapter 1. However, this was tainted with the doctrine of assurance which Wesley preached after his conversation with Peter Böhler,[212] a more recent doctrine which proved popular amongst the piety of the societies and groups he was invited to meet.

One of the keys of the Methodist movement from 1740 was Wesley's allegiance to the doctrine of perfection. This doctrine, like much of Wesley's inheritance, did not develop from one single strand of religious experience or teaching; rather, it grew in a cross-fertilization of Puritanism, Pietism, and Catholicism. In each tradition, perfection theology arose from a desire for a more intimate union with God.

As previously mentioned holiness brought the Puritan Christian to an understanding of *being*, rather than simply *doing* as the goal of life. The shift into mysticism resulted from the desire to be inwardly holy. Mystical Puritanism was subjective; devotion to God, leading to a union with God. Coats argues: "Mysticism as a form of piety is the passion and hunger of the soul for immediacy of access to the Father, and the all-

---

210. Heitzenrater, *Wesley and the People Called Methodists*, 140.

211. Wesley, *Works [BE]*, Vol.19, 383. April 1st 1739: Mr. Deschamps (thirty there.) April 6th: Mr. Williams,' 393. June 9th: Mrs. Williams' (ten there), 399. July 22nd: Mr. Willis' (twenty-five there), 400. July 28th: Mrs. Willis' (fifteen there), 401. August 4th: Mrs. Williams' (nine there), 403. August 15th: Mrs. Grace's (nine there), 403. August 18th: Mrs. Williams' (fourteen there), 404. 19th August: Mrs. Willis' (twenty-two there), 404. 22nd August: Margaret Somerel's (nine there), 411. 13th October: Mrs. Williams' (twenty there), 411. 14th October: Mrs. Willis' (fifty-six there).

212. Wesley, *Works [BE]*, Vol. 18, 228. The conversation took place on the 4th March 1738.

satisfying vision of his eternal glory."[213] Wesley turned the introspective perfection of Puritanism into a world-affirming understanding, wherein the freedom from outward sin did not remove the individual from interaction with the world. In effect, for Wesley, love, experienced through perfection, replaced sin.

Wesley undoubtedly acquired a form of perfection theology from the Catholic Marquis de Renty that was inextricably linked with the pursuit of good works. De Renty, a seventeenth-century French nobleman, began small classes for those who wrote to him for spiritual advice, and through personal example encouraged people to undertake pietistic works. Orcibal notes that Wesley's letters frequently referred to the work of the Marquis, and Wesley felt his life was one of "noble simplicity . . . and . . . extraordinary intimacy of union with God."[214]

Wesley's understanding of perfection was first articulated in the 1733 sermon, *The Circumcision of the Heart*. As previously quoted, perfection, or spiritual circumcision, leads the Christian to be clean from sin and hold the nature of Christ, such that an individual becomes "perfect as our Father in heaven is perfect."[215] By 1733 Wesley had come to hold a doctrine of Christian perfection that was to remain with him through his life, and which was to influence the classes and bands, even though he remained unsure of his spiritual state until 1738.

The mystics, with the exception of de Renty, were jettisoned by Wesley while in Georgia, explaining to his brother that they had served only as rocks on which he almost shipwrecked his soul.[216] This careful appraisal and ultimate rejection of one form of doctrine enabled Wesley's inheritance to be highly personal, yet would prove effective for the Methodists he would lead for a large part of the eighteenth century.

CHAPTER SUMMARY

The Wesleyan schema of faith was predominantly laid by the time of the "Aldersgate experience." Reason, experience, tradition were understood in relation to Scripture—to which Wesley had resolved to be "homo unius libri." If Scripture offered the foundation of the life he would lead

213. Coats, *Types of English Piety*, 156.

214. Orcibal, "The Theological Originality of John Wesley and Continental Spirituality," 90.

215. Wesley, *A Plain Account*, 7.

216. See Wesley, *Works [BE]*, Vol. 25, 487.

after his experience, it would not be a sandy foundation, as every aspect of faith and spirituality would be tested. Hempton properly writes that in reality, to see Scripture, reason, tradition, and experience as a "quadrilateral"[217] is inadequate. Having dismissed Albert Outler's description, he writes:

> If Wesley's theology must be reduced to a model, one that offers better explanatory power than the quadrilateral is to see it more as a moving vortex, fuelled by scripture and divine love, shaped by experience, reason and tradition, and moving dynamically toward holiness or Christian perfection.[218]

The Fetter Lane Society was the final building block prior to the foundation of the Wesleyan movement. In this society, of which he was both member and leader, he noted flawed Pietsm that gave up the means of grace, and which would not engage with works of mercy. For Wesley, whose faith demanded rigorous discipline and social outreach, this was ultimately unsatisfying, and the permission to travel to Bristol in 1739 opened a new dimension in his life. Wesley began societies based on his own model: a model that would give rise to the class meeting, the crown and cross of Methodism; a model that did indeed allow Hempton's "vortex" full expression for the earliest Methodist people. Yet it was a vortex that would become a schema set as Outler described, a "quadrilateral," based not on the dynamic experiences through which Wesley had been, but on the settled life of a class, in which dynamism gave way to routine, and the settlement of a received doctrine.

---

217. Albert Outler, (1908–1989) was an American Methodist minister. He taught at Yale, Duke and Southern Methodist Universities. He coined the term of "Wesley's quadrilateral" which has become widely known within the field of Wesleyan studies.

218. Hempton, *Methodism Empire of the Spirit*, 57.

3

Religious Societies in England from 1678

CONTEXT

RELIGIOUS SOCIETIES IN ENGLAND can be traced to the foundation of the Savoy Society in 1678. The English societies did not emerge in a vacuum, but as the result of, or as descendants of, previous models of Christian expression discussed in chapter 1. In the sixteenth century the English Church held a significant part in local life, as Clark stresses: "The most important covered space in a community was the parish church,"[1] providing a meeting place for social and liturgical purposes.

Post-Reformation, the social function of the church waned. However, the church did not lose its hold on community life. During the reign of Elizabeth I, market and fast days were marked by extended preaching and "prophesying services," which later became "combination lectures"[2] intended to improve spiritual standards. Laymen also met at private prayer meetings, and while these were mainly conformists, Puritans, Dissenters, and Catholics also met in groups. Two societies existed within the ecclesiastical framework of the Church of England prior to 1678: Nicholas Ferrar's society at Little Gidding[3] and the Company for the Propagation of the Gospel in New England.[4]

THE SAVOY SOCIETY AND THE POPLAR REGULATIONS

The English Religious Society can be traced to Anthony Horneck, born in 1641 at Bacharach. After studying at Heidelberg and Wittenberg

---

1. Clark, *British Clubs and Societies*, 32.
2. Ibid., 34.
3. Bullock, *Voluntary Religious Societies*, 121–22.
4. Ibid., 123–24.

Universities he traveled to England, studying at Queen's College, Oxford (completing the Master's degree begun in Wittenberg). He was ordained in the Church of England, and after a period at the court of the Elector Palatine returned to England to take up a post at the Savoy Chapel. While at the Savoy he was awarded the degree of Doctor of Divinity by Cambridge University.

Bullock offers a suggestion of the Unitary society's purpose: "Horneck's pastoral work and sermons so moved a large number of young men that they began in 1678 to meet together with him weekly for devotional purposes and for mutual instruction in *The Principles* of the faith."[5] Portus echoed this, and suggested that the Savoy Society began because young men were approaching their ministers "concerning their awakened state."[6] The Savoy Society was concerned with poor relief[7] and two members were elected to act as Stewards, responsible for the administration of funds. Josiah Woodward gave them an alternative title, "*Managers* of their charity."[8]

Savoy Society membership was confined to confirmed Anglicans. In addition, as the first rule indicated, prospective members had to "resolve upon a holy and serious life."[9] The rules were also heavily influenced in favor of the presiding minister having a veto on prospective members.[10] The local clergyman who led and directed the society acted as "president." Horneck's rules are general as to the choice of minister, which was open to the society members, but once appointed, he directed business and regulated admission. There were no lay leaders in his society.

Bullock described Horneck's role as "general spiritual adviser,"[11] and this role can be seen in the rules which he drew up.[12] Horneck was not automatically the Director of societies he founded. If, as Bullock states, citing Dr. Richard Kidder, Horneck "had the care of several societies of

---

5. Ibid., 127.
6. Portus, *Caritas Anglicana*, 10.
7. See Appendix 1.
8. Woodward, *An Account of the Rise and Progress of the Religious Societies in the City of London &C. And of the Endeavours for the Reformation of Manners Which have been made Therein*, 37.
9. Appendix 1: Rule 1.
10. Appendix 1: Rule 14.
11. Bullock, *Voluntary Religious Societies*, 128.
12. See Appendix 1.

young men"[13] he would have been anxious to create rules which could be used at any number of societies.

The significance of membership is further evidenced by the weekly payment toward a "poor fund."[14] Funds were increased by fines paid by members who absented themselves from meetings,[15] and by the "fine" of five shillings paid to leave the society.[16] This undoubtedly increased the value of membership, and ensured that members took the pursuit of seriousness and holiness with due diligence.

The philanthropic nature of these early societies grew, and as the number of societies increased, so did the work they accomplished through their weekly giving. Societies distributed monies to the poor, to widows and orphans and provided money for a funeral sermon for any deceased member.[17] Woodward wrote:

> at every meeting (as it was advis'd) they consider the Wants of the Poor, which in time amounted to considerable sums, that thereby many *poor families* have been reliev'd, some *poor people* set into a way of Trade suitable to their Capacities, sundry *Prisoners* set at liberty, some poor *Scholars* furthered in their Subsistence at the University, several *Orphans* Maintained.[18]

Bullock believed Spener's *Collegia Pietatis* influenced the design and nature of Horneck's society. Horneck was in the service of the Elector Palatine from 1669 to 1671, and Spener had been tutor to the Palatine princes some years before. His belief is speculative: "probably the Elector remained in close sympathy with his old tutor's ideals,"[19] and "it would appear very likely that Horneck would go to that city, (Frankfurt)."[20] The argument rests upon the assumption that Horneck heard about Spener's work and remembered it.

Bullock also asserted that Horneck probably read Spener's *Pia Desideria* and that he was in correspondence with others in Germany

---

13. Bullock, *Voluntary Religious Societies*, 128.
14. Appendix 1: Rule 11.
15. Appendix 1: Rule 10.
16. Appendix 1: Rule 16.
17. Portus, *Caritas Anglicana*, 17–18.
18. Woodward, *An Account*, 36.
19. Bullock, *Voluntary Religious Societies*, 130.
20. Ibid. (Words in brackets mine)

who knew of Spener's work and the *Collegia Pietatis*.²¹ Woodward's *Account* supports Bullock's argument. The second edition was published in 1698, but the first edition had already been widely read:

> Since the first edition of this *Account*, I have understood in my conversation with many Divines in and about this city, and by Letters from the remotest parts of this Land . . . that the Piety of many Persons, especially the younger sort, has been evidently enlivened thereby; and that it has been read by them *with a very Surprizing Joy.*²²

Likeminded people in other areas of England were picking up the patterns established in London, and knew of Horneck's society by the time the second edition was published. Samuel Wesley knew of Woodward's book by 1701, asking for a copy in a letter to the SPCK in June 1701, and writing in his own *Account of the Religious Society begun in Epworth* that he read "over with more attention then (sic) formerly Dʳ Woodward's Book of the Religious Societys Edit: 3."²³

Bullock noted similarities from the general design of the rules to further support his argument. These included the need for an ordained director; the encouragement of holiness; the avoidance of controversy; the need for confirmation; the assistance of the poor; self-examination, and loving one another. There are points at which Spener's rules diverge, but Bullock wrote: "Their similarities are far closer than their differences, and the resemblances between them do seem too close to be purely accidental and un-associated."²⁴ This point is interesting, and if true, it serves to emphasize the associations that were being made amongst Christian groups. This is not to say that they were by any means slavishly adopting another group's rules and style, but that a pre-existing society provided the base for a new society with its own distinctive ethos. Such a move will be seen through the formation of the rules at Fetter Lane. Although not a Moravian society at the outset, there were many similarities with the Herrnhut rules.

---

21. See O'Brien, "Eighteenth Century Publishing Networks in the First Years of Transatlantic Evangelicalism," 38–57.

22. Woodward, *An Account*, 18.

23. Allen and McClure, *Two Hundred Years: The History of the Society for Promoting Christian Knowledge. 1698–1898*, 89.

24. Bullock, *Voluntary Religious Societies*, 131.

Portus, charting the life of the Savoy Society, noted two events that occurred after the accession of James II.[25] First, societies which "enjoined that strangers were only to be admitted to meetings with extreme caution, and membership was only accomplished after private discussion of a candidate's fitness,"[26] were open to attack as secret Catholic societies. While this caused some members to leave the societies, it resulted in a second effect: the creation of societies expressly founded to combat Catholicism,[27] through endowments for the provision of preachers, and the establishment of regular lectures, prior to holy communion. These endowments were anti-Catholic.

Secondly, as a result of suspicion many religious societies moved from private to public meetings, becoming "clubs." These meetings could be in public houses, where "spending the odd shilling in drink, they continued to remain unmolested."[28] This contrasted with the Poplar Regulations, which expressly urged members to avoid public houses and playhouses. By the time the Poplar Regulations were written, religious societies had embraced characteristics of the *Societies for the Reformation of Manners*, and lewd and profane behavior was no doubt believed to have been most rife in those places. These new "clubs" are written up in Portus' account of the early societies. Of fifteen societies, only one met in church. The others met in "private chambers or taverns."[29]

Over time, societies came to be regarded as an element of church life for young men, and Bishop Compton of London and Archbishop Tillotson of Canterbury approved of them.[30] After Horneck's death, other societies were founded to achieve similar aims to those of the Savoy Society. Josiah Woodward provided the most informative account of the

---

25. Woodward, *An Account*, 38. Woodward gives a short, yet graphic account of the executions that took place after the accession of James II in 1685.

26. Portus, *Caritas Anglicana*, 12–13.

27. Woodward, *An Account*, 39–41.

28. Portus, *Caritas Anglicana*, 14. See also Woodward, *An Account*, 42.

29. Ibid., 20–21.

30. Ibid., 15. Compton stated "God forbid that I should be against such excellent designs." Tillotson stated "these *Societies* were a support to our *Church*." See also Woodward, *An Account*, 50–65. In chapter III "An Account of the Progress of These Societies; and of the Real Aim and Design" Woodward details the progress of the societies and within the chapter relates the difficulties initially faced by them in relation to the established church.

earliest societies. He was involved with a religious society in Poplar,[31] the London parish of which he was vicar. The rules of his society are fuller than those of the Savoy Society, and chart a development in thinking and practice in the purpose of a religious society.

Woodward's Society had similar rules to Horneck's but elaborates the recommendations relating to personal conduct. The Poplar Regulations are as much concerned with behavior in society, especially to frequenting public houses and taverns, the avoidance of gambling "ale-house games"[32] and "lewd play-houses"[33] as they are with behavior within the society itself. Scriptural warrants are applied to some of the rules, perhaps to give them greater strength with the membership. This is especially true of rule 10, with 20 numbered sub-headings, 17 of which have one or more passages of Scripture annexed.

Bullock suggested two significant changes developed in later societies, especially Fetter Lane: lay leadership and the opportunity for deeper spiritual conversation. I suggest there is a third, drawn from Woodward's model; the abstention from licentious behavior, coupled with a keen interest in the maintenance of public morality.

Lay leadership was exercised through elected stewards[34] who oversaw the distribution of monies to the poor and regulated entry into the society.[35] Stewards also had authority to "exclude any member proved guilty of any mis-behaviour, after due admonition, unless he gives sufficient testimony of his repentance and amendment, before the whole Society."[36]

Poplar Society stewards have no social function related to their role to distribute funds to the poor, as in Horneck's Savoy Society.[37] They are elected to fulfill a quasi-judicial role in the admission and exclusion of members. Woodward's *Account* also indicated that when the Society director, an ordained minister, was not present, a Steward might fulfill the director's duties at the meeting. Guidelines were laid down for the execution of this role:

---

31. These rules, called *the Poplar Regulations* are annexed at Appendix 2.
32. Appendix 2: Rule 9.
33. Ibid.
34. Appendix 2: Rule 5.
35. Appendix 2: Rule 8.
36. Ibid.
37. Appendix 1: Rule 12.

one of the Stewards (if the director be absent), or any other person desired, may begin the conference thus–there follows an exhortation and form of prayers, then a reading from Scripture with pauses, so that any member can interject a remark if he so desires, "or some part of an approved exposition on the Holy Scripture or on the catechism may be read."[38]

The lay leader at that meeting could also decide on the subject for the following week's meeting.

Spiritual conversation was encouraged and achieved by allowing members to comment during the reading of Scripture, and through the detailed subheadings of rule 10, which indicate that personal spiritual advancement was not achieved at society meetings alone but during private devotions, public prayer, and attendance at the Lord's Supper.

The final major development was the interest and requirement placed upon members to be involved with the reformation of public morals and manners. This development is significant as the Savoy Society was founded merely for those resolved "upon a holy and serious life."[39] The members who accepted the Poplar Regulations as societal government acquiesced to abstention from attending taverns and theaters,[40] and a pro-active role in promoting public morals and the maintenance of social order.[41] Again, scriptural warrant is given to this element of the society's business. Here, for the first time, the religious society is not merely for the purpose of private advancement in faith, but for the upholding of the social status quo, as an outworking of the designs of the Kingdom of God.

By the time the Poplar Regulations were codified, there were many societies formed with the purpose of reforming public morals: "During the reigns of Charles II and James II, profanity, drunkenness, immorality, and excessive gambling were particularly rife. Sunday observance was very slack."[42] The *Societies for the Reformation of Manners*, which flourished from 1691, used many tactics to achieve their stated aim including informing on offenders.

---

38. Bullock, *Voluntary Religious Societies*, 143.
39. Appendix 1: Rule 1.
40. Appendix 2: Rule 9.
41. Appendix 2: Rule 11.
42. Bullock, *Voluntary Religious Societies*, 135.

There was a cross-fertilization between the two distinct groups, and from the Poplar Regulations it is apparent that religious societies adopted one aspect of the work of the reforming societies: the moral imperative for improving public behavior, by personal adherence to the law, and through societal action to procure adherence to the law.

In 1693, Dissenters were allowed to join the reforming societies; the first time Anglicans and Dissenters shared a common purpose. This mutuality extended only to the *Societies for the Reformation of Manners*. The next time such a union would occur would be in Fetter Lane 45 years later, in a religious, rather than a reforming society.

THE SOCIETY FOR THE PROMOTION OF CHRISTIAN KNOWLEDGE

The Society for the Promotion of Christian Knowledge (SPCK), founded in 1698, is the only surviving religious society from the early period of religious association.

The SPCK first met on March 8th 1698–1699. Amongst the founders was "The Right Honble the Lord Guildford, Sr Humphrey Mackworth, Mr. Justice Hook, Dr. Bray, Co. Colchester."[43] This society is distinctive in that its founders were gentlemen. Among the early corresponding members was the Reverend Samuel Wesley.

The purpose of the SPCK was the furtherance of the gospel, both in Britain and overseas. It supported missionaries abroad, and provided publications to create "Parochial Libraries throughout the Plantations."[44] Smaller parishes in Britain were to be endowed with "catechetical Libraries"[45] to encourage young people to be taught the Christian religion. These were enhanced with the provision of schools to educate poor children to read and write. The schools were aimed at eradicating vice and debauchery, and overcoming gross ignorance of Christian principles.[46]

Portus contended that the SPCK sought to achieve the same aims as the reforming societies by approaching the problem through education and publication. He stated: "It attacked the cause rather than the

---

43. Allen and McClure, *Two Hundred Years*, 13.
44. Ibid., 22.
45. Ibid., 23.
46. Ibid., 27. See the order for Charity Schools.

result of the evil which was manifested in contemporary manners, and therefore it gradually supplanted the Reforming Societies."[47] The SPCK did not act as a religious society. Today the SPCK might be termed as a "para-society," which works above the grass roots of societal structure.

Peter Clark argues that although the influence of the moral reform societies was waning, the SPCK was providing financial and institutional support for the continuing societies in London and beyond.[48] He also argues that the SPCK alone withstood the decline of moral reform societies. This was possible because of its "extensive institutional structure."[49] Through this, the SPCK was able to be:

> Active in fostering local religious societies and charity schools, the SPCK provided continuing support for moral reform during the first half of the eighteenth century.[50]

Religious societies began outside London once the SPCK began distributing publications, and of note is the Epworth Society of the Reverend Samuel Wesley.

THE EPWORTH SOCIETY

Samuel knew of the work of the religious societies, and wrote an article about their design in *A Letter Concerning The Religious Societies*. (An appendix to *The Pious Communicant Rightly Prepared*). Wesley believed societies were helpful to members and clergy of large parishes. Membership was a guard against the world: "these Christian societies now erected namely to make a stand for religion and virtue, so many redoubts against an encroaching world."[51]

Membership was limited to communicants, and met "wholly upon a religious account to promote true piety in themselves and others and all of them are strict members of the Church of England."[52] In the article, Samuel Wesley mentioned the Marquis de Renty's religious societies. Though he was a Catholic, Samuel considered de Renty:

---

47. Portus, *Caritas Anglicana*, 62.
48. Clark, *British Clubs and Societies*, 75.
49. Ibid., 434.
50. Ibid., 434.
51. Wesley, *A Letter Concerning The Religious Societies*.
52. Ibid.

The noble and pious de Renty in France was of this number. He employed much of his time in this happy exercise particularly at Caen, where he settled many societies of devout persons to meet weekly, and consult about the relief of the poor and preventing offences against God.[53]

Samuel understood the society's purpose was not to create schism or new churches from existing congregations, "but rather to promote the glory of God in the practice of humility and charity."[54]

Wesley began a society in Epworth after reading Woodward's *Account*.[55] His parish had around 7,000 inhabitants in 1701[56] and he had no curate. His aim was to reform manners and increase spirituality. Samuel Wesley did not use informers, but education and religious devotion. Wesley sought and received the agreement of his bishop to begin a society. The first Epworth meeting was held on the 7th February 1701, with eight people. These were young men, and at least one (if not all) was in the choir.[57]

Samuel Wesley's report to the SPCK states, "There are I believe 30 or 40 other sober persons in the Town who would be glad to enter the society."[58] Lay leadership was allowed when Samuel Wesley could not be present. "The members of the Society promis'd to continue in my absence."[59]

Eventually, as the need for more groups emerged, others were put into leadership of new groups. New members were admitted only by unanimous consent.[60] The results were notable, members becoming "much more careful of their lives and conversations."[61] Rack remarks that the meetings were not solely for personal edification and spiritual

---

53. Ibid.
54. Watson, *The Early Methodist Class Meeting*, 72.
55. Portus, *Caritas Anglicana*, 146. See also Allen and McClure, *Two Hundred Years*, 89. The addition of the work of the society in Old Romney spurred Samuel Wesley to form the Epworth Religious Society.
56. Allen and McClure, *Two Hundred Years*, 88.
57. Ibid., 90.
58. Ibid., 91.
59. Ibid., 90.
60. See Appendix 3: Rule III.
61. Watson, *The Early Methodist Class Meeting*, 72.

growth. He writes, "They intended to help the poor and to correspond with similar societies abroad and translate their tracts."[62]

The Epworth Society took a cautious approach to admission to the group, restricting membership to those who had themselves been converted and were serious about spiritual growth. A regular collection was taken which was used to educate the poor, purchase treatises, correspond with other societies and care for the poor and sick. Samuel's Society met to nourish the individual soul and provide a form of social service. This was to be further advanced by the erection of a charity school in the parish.

JOHN WESLEY AND THE RELIGIOUS SOCIETIES

There is little available detail about the work of Anglican religious societies up to 1738 when John Wesley returned from Georgia, and it is Wesley's *Journal* and *Diary* which offer the greatest amount of information about these societies in the second quarter of the eighteenth century. From May 1st 1738, Wesley became involved with the Fetter Lane Society. However, he remained an assiduous preacher at numerous societies across London. There had clearly been some developments in societal meeting by 1738 as Wesley records meetings in homes and taverns.

Wesley was regularly present at meetings at Mr. Exall's[63] home on a Saturday evening. Wesley's correspondence to his brother indicates this was not a small band-like group: "Many were cut to the heart, both here (at Lady Hume's) and at Mr. Exall's."[64] Exall belonged to Fetter Lane, and remained with Wesley after his separation from that society.[65] John Bray held a meeting in his home[66] and Thomas Crouch,[67] organized a society at Dowgate Hill, with regular visitation from John Wesley.

Wesley was also involved with traditional societies across London, most of which followed traditional rules. Rack points out that while

---

62. Rack, *Reasonable Enthusiast*, 53.
63. Wesley, *Works [BE]*, Vol. 19, 13.
64. Wesley, *Letters [SE]*, Vol. I, 337.
65. Libby, "The Personnel of the Fetter Lane Society," 145.
66. See Appendix 9. The *Diary* entry for the same day, shows Wesley "at home; Society" at 6pm. See Wesley, *Works [BE]*, Vol. 19, 406.
67. See Appendix 9. Wesley later records attending meetings at Dowgate Hill. Wesley, *Works [BE]*, Vol. 19, See 375, 377, 407 & 415.

Fetter Lane was a break from the societies that preceded it, other "traditional" societies were beginning at the same time:

> In fact a new crop of societies was beginning to emerge, and these as well as some of the old ones would be infiltrated by the Moravians and Whitefield converts, reflecting the doctrine and priorities of the "new birth."[68]

The Aldersgate Street Society was founded by James Hutton and it was here that John Wesley found his heart strangely warmed in May 1738. He attended it at least twice after his return from Germany in 1738.[69] The entries for this society are interesting, as on the first occasion (20th September 1738) the *Journal* reads, "I spoke the truth in love at a society in Aldersgate Street,"[70] while the *Diary* records "6 At James Hutton's, Mrs Claggett,[71] etc; sang; religious talk; prayed."[72] On the second occasion (Sunday 11th February 1739), it appears Wesley led a traditional preaching service there: "3 At Aldersgate, read Prayers, Sermon."[73] Wesley's *Journal* and *Diary* agree on the societies that he visited. Although the *Diary* names more societies, the *Journal* adds notes about Wesley's relationship with these societies.

Some societies clearly hired rooms over public houses: "8 At the Green Man, religious talk";[74] "4 Plaistow, The Ship; Mr Bray etc, teas, religious talk,"[75] "1 At The Three Cups, religious talk, dinner, prayed."[76] In all, Wesley attended and spoke at 32 societies[77] across London between September 1738 and July 1740, most regularly at the Savoy Society.[78]

---

68. Rack, *Reasonable Enthusiast*, 141. Rack cites Podmore's article in the *Proceedings*, Vol. XLVI. 1988, part 5, 125–153. as a definitive account of these new societies.

69. See Appendix 9. See also Wesley, *Works [BE]*, Vol. 19, 375.

70. Wesley, *Works [BE]*, Vol. 19, 13.

71. Mrs. Claggett's personal testimony is contained in the *Early Methodist Volume* held at the John Rylands University Library Manchester, 41.

72. Wesley, *Works [BE]*, Vol. 19, 354. For further information about the site of the society that met here see Wesley, *Journal [SE]*, Vol. II, 475. Footnote 1.

73. Appendix 9, Wesley, *Works [BE]*, Vol. 19, 375.

74. Appendix 9. See Wesley, *Works [BE]*, Vol. 19, 393.

75. Ibid., 407.

76. Ibid., 408.

77. See Appendix 9.

78. Wesley, *Works [BE]*, Vol. 19, 354. Wesley attended this society seventeen times, always on a Thursday.

As a clergyman without a parish living, Wesley was free to visit Anglican societies. This became more important to Wesley as incumbents who considered Wesley to be an enthusiast closed their pulpits to him. From September 1738, frequent notes in the *Journal* show that Wesley was welcomed at fewer and fewer churches:

> Sunday 5, (November) in the morning at St. Botolph's, Bishopsgate, in the afternoon at Islington, and in the evening to such a congregation as I never saw before at St. Clement's in the Strand. As this was the first time of my preaching here, I suppose it is to be the last.[79]

One Sunday, Wesley preached in Spitalfields in the morning and afternoon, but the invitation to conduct the evening service was withdrawn. Wesley notes that this gave him, "a good remembrance that I should, if possible, declare at every time the *whole* counsel of God."[80] Benham's *Memoirs* of 1856 related the closure of pulpits to "negligence and unconcern"[81] on the part of the clergy. However, he accused the Methodists of "misguided zeal and unexampled indiscretion."[82]

John Walsh addressed the issue of membership in the Anglican societies to 1740, when Wesley broke away from Fetter Lane, and the Methodist movement began. Prior to the field preaching of Whitefield and Wesley, Walsh states: "recruitment to the societies had been aimed at the urban, literate and respectable of Dr Woodward's social milieu,"[83] the new Methodists in contrast attracted "the 'outcasts', 'the forlorn ones'; the marginalized who squatted on the edges and in the gaps of the parochial system."[84]

To that must be added Methodism's ability to cut into existing societal life. Walsh's comment is stark:

> The rapidity with which early Methodism established itself owed a great deal to its ability to cannibalise the religious societies of London, Bristol and elsewhere.[85]

---

79. Ibid., 20.
80. Ibid., 35. The chapel was in the patronage of Sir George Wheeler's family.
81. Benham, *Memoirs of James Hutton*, 42.
82. Ibid., 42.
83. Walsh, "Religious Societies: Methodist and Evangelical 1738–1800," 286.
84. Ibid., 286–87.
85. Ibid., 284.

The first Methodist society in St Ives, Cornwall, began after visits by Joseph Turner. At his initial visit in 1743 he met with a distinctly Anglican Society. Simon comments that their rules were "founded probably on Dr Woodward's plan."[86] After visits by two lay preachers and Charles Wesley in that year, the group became a Methodist society.

Anglican opposition to the new "enthusiasts" was vigorous and vociferous. Thomas Bullock received widespread support from lay leaders of the older religious societies in London in 1743, when at the behest of the Bishop of London, he publicly opposed the Moravians. The stewards of the older societies also acted to remove those who attached themselves to Whitefield, or other enthusiasts.[87] In 1759, there were still 14 "old style" religious societies in London, and older pre-1740 societies continued to exist without Methodist or Evangelical Anglican influence. Rack cites the *Diary* of Thomas Day, a Methodist, who in 1756 met three "old style" societies in Southwark.[88]

To address, or perhaps offer, an apologia for his role amongst the new societies, George Whitefield wrote a public letter in 1740, outlining the differences between the old and new societies. Whitefield stated his fondness for the old societies which had been overshadowed by new societies. Rack mentions Whitefield's comment that the new societies offered the opportunity of "confessing your faults and communicating your experiences to one another."[89] This same opportunity was a major stronghold of Wesley's *Rules of the Band Societies*[90] written in December 1738.

ANGLICAN RESPONSES TO METHODISM

Unsurprisingly within Anglicanism there was a move to counter Methodist societies as evangelical clergy began to fill parishes. Their presence aroused parishioners' desires for more than the Sunday services, and in response, the evangelicals of the Church of England adopted

---

86. Simon, *John Wesley and the Methodist Societies*, 139.

87. Bullock, *Voluntary Religious Societies*, 200.

88. Rack, "Religious Societies," 583.

89. Ibid., 586. Rack cites from Whitefield's *Letter to the Religious Societies lately set on foot in several parts of England and Wales*. Extracts of this letter are contained in Luke Tyerman's *Life of George Whitefield* published in 1877 (pp. 317–19).

90. Wesley, *Works [SE]*, Vol. 9, 77–78. See also Appendix 11 rules 4, 6, and 11. The openness of conversation in the Bands was its hallmark. All conversation *in band* was confidential.

the society system. These clergy were well aware that failure to satisfy their parishioners' needs would only lead to Dissenters and Methodists doing that for them.

William Grimshaw began religious societies in Rochdale in 1741. After meeting Benjamin Ingham, William Darney, and John Nelson, he began classes modeled it seems upon the Methodist pattern in Howarth:

> I joined people (such as were truly seeking or had found the Lord) in Society . . . These meetings . . . are held once a week, about two hours, and are called "Classes," consisting of about ten or twelve members each.[91]

Thomas Vivian[92] in Cornwood organized his societies directly on the Methodist model, even using Methodist hymnody.[93] Others formed societies that were very different. For example, Hervey's Society in the Northampton area required members to bring copies of the New Testament in Greek to meetings.

The parish system with its vagaries of size and location frequently dictated how religious societies should be organized. In a compact parish, clergy supervision was reasonably simple, and the strict clerical hold over the business of each meeting was maintained. For Henry Venn, vicar of Huddersfield, however, clerical authority was tempered by the vastness of his parish. Walsh writes, "Their (the classes) remoteness meant that Venn could only visit them monthly and had to recognize their self-governing autonomy."[94] Venn was in contact with John Wesley from 1754, and they met in 1759. The Methodist society which met within his large parish existed before Venn took the incumbency; Wesley refused to disband it and a compromise was reached that Methodist preachers would enter the parish only monthly. In 1771 Venn[95] moved to Yelling, and his successor who was not of the same evangelical fervor soon found

---

91. Bullock, *Voluntary Religious Societies*, 203.

92. The Reverend Thomas Vivian (1720–1793) was vicar of the parish of Cornwood, a small village near Ivybridge, Devon. Vivian was in correspondence with Wesley, and had been ejected from his curacy in Redruth owing to his sympathetic stance towards Methodism. See Wesley, *Works [BE]*, Vol. 20, 402–3. See footnote 45.

93. See Walsh, "Religious Societies," 296.

94. Walsh, "Religious Societies," 296. (Words in brackets mine.)

95. Pawson, "The Life of John Pawson," 34. Pawson recounts the Conference decision to begin preaching in Venn's parish after his move to Yelling.

the societies failing. Members left the Church and joined other churches, while others formed a separate meeting. Even though this vicar left after two years, Venn's work could not be re-established.

In Truro, Cornwall, Samuel Walker, curate at St Mary's, organized religious societies[96] based upon Woodward's model. Walker restricted membership to regular communicants. He ran the society formally, allowing no extempore prayer and no one other than the director or the deputy could speak.[97] The aim of the Truro religious society was threefold: "to glorify God—to quicken and confirm ourselves in faith and holiness—and to render us more useful among our neighbours."[98] Unwritten, but clearly intended, was the preservation of the Established Church.[99]

Samuel Walker borrowed the band system and allowed freedom of speech in the small segregated groups, forbidden in the meeting of the society. Personal behavior was the major topic of discussion, and members were free to encourage or reprove others. Walker published a small book to help these bands in their business, as he was not present at the smaller meetings.[100] The deputy mentioned in rules 5, 10, and 11 of appendix 5 might have functioned as "band leader." Samuel Walker was highly directive in the business of the Truro Society bands, but in allowing the creation of this sub-group, he was seeking to enable deeper Christian discipleship, or trying to beat the Methodists at their own game.

In 1755, Walker urged Wesley not to found Methodist societies in parishes where there was an evangelical incumbent, and to ensure that the Methodist movement did not separate from the Church of England. Wesley refused to accept the suggestion on the grounds that when a clergyman moved away his successor might not be evangelical.

---

96. See Appendix 4.
97. See Walsh, "Religious Societies," 297.
98. Bullock, *Voluntary Religious Societies*, 206.
99. There is a shorter and possibly earlier set of rules held at Lambeth Palace Library in the *Lavington Papers*. These rules expressly direct the manner of business to be conducted, and print the prayers and collects which were to be used. See *Articles of the Religious Societys at Truro* Lambeth Palace Library, Secker 8.16, Lavington Papers. These are annexed at Appendix 5.
100. See Bullock, *Voluntary Religious Societies*, 210–11. Sidney's book *The Life, Ministry and Selections from the Remains of the Rev Samuel Walker* was published in 1835.

James Hervey, a Holy Club member and clergyman, who began societies during his ministry, was believed to have written to Wesley asking why he allowed Methodist societies in parishes of which he was not incumbent. Wesley's reply contains the phrase "I look upon all the world as my parish."[101] Although it is not now clear to whom Wesley was replying, he is plainly arguing that his commission under God to preach the gospel is greater than the niceties of parish convention.

Hervey became an evangelical in 1741, and agreed with Methodist principles. Like Walker, Hervey began his own society, an *Assembly for Christian Improvement*.[102] Members paid fees for belonging and fines for non-attendance to the treasurer to be used for charitable purposes. Meetings were held at inns and the times of commencement and finishing were clearly stated. As mentioned above, this society heard readings in New Testament Greek. A working knowledge of Greek was unusual, and may have limited membership to clergy and gentlemen. Hervey later met Samuel Walker and declared that a society formed upon his rules was "productive of great good, and in some degree revives the dropping interest of Christianity, wherever it was prudently managed."[103]

From 1740, the Anglicans did not stand by and watch the Methodists use the Religious Society for their own ends. Evangelical Anglican clergy realized that their preaching and ministry required parishioners to meet midweek for instruction and support, if they were not to be lost to the Methodists. In contrast, the older, High Church societies waned in influence as their purpose of promoting holiness of living and the reformation of society lost impetus.

For many evangelical clergy the problem with Methodism lay in its aggressive growth and refusal to stay away from evangelical parishes. Many clergy who were in sympathy with the aims of Methodism became wary when Methodism became embroiled in discussions over administration of the sacraments, and the resulting possible consequence of separation from the Church of England.

---

101. Wesley, *Works [BE]*, Vol. 25, 616. For the *Journal* entry see Wesley, *Works [BE]*, Vol. 19, 67. The letter that Wesley wrote to Hervey on March 20th 1739, previously thought to contain this phrase has now been found. See Wesley, *Works [BE]*, Vol. 25, 609–10. The recipient of this letter may have been John Clayton.

102. Bullock, *Voluntary Religious Societies*, 214. See Appendix 5.

103. Ibid., 216.

However, Anglicanism's failure lay in an inability to organize a system of quasi-connexional religious societies across the country, offering an alternative to Methodism clearly within the Established Church. There are three main reasons for this: the broadness of Anglican churchmanship; the right to the freehold of the parish afforded to the clergy, which often meant incumbents remained in post for many years;[104] and the inability of parish clergy to reach those whom Bishop Butler had described as "the rabble."[105]

Rack poses two interesting arguments which further account for the decline in Anglican societies. The first is simply that the Anglicans sought to change society through influence in the upper echelons of society, including the royal family. Lady Huntingdon hoped for preferment for George Whitefield to the episcopacy and she "did her best to insinuate evangelicalism into the prince's circle."[106] Secondly, the inherent Calvinism of the Anglican Evangelicals meant they had no need to subdivide their societies into small groups for discipling and spiritual growth; rejecting any form of perfection negated any need of meeting in societies. In Methodism, a member had a personal goal to aim for perfection, and the achievement (or failure) of that goal was seen in band and select band membership.

The English religious movement that began in earnest with Horneck's Savoy Society developed from the Restoration. Anglicanism post-1660 was concerned with maintaining its fragile place as state church, and the Non-Juring ejections of the period, combined with the later societies, were intended to impose Anglican doctrine and order on post-Commonwealth England. The Piety and Puritanism which Anglicanism intended to overcome could never be assuaged, and even in Horneck's Society, overtones of Dissenting doctrines can be traced, although Dissenters could not belong. This derived in part through the recent Puritanism of the Commonwealth and the sixteenth-century thinking on which it fed. It also developed through the increasingly associational and mobile leaders of religious thought who corresponded

---

104. For example, The Reverend Samuel Wesley was rector at Epworth for 40 years (1695–1735). Likewise Thomas Vivian was vicar of Cornwood for 46 years (1747–1793). Both remained in their parish until their deaths.

105. Walsh, "Religious Societies," 287.

106. Rack, "Religious Societies," 592. This was Prince Frederick, Prince of Wales, the eldest son of George II. The prince died in 1751.

with and visited other Christian leaders whose novel doctrines or practices could be considered and used in other countries.

Thus far, I have outlined the development of the Unitary societies from the Savoy Society of 1678. With the foundation of the SPCK the purposes of the Unitary societies became widely known. Samuel Wesley's Epworth Society was modeled on the Poplar Regulations of Woodward. The rules of the societies charted in this chapter[107] show that within the Unitary system the purpose of meeting developed over time; Horneck's Society provided the basis for the rules of the other societies.

THE DISTINCTIVES OF THE UNITARY SOCIETIES

This chapter turns now to consider the aspects of societal life that were common to all the societies from 1678 to the founding of Fetter Lane in 1738. I have shown that Unitary societies continued post 1738, and these distinctives can be seen in those societies that were not touched by the doctrines of New Birth, felt assurance or perfection.

The turn to seriousness and holiness

The rules of the Savoy Society and the Poplar Regulations countered a prevailing trend away from religion that arose during the Restoration. Clark argues that the ascendancy of Catholicism in the Court and growing numbers of Dissenters gave impetus to the desire to encourage young men to remain within the Church of England. With the passing of the Toleration Act in 1689, Dissent gained a more stable position, which encouraged the building of new chapels for worship. The need therefore to encourage young men to remain Anglicans was all the greater after the Glorious Revolution.

In an England which had come through a period of civil war and the Commonwealth, the Anglican Church was no longer the sole repository of faith and teaching. Puritanism had replaced Anglicanism during the Protectorate, and although the Restoration ensured there was a return to the established order, the "old order" could not be wholly reconstituted. The Puritans, instrumental in the Restoration, were not going to surrender their gains quietly:

---

107. See Appendices 1 to 5.

The Presbyterians had played an important part in the Restoration, and appeared to be firmly entrenched in positions of power.[108]

For this reason amongst others, the Church was anxious to ensure that young men turned toward the Church of England. Even though the Test Act prevented Catholics from holding positions of authority, and Dissenters were sporadically persecuted, there was still a danger that some might be drawn toward the practice of religion beyond the Church of England.

The seriousness required from the Poplar Regulations placed a duty upon individual members to practice their faith beyond the society and the organized church, and rule 10[109] which has 20 subsections, was no doubt intended to offer members a yardstick by which to measure their progress. John Wesley's turn to seriousness in 1725 was said by him to have been occasioned by reading à Kempis. However the Poplar Regulations have a very similar aim to those he expressed in his retrospective account of May 1738.[110] Wesley's turn to a devoted and holy life bear a remarkable likeness to these subsections.[111]

Reformation of manners

A development of the personal resolution to holiness, seen in the Poplar regulations, was the desire to reform the behavior of others. The Savoy rules do not envisage the need to reform the behavior of others, and concentrate wholly on the member's personal living. Samuel Wesley's society takes a similar line, but coming from the early SPCK tradition the desire to reform manners was evidenced by the distribution of tracts and pamphlets, and the opening of charity schools, rather than by using informants as the *Societies for the Reformation of Manners* did.

The desire to reform manners, evident in the Poplar Regulations, is not obvious. It may be that as societies which sought to reform manners became popular, religious societies lost members, and these new rules encouraged members to remain by including the business of reforming society to the business of reforming self.

---

108. Cragg, *The Church & the Age of Reason 1648-1789*, 50.
109. See Appendix 2.
110. Wesley, *Works [BE]*, Vol. 18, 244.
111. Appendix1: Rule 10.

Young membership

The societies founded by Horneck and Woodward were aimed at young men, over sixteen,[112] confirmed into the Church of England. Clark argues that these men, predominantly apprentices, were using the society structure in the manner of the earlier trade guilds for career advancement, and spiritual development.[113] Samuel Wesley may have had members younger than this.[114] Common to all the annexed rules is the individual's need to express a desire to join the society. It is clear that belonging was a voluntary, and perhaps in some places enviable status, especially if Clark is correct and advancement in business could be found in a Unitary society.

Rules of entry

At a time when, as Woodward, Portus, and others pointed out, society was in need of religion, it may seem surprising that membership was strictly controlled. In the Savoy Society, the presiding clergyman controlled entry to the society[115] although the choice of presiding clergyman seemed to be made by the society members.[116] Under the Poplar regulations entry was controlled by elected stewards and the society,[117] but only after a careful examination of the applicant's reasons for joining. Samuel Wesley's Society allowed new members entry only with the unanimous consent of the existing membership.[118] The reason for this rule is simply the prevention of admittance to "a little leven" which would "spoil the wholelump."[119] Samuel Wesley's Society allowed subdivision when the group became larger than twelve.[120]

In time, joining a society was not simply an act of accepting regulations covering personal religious development. As some societies began to meet in public houses, or chose to meet away from church

---

112. Appendix 1: Rule 2.
113. Clark, *British Clubs and Societies*, 55.
114. Allen and McClure, *Two Hundred Years*, 90. Samuel Wesley approached a young man who was "sober and sensible" from amongst his singers.
115. Appendix 1: Rule 14.
116. Ibid., Rule 3.
117. Appendix 2: Rule 8.
118. Appendix 3: Rule III.
119. Ibid., Rule III. See also Rule V.
120. Ibid., Rule IIII.

buildings, rules expressely forbade vice, gambling, and drinking.[121] Moral uprightness might have occurred because societies which chose to meet openly in public houses were no longer fulfilling their primary aim of personal holiness.

Ordained/lay leadership

The developing role of the leaders of religious societies is easily traced through the annexed rules. In some respects, Samuel Wesley's Society is the most developed, for it allows for subgroups, using members of the earlier group as leaders of the new society.[122]

Horneck could not act as director of all the groups formed using the Savoy Rules, acting rather as a "spiritual advisor"[123] to a number of societies. The rules associated with the name of his church allowed only an ordained clergyman[124] as director. Presumably this rule was created to prevent dispute in theology and discussion of politics. The clergyman was also required for those elements of the liturgy reserved to the ordained priest.[125] Lay leadership was encouraged under the Poplar Regulations with elected stewards who acted as administrators and leaders in the absence of the clerical director. Horneck's society appointed stewards in an administrative position. Woodward required ordained clergy only for amendments of the rules.[126] Woodward envisaged each member of the society being a catechiser of "young and ignorant people in their families,"[127] a role enshrined by Samuel Wesley in his rules as a duty of membership.[128]

Allowing men to lead the societies formed from the first Epworth Society developed the role of lay leaders.[129] Samuel Wesley was forced to take this action as he was in a rural parish without clerical assistance.

---

121. Appendix 2: Rule 9.

122. Appendix 3: Rule IIII.

123. Bullock, *Voluntary Religious Societies*, 128. Bullock cites Dr. Richard Kidder who wrote that Horneck "had the care of several societies of young men," 128.

124. Appendix 1: Rule 3.

125. Ibid., Rules 4, 5 and 6.

126. Appendix 2: Rule 13.

127. Ibid., Rule 12.

128. Appendix 3: Rule VIIII.

129. Ibid., Rule IIII.

Henry Venn, vicar of the massive parish of Huddersfield, needed to staff the rural societies he had begun, and had no additional clerical help.

Walker's rules of 1754[130] allowed little lay participation in the Truro Society. He wanted Wesley to hand over the lay-led Methodist societies to local clergy, in part to prevent separation from the Church of England.[131] Wesley refused this request. Walker's fiercely prescriptive and protective rules for his own Society prevented any external interference.[132]

It is often asserted that John Wesley was responsible for the introduction of lay leadership and disciplined rules as standards for his societies from the early 1740s. It can be seen that over 50 years before, religious societies developed rules of government and organization. Their growth led to lay leadership through elected stewards, family catechists, and disciplined regulation. John Wesley distilled the rules of these early societies with the lessons learned from Fetter Lane into the rules of the United societies.

After 1738 the Fetter Lane Society eclipsed its predecessors and moved societal life forwards. Fetter Lane admitted women and Dissenters to the Society. Horneck and Woodward assumed that women would not be admitted, while Samuel Wesley expressly forbids their membership.[133] Samuel Walker allowed women to belong to a segregated Society in Truro, probably because the Methodist societies admitted women.[134] Dissenters were not admitted to any Unitary society, although Woodward's Regulations invited members to "express due Christian charity, candour and moderation to all such Dissenters as are of good conversation."[135]

From the early eighteenth century, the impetus of the religious societies to promote religion and reform manners began to wane, in part due to religious apathy. Many members held Jacobite views, which sat uneasily with the Hanoverian succession of 1714. The society meeting at St Giles Cripplegate specifically included a declaration of loyalty to King

---

130. Appendices 4 & 5.

131. Wesley, *Works [BE]*, Vol. 26, 582–86; 592–96 and 606–8. See also Wesley, *Letters [SE]*, Vol. II, 192–96.

132. See Rack, *Reasonable Enthusiast*, 300.

133. Appendix 3: Rule VIIII.

134. Appendix 4: Rules 1 and 2. Appendix 5: Rule 1.

135. Appendix 2: Rule 2.

George I, and Non-Jurors were ejected if they could not assent.[136] Portus suggested the declaration was required by outside authority.[137]

JAMES HUTTON AND THE UNITARY SOCIETIES

Many of Fetter Lane's leaders were actively involved in societal life before 1738. The Wesleys have already been considered in detail. James Hutton founded societies in London prior to 1738; one to read correspondence from the Wesleys while they were in Georgia. This meeting included "prayer, Bible study and mutual counsel."[138] Bullock asserted that John Wesley's letters to the Society influenced Hutton, especially as he was as dissatisfied with his own spiritual state as John Wesley was with his. He also founded the Society in Aldersgate Street.

Hutton's societies differed from the Unitary societies. He allowed members of the older societies to attend them by arranging different meeting times. The Reverend George Whitefield, who would lead his own branch of the revival, was known within Hutton's circle. He stirred people up and encouraged them to join Hutton's new societies. Whitefield also affected renewal amongst the older societies:

> When they applied to him personally for advice, he . . . recommended them to the society raised by Hutton and his friends, by which it was much increased, and so extensively made known that even the wardens of the original societies [the older religious societies], entreated Whitefield to preach their quarterly sermons before them.[139]

Portus attributes the introduction of extempore prayer to Whitefield, a feature that would be a mark of Methodism. The earlier religious societies had expressly forbidden extempore prayer as this was a Puritan practice, and a mark of Dissent.

CHAPTER SUMMARY

I have shown that by 1738 the religious associational milieu was untidy, having diversified from meetings at the Savoy Chapel to homes, public houses, and clubs. Societal life was no longer confined to young

136. Bullock, *Voluntary Religious Societies*, 165.
137. Portus, *Caritas Anglicana*, 195.
138. Bullock, *Voluntary Religious Societies*, 171.
139. Portus, *Caritas Anglicana*, 201.

men, as women who sought religious association were meeting beyond the traditional Unitary societies. Wesley attempted to meet that novel requirement. The foundation and life of the Fetter Lane Society encouraged religious association in a model of meeting which drew together Anglican and Moravian teaching and life.

This chapter has analyzed the purposes of the Unitary societies in their historical context. This approach is used in the next chapter, and will assist in understanding the new mode of association experienced at Fetter Lane.

The original approach of chapters 2 and 3, offers insights into the model of association found within the Wesleyan societies, and sets out clear indicators of the origins of the Methodists, and Wesley's openness to novel ideas, practices, and methods of religious awakening, justification, and discipleship. This openness would mean Wesley embraced the possibilities which the class meeting presented when suggested in 1742.

4

The Fetter Lane Society

CONTEXT

THE PREVIOUS CHAPTER OUTLINED the Wesleys' involvement with Anglican societies across London. This association continued during the Fetter Lane period, when John and Charles Wesley mixed not only in warm hearted, Pietist circles, but also with the Unitary societies, to whom they preached a gospel of justification by faith alone. It was this doctrine that caused pulpits to be closed to them, and the charge of enthusiast to be laid against them. Wesley was a tireless society preacher and was meeting with small groups, predominantly women, at his own home, and those of others.

THE FOUNDATION OF THE FETTER LANE SOCIETY

On the 1st May 1738 John Wesley was present at the foundation of what became the Fetter Lane Society, in the home and shop called the "Bible & Sun" of James Hutton, a bookseller. This was in Little Wild Street, now Keeley Street.[1]

Charles had returned to James Hutton's on the 28th April, and was immediately taken ill: "No sooner was I got to James Hutton's having removed my things thither from his father's, than the pain in my side returned, and with that my fever."[2] John traveled to Hutton's to visit Charles, and was present on the evening of the 1st May when the group met.

---

1. Watson and Heitzenrater state that this meeting occurred at the home of the Reverend John Hutton. This is incorrect. See Watson, *The Early Methodist Class Meeting*, 80. See also Heitzenrater, *Wesley and the People Called Methodists*, 79. However, Heitzenrater's incorrect name may simply be a typographical error.

2. Wesley, *Journal*, Vol. I, 85.

John Wesley records the creation of the Fetter Lane Society quite simply with the words, "This evening our little society began which afterwards met in Fetter Lane."[3] Peter Böhler convened the group but did not assume leadership. He was preparing to leave for America on the 4th May. Benham wrote of the first meetings, "During the stay of Peter Böhler in England, he made certain regulations among those who desired to walk in conformity to the mind of Jesus; and who at first consisted of six or eight persons in whom he had confidence."[4]

Present with Böhler (Moravian) and Wesley (clergyman) were James Hutton (bookseller) John Bray (brazier) Shepherd Wolf (barber) John Edmonds (poulterer) William Oxlee (clog-maker) William Hervey (wine-cooper) Matthew Clarke (barber) John Shaw (attorney, retired).[5] Curnock incorrectly suggests that Charles Wesley and Henry Piers, vicar of Bexley were present.[6] Podmore states the facts succinctly: "John Wesley was present only by chance, Charles Wesley ill in bed, and the vicar of Bexley, Henry Piers, miles away."[7]

Böhler did not expect John Wesley to be present at James Hutton's home. Wesley would have been in Oxford but for Charles' illness.[8] Others, however, were invited to Hutton's that evening and two additional names, other than those mentioned above, are included in Böhler's *Diary* entry:

> For just that time the brethren had been summoned who are of one mind and seek closer fellowship with each other and therefore want to form a band with each other, that is Hutton, Bray, Edmonds, Wolf, Clark, Oxlee, Procker, Harvey, Sweetland and Shaw and the elder Wesley.[9]

It is clear that Böhler's use of the word *antreffen* (meet, chance upon, unexpectedly) indicates Wesley's presence was chance. Böhler's *Diary* is positive about the future for this group; referring to men who may want

---

3. Wesley, *Works [BE]*, Vol.18, 236.
4. Benham, *Memoirs of James Hutton*, 29.
5. Trousdale, "The Moravian Society. Fetter Lane–London," 30.
6. Wesley, *Journal [SE]*, Vol. I, 458. Footnote 1.
7. Podmore, *The Moravian Church*, 40. The view that Henry Piers was present was re-stated in Bullock, *Voluntary Religious Societies*, 174.
8. Böhler, *Peter Böhler's Diary*, 1st May 1738 The original diary is in the Unitatsarchiv Herrnhut, and a copy is held at Moravian Church House. Ref: AB43.A3.
9. Ibid.

to join, "Fisch, Braun, Hartley, Greenich and others."[10] Fisch [or Fish] and Hartley are signatories to the letter of the 2nd May to Zinzendorf, asking that Böhler should remain amongst them.[11] The letter has a further six signatories, none of whom were present on the 1st May. For this reason the group can properly be described as a "band."[12] An indication of the age of these people is given by Böhler, "they will divide themselves and the youths and the men will meet separately. But every four weeks both classes will have a meeting together."[13]

George Whitefield's first contact with Fetter Lane came in December 1738 when he returned to England from America. His *Journal* gives the impression that Fetter Lane was the result of his own preaching and ministry: "In the evening went to a truly Christian Society in Fetter Lane, and perceived God had greatly watered the seed sown by my ministry when last in London."[14]

THE FETTER LANE RULES

There are three forms of rules for this group, but only two rules (created under the advice of Peter Böhler)[15] operated at the outset.[16] They were:

> That they will meet together once in a Week to confess their Faults one to another, and to pray for one another that they may be healed. [cf. James 5.16]
> That any others, of whose Sincerity they are well assured, may if they desire it, meet with them for that purpose.

The second part of rule 1, that society members should "confess their Faults one to another, and to pray for one another that they may be healed," bears a striking similarity with the wording of the Moravian band rule recorded by Wesley in his *Journal*[17] during his visit to Herrnhut some weeks later.

10. Ibid.,12th May 1738 (old style) 1st May 1738 (new style)

11. Benham, *The Memoirs of James Hutton*, 32.

12. Podmore, *The Moravian Church*, 400–411. Podmore notes that this initial group numbered only ten people. The letter to Zinzendorf has a further six signatories.

13. Böhler, *Peter Böhler's Diary*, 12th May 1738 (old style) 1st May 1738 (new style)

14. Whitefield, *George Whitefield's Journals*, 193.

15. Wesley, *Works [BE]*, Vol. 18, 236.

16. Wesley, *Works [BE]*, Vol. 9, 6.

17. Wesley, *Works [BE]*, Vol. 18, 292. See rule II part 3 "ninety bands, each of which

John West, describing the early meetings ascribes the creation of bands to Böhler, "At our request he (Böhler) formed us into bands."[18] West, like others, was influenced by Böhler's preaching, and although Böhler spoke only broken English, his words "came home with power to those who heard him."[19]

Trousdale's *Proceedings* article adds a further 28 rules according to a manuscript he accessed at the Moravian archives in Herrnhut,[20] and a further 31 rules according to the account in Benham's *Memoirs*.[21] Wesley's *Journal* records 11 rules under the date, 1st May.[22]

The rules of the Herrnhut manuscript (*Rules A*) and the *Memoirs* (*Rules B*) are the result of a process. These clearly show that on the 29th May a further three rules were added. On the 20th September (*Rules B* only) yet another rule was added. On the 26th September, final rules were included.

Wesley was absent when the 20th September rule was added, but present on the 26th September.[23] These additions took care of the creation of the society into bands (29th May) the nature of the band leader's role (20th September) and the conditions for entry to the bands and the society (26th September). As Podmore suggests, this was a society that was Anglican in membership but Moravian in organization.[24] There are rules common to them all, and *Rules A* and *Rules B* are considerably more detailed than Wesley's own *Journal* account in *Rules C*. Bullock pointed out that the *Journal* form of the rules noted only those which were considered "fundamental."[25]

Wesley left for Germany on the 14th June 1738 returning on the 16th September. The rule added on the 20th September (*Rules A*: 6) is

---

meets twice at least but most of them three times a week, to 'confess their faults one to another, that they may be healed."

18. "Memoirs of Brother John West," 238. (Name in brackets mine.)

19. Ibid., 238.

20. Appendix 6. Rules A. See Trousdale, "The Moravian Society. Fetter Lane–London,"

21. Appendix 7. Rules B. See Trousdale, "The Moravian Society. Fetter Lane–London," 32–35. See also Benham, *Memoirs of James Hutton*, 29–32.

22. Appendix 8. Rules C. See Wesley, *Works [BE]*, Vol. 18, 236–37.

23. Watson, *The Early Methodist*, 173. Endnote 70.

24. Podmore, *The Moravian Church*, 39–41.

25. Bullock, *Voluntary Religious Societies*, 176.

similar to that recorded in the *Journal* for the Moravians.[26] The elders of the Moravians held a weekly conference to discuss the "state of souls"[27] and the Fetter Lane rule emulates this. Similarly, the later rules, added on the 26th September, have overtones of Wesley's own experience while amongst the Moravians. The day of general intercession (*Rules A*: 25 and *Rules B*: 27) was one of Wesley's first experiences during his journey.[28] These days were an opportunity for the community to pray for the needs of others over a 24 hour period. Likewise love feasts, integral to Moravian community life, became part of Fetter Lane practice (*Rules A*: 26 and *Rules B*: 28) and had been held in Wesley's absence.[29] Wesley's *Journal* records witnessing, but presumably not sharing in, a love feast[30] for the "married men."[31] He had already experienced a German love feast in Georgia.[32] Philip Hardt, commenting on the development of Methodist structures, notes what he believes to be a change from Moravian practice. "Wesley . . . departed from the Moravian model. First, he allowed all society members to attend the love feast; the Moravians restricted attendance to only band members."[33] In reality, the Moravians held love feasts for the choirs which were single sex, and for the Congregation, which included everybody. In the same way, the Moravian custom of continual intercession (which began at Herrnhut in 1727)[34] was included in Fetter Lane practice during Wesley's absence[35] (*Rules A*: 29 and *Rules B*: 29).

Böhler's authority and knowledge of Moravian life meant that before Wesley's journey, aspects of these later rules were already Fetter Lane

---

26. Wesley, *Works [BE]*, Vol. 18, 292. This rule, numbered III in the Moravian discipline was recorded by Wesley during his visit to Herrnhut.

27. Wesley, *Works [BE]*, Vol. 18, 292.

28. Ibid., 256. See also 260, (conference for strangers), 272, and 293.

29. Podmore, *The Moravian Church*, 44.

30. Heitzenrater, *Wesley and the People Called Methodists*, 85. Heitzenrater suggests that Wesley did participate in a love feast, but as the Journal only records one instance of a love feast for married men it is not likely that he shared the meal.

31. Wesley, *Works [BE]*, Vol. 18, 267.

32. Wesley, *Journal [SE]*, Vol. I, 377.

33. Hardt, *The Soul of Methodism. The Class Meeting in Early New York Methodism*, 12.

34. Wesley, *Works [BE]*, Vol. 18, 295. This was extracted by Wesley from the "Constitution of the Moravian Brethren 1733." It is paragraph 10.

35. Podmore, *The Moravian Church*, 44.

practice, if not codified by the leadership. Wesley wrote to his mother,[36] brothers,[37] and at least James Hutton[38] during his visit to the Moravians, and elements of his experience reflecting Fetter Lane life are seen in this correspondence. Much of the correspondence sent from Germany has not survived.[39]

FETTER LANE AND THE OXFORD METHODISTS COMPARED

For the Wesleys, the life of Fetter Lane was not a complete break with the Oxford Methodists who had met between 1729 and 1735. Rack records that Wesley wished to bring some of the rigorous exercises of the Oxford Methodists into Fetter Lane; Wesley "would have liked the Fetter Lane members to do the same (fast)."[40] In personal practice, Wesley maintained his regular fast days,[41] his attention to prayer,[42] and to reading the Scriptures.[43] He also received holy communion regularly. In the days around Christmas 1738, he received the sacrament daily.[44] Writing on the 1st December 1738 to James Hutton he explicitly states he wants the Friday fast introduced.[45] By August 1739, Wesley had established this practice and a shortened general intercession into the Bristol society.[46]

The Fetter Lane Society was in contact with the Oxford work and J. Hutchings, who was at Pembroke College, wrote regularly to James Hutton. On the 23rd July 1738,[47] he wrote to Hutton about a society he

36. Wesley, *Works [BE]*, Vol. 25, 556–7.

37. Ibid. Wesley wrote to Charles on the 7th July 1738, (old style) 557–58, and the 4th August 1738, (old style) 560. Wesley wrote to Samuel on the 7th July 1738, (old style) 558–59.

38. Wesley, *Works [BE]*, Vol. 25, 561–562. Wesley wrote to James Hutton on the 4th August 1738 (old style).

39. Wesley, *Journal [SE]*, Vol. II, 12.

40. Rack, *Reasonable Enthusiast*, 188. (Word in brackets mine.)

41. Wesley, *Journal [SE]*, Vol. II, 79. See also, 82, 88, and 96.

42. Ibid., 89. See also 83, 88, and 93.

43. Ibid., 88. See also 93.

44. Wesley, *Works [BE]*, Vol. 18, 367–468. From the 21st December until the 29th December he communicated every day except Christmas Day. See also Rack, *Reasonable Enthusiast*, 188. Also Wesley, *Journal*, Vol. I, 139.

45. Wesley, *Works [BE]*, Vol. 25, 594–95. See MCH. AB100.A.3

46. Wesley, *Works [BE]*, Vol. 18, 88.

47. Hutchings J. to Hutton J. 23rd July 1738. MCHp88A.3 [folder 13].

had begun in Woolmistone. The reverse of the letter has the names of members, who presumably were passed the letter to read in a "round robin" fashion. Among the names were Thorold, Hutchings, Ingham, Shaw, Wesley, and Böhler. There is also a note "where's Mr C Wesley?"[48] An undated letter from George Whitefield to James Hutton has similar annotations.[49]

The social outreach of Oxford Methodism was not integrated into the life of Fetter Lane. Böhler and others visited condemned prisoners, but this was to win their souls for Christ before execution, a practice Wesley initially found hard to bear, as he could not accept death bed repentance as genuine:

> The first person to whom I offered *salvation by faith alone* was a prisoner under sentence of death. His name was Clifford. Peter Böhler had many times desired me to speak to him before. But I could not prevail on myself so to do, being still (as I had been many years) a zealous asserter of the *impossibility of a death-bed repentance*.[50]

Although the social work of the Oxford Methodists was dying out by the time Wesley commented in his *Journal* on the 3rd October 1739: "I had a little leisure to take a view of the shattered condition of things here"[51] there was never a comparable work from Fetter Lane amongst poor or uneducated people.

WESLEY THE ANGLICAN AND FETTER LANE

Wesley continued to adhere to his Anglicanism, most notably in his conformity to recognized forms of clerical authority. James Hutton proposed a Moravian[52] structure of leadership for Fetter Lane, suggesting the appointment of monitors, and a president[53] elected annually by lot.

---

48. Ibid.
49. Whitefield G. to Hutton J. undated MCHp91A.3 [folder21].
50. Wesley, *Works [BE]*, Vol. 18, 228.
51. Wesley, *Works [BE]*, Vol. 19, 100.
52. Wesley, *Works [BE]*, Vol. 18, 294–7. Wesley records the organisation of the Moravian settlement in Herrnhut. The Herrnhut community has the post of *monitor*. See rule 8.
53. See Bullock, *Voluntary Religious Societies*. Bullock states that Hutton acted as president while John Wesley was in Germany and that Wesley assumed this position upon his return. This cannot be correct as correspondence indicates the office of presi-

Wesley was unhappy with this plan: "What is proposed as to casting lots concerning a president . . . Would that not [require] more particular consideration?"[54] He was also concerned that the president had no formal role. Monitors were to have responsibility for telling others their faults. He held that monitors would simply do away with the need for bands, as group accountability would be nullified. "Every man in my band is my monitor, and I his; else I know no use of our being in Band."[55] He also believed his ordination afforded the position of "monitor."[56] Monitors never appear in any rules as Podmore noted: "It may be that his (Wesley's) viewpoint won in the end, since monitors are mentioned in neither version of the rules."[57]

Watson believes that Wesley's *Rules of the Band Societies* countered the fault in leadership and mutual responsibility he saw in the Moravian system. Wesley's own bands were to be based on "mutual confession and accountability."[58] Similarly, Martin Schmidt wrote, "The basic principle which he expressly put into effect was the mutual responsibility which no one could transfer to or take, from another."[59] The appointment of monitors would have removed mutual accountability, fundamental to the later Methodist class and band system.

Wesley's understanding of the society's relationship to the Church of England is seen in a letter of the 27th November to Hutton. Wesley wrote, "I believe bishops, priests, and deacons to be of divine appointment, though I think our brethren in Germany do not."[60] Wesley understood the Fetter Lane Society to be submissive to the Church of England, and in correspondence with James Hutton in late 1738, he refers to the authority of the Church as guiding the members of the society: "Are we

---

dent was an innovation. See 178–179. See also Benham, *Memoirs of James Hutton*, 41. Benham states that Wesley presided over meetings when in London, and in his absence, Hutton presided. This does not however mean that either was "president."

54. Wesley, *Works [BE]*, Vol. 25, 590–2. See MCH. AB100.A.3.
55. Ibid., 591.
56. Ibid., 592.
57. Podmore, *The Moravian Church*, 46. (Italics mine.)
58. Watson, *The Early Methodist Class Meeting*, 83.
59. Schmidt, *John Wesley A Theological Biography; Volume II, Part I*, 20.
60. Wesley, *Works [BE]*, Vol. 25, 593. See MCH. AB100.A.3.

members of the Church of England? First, then, let us observe her laws, and then the by-laws of our own Society."[61]

However, Wesley's Anglican outlook and practice was not imposed upon the Fetter Lane membership. He did not compromise his position as a clergyman, or promote himself to leadership over any other member, and was sensitive to the suggestion that the membership required pastoral oversight.[62] James Hutton by contrast was seeking to make decisions affecting the society without consulting the whole membership,[63] which Wesley seemed anxious to avoid. Wesley's loyalty to the Church of England subordinated the Fetter Lane rules to "by-laws."[64]

Wesley was seeking to work out his own faith after May 1738, and how and where that faith might be used. While he was an Anglican, which guided much of his life and practice, the Pietists of whom he had read and whom he had met heavily influenced him. Wesley's views can be observed in two statements; the first relating to his Anglicanism, "A serious clergyman desired to know in what points we differed from the Church of England, I answered: "To the best of my knowledge, in none. The doctrines we preach are the doctrines of the Church of England."[65] The second statement related his warmness to Moravian Church practice. "What unites my heart to you is the excellency (in many respects) of the doctrine taught among you."[66] These preface the fourth part of the *Journal*. He found no difficulty being a clergyman of the Church of England, who was involved with Pietsm, a charge many others held against him.

DISAGREEMENT AT FETTER LANE

The Society grew and in September 1738, after Wesley returned from Herrnhut he recorded in his *Journal*, "I rejoiced to meet with our

---

61. Wesley, *Works [BE]*, Vol. 25, 592–3. See MCH. AB100.A.3.
62. Ibid.
63. Wesley, *Works [BE]*, Vol. 25, 590–2. See MCH. AB100.A.3 This correspondence deals with the exclusion of women from the general meeting and the appointment of monitors and a president.
64. Ibid., 595. See MCH. AB100.A.3.
65. Wesley, *Works [BE]*, Vol. 19, 96. The fuller response to the clergyman is found on pp. 96–97.
66. Ibid., 117. The fuller letter is found on pp. 116–18.

little society, which now consisted of thirty-two persons."[67] Between September and October the *Journal* shows that Wesley was present at twenty society and band meetings in London and Oxford beyond the Fetter Lane Society. His life was centered on the growing society but he was by no means confined by it. By January 1st 1739, there were at least 60 members,[68] and at a love feast at around three in the morning, the "power of God"[69] broke out amongst those present. The briefly described scene of crying out and falling to the floor was to become a "hallmark" of much of Wesley's early ministry.[70]

From 31st March to 13th June, Wesley was in Bristol, having been given permission by the leadership to accept George Whitefield's invitation to take over the work there. Wesley received a letter[71] on the 11th June about problems in London and returned within two days. That evening he met with the women of Fetter Lane at 6pm and the men at 8pm.[72] The causes for concern, recorded in Charles Wesley's *Journal*, were the influence of the French Prophetess Lavington,[73] the claim by John Shaw that he had authority to administer the sacraments without

---

67. Ibid., 12.

68. Ibid., 29.

69. Ibid., 29.

70. In a letter from John Thorold to James Hutton dated the 23rd October 1738, it appears that a similar (though smaller) occurrence had happened there. Thorold wrote that amongst "the great crowd of people that was there the Thursday before, the fainting away of 2 people." MCHp88A.3[packet 13].

71. Wesley, *Journal [SE]*, Vol. II, 216. Footnote 1.

72. Wesley, *Works [BE]*, Vol. 19, 69.

73. Wesley, *Journal*, Vol. I, 152–53. See Schwartz, *The French Prophets: The History of a Millenial Group in Eighteenth-Century England*, 72–113. This offers an overview from their arrival in England in 1706. See 205–7. This describes Welsy's opinion of the French Prophets during the Fetter Lane Period. A brief discussion of the French prophets can also be found in Symonds, *Thomas Brown and the Angels*. Charles Wesley spent time and effort in ascertaining Prophetess Lavington's background which he then spent time telling the society, and any who would hear him. John Bray was under the influence of Prophetess Lavington.

being ordained,[74] a dispute regarding lay preaching,[75] and the disavowal by two members (Shaw and Wolf) of their membership of the Church of England.[76] At a meeting of the society on the 13th June, the society disassociated itself with Prophetess Lavington and expelled[77] John Shaw and Shepherd Wolf. John Bray, another founder member, was "humbled."[78]

The issue of lay preaching arose after George Whitefield preached in the open air in Islington, London. Whitefield had already preached in the open air in Bristol; breaching the order of the Church of England. After Whitefield preached on the 28th April, a layman, Thomas Bowers[79] got up to preach. Charles Wesley unsuccessfully tried to restrain him, and left along with others from the society. The issue did not die away, and was raised at a later meeting. Bray and Shaw, two founders of the society spoke for it, while Charles Wesley and George Whitefield spoke against. The Moravians were against preaching in the open air, and the Church of England would not allow open air preaching without a licence. This development was irregular.

John Wesley's actions were not an attempt to exert clerical authority. He returned as a result of a request. The meeting's decisions appear to have been corporate, with no one individual's opinion taking precedence over any other. Some five days later, a former Fetter Lane member, Richard Tompson, who had previously left the society and the Church of England, was readmitted.[80]

---

74. Wesley, *Journal*, Vol. I, 151. Shaw accused Charles Wesley of seeking pre-eminence amongst the society. One Mr. Fish considered Charles was under the influence of the devil. Fish, (along with Shaw and Wolf) disassociated himself from the Church of England, but is not recorded as having been expelled on the 13th June. Ward & Heitzenrater indicate that Shaw and Wolf were Moravians. This cannot be the case, as the Moravians had no members in England. See Wesley, *Works [BE]*, Vol. 19, 69. Footnote 51.

75. Wesley, *Journal*, Vol. I, 149.

76. Ibid., 153.

77. Ibid. Charles Wesley states that their names were "erased out of the society-book."

78. Ibid.

79. Bowers did not cease lay preaching. Charles Wesley records that Bowers' preaching in Wycombe, prevented him from being able to preach there. See Wesley, *Journal*, Vol. I, 160.

80. Wesley, *Works [BE]*, Vol. 19, 71. The diary shows the meeting occurred at Mrs. Mills', 394.

Benjamin Ingham, who was a member of the society, but in ministry in the North of England, wrote an insightful letter to Hutton after these events: "All the confusion that has happened, has been owing to people's rashness and forwardness, leaning more to their own understanding and self will, than to sober advice."[81] He concluded that there was a need for, "somebody at the head who is able to direct and govern, and willing also to be directed and governed."[82]

By Monday 18th June, Wesley had left London for Bristol, returning at the end of August. On the 9th September he attended Fetter Lane and "exhorted them to love one another."[83] Seemingly, there was little love amongst the members. While still in London, Wesley heard for the first time the issue that led to his separation from Fetter Lane. At the home of Mrs. Stover, Wesley met with Mrs. Crouch who, under the advice of Mr. Delamotte[84] had ceased to receive communion.

> Thur. 20. Mrs C[rouch], being in deep heaviness, had desired me to meet her this afternoon. She had long earnestly desired to receive the Holy Communion having an unaccountably strong persuasion that God would manifest himself to her therein and give rest to her soul. But her heaviness being now greatly increased, Mr. D[elamotte] gave her that fatal advice not to communicate till she had living faith. This still added to her perplexity. Yet at length she resolved to obey God rather than man. And "he was made known unto her in the breaking of bread."[85]

This early meeting with stillness for Wesley is not mentioned by Podmore and preceded the visit by the German Moravians of November 1739, which led the society into crisis. The doctrine of stillness began to

---

81. Ingham B. to Hutton J. 23rd June 1739 MCHpp88–89A.3 [folder 14] Ingham's letter raised the issue of Thomas Broughton's views on baptismal regeneration: that a person was forgiven and born again in baptism, and any sin committed after that date required repentance. See Wesley, *Journal [SE]*, Vol. I, 456. (Footnote 2), and Wesley, *Works [BE]*, Vol. 18, 234. See footnote 89. He also referred to Charles Kinchin's resignation as an Oxford fellow and his intention to sell his living.

82. Ingham B. to Hutton J. 23rd June 1739. MCHpp88–89A.3, [folder 14].

83. Wesley, *Works [BE]*, Vol. 19, 95.

84. Wesley, *Works [BE]*, Vol. 19, 98. Footnote 42 states that this may have been Charles Delamotte. Ward and Heitzenrater indicate Charles Delamotte had become a Moravian. This is not so. He was influenced by the Moravians, but was not received into the Moravian Church at that time. Charles Delamotte was received into the Moravian Church in 1761. See Lineham, "Charles Delamotte," 307–8.

85. Wesley, *Works [BE]*, Vol. 19, 98.

pervade the society after a visit by Phillpp Heinrich Molther. Molther was introduced to Moravianism by Zinzendorf's son, Christian Renatus. He was appointed to lead the Moravians in Pennsylvania, and came to London *en route* for the colonies. He was held up in London, as there was no ship able to take him to America until the next year. At the same time, Spangenberg returned from America.

Podmore disagrees with the accepted argument that Molther introduced stillness to the Fetter Lane members, arguing that Spangenberg spoke of "the deep repose to be found in the blood of Christ,"[86] and that Molther spoke little English. However, Charles Delamotte was speaking about the doctrine (at least to individuals) before Molther and Spangenberg arrived in London, and it was the English members of Fetter Lane who took stillness to extremes.

Molther's reaction to the members' behavior is noted by Podmore. "He was shocked by what he found: the groaning, crying, contortions, and strange gestures at the meeting were," he remarked, "enough to bring one out in a cold sweat."[87] It was Spangenberg, however, who addressed the society about stillness in definitive terms that until there was a certainty of faith, the individual should refrain from using the means of grace.

Podmore stresses that it was not Molther, as Wesley suggests in his *Journal*, but Spangenberg who first raised stillness with the society as a whole. Wesley was already aware of this doctrine from his meeting with Spangenberg in Georgia. The *Journal* gives the impression that stillness had not been mentioned to the society before Molther's arrival. This is not, however, correct—stillness was a tenet of Moravianism and Böhler had advocated waiting upon God before the Fetter Lane Society began.

Wesley's *Journal* from the 3rd November 1739 related how the first person he met on returning to London from Bristol had been influenced toward stillness. She was previously a zealous woman, who now believed she had never had any faith at all.[88] The teaching also influenced John Bray. Attending the society on the 4th November Wesley recorded how they "continued *silent* till eight. One then spoke of 'looking unto Jesus' and exhorted us all to 'lie *still* in his hand.'"[89] On the 7th November,

---

86. Podmore, *The Moravian*, 60.
87. Podmore, *The Moravian*, 59.
88. Wesley, *Works [BE]*, Vol. 19, 119.
89. Ibid. See also the following pages.

Wesley held a conference with Spangenberg, and while they agreed on much, there was no agreement about stillness.

Abstention from the means of grace was anathema to Wesley whose background and previous experience gave these a high value in the quest for faith. This does not mean the Moravians held a low view of communion; rather, their argument that it should not be received until a person had faith signals a high view of communion as a confirming ordinance.

On the 10th November, Wesley met with a woman who had received assurance while receiving communion, and from this he drew the conclusion that communion was not merely a confirming ordinance, but a converting ordinance.[90] Here he was moving away from accepted Anglican teaching. His mother would later write to Wesley of her similar experience.

However much the teaching on stillness concerned Wesley, he still left for Oxford on the 12th November, traveling to Tiverton soon after as his brother Samuel had died. On the journey to Tiverton, he stopped in Bristol to speak and preach against stillness.[91] Wesley returned to London on the 19th December, perhaps in part precipitated by the reports he was receiving from Fetter Lane "I received several unpleasing accounts of the state of things in London."[92] One report suggested that Fetter Lane members were leaving the meetings after recording their attendance and that Molther was meeting with a group of Fetter Lane members at the home of Matthew Clarke.[93] Another report suggested that Hutton, Bray and Edmonds, under Molther's direction, were planning to "raise a church."[94]

The *Journal* indicates that Wesley was more concerned with the effect stillness was having upon the membership at Fetter Lane rather than the doctrine itself: "I found every day the dreadful effects of our brethren's reasonings, and disputing with each other. Scarce one in ten retained his first love, and most of the rest were in utmost confusion, biting and devouring one another."[95]

90. Ibid., 121. See also 158.
91. Ibid., 122.
92. Ibid., 128.
93. Ibid., 129. See footnote 56.
94. Ibid., 130.
95. Ibid.

The Fetter Lane Society   115

A clue to Wesley's withdrawal is found in the *Journal* entry for Monday 24th December. Molther and Spangenberg's insistence on stillness may have rested on a desire to curb the excesses of the Fetter Lane members, first seen at the meeting of the 1st January 1739, as on abstention from the means of grace *per se*. Wesley's *Journal* records a meeting where one individual was "overwhelmed with joy and love, and could not help showing it by strong cries and tears."[96] Another at the meeting declared this to be "nature, imagination and animal spirits."[97] It seems Wesley was willing to allow the quasi-pentecostal outburst as a degree of faith, and an expression of God at work. Although his own experience of the 24th May 1738 was not as expressive, he could not see how, in the light of his experience, such behavior was merely "human." This must be held in "tension" so to speak, with his view of the spiritual excesses of the French Prophets (especially Prophetess Lavington) about whom Wesley was at best skeptical.

Stillness boiled down to a clear doctrinal difference between the Wesleys on one side and the majority of the English leadership on the other. The Germans present in London were not part of this division. They were passing through London and were not as extreme about stillness. To this major problem should be added the nature of reception of New Birth and assurance, and perfection. Holland's account picks up these issues:

> It was now (1740) a great dispute arose in our Society, some speaking as if there was no Means of Grace and left off coming to the Church and Sacraments expecting to find the Lord sooner by stillness–Some declared that after we were justified there was generally an intermediate space before we received the witness of the Spirit. Others that we were justified and had the witness of the Spirit at the same time.[98]

After meeting with Molther on the 31st December, Wesley wrote down what he "conceived to be the difference between us."[99] He laid five

---

96. Ibid., 131.

97. Ibid.

98. Holland, *Extract of a Short Account of Some Few Matters Relating to the Work of the Lord in England 1745*. (Manuscript document annexed into the Fetter Lane Congregation Book for 1742) MCH.

99. Wesley, *Works [BE]*, Vol. 19, 131.

charges against the Moravians and five replies.[100] Essentially, they were unaltered from Wesley's first objection to stillness, relying on his understanding of degrees of faith, justification and the work of the Holy Spirit (the gift of God).[101] There is, however, an additional charge, the use of guile.[102] Molther had suggested to Wesley that certain fabrications could be told to hearers that they might seek to attain beyond their present state.

By the 3rd January 1740 Wesley was again traveling, returning to London to minister to Gwillam Snowde, a condemned prisoner at Newgate, on the 5th February. Wesley found himself at odds with the Society over the issue of plain speaking, and "leaving off the ordinances of God."[103] He was content to allow any who wished to abstain from the means of grace to do so, but he was not prepared to allow others to harass those who chose to use the means of grace.

By March the situation at Fetter Lane was serious. Charles Wesley visited the Morgan family,[104] who, having spent a week with John Bray in London, were now convinced the means of grace were unnecessary. Bray had persuaded Mrs. Morgan to cease attending church, praying, reading the Bible or receiving communion. She was content to wait for religion to come "when it will." Mr Morgan was dissuaded from preaching or leading family prayers. The influence of Bray and others in the society by then was such that George Whitefield and the Wesleys were considered mischievous because of their preaching. Charles Wesley expressed his view of stillness as: "a Christianity which had no cross in it, no work of faith, no patience of hope, no labour of love."[105]

SEPARATION

By April, Charles Wesley concluded, "A separation I foresee unavoidable."[106] On the 6th April, John Bray threatened Charles with ex-

---

100. Ibid., 131–34.
101. Ibid., 132.
102. Ibid., 133.
103. Ibid., 140.
104. Wesley, *Journal*, Vol. I, 200.
105. Ibid., 201.
106. Ibid., 207. Charles' *Journal* for the days preceding that entry records several accounts of members abstaining from the means of grace.

pulsion from his band[107] unless he attended it the next day. John Wesley returned to London after receiving a letter from John Simpson asking him to prevent Charles from "preaching up the ordinances."[108] John and Charles met with Molther on the 25th April, without agreement. Charles was aware of the seriousness of the dispute and the entrenched positions of both sides: "I see no middle point wherein we can meet."[109]

The female bands at Fetter Lane were well disposed to the Wesleys, and were in danger of expulsion from the society because Thomas Maxfield[110] was present at their love feast. Pre-emptively, the Wesleys removed them from Fetter Lane's authority. Charles records that they: "rescued our lambs out of their hands."[111] This course of action was possible, as they had taken a lease on a disused foundry. The female bands moved from Fetter Lane discipline to the new Wesleyan discipline drawn up on Christmas Day 1739. Ostensibly, the unity of the society was at an end.

An attempt to visit Molther on the 5th June in Islington was unsuccessful as he was ill. Neither Spangenberg, nor Böhler were in London at the time and the society was in the hands of John Bray[112] who was joined by: "John Simpson and George Stonehouse (both clergymen), Charles Delamotte, William Oxley, and Richard Bell."[113] These leaders attempted to prevent Charles Wesley from preaching at the society, ensuring Fetter Lane meetings coincided with those of the Foundery.[114]

---

107. Ibid., 210. See also, 222. John Bray reproved Charles for not attending his band. At the same meeting Bray expelled a member from the society meeting.

108. Wesley, *Works [BE]*, Vol. 19, 146. Simpson had spoken publicly at the Fetter Lane meeting against Charles Wesley's preaching on the ordinances. See Wesley, *Journal*, Vol. I, 212. See also 221. Charles Wesley did not help matters by composing a hymn entitled *The Means of Grace*.

109. Wesley, *Journal*, Vol. I, 223. See also Wesley, *Works [BE]*, Vol. 19, 147. This gives John Wesley's account of this meeting.

110. Maxfield, a member of John Wesley's Bristol society had traveled to London with Wesley and attended a meeting of the female lovefeast.

111. Wesley, *Journal*, Vol. I, 223. The *Journal* for the ensuing days shows that Charles Wesley met with many of the female bands who had joined the Foundery society.

112. Podmore, *The Moravian Church*, 67. Podmore's footnote 218 to Charles Wesley's *Journal* suggests the 23rd April. There is no date in the *Journal* beside the appropriate entry but John Wesley's *Diary* relates the meeting at Fetter Lane "our society" to that date. See Wesley, *Works [BE]*, Vol. 19, 417.

113. Podmore, *The Moravian Church*, 68.

114. Wesley, *Journal*, Vol. I, 229.

John Wesley sought to accommodate the differing opinions of the Fetter Lane Society, by dividing bands along doctrinal lines. Those who wished to follow stillness could do so in a band of like-minded people, and those who wished to use the means of grace could join a similarly "exclusive" band: "My brother proposed new-modelling the bands, and setting by themselves those few who were still for the ordinances."[115] This proposal was accepted after Benjamin Ingham had seconded it, and "as many as were aggrieved put into new bands."[116]

From the 22nd June onwards, Wesley used the morning Bible study to "expound the basic Christian teaching as he understood it."[117] On the 16th July matters came to a head, when it was asked whether Wesley would be allowed to preach in the new building. The society had leased another building "the Great meeting House," and this had until then been used by the society. He was refused, being told "This place is taken for the Germans."[118] Wesley, after debate "gave them up for God."[119]

Within a week, after a meeting at which his mother was present, it was decided to leave Fetter Lane.[120] At the conclusion of a love feast Wesley read a statement and invited any who agreed with him to follow him: "nothing now remains but that I should give you up to God. You that are of the same judgment, follow me."[121] Some 18 or 19 followed him from the society. Hutton recounts that Wesley left the meeting without his hat, as it had been hidden.[122] The Foundery society, which met on the 23rd July, recorded 25 male and some 48 female former Fetter Lane members. The number of women was higher due to their separation after Maxfield's presence at their love feast.[123]

James Hutton's own memoir of the separation is telling for its candor, and propaganda:

115. Ibid., 239.

116. Ibid., 239.

117. Wesley, *Works [BE]*, Vol. 19, 153. See footnote 75. The notes of these Bible studies are contained in the *Journal* on 153–9.

118. Ibid., 161.

119. Ibid., 161.

120. Ibid., 427. The *Diary* for the 18th and 20th July gives little detail. The *Diary* for the 18th reads "agreed to leave the Society!" while for day on which he left Fetter Lane he wrote, '8.15 Fetter Lane; Love-feast; parted!'

121. Ibid., 162.

122. Hutton, *History of the Moravian Church*, 299.

123. See footnote 110 above.

Wesley became hostile, partly through our imprudent behaviour towards him, partly from inability to bear that he should be less thought of amongst us than Br. Molther. In short he broke off from us, contradicted our teaching publicly, but we contradicted his only quietly. He took away from us almost all of the women folk who then belonged to us, but only some 14 men. He became our declared enemy.

During Br. Molther's illness our meeting became very small, and Wesley gave opportunity for those who were unsound and wished to remain so, to leave us.[124]

Annexed to the notes of a Prayer Day held on the 17th September 1740 is a letter from Molther to Fetter Lane dated 20th October 1740. Molther reflects on the issue that had brought about the separation:

> When the Saviour is a pulling down of them and giveth them a deep sense of their misery and sinfulness, then people, who besides the Lord have a great many means to help themselves, fly to them, instead of lying still, and being helped by the Lord Jesus, get into self working force themselves to pray and sing hymns, till they have got rid of the Pain, they have upon their hearts, and got up from the dust when the Lord would have them continue there ... but also on the other hand empty of all means to help yourself, and of all workings of your own. He is able to save you alone, without your assistance, and will have the glory alone.[125]

Wesley wrote to Zinzendorf on August 8th 1740 setting out his view of the Moravians. Molther's letter may be a reply to that. The front page of the Prayer Day notes has pencilled "Brother Hutton is to take a copy of the answer to Mr. Wesley's letter."[126] Molther's annexed letter was intended only for Fetter Lane, and he makes no apology for the doctrine of stillness, inviting the reader to "lie still at the feet of our Saviour."[127] It was only by recognizing personal sinfulness and being still that an individual came to faith. Molther's understanding of stillness is not as extreme as the English leaders, and while his feelings about the use of the means of grace are clear in the letter, his argument against using the means is that they hinder the acceptance of faith.

124. Libby, "James Hutton's Account of 'The Beginnings of the Lord's Work in England to 1741,'" 188.
125. Philip Molther's Letter to the Fetter Lane Society, MCHp43A.3.
126. Prayer Day notes, MCHp43A.3.
127. Philip Molther's Letter to the Fetter Lane Society, MCHp43A.3.

Wesley's letter laid before Zinzendorf the faults of doctrine he saw within Moravianism.[128] This letter was the subject of a conversation between Zinzendorf and Wesley just over a year later.[129] He did not apologize for the separation, but set out his charges against Moravian practice and discipline. Wesley's apologia is contained in the preface to the fourth part of his *Journal*,[130] published in 1744, after any possibility of reconciliation with the Moravian Church had passed.

Podmore's comment on the separation is poignant: "Little more than two years after its inception, the Fetter Lane Society's unity was at an end, and the revival movement was divided–as it turned out, permanently."[131] Perhaps Wesley precipitated the separation through his reading an excerpt from *The Mystic Divinity of Dionysius*,[132] but there was no middle ground upon which to build. Relations within Fetter Lane had been disintegrating for some time, and the separation cannot have been a surprise, "the temporary partnership between the two wings of the army of revival was dissolving throughout 1739 until the final breach in July 1740."[133]

Benham's *Memoirs* illustrate the revival's division. In 1740, after Whitefield returned from America, and Wesley had separated from Fetter Lane, Whitefield asked Hutton to publish a Calvinist tract in response to one of Wesley's anti-Calvinist sermons.[134] Hutton declined on the basis he could not accept Calvin's doctrine of predestination: "Whitefield at this took offence against the Brethren as well as against Wesley, and thus the Methodists not only quarreled with the Brethren but wrangled among themselves."[135]

Walsh captures the division:

---

128. Wesley, *Works [BE]*, Vol. 26, 24–31.
129. Wesley, *Works [BE]*, Vol. 19, 211–24.
130. Ibid., 116–18.
131. Podmore, *The Moravian Church*, 70.
132. Wesley, *Works [BE]*, Vol. 19, 160. Wesley read an excerpt which denied the value of using any means of grace prior to conversion. He invited the members present to assent to or deny whether they agreed with the excerpt. Mr. Bell responded that it was right, and that using the means prior to conversion prevented coming to faith.
133. Addison, *The Renewed Church*, 84.
134. Whitefield published a tract in response to Wesley's sermon on *Free Grace*. See Wesley, *Works [BE]*, Vol. 3, 542–63.
135. Benham, *Memoirs of James Hutton*, 53.

Emotions ran high. Feelings of Pentecostal fraternity coincided with a combativeness that split Methodist from Moravian and Arminian from Calvinist. There was a movement to and fro, much spiritual wayfaring–a very rapid turnover of membership in the societies, as converts were not only won but lost.[136]

This wayfaring was felt by John West who wrote after the Wesleys' departure for the Foundery, "After Mr Wesley withdrew from us, I was in a great strait whom to follow but finally concluded it was best for me to join the Brethren."[137]

THE DISTINCTIVES OF FETTER LANE

The second section of this chapter echoes the analysis of the distinctive features of the Unitary societies discussed in chapter 3. Fetter Lane modeled its rules upon those of the Moravian Church. Two pillars assisted the membership develop as Christians: the band, a close-knit community of people, sharing problems and issues together; the society, a large-scale meeting at which preaching and teaching would take place. Within the society disputes could be aired and individuals or groups taken to task and even expelled.

The society also introduced love feasts, prayer days and general intercession days into English religious life and stressed the importance of fast days, an established practice for High Anglicans, but with the introduction of a continual fast changed the pattern of fasting. These practices added to the sense of community amongst the society members, but were not compulsory.[138]

The following headings expand those elements of Fetter Lane life that were new to the English scene. These distinctives illustrate a clear progression from, if not a break with the unitary system.

Communal pattern

The society functioned with a particular model of religious life:

Band meeting—Monday evenings, and one other night by agreement. New members would be formed into "trial bands." If no objections

---

136. Walsh, " 'Methodism' and the Origins of English Speaking Evangelicalism," 23.

137. West, "Memoirs of Brother John West," 238.

138. Appendix 6: (Rules A): Rule 16 and Appendix 7: (Rules B): Rule 18.

were raised to an individual, full membership of the society would be granted one or two months later.[139] (Segregated by age, sex and marital status.)

Society meeting—Every Wednesday at 8pm. New members proposed once a month, and maximum meeting length of two and a half hours.[140]

General Intercession—One Saturday a month.

Love feast—Sunday evening, seven days after the General intercession. (Segregated by sex.)

Continual intercession—each member would spend an hour every day praying for other members.

Continual fast—three members each day fasted except on Sundays and holidays.

This exacting pattern of meetings suited the settled community of Herrnhut where the community lived and worked within community boundaries. However, it was a very different matter for those who did not live in community, and worked as employees or self-employed artisans to follow such a rigorous pattern. Heitzenrater is right when he states that the formation of religious bands within a settled community at Herrnhut was not "well suited to the needs of working-class English people who faced the hardships of changing social and economic conditions of the workaday world."[141]

It is not easy to ascertain how successful the bands and society were in fulfilling the functions that it laid down, or in regulating members and their activities. From October 1742, when Fetter Lane became a Moravian congregation, there is a wealth of documentary evidence which helps to establish the society's success. Prior to 1742, no records survive. There was a society book, as Charles Wesley refers to the names of Thomas Shaw and Shepherd Wolf being "erased out of the society-book,"[142] but this is not extant.

---

139. *Rules* A: 24 one month, *Rules* B: 26 two months.
140. *Rules* C: 14.
141. Heitzenrater, *Wesley and the People Called Methodists*, 108.
142. Wesley, *Journal*, Vol. I, 153.

How many bands can be identified?

William Holland noted that in 1732 there were "thirty or forty of these societies in the City and suburbs of London,"[143] and Fetter Lane was one of a "network" of societies in London in 1738.

James Hutton's account of the origins of Fetter Lane recollects the earliest days of the society:

> Böhler before he left, made some rules for those who had grace, and to begin with formed only one Band, out of 6 or 8 in whom he had the most confidence. This gradually increased, out of the first new Society founded by the Bookseller, etc., and from other souls lately awakened, and met in the Bookseller's house, when they wished to meet apart.[144]

While Wesley was in Germany with Ingham and Töltschig, the society consisted of "some 30 or 40 hearers, with the Bookseller, who, in Wesley's absence, held the meetings for edification."[145] Returning from Germany, John Wesley visited some 20 societies and bands in London and Oxford.[146] Some, identifiably predating Fetter Lane, are generally referred to by place name. "I went to a society in Bear Yard,"[147] rather than by a personal name: "at Mr E[xall]'s society."[148]

In a letter to the Herrnhut leaders, shortly after his return from Germany, Wesley stated: "Fourteen were added to us since our return, so that we have now eight bands of men, consisting of fifty-six persons; all of whom seek salvation only in the blood of Christ."[149] At this point there were only two female bands. By January 1739 Abraham Richter noted,

---

143. Holland, *Extract of a Short Account*, 1.

144. Libby, "James Hutton's "Account of the Beginnings of the Lord"s Work in England to 1741,'" 185.

145. Ibid.,185.

146. Wesley, *Works [BE]*, Vol. 19, 12. Bear Yard, 13. Aldersgate Street; Gutter Lane; Savoy, and Mr. Exall's, 14. Bow (this may have been a number of societies meeting together), 16. Wapping, 19. Mrs. Fox's (three times in one day), Mrs. Mear's, Westminster, 355. The Minories; Savoy Chapel, and Mr. Wolfe's, 356. Bear Yard, Mr. Brockmer's, Mr. Parker's, 357. Mrs. Fox's, Mrs. Ford's, 358. Mr. Washington's (this may have been a Holy Club meeting. See Wesley, *Journal [SE]*, Vol. II, 88).

147. Wesley, *Works [BE]*, Vol. 19, 12. See also 354.

148. Ibid., 13. See also footnote 36. William Exall was a member of the Fetter Lane Society.

149. Wesley, *Works [BE]*, Vol. 25, 572.

"gatherings several hundred strong were not unusual."[150] An exhaustive study of Wesley's *Diary* names individuals,[151] all women, who led bands. This may simply reflect the opportunity that Fetter Lane offered women. Whitefield's *Journal* for the 28th April 1739 records his preaching before a "thronged society of women at Fetter Lane."[152]

John Wesley belonged to a band, and from the *Diary* his leader appears to have been James Hutton.[153] It certainly met at Hutton's home. A band also met at his home.[154] Charles Wesley belonged to Mr. Bray's band. The *Diary* mentions several other people whom Wesley met at home, but these meetings are not referred to as "band meetings." The basic requirement for a band meeting was that they should begin and end with prayer and singing, and contain an opportunity for free and honest speech.[155] Using these rules as a basic guide, and allowing for Wesley's abbreviation of the phrase "sang, prayed, religious talk, sang, prayed"[156] to anything as short as "sang etc."[157] there is a number of groups which fulfilled a function similar to that of a band but which may not have

---

150. Podmore, *The Moravian Church*, 47. Podmore cites Richter's diary entry for the 3rd January 1739.

151. Wesley, *Works [BE]*, Vol. 19. Many of those mentioned by name have multiple references. For the purpose of this footnote, each individual is mentioned only once. *Diary*: Monday 18th September 1738 "Mrs Wolf," 367. Monday 15th January 1739 "J[enny] Loyd," 371. 5th February "Mary Hanson," 374. Saturday 17th February "Mrs Chambers," 376. Wednesday 21st February "Mrs West," 377. Thursday 22nd March "Mrs Thacker," 381. Friday 23rd March "Mrs Mills," 381. Wednesday 28th March "Mrs Sellars," 382. Tuesday 4th September "N Tilson," 406. Tuesday 18th September "Mrs Soane," 408. Friday 21st September "Mrs Dixon," 408. Wednesday 7th November "Sister Hodges," 415. Thursday 8th November "Mrs Vaughan," 415.

152. Whitefield, *George Whitefield's Journals*, 260.

153. Wesley, *Works [BE]*, Vol. 19. Wesley records meeting at Hutton's on the following days: Monday 18th December 1738, 367. Thursday 28th December, 368. Monday 8th January 1739, 370. Monday 15th January, 371. Thursday 18th January, 371. Monday 22nd January, 372. Thursday 25th January, 373. Thursday 1st February, 374. Monday 3rd September, 406.

154. Wesley, *Works [BE]*, Vol. 19, 356. This band met regularly on a Sunday evening.

155. *Rules* A: 10 & 11. *Rules* B: 9 &10.

156. Wesley, *Works [BE]*, Vol. 19, 354. See the entry for 8.30am on the 18th September. Like many entries the basic band requirements are interspersed with other phrases.

157. Wesley, *Works [BE]*, Vol. 19, 356. See the entry for 5.30pm on the 11th October.

actually been recorded as bands of the society proper.[158] Some of these can be identified as members of the Fetter Lane Society.[159]

Faith development

At a basic level, the bands offered a platform for faith development. Charles Wesley's *Journal* noted that an individual's declaration of faith occasioned a general thanksgiving. "In the bands, one witnessed her having received her pardon. We gave thanks with her, whom the Lord hath redeemed."[160] Conversion was not experienced in isolation, as the whole group shared the moment of witness.

From early 1740, Charles held "conferences" in which men and women expressed their spiritual state to him. These conferences appear to have been one-on-one conversation: "From eleven to one is devoted to conference. The first that came was Stephen Dupee, a soldier, who informs me he received forgiveness this week in hearing the word."[161]

A conference was an opportunity for Charles Wesley to collect evidence of the progress of a society member, and possibly counter stillness. However, they also provide an understanding of the work of the bands as faith-development groups: "In the hours of conference Eliz. Holmes informed me, she had been filled with the spirit of love while we were praying at S. Anderson's."[162]

The bands also gave opportunity for the teaching of catechumens. The rules of the society[163] allowed faith seekers to join on probation, varying between one and two months "on trial." These "on trial" bands

158. Wesley, *Works [BE]*, Vol. 19. See Monday September 18th 1738 "Mrs Delamotte," 354. Wednesday 20th September "Mr Harris," 354. Also Wednesday 27th September, 355. Thursday 28th September "Mr Brockmer," 355. Saturday 7th October "Mr Summers," 357. Sunday 22nd October "Mr Hodge"s,' 359. Wednesday 25th October "James Ha[rris]," 359. Friday 3rd November "Mrs May," 361. Tuesday 7th November "Mrs Duzzy" "Mrs Ironmonger" "Mrs Claggett," 361–62. Friday 22nd December "Mr Parker," 367. Friday 26th January 1739 "Mr Abbott," 373. Saturday 27th January "Mr Agutter," 373. Tuesday 20th February "Mr Savage," 376–77. Tuesday 21st March "Mr Hastings," 381. Saturday 15th September "Lady Hume," 407. Monday 17th September "Mr Bowe"s,' 408. (See also the entry for Monday 24th September, 409. Here the name is given as "Mr Bowers.")

159. Libby, "The Personnel of the Fetter Lane Society," 144–47.

160. Wesley, *Journal*, Vol. I, 158.

161. Ibid., 207.

162. Ibid., 227.

163. Appendix 6: Rules A: nos. 19 to 24: Appendix 7: Rules B, nos. 21 to 26.

provided a place where the stirrings of faith could be nurtured. The questions asked of the "on trial" members introduced potential new members to the rules and discipline of the society from the outset. John Wesley's view on this group is shown in his letter of October 1738 to Herrnhut: "there are many others who only wait till we have leisure to instruct them how they may most effectually build up one another in the faith and love of Him who gave himself for them."[164] The implication being that these individuals were not settled into "on trial" bands.

More than that, however, the "on trial" period allowed for new Christians to undergo baptismal initiation into the Church of England after instruction. John Wesley's *Journal* relates the baptism of five adults at St. Mary's Islington[165] on the 25th January 1739. The *Diary* entry for the same day reads "8.30 The catechumens came, sang prayed."[166] Charles Wesley also baptized adults, who had presumably been through a similar catechumenate period.[167] During the early life of the Fetter Lane Society, at least one request for baptism was received from a woman, previously baptized by a Dissenter. Charles Wesley conferred about this with the Bishop of London, who in a stormy meeting was equivocal.[168] Later that day he did baptize. "I read prayers at Islington, and baptised an adult; Mr. Stonehouse, M. Sims and M. Burton, being the witnesses."[169] The register shows that Ann Fillney was baptized that day. If, as seems probable, the

---

164. Wesley, *Works [BE]*, Vol. 25, 571–73.

165. Wesley, *Works [BE]*, Vol. 19, 32. The five adults are John Smith, Ann Turner, Sarah Pappet, Judith Probert, and Anna Taylor. (From baptismal registers of St Mary's Church Islington, held at The London Metropolitan Archives. Reference X085/079)

166. Ibid., 372–3. See also 374. The Diary relates the christening of Mrs. Dymox. There is another occasion when he baptized three women on the 9th July 1740 (see 426.) these were probably Foundery members rather than Fetter Lane members.

167. Wesley, *Journal*, Vol. I, 151. On this occasion Charles Wesley did not perform the baptism, but there are other occasions when he did. Towards the end of the Wesley's association with St. Mary's Islington, the wardens refused to allow Charles Wesley to baptize Bridget Armstead (227. 9th May 1740). He had to wait until the 21st May, when she was baptized by the minister of Bloomsbury Church (235. 21st May 1740).

168. Ibid., 135–36.

169. Ibid., 136. Ann Fillney's name is the sole entry for the 14th November 1738. (From the baptismal registers of St Mary's Church Islington, held at The London Metropolitan Archives. Reference X085/079.) Charles Wesley's *Journal* also indicates the baptism of two women at Islington on the 11th March 1739. There is no record of these in St Mary's registers. The only entries for that day relate to two male children, John Johnson and Joseph Gardner. (Also from the baptismal registers of St Mary's Church Islington, held at The London Metropolitan Archives. Reference X085/079.)

women's bands were proving successful in reaching people previously neglected by the religious societies, then the need for baptism as part of the faith development process was a very real issue for the society. The assumption is that John and Charles Wesley had responsibility for the catechumen's progress, at least to baptism.

Gradually a dichotomy arose over degrees of faith. Wesley's allowance for the young, growing Christian, who was justified, but not fully sanctified, highlighted the difference between his theology and Moravian theology. Heitzenrater, succinctly expresses this:

> Wesley was clearly differentiating between justification and sanctification and becoming more positively inclined to value the experience of the "almost" Christians.[170]

Moravianism did not accept the bands as a place where faith was steadily developed. Rather, the tendency toward stillness, simultaneous justification, and assurance did away with any need for growth in faith and negated the purpose of the bands themselves. Heitzenrater comments that Wesley "represents a direct challenge to the Moravian's unitary concept of faith."[171]

Assurance was central to eighteenth-century evangelicals. Bebbington contends that this bound up the strands of discontinuity evident in early eighteenth-century conservative Protestantism.[172] However, this doctrine added to those about which Wesley disagreed with the Moravians. Heitzenrater states that even though there was a widening gap between Wesley's thinking and that of the Moravian teachers, he still preached "the necessity of full assurance of faith and actual freedom from sin as the true ground of a Christian's happiness."[173] Wesley came to understand that the "assurance of salvation was an essential complement to justification."[174] This assurance would elicit the fruit of the Spirit in the life of the believer, and would also lead the Christian to know that the Spirit was witnessing with his/her spirit. Randy Maddox makes the point that in private correspondence Wesley spoke of "degrees of faith, as well

---

170. Heitzenrater, *Mirror and Memory*, 139.
171. Ibid.,141.
172. Bebbington, *Evangelicalism*, 42.
173. Heitzenrater, *Mirror and Memory*, 126.
174. Rack, *Reasonable Enthusiast*, 393.

as *degrees* of assurance. In short, he was allowing that someone could be *truly* Christian (albeit, imperfect) who was not yet *fully* Christian."[175]

In this the band played an important role, as some, who had a "higher" degree of faith, would encourage even the newest seeker. This contrasted with the Moravian requirement of assurance being evidenced by the fruit of the Spirit, as the expectation of the true Christian.[176] Wesley used others' experience to evidence his views, which Heitzenrater succinctly details.[177] As the work of the Holy Spirit was evident in the lives of his hearers, so their witness increased his confidence. These were "living arguments."

Wesley also produced some form of material to be used in the band meetings.[178] However, with the emphasis of the bands on small group experience and growth, this may have been study or discussion material.

Female membership

A unique feature of Fetter Lane was the full inclusion of women. Previously women had been catechized at home by male relatives, who led family prayers. In October 1738 there were two female bands: "As yet we have only two small bands of women–the one of three, the other of five persons."[179] By November the number had increased to six settled bands.[180]

On two occasions in the *Diary* John Wesley indicates the formation of new women's bands. One met at Mr. Thacker's home, led by

---

175. Maddox, *Responsible Grace*, 126.

176. SeeHeitzenrater, *Mirror and Memory*, 127. The dilemma Wesley faced in this regard showed itself in self examination. On this topic, see also Heitzenrater, *Wesley and the People Called Methodists*, 87–89.

177. Ibid., 131–32. The evidence to which Heitzenrater points show how Wesley tested the spirits, to ascertain how real the experience claimed was. In the case of the French Prophets, he would not allow their claims to divine revelation.

178. Wesley, *Works [BE]*, Vol. 19, 408. (September 18th) Wesley also recorded writing for the society. These entries occur from April 1740 and probably relate to the Foundery. See 417. 26th April 1740, 423. 12th June 1740, 424. 26th June 1740, 425. 30th June 1740, and 1st July 1740, 426. 8th July 1740.

179. Wesley, *Works [BE]*, Vol. 25, 572.

180. Ibid., 591. This letter was written after women had been separated from the general meeting. Wesley thought the bands he settled had not been successful, having been allowed to fail.

Mrs. Thacker.[181] He was the only male allowed, other than the leader.[182] Her band needed division, and Mrs. Chambers[183] was to lead the new band formed from it. In March he was also present at Mrs. Sellar's, "the new band."[184] John Wesley wrote the rules which governed the women's bands.[185]

Hutton's suggestion in November 1738 that the women should meet separately from the men was met with a stern response from Wesley.[186] Hutton was concerned that the women were causing familiarity. Wesley suggested appointing their own meeting, although this would cause them offense, "at least, unless you *first* fix a night for them to come by themselves–which I firmly believe will give more offence."[187] The desire for them to meet separately prevailed and Wesley frequently records for Wednesday evenings, "5.30 Fetter Lane [women]. 8 Fetter Lane [men]."[188]

After the separation of the women's meeting from the men's Wesley wrote to George Whitefield: "On Wednesday at six we have a noble company of women, not adorned with gold or costly apparel, but with a meek and quiet spirit and good works."[189] Women were afforded leadership amongst the bands, and again, it is John Wesley who records meeting the women leaders. On the 12th September 1739, Wesley's *Diary* records, "3.45 The women leaders, necessary talk (religious)."[190]

Charles Wesley was the catalyst for the separation of the women from Fetter Lane. On the 5th April, in conference with sister Jackson, he was told most of the women had given up the ordinances, and that sister Munsey had left the society over the treatment meted out to the Wesleys.[191]

181. Appendix 6: Rules A: Nos. 17 & 18
182. Wesley, *Works [BE]*, Vol. 19, 381. (22nd March 1739.)
183. Ibid., 376. (17th February 1739.)
184. Ibid., 382. (28th March 1739.
185. Ibid., 372. (25th January 1739.)
186. Wesley, *Works [BE]*, Vol. 25, 588.
187. Ibid.
188. Wesley, *Works [BE]*, Vol. 19, 393. 13th June 1739. See also the entries for the 5th September, 406. 12th September, 407. 19th September, 408. 26th September, 409. 7th November, 415.
189. Wesley, *Works [BE]*, Vol. 25, 602.
190. Wesley, *Works [BE]*, Vol. 19, 407. There are other *Diary* entries that show this was a regular meeting. Wesley also met the male leaders regularly.
191. Wesley, *Works [BE]*, Vol. 25, 487.

The following day, Charles Wesley, in company with Thomas Maxfield[192] and some of the women, were denied entry to Bowers's Society. Charles Wesley and Maxfield went to John Bray's with the women, and Maxfield was allowed to remain, breaching the rules.[193] Wesley, when confronted, asked the women what they wished. They asked Maxfield to stay, accepting the breach. Bray was ready to give up his care of the bands, unless Maxfield was excluded.[194]

Matters came to a head on the 30th April, when Charles Wesley was castigated for the new rule amongst the women. "They fell upon me about the women reading *their* rule for the exclusion of the brethren."[195] Wesley responded by questioning the society's authority, and removing them from the oversight of Fetter Lane altogether: "We answered, 'Whence had you your authority over them? We will save you any farther trouble, and do now take them out of your hands.'"[196] In early 1740, Hutton wrote to Zinzendorf, and referred to the obvious charm which the Wesleys exercised among the women, "J.W. and C.W., both of them are dangerous snares to many young women; several are in love with them. I wish they were once married to some good sisters, but I would not give them one of mine if I had many."[197]

Oversight and leadership

From May 1738, John Wesley was largely itinerant, traveling to Germany in July, Oxford later that year, and finally from March 1739, Bristol, which occupied much of his time. Between journeys Wesley assumed a leadership role amongst the bands and society of Fetter Lane. He also regularly visited other societies.

James Hutton's *Account* describes Wesley's itinerancy: "Shortly after Wesley and Ingham's return from Germany (Wesley was seldom with

---

192. See McGonigle, "Maxfield, Thomas," 225. Maxfield was converted under John Wesley's preaching in Bristol in 1739.

193. See Appendix 6, Rules A. After the rule relating to admission of women, the rules state, that "no men be present except their respective husbands, & the Persons who pray and Expound the Scriptures."

194. Wesley, *Journal*, Vol. I., 209.

195. Ibid., 223.

196. Ibid., 223.

197. Benham, *Memoirs of James Hutton*, 46.

us in London, and Ingham went to Yorkshire)."[198] He also wrote of both John and Charles: "The brothers Wesley visited us from time to time."[199] Of the same period, however, Wesley gives the sense that he and his brother were anxious to return to London from Oxford. "My brother and I are partly here and partly in London, till Mr. Whitefield or some other is sent to release us from hence."[200]

The Wesleys constant traveling may have caused the early pastoral and doctrinal problems, and eventually allowed stillness to become a popular doctrine. Hutton stated of the summer of 1738: "We fell into one confusion after another."[201] After January 1739, a number of Anglican clergymen could have been called upon for advice.[202] Whitefield was itinerant, but Ingham,[203] Hutchings,[204] Kinchin,[205] Simpson, Stonehouse, and Gambold[206] all of whom came to accept Moravian doctrines,[207] could have been consulted.

When in London, the Wesleys were assiduous members of the society. *Journal* and *Diary* entries show evidence of meeting bands and the society on the appointed nights (Monday for the bands and Wednesday for the general meeting) and visiting bands on their second meeting night. They also attended love feasts and John Wesley attended the prayer days, usually visiting Fetter Lane three times in the day.[208] This was combined with regular preaching and exhorting at other societies. For the Wesleys, Fetter Lane, while important, was not the center of their activities, implying that they were not careful to maintain the primacy of Fetter Lane.[209]

198. Libby, "James Hutton's 'Account,'" 186.

199. Ibid.

200. Wesley, *Works [BE]*, Vol. 25, 571. The letter is dated October 13th 1738.

201. Libby, "James Hutton's 'Account,'" 186.

202. Podmore, *The Moravian Church*, 47. See also Wesley, *Works [BE]*, Vol. 19, 29. Wesley indicates that seven clergy were present at the love feast.

203. Rose, "Benjamin Ingham," 590–91.

204. Skevington Wood, "John Hutchings," 587.

205. Charles Kinchin to Count Nicholas Ludwig Von Zinzendorf. One of the transcripts of the letters read at the Herrnhag Prayer Day on 15th October 1740. MCHp43.A3.

206. Podmore, "John Gambold," 422–33.

207. Libby, "James Hutton's 'Account,'" 145–46.

208. Wesley, *Works [BE]*, Vol. 19, 373. (Saturday 27th January 1739.)

209. Appendix 7: Rules B; No. 17.

John Wesley was active amongst the band leaders at Fetter Lane, meeting the leaders on a regular basis, at his home,[210] and at the society room.[211] Charles Wesley's *Journal* refers only once to meeting the female band leaders on the 11th May 1740.[212] He also records meeting the male band leaders once.[213] At that meeting he discovered Fetter Lane were holding meetings contemporaneously with the Foundery to prevent Fetter Lane members attending.

The Wesleys' pastoral and spiritual role amongst the bands can be clearly defined. Their presence at the women's bands was allowed as they would expound the Scripture and lead in prayer. In the final months of the Wesleys' membership at Fetter Lane, Charles Wesley anguished over the women's bands and he removed them from society control.

Whether John Wesley considered himself leader or "spiritual counsel" is unclear. He took an active part in speaking against stillness, was consulted about the separation of females from the general meeting, and the posts of monitor and president which indicate a leadership role. In *The Principles of a Methodist Farther Explained*, Wesley described himself as "having been 'but a single, private member of that Society.'"[214] Podmore states that unlike previous religious societies, Wesley's status did not even afford him the role of "clerical director envisaged in the rules of the older societies."[215] This view echoes Martin Schmidt's assertion that John Wesley's role was pastoral over all other things, "Much time was taken up by correspondence which was of a more pastoral nature than it had previously been."[216] Molther, however, affords a leadership role for John and Charles: "the society in Fetter Lane had been under the care of John and Charles Wesley."[217] Martin Schmidt, citing

---

210. Wesley, *Works [BE]*, Vol. 19, 372. (Wednesday 24th January 1739.) Wesley also met with the women leaders on the same day as the men. See 407. (Wednesday 12th September 1739.)

211. Ibid. (Wednesday 21st February 1739.)

212. Wesley, *Journal*, Vol. I, 228. (Sunday May 11th 1740.)

213. Ibid., 229. (Tuesday May 13th 1740.) Wesley noted "above twenty of the still brethren there."

214. Wesley, *The Principles of a Methodist farther Explained*. From Wesley, *Works [BE]*, Vol. 9, 172.

215. Podmore, *The Moravian Church*, 45.

216. Schmidt, *John Wesley*, Vol. II, Part I, 16.

217. Benham, *Memoirs of James Hutton*, 53. (See also, *The Life of Philip Henry Molther* Moravian Messenger, 1876.)

the account of the Moravian Church in England of 1747 and signed by leading Moravians, stated that if Molther had given John Wesley leadership, the separation might not have occurred.[218] Their position within the society then remains unclear.

The society lacked a clear leadership structure. Perhaps leadership was collegial. This is implied by Wesley's response to the issue of the exclusion of women from the general meeting, "I wish it might not be done before we have talked together."[219] Once the issue was settled, without Wesley's attendance at a meeting, he accepted the decision. Similarly Wesley believed the issue of president needed more thought: "Would not that [require] more particular consideration?"[220] During Wesley's absence from London in the summer of 1738, James Hutton felt the society required spiritual direction but not leadership.[221]

While Molther was ill (from April 1740), leadership lay with John Bray, George Stonehouse, John Simpson, Charles Delamotte, William Oxley, and Richard Bell. These leaders were amongst the group of whom Wesley wrote in his *Journal* "I had a long conference with those whom I esteem very highly in love."[222]

The German brethren's involvement at Fetter Lane was spiritual rather than temporal, although there were several Germans in London during the life of the society. Prior to July 1740, Molther, Böhler, Spangenberg, Töltschig, and Cossart visited the society, because they had come to London or Oxford, or because they were traveling to and from the colonies. Richter and Piesch, who were in London for longer periods, devoted their time to the Germans as their English was not good enough to have involvement with Fetter Lane.[223] Böhler left London for America on 4th May 1738, and Molther was in London for a protracted period between 1739 and 1740. Podmore states clearly that the Germans

---

218. Schmidt, *John Wesley*, Vol. II, Part I, 41. See Schmidt's footnote numbered 85 on p. 241. Schmidt states this view was a misjudgment of the real situation, but nonetheless a view held by the Moravians.

219. Wesley, *Works [BE]*, Vol. 25, 588.

220. Ibid.

221. Libby, "James Hutton's 'Account,'" 186.

222. Wesley, *Works [BE]*, Vol. 19, 139. (Entry for the 21st February 1740.)

223. Podmore, *The Moravian Church*, 51.

were not the final cause of the separation of Fetter Lane.[224] Therefore their influence can be taken as limited.

Ingham's letter to Hutton of the 23rd June 1739 highlighted the lack of decisive leadership, English, or German.[225] Without a single guiding hand, problems were inevitable. It was not until Fetter Lane was organized and led as the Brethren's German congregations were, that ordered leadership was exercised in a disciplined manner.

Lay leadership

The responsibility given to lay people, both male and female, in Fetter Lane's organization was exercised in two distinct areas: band leadership and the admission of members.

The bands met regularly and these were in the care of individuals, charged with the task of ensuring the meeting began punctually,[226] "interrogating"[227] the other members of the band and collecting the payments toward the "Common Stock."[228] Leaders also had the task of admonishing those members who failed to attend their band without good reason.[229] Prior to the Wednesday general meeting the leaders met to discuss the bands[230] and any action they were to take in connection with them. This action was to be reported back the following week. At this meeting, leaders were appointed to settle new bands and visit them. Originally, the leaders were to meet at "Mr Bray's,"[231] but these meetings often occurred at Wesley's home, or the Society Room. The leader's role was threefold: functionary, ensuring the regulation of a band; spiritual, hearing others speak of their Christian journey; disciplinary, discussing problems and any action to be taken.

The admission of individuals was the second area in which lay leadership was exercised. This is noted because admission was not subject

---

224. Ibid., 67–71.

225. B. Ingham, to J. Hutton, 23rd June 1739. MCHpp88–89A.3 [folder 14]; Ingham was concerned that there should be "somebody at the head."

226. *Rules* A; no. 9, *Rules* B; no. 8.

227. *Rules* A; no. 5, *Rules* B; no. 5. See also *Rules* A; no. 11, *Rules* B; no. 10.

228. *Rules* A; no. 27, *Rules* B; no. 31.

229. *Rules* A; no. 16, *Rules* B; no. 18.

230. *Rules* A; no. 6.

231. Ibid. This was John Bray. Charles Wesley's *Journal* mentions meeting the male leaders at Brays. See Wesley, *Journal*, Vol. I, 229.

to a clergyman's veto, as under the rules of the Unitary societies. There is similarity with the later Poplar Rules, where a majority of members admitted new members. Those who wished to join the society were mentioned by name at the Wednesday general meeting and answered set questions,[232] following which objections were raised and the prospective member was questioned. If the society was satisfied after a period "on trial," final admission was allowed, but only after opportunity was given to once more raise objections.[233] This gave the lay members of the society the right to object to any person, lay or ordained, and thereby, deny access to the society. In discussion of the Methodist classes, I will show that admission into the class "on trial" was not predicated on interrogation prior to joining, but continuance as a member was subject to showing a developing awareness of sin, awakening or justification.

Discipline

Discipline was exercised on two levels. At a routine level, the regularity of the society's meetings, and the obedience expected of members to meet in band or society as a priority over any other club or society, meant that in Fetter Lane, society members were separated from society in general. The rules drew members away not only from other religious societies, but also from clubs[234] and companies that were not conducive to a Christian life. Fetter Lane's rigorous schedule of meetings separated members from the world, in a manner that Herrnhut achieved through a settled community. Amongst the Fetter Lane membership, regular meetings replaced communal life.

To fail to attend either a general meeting or band meeting was a matter of concern and such behavior resulted in private and public reprimands.[235] Expulsion from the society was the final sanction. Charles Wesley was threatened with expulsion from his band by John Bray,

> J. Bray asked me whether I should come to my band on Monday. I answered, "No." He modestly replied, "Then you shall be expelled."[236]

---

232. *Rules* A; no. 19, *Rules* B; no. 21.
233. *Rules* A; nos. 21–24, *Rules* B; nos. 23–26.
234. *Rules* A: no 15; *Rules* B: no 17.
235. *Rules* A: no 16; *Rules* B: no 18.
236. Wesley, *Journal*, Vol. I, 210.

Expulsions were dealt with on a Wednesday evening. It was at a general meeting that Fish and Shaw were expelled and at the same meeting, Bray and Bowers' were publicly admonished over their adherence to the French Prophets.[237] At one meeting, Richard Tompson was readmitted. John Wesley met with him and after "the scales fell off from his eyes. He gladly returned to the Church and was in the evening re-admitted into our society."[238] Whitefield's *Journal* gives the impression that those who left the society over doctrinal issues constituted a "purging" of the society.[239]

No prospective member could be in any doubt of the society's codified expectations.[240] An individual's religious affiliation or state of faith was unimportant as the latter was tested during the "on trial" period. Rather, the questions asked about sincerity of purpose, openness, honesty, and submission to others were important to move from "on trial" to full membership.

On a deeper level, members were expected to be committed to the society. Here discipline surrounded the secrecy toward non-members about the matters discussed in band, society meetings, and love feasts. Confidentiality allowed openness amongst members in every aspect of their life, knowing that even those with whom a member shared a family or working bond would not divulge to any other person any matter mentioned.

Such closeness and secrecy allowed for antagonists to raise any number of accusations against the society. Charles Wesley's *Journal* notes the Reverend Henry Piers, Vicar of Bexley, ceased meeting "through fear of the world's threatenings."[241] Perhaps his inability wholly to explain the proceedings of the society may have provoked an adverse reaction from his congregation.

Fetter Lane always faced the possibility of being termed a conventicle, or Dissenter's meeting. The Wesleys met Bishop Gibson of London[242] and inquired whether religious societies were conventicles.

---

237. Wesley, *Journal*, Vol. I, 153. See also J. Wesley, *Works [BE]*, Vol. 19, 69.
238. Wesley, *Works [BE]*, Vol. 19, 71. See footnote 59.
239. Whitefield, *George Whitefield's Journals*, 261.
240. *Rules A*: no 19; *Rules B*: no 21.
241. Wesley, *Journal*, Vol. I, 134. Henry Piers also closed his pulpit to Charles Wesley.
242. Ibid., 133. John Wesley does not refer to this meeting either in his *Diary* or

Bishop Gibson's response was, "No; I think not: however, you can read the acts and laws as well as I: I determine nothing."[243] Over time, their position became more difficult as neither brother was licensed to a parish. Bullock pointed out that their work amongst the societies was irregular, and he argued that this was one reason for the closure of London pulpits to them.[244] Early in 1740 the Foundery was presented as a "seditious assembly"[245] to a local court. This society also had rules relating to openness in conversation at meetings.[246] While there was no explicit direction to privacy, it may be assumed that this was expected. The Foundery, like Fetter Lane, laid itself open to accusations of sedition. The main problem was simply whether the societies were public or private meetings. Whitefield believed they were private "in imitation of the primitive Christians."[247] Those who allowed societies to meet in private homes were also threatened with prosecution.[248]

Discipline was further exercised by continual fast and continual intercession.[249] No doubt for John and Charles Wesley these repetitive activities, when added to observance of the means of grace, assisted in the acquisition and development of faith. One can only presume that the doctrine of stillness, when readily accepted amongst the society members, affected not only observance of the means of grace but also observance of these early rules.

The Fetter Lane Society progressed members' religious life beyond the experience of the Unitary societies. Societies which had met to deepen personal piety and perhaps advance trade were superseded by a society that met to create a community of warm-hearted Christians whose entire life centered on the society, and the living of a regulated Christian life beyond the society's walls.

---

in the *Journal*. Susanna Wesley's involvement in the "Evening prayers controversy" in 1711 and 1712 was a cause of concern for Samuel Wesley, as he believed that the prayers at the Epworth rectory might have constituted a conventicle. See S. Wesley, *Susanna Wesley*, 78–83. Note especially Susanna's reply to her husband dated 25th February 1711/1712, 81–83.

243. Wesley, *Journal*, Vol. I, 133.
244. Bullock, *Voluntary Religious Societies*, 178.
245. Wesley. *Journal*, Vol. I, 236.
246. Wesley, *Works [BE]*, Vol. 9, 77–78.
247. Whitefield, *George Whitefield's Journals*, 202.
248. Ibid., 204.
249. *Rules A*: nos. 29 and 30; *Rules B*: nos. 29 and 30.

Communal living

A striking development in societal organization was the "The House," a "quasi-Moravian" community in Islington, where "members could experiment with community life."[250] Whitefield was initially against this development, believing servants would renounce their employment, and that a new congregation would be formed with no allegiance to the Church of England. He was also concerned that William Seward, who was working with Whitefield in Bristol, would be the sole financial support for the venture.[251] Seward wrote that neither he nor Whitefield could "see the expediency of this House at Islington."[252] Whitefield later wrote that he hoped the venture would succeed, and commented that as "Brother Paterson, and Brother and Sister Ansel I find are engaged there, so that I now propose, God willing, taking a young man of their profession."[253]

The House was leased in the Cambridge Road, and named "Shiloh."[254] Joseph Periam, a resident of the House, was apparently unhappy with the rules imposed upon the residents. Whitefield wrote to him:

> It is, no doubt, your duty, whilst you are in the house, to submit your self to the rules of it; but, then, you may use all lawful means to get yourself out. I have just now been with your sister, and will see what can be done further. Watch and pray.[255]

Wesley did not take this aspect of Fetter Lane's life into his own structure, although his early societies at Kingswood, Newcastle, and London provided for a "housekeeper."

---

250. Podmore, *The Moravian Church*, 52.

251. George Whitefield to James Hutton, 14th March 1739, (AB106.A3.14.33). Whitefield was also concerned that enemies of the Fetter Lane Society would have good reason to complain about the society, and that the membership might show disaffection to King George III and the Church of England through the leasing of the house.

252. William Seward to James Hutton, 11th March 1738 (1739), (AB101.A3.4.13).

253. George Whitefield to James Hutton, 22nd March 1738 (1739), (AB101.A3.4.17).

254. Podmore, "The Fetter Lane Society, 1739–1740," 161.

255. Whitefield, *The Letters of George Whitefield*, 497.

CHAPTER SUMMARY

At the separation from Fetter Lane in 1740, a unique society, which broke the mold of the religious life in England, came to an end. This chapter has traced the development and major emphases of the Fetter Lane Society, and discussed how Fetter Lane offered a deeper experience of faith to men and women, influencing not only contemporaneous societies, but also the later Anglican societies. Fetter Lane's foundation awakened the need for a fuller experience of faith, based upon the previously unpopular doctrines of New Birth, justification, and assurance.

Fetter Lane offered to English religion the warm piety of Moravianism, which was countered both by Wesley's own Anglicanism expressed through the Methodist movement, and by the established Church, who assimilated Pietst doctrine without the organizational structure. Although the Unitary societies survived, the pattern of religious life irrevocably changed with the introduction of the Moravian Church into England from 1740, and the growth of the Methodist movement.

Part Two will chart the development of the Methodist societies and analyze the distinctive aspects of the Methodist class meeting. From 1740, once Wesley was free to pursue his own movement without the hindrance of the Established Church, or the indecisive leadership of Fetter Lane, the resultant movement was a unique contribution into English religious life.

This section has mapped the origins of Wesley's theology, doctrine, and practice, by grounding the same within the religious and social milieu of his period, his familial background, and the religious associations of which he was aware, or was actively involved with. The context of this section sets into their proper places Methodism and the class meeting in the eighteenth-century Evangelical Revival. The uniqueness of the approach I have taken so far, to scrutinize, chronologically and analytically, the precursors to Methodism enables the following sections to be more fully understood, and appraised for their originality and discussion of the class both as *crown* and *cross*.

Part Two

Introductory Comments

THE FOLLOWING CHAPTER COMPRISES Part Two of the book. Within the chapter is a chronological study of the origins and development of the class meeting. This will show that the class did not begin until 1742, two years after Methodism's inception, and that its initial purpose was financial, rather than pastoral, experiential or affective.

Methodism was as regulated as its earlier counterparts. The chapter contains an original comparison of the Methodist's rules with those of Samuel Walker, who ran a contemporaneous society with Wesley's in Truro, and with Fetter Lane, the society Wesley left to form his own movement. Once Wesley recognized that the class meeting could provide a level of support, discipline, and disciping not found in the extant movement, he quickly realigned Methodism to include the class as the introductory group to which all aspiring Methodists had to belong.

The subsequent analysis of the purpose of the class, detailed in four subsections—fellowship, conversion and discipleship, financial accountability, and discipline—allows the book's development and fully assesses the class meeting as the "crown" of Methodism's life. The meeting was genuinely affective for those who came to faith in the "first wave" of Methodism's life, or who came to Methodism during periods of dispute or persecution.

A review of the class meeting is followed by a study of Methodism using two approaches within social science: social identity and group processes. The processes that occur within these two methodologies offer further insight into the success of the class as a "crown" for Methodism. Through these two aspects of the book, I show how prospective early Methodists actively chose to join a local society, having appraised the opportunities which membership offered, and subsequently having joined, how individuals became aligned within the class to hold the same beliefs, values, and opinions.

5

The Classes of Methodism

CONTEXT

WITH THE BREAK FROM the Moravians at Fetter Lane and the Calvinists under George Whitefield,[1] Wesley was free to pursue the development of Methodism without the checks and balances of other individuals or groups. From 1740 he would remain firmly in control of the polity and practice of the Methodist people, not only through his leadership of the later Conference but also through his publications, and regular visitations to societies around the developing Methodist Connexion.

In 1740 the Wesleyan movement ran along an east-west axis between London and Bristol, with the major centres being England's two largest cities of the time, with some societies dotted along the road between them. Once free to pursue his own movement's aims, Wesley lost no time in seeking to expand the movement throughout Britain.

Just as in London and Bristol, Wesley seized opportunities to take over pre-existing societies in the process of expansion. Henry Rack's description of John Wesley is apt: "Wesley, to put it rather brutally, was a great cannibalizer."[2] This can be seen in the assimilation of William Darney's societies in Yorkshire. Darney, a Scot, knew William Grimshaw of Haworth, and in 1747 his societies were offered to Benjamin Ingham. Ingham refused to take them. Shortly afterwards, when Charles Wesley

---

1. Wesley, *Works [BE]*, Vol. 19, 260. After meeting with George Whitefield on the 23rd April 1742 Wesley decided he would act independently of Whitefield, "I go on my way, whether he goes with me or stays behind."

2. Rack, *Reasonable Enthusiast*, 214.

visited Grimshaw, there was no such reluctance, and Darney's societies came to the Methodists.³

Attention here will be given to the creation of classes and bands, and the process of visitation to the Methodist societies. Personal testimonials and Wesley's own pronouncements through letters, publications, and the Conference will help to show how the classes and bands remained the focal point of the Wesleyan movement.

EMERGING WESLEYAN REGULATION

The geographical rise of Methodism is not within the remit of this book, but it is important to note the development of Methodism to the opening of Wesley's northern base, the Orphan House in Newcastle. In May 1742, Wesley visited Donnington Park, home of the Countess of Huntingdon, for the first time. From there, he started out with John Taylor, a servant of the Countess, toward Yorkshire.⁴

In Wakefield, John Wesley met John Nelson, a stonemason who had been converted through his preaching at Moorfields. Nelson returned to Yorkshire, feeling called to do so while receiving communion in St Paul's Cathedral.⁵ The closeness of the evangelical circle can be seen from Nelson's disappointment that more of his family had not been converted by the Reverend Benjamin Ingham.⁶

Nelson's preaching was successful,⁷ but he soon fell out with Ingham, whose own religious societies were growing across Yorkshire. It was at one of Ingham's societies that Nelson met David Taylor, John Taylor's brother. Nelson described David Taylor's preaching as a "dry morsel."⁸ John Nelson's account of an Inghamite society meeting shows that they were very similar to unitary Anglican societies:

---

3. Baker, *William Grimshaw 1708–63*, 101.

4. Wesley, *Works [BE]*, Vol. 19, 266. See footnote 66 for a short biography of John Taylor. See also Wesley, *Works [BE]*, Vol. 26, 76. Lady Huntingdon described John Taylor as possessing "a sweet and humble spirit."

5. Nelson, "The Journal of John Nelson," in *Preachers*, Vol. I, 37. See also Wesley, *Works [BE]*, Vol. 9, 434. (*A Short History of the People Called Methodists*.)

6. Nelson, "The Journal of John Nelson," 37. "I was greatly disappointed; for I expected to find many of my relations converted, as I understood they attended Mr. Ingham"s preaching.

7. Wesley, *Works [BE]*, Vol. 19, 267.

8. Nelson, "The Journal of John Nelson," 38.

> I went afterwards to a meeting of Mr Ingham's, where one read in an old book for nearly an hour; then sung a hymn, and read a form of prayer.[9]

Wesley was not breaking new ground in the evangelical revival, as John Nelson, Benjamin Ingham, and David Taylor were all preaching in England, and Ingham at least was forming societies. Howel Harris[10] and Daniel Rowland[11] were preaching in Wales, and Harris would later be active with the Calvinistic Methodists.

Benjamin Ingham remained in contact with the Moravians and Peter Böhler came to minister in Yorkshire in Ingham's absence. Böhler did not initially espouse stillness, appearing, according to Nelson, to preach "Wesley's doctrine."[12] It was only later that Böhler began to advise Ingham's followers to be still. At Ingham's invitation the Moravians moved into his societies.[13] "The Moravians themselves, who had commissioned workers to go to Yorkshire in May 1742 and sent them off a few weeks later, were going in a response to an invitation from Ingham to take over a group of societies he had founded."[14] That journey concluded in Bristol in late June 1742.

Wesley's ministry centered as much on "putting out fires" as on evangelism. The return to Bristol was marked by disputes and he spent five days[15] resolving those disagreements before traveling to a society in Cardiff and later returning to London. While in London, Wesley's mother Susanna died. John's letter to his brother informing him of his mother's death is almost matter-of-fact. After briefly describing his mother's last moments, he asks his brother: "Now, I would have you send me word immediately, whom I shall take into the house, to keep the accounts . . . And what [[woman, young or old, in the place of Betty Brown]]? I wait your answer."[16] The letter concludes, "She is to be buried tomorrow evening. Adieu!"[17]

9. Ibid., 39.
10. See Tudur, "Howel(l) Harris," 149–50.
11. See Tudur, "Daniel Rowland," 301–2.
12. Nelson, "The Journal of John Nelson," 48.
13. Nelson, "The Journal of John Nelson," 50–57.
14. Rack, *Reasonable Enthusiast*, 216.
15. Wesley, *Works [BE]*, Vol. 19, 282.
16. Wesley, *Works [BE]*, Vol. 26, 82. See also Wesley, *Works [BE]*, Vol. 19, 282–91. This is the *Journal* account of his mother's death, and burial and is followed by two letters Susanna had written to her son.
17. Wesley, *Works [BE]*, Vol. 26, 83.

In early August, Wesley was again journeying to Bristol, having removed some from the London societies who did not "show their faith by works."[18] Wesley records an incident with one Mr. Graves who had repudiated any allegiance to the Methodists, and who subsequently "recanted" of the repudiation. Wesley "regulated"[19] the Kingswood society and returned to London. Once again in London, problems arose with the Foundery Society, in the form of stillness which despite the separation from the Moravians had not been overcome.[20]

At this time, Lucy Godshall, an early member of the bands at Fetter Lane, died. Wesley had removed her from the bands after about two years, as he believed she was "weary and faint in her mind."[21] This action caused her to reappraise her state and she was eventually readmitted. Her experience is highly charged. She felt Satan was sifting her as wheat, which led to her whole being coming under "darkness and heaviness."[22] She eventually found peace and died. Wesley's defense of Lucy Godshall's experience led to an accusation of enthusiasm.[23]

The charge of enthusiasm was not unusual in Wesley's experience, and neither was the report to him a few days later from a woman (probably Mrs. Sparrow) who accused him of being a papist. In a conversation with another woman (Miss Gregory), Mrs. Sparrow was told that Wesley had rocked the cradle on Christmas Eve, and had taught Miss Gregory while she was in the bands to pray to the saints and the Virgin Mary. Mrs. Sparrow's response was to inquire why no other members of Miss Gregory's band accepted the same teaching and believed Wesley to be a papist. Miss Gregory stated that Wesley's religion was a "secret yet"[24] and that one had to belong to the bands for a while before this was made clear.

The growth of the societies was hindered by personal accusations made against Wesley, which clearly left some uneasy, despite being attracted to the movement. Notwithstanding the clear prejudice leveled against Wesley and the early Methodists, it is clear that many found an

18. Wesley, *Works [BE]*, Vol. 19, 291.
19. Ibid., 294.
20. Ibid., 296. See the entry for September 8th.
21. Ibid.
22. Ibid.
23. Ibid. See footnote 76.
24. Ibid., 298–99.

experience of God which was personal and life-changing. On traveling to Bristol in September 1742, Wesley received notes from society members who wanted to thank God for mercies they had received through faith.[25] These thanksgivings range from a new understanding of the love of God, to a sense of personal forgiveness. It is surely in these simple personal testimonies that one of the keys to the structure of Methodism lay. Within a close and watchful system where each individual is personally accountable, and where the experience of others is publicly known (and possibly seen), faith was not merely cerebral but a warmed heart experience.

Similar experiential accounts can be found in the *Early Methodist Volume*.[26] These accounts, primarily from the early 1740s were written to Charles Wesley.[27] In part, they are intended to be used as encouragement for other society members: "I doubt not that you will allow this written admission into the close band. I have *no* doubt."[28] The testimonies also provided anecdotal evidence to rebut arguments in favor of stillness. It is also clear that the writers have much from their personal experience to thank God for. The death account of Joanna Barber shows how her faith was assured: "When the time came that the Lord was about to take her to himself . . . being asked if she had anything that burthen'd her mind she answer'd no, she knew that Christ had taken away all her sins."[29] The phrase used by Wesley of his conversion experience: "A brand plucked from the burning," was used by others of their conversion.[30] For Samuel Webb, the thanksgiving, which he owed to God for his salvation, translated into a desire to evangelize others:

---

25. Ibid., 297–98.

26. The *Early Methodist Volume* is part of the Special Collection at the John Rylands University Library, Manchester.

27. See also the personal testimonies contained within Morgan, "Methodist Testimonials for Bristol Collected by Charles Wesley in 1742."

28. Testimonial: Joseph Carter to Charles Wesley, November 1741. *Early Methodist Volume*, 17. See also the note to Mary Fletcher regarding Rebecca Lloyd's sanctification in The *Fletcher Tooth Collection* at the JRULM. MA Fl. 38.1 The note was intended to be read publicly.

29. Testimonial: Account of the death of Joanna Barber to Charles Wesley, February 1752, 22. Joanna Barber had been a follower of John Wesley before the split from Fetter Lane. From the *Early Methodist Volume*.

30. Margaret Austin, 19th May 1740, 1. Catherine Gilbert, 1740, 6. Both are from the *Early Methodist Volume*.

I believed in the witness of the Spirit accordingly I declared it to brother Cooper in Band and from that time for 3 months (to the best of my remembrance) I had such a glowing a bigness in my breasts that I thought it my duty to invite all men to seek the Lord.[31]

In November 1742 John Wesley visited the young Newcastle Society. The period spent in Newcastle from 13th November to 30th December,[32] gives a picture of the method which Wesley used to encourage and evangelize. Days were spent field preaching, preaching to the society, meeting with the society and individual members, preaching at the local hospitals, and traveling around the surrounding area of Newcastle to preach and meet with other societies.

Wesley reported the people of Newcastle to be less convinced of sin than in other places where the Methodists were at work, but declared the work which was underway to be "evenly and gradually carried on. It continually rises step by step."[33] However, there was one instance of enthusiasm, when John Brown[34] rode through town, declaring he had received a revelation from God. Wesley's response was to rebuke him and send him home.[35] The building of the Orphan House began on the 20th December[36] and provided a base in the north of England.

Wesley's practice of regularly examining the spirituality of society members is seen through the few days spent in February 1743 in the London Society. With Charles, John Wesley met with the members to examine their spiritual state: "My brother and I began visiting the society together, which employed us from six in the morning every day till near six in the evening."[37] Charles Wesley's *Journal* gives a fuller account of this visitation, and he seems to have been stricter in examination than his brother; for he writes of one woman who told John Wesley that she had a "constant sense of forgiveness."[38] Charles' deeper questioning of

---

31. Samuel Webb to Charles Wesley: 20th November 1741, 18. *Early Methodist Volume*.
32. Wesley, *Works [BE]*, Vol. 19, 301–9.
33. Ibid., 303.
34. Ibid., 303–4. See footnote 3. Brown became an evangelist and began societies.
35. Ibid., 304.
36. Ibid., 305.
37. Ibid., 314.
38. Wesley, *Journal*, Vol. I, 305.

her led to the startling admission that she despised a fellow member. The remedy in this instance was prayer, but Charles makes the comment "I fear we have many such believers among us."[39]

By now, the organization of Methodism as a distinct group within the evangelical revival needed structured guidelines. Wesley had already published the *Rules of the Band Societies* in December 1738. In Newcastle in early 1743 Wesley published *The Nature, Design and General Rules of the United societies in London, Bristol, Kings-wood and Newcastle upon Tyne*.[40] The *Rules* were first read on the 6th March 1743 to the Newcastle Society. Wesley's intention in publishing them was to stir the society in that he "desired everyone seriously to consider whether he was willing to conform thereto or no. That this would shake many of them I knew well."[41] The next day, Wesley began visiting the classes to reinforce his intention that these rules should be followed.

There is a degree of apologetic within the preamble to the *Rules* setting out the rise of Methodism and the purpose of the *Rules* themselves. Once published, the *Rules* became a public document, and therefore Wesley may have been anxious to preface his own, quite distinct organizational rules with a statement outling the need for them.

It is quite obvious from the preamble that Wesley's creation of societies was in his view the result of a few individuals coming to him.[42] This is not wholly true. However, the reason for the desire to create these societies was far different from the Anglican Church's reasons to create societies. Methodists had to actively seek Christ and salvation, and pursue a holy life.

For Wesley, entry into a society was open; men and women, young and old, could meet together and seek to become holy through personal piety and communal meeting, prayer, worship, and study. Growth as a Christian in the Methodist society was not accomplished alone; rather it was to be a mutual experience through regular meeting, and as the preamble states, members were to "watch over one another in love, that they may help each other to work out their salvation."[43] The first subdivision of the society according to the 1743 *Rules* was the class, and in this

---

39. Ibid.
40. Wesley, *Works [BE]*, Vol. 9, 67–75. See Appendix 10.
41. Ibid., 317.
42. Appendix 10: Paragraph 1. See also Wesley, *Works [BE]*, Vol. 9, 69.
43. Appendix 10: Paragraph 2. Wesley, *Works [BE]*, Vol. 9, 69.

small group it could be "more easily discerned whether they are indeed working out their own salvation."[44]

There was a single reason for admission. "A desire to flee from the wrath to come, to be saved from their sins."[45] The corollary to such an open membership policy was that those who wanted to remain in membership should be "doing no harm,"[46] "doing good,"[47] and "attending upon all the ordinances of God."[48] Membership of a class was the way in which these rules were worked out in daily living. In case there were any questions, however, the subdivisions of each of the three "rules" were highly prescriptive, covering everything from "buying or selling spirituous liquors; or drinking them"[49] to regularly attending "The Supper of the Lord."[50]

METHODIST RULES AND WALKER'S RULES COMPARED

Wesley's *Rules* contrast with the rules of the Reverend Samuel Walker's Truro Society.[51] However, both sets of rules envisage that members should affect a particular behavior. Rule 9 of Appendix 5 is the single rule dealing with personal, social conduct. In the longer rules of Appendix 4 the entire preamble[52] is concerned with the manner in which members behave, and these are similar to the Methodist rules of 1743. The rules also deal with personal conduct, but from a more disciplinarian stance.[53]

Samuel Walker's Truro Society accommodated women, but the rules in both appendices ensured that single men and women were in separate societies, and Walker did not have classes or bands on the Methodist pattern. In the Methodist societies, men and women were together at society meetings, and in classes but segregated in the band.

Walker's rules contain the written prayers that are prescribed for use by society members at meetings. One can assume that Walker

44. Appendix 10: Paragraph 3. Wesley, *Works [BE]*, Vol. 9, 69.
45. Appendix 10: Paragraph 4. Wesley, *Works [BE]*, Vol. 9, 70.
46. Appendix 10. Wesley, *Works [BE]*, Vol. 9, 70–72.
47. Appendix 10: Paragraph 5. Wesley, *Works [BE]*, Vol. 9, 72.
48. Appendix 10: Paragraph 6. Wesley, *Works [BE]*, Vol. 9, 73.
49. Appendix 10: Paragraph 4. Wesley, *Works [BE]*, Vol. 9, 70.
50. Appendix 10: Paragraph 6. Wesley, *Works [BE]*, Vol. 9, 73.
51. See Appendices 4 and 5.
52. See Appendix 4: 389–93.
53. See Appendix 4: rules 7 and 8

wanted to ensure there was no place for extempore prayer. Wesley's societies allowed extempore prayer in society, class, and band meetings. The Methodists were also intended to form an interdependency not envisaged by Walker. Walker's presence was required for all matters of society discipline. This was not so for the Methodist societies. Rule 7 of the *General Rules* show a form of dependence that allows for one to speak to a "rule breaker" and ultimately to a leader so that action may be taken.[54] This rule shows an accountability that was not seen in any other society. Members are not merely watching each other for disciplinary purposes, but for salvific reasons: "an individual's salvation may rest upon your speaking or remaining silent." The member who errs is given the opportunity to repent and rejoin the society. It was mutually important for each member to ensure his or her neighbors were walking in an orderly manner, for this ensured each member did so.

Walker sought exclusivity for his society, refusing his members' involvement with any other society. Rule 4 details stringent entry requirements, and confined membership to inhabitants of Truro. Fetter Lane[55] had a similar rule, although this was not as prescriptively written. Walker wanted to ensure his society remained Anglican, as he saw the Methodists as a threat to the stability of his parish and his congregation. Samuel Walker referred to the earliest Unitary society rules, which had exactly the same prescriptive membership requirement.

METHODIST RULES AND FETTER LANE'S RULES COMPARED

What are the differences between the 1743 rules, which Wesley introduced, and the earlier rules of Fetter Lane, rules to which Wesley acquiesced? As there are three sets of rules, I shall compare the Methodist rules with the longest set of Fetter Lane rules.

Of primary interest is the difference in the method of rule creation. The leaders at Fetter Lane created their rules in an *ad hoc* manner. Initially consisting of rules 1 and 2,[56] later the growing society was subdivided into

---

54. Appendix 10: Rule 7. "If there be any among us who observe them not, who habitually break any one of them, let it be made known unto them who watch over that soul, as they that must give account. We will bear with him for a season. But if then he repent not, he hath no more place among us. We have delivered our own souls."

55. See Appendix 7: Fetter Lane Rules; Rule 17.

56. See Appendix 7. These two rules set the standard for the earliest admissions to

bands, and leaders appointed. At that time 3 further rules were added. On September 26th 1738,[57] a further 28 rules were added,[58] governing the time and nature of band meetings, and the other associated meetings of the society. Some rules dealt with the operation of the bands.[59]

Wesley's rules were handed to the United societies in a completed form. The only names which appear at the end of the rules are his own and his brother's. Here is a complete system of organization and discipline delivered to a new and growing organization, which needed some definitive regulations to govern the organization not simply in one place but in four distinct centres: London, Bristol, Kingswood, and Newcastle upon Tyne. Wesley carried into his societies some of the aims of Fetter Lane, and abandoned others. In 1743 he established rules asserting his leadership and authority over the United societies, an opportunity he did not have in the more "egalitarian" leadership of Fetter Lane.

In paragraph 2 of Wesley's *Rules*, the sentiments of the Fetter Lane Rules (Appendix 7: Rules 1 and 2) are picked up. The earlier 1738 attitude, which allowed members to meet in a spirit of openness and honesty, to confess sins and pray for one another, continued into Methodism. From that point it becomes a little more difficult to correlate the rules with each other as Fetter Lane subdivided into bands, and the Methodists in 1743 were initially subdividing into classes.[60] However, some general points can be made.

Fetter Lane members, like the Methodists, made regular financial contributions. At Fetter Lane these contributions were for the "general charge of the bands."[61] Monetary contributions paid to class leaders were

---

the Fetter lane Society. Later arguments over stillness were not envisaged.

57. This date is incorrect and should be the 25th September (a Monday) as shown in Wesley's *Journal*.

58. The shorter Fetter Lane Rules, (Herrnhut: 30 rules) have an additional insert on the 20th September which appointed the society leaders to meet with the leaders of the bands and discuss each band member and to decide what else might need to be undertaken to ensure the running of the society and appoint a leader for and create female bands. This is rule 6 in the shorter rules. Despite John Wesley's name appearing in that rule, he was not present when it was created.

59. See Appendix 7: Rules, 12, 13, 14, 15 & 16.

60. The Fetter Lane Rules lie more closely with the earlier Band rules drawn up by Wesley in December 1738.

61. Appendix 7: Rule 31.

used for a variety of purposes, and are mentioned only in the duties of class leaders.[62]

Wesley's openness toward lay leadership of the classes (and the bands) began at Fetter Lane. Rule 5 of the Fetter Lane Rules[63] allowed laymen and women to have an active part within the leadership. The *Herrnhut Rules* indicate band leaders were under the direction of the society leaders.[64] Wesley maintained a strict control over his leaders, meeting them frequently.

As the only rule of admission to the Methodist Society was "a desire to flee from the wrath to come, to be saved from their sins,"[65] the way in which this desire was evidenced was through the life of the society and class as the first subdivision of the society. The earlier Fetter Lane rules have only one rule for admission,[66] which Wesley appears to expand throughout his *General Rules* into a series of behavioral rules covering social, personal, spiritual and commercial conduct.[67]

The notable difference between Wesley's 1743 *Rules* and the Fetter Lane rules of 1738 is the clear prescription to attend "upon all the ordinances of God,"[68] included here as an "antidote" to stillness which had spread through Fetter Lane and eventually brought about division. John Wesley also included a reference to the need for good works.[69] In 1740, he had written to Zinzendorf and the Herrnhut Church a long letter outlining his grievances against Moravianism.[70] He protested:

> Hence lastly you undervalue good works (especially works of outward mercy), never publicly insisting on the necessity of them, nor declaring their weight and excellency. Hence when some of your brethren have spoken of them they put them on a wrong foot, viz. If you find yourself moved, if your heart is free to

---

62. Appendix 10: Rule 3, paragraph numbered 2.
63. Appendix 7: Rule 5 The person placed in charge of the small group was the band leader.
64. Appendix 6: Rule 6.
65. Appendix 10: Rule 4.
66. Appendix 7: Rule 21.
67. Appendix 10: Rules 4 to 6.
68. Appendix 10: Rule 6.
69. Appendix 10: Rule 5.
70. Wesley, *Works [BE]*, Vol. 26, 24–31.

it, then reprove, exhort relieve. By this means you wholly avoid the taking up your cross in order to do good.[71]

This grievance for Wesley was as fundamental a failing as stillness, and is set right explicitly within the *General Rules* where good works are an evidence of salvation. The mutual reproof and instruction which Wesley envisaged for the good of a brother or sister could be given in the class, band or privately.

WESLEY'S RULES AND PERFECTION

Alongside the *General Rules* stood the earlier *Rules of the Band Societies* drawn up in 1738. Once the *General Rules* were published, the earlier *Rules of the Band Societies* became subservient to the *General Rules* and governed the conduct of the subdivision of the class into a smaller, more intimate group, the band. The class, or rather the class-leader, touched with the membership on the individual's spiritual state[72] within a communal meeting where reproof or congratulation was shared equally among the group as encouragement or warning. The band meeting took this mutual accountability deeper in the quest for perfection, or perfect love (also called sanctification).

The rules show that the band was an egalitarian meeting with each person able to question and speak to others (although there was a band leader). Prior to admission each person was asked the questions which set the nature of the band meeting before the prospective member.[73] There were a series of standard questions asked of each member at each meeting. These questions required honest and full answers and were a part of the process of sanctification. Again, members learned from one another's experience and supported one another in a close fellowship striving for the same ultimate experience, having begun the journey from the same place, often a moment of crisis conversion. In 1744 further *Directions*[74] were issued to the band societies.

The *Directions* have overtones of Wesley's turn to seriousness of 1725, and his quest for primitive Christianity between 1735 and 1737. His quest for a holy life led him to keep a detailed record of his actions

71. Wesley, *Works [BE]*, Vol. 26, 30.
72. Appendix 10: Rule 3, paragraph 1.
73. Appendix 12: Rules 1–11. (Second section.)
74. See Appendix 12.

and thoughts across each day, and to live in an ascetic manner. While these *Directions* do not have quite the same requirement to document the use of time, section II[75] (Rules 1, 2 and 3) indicates a turning away from anything that might be considered as lightness toward a defined lifestyle, which would be noticeably different to the majority of a community and possibly noticeable even amongst society members. In this lifestyle, a practical, outward piety was envisaged, experienced by Wesley from 1725. In some respects, Wesley was creating for others a practical piety, which he had developed having read à Kempis, Taylor, and Law.

In the *Directions* Wesley is laying down a simple and effective method of living; ascetic, devoted, and useful. These three elements were surely the very things for which Wesley strove as a younger man in Georgia as he sought out the life, worship, and practices of the very earliest apostolic Christians, and longed to recapture this primitive Christianity for himself.

The journey toward entire sanctification or perfection can be found through the *Directions*. If these *Directions* are seen as a codification of John Wesley's turn toward a serious life, his reflection, and assimilation of the authors who brought it about, and the experience of Georgia, the underlying strand of the need for perfection (or perfect love) runs through each of the three sections.

Despite Wesley's feeling that the mystics had almost caused him to flounder spiritually,[76] he never denied the doctrine of perfection which they espoused, and integrated the need for growth toward perfection into the bands. While the class was not specifically for those actively seeking perfection, those made perfect were members of classes.

By rejecting the mystics' insistence upon the spiritual life as an introverted journey, yet maintaining the importance of perfection, Wesley wove together a form of communal and personal life that promoted the need for the means of grace and good works. Perfection was, for Wesley, the end result of the process of sanctification, and it was a state that each believer could attain following justification. Watson describes perfection thus: "it was no more than the corollary of his distinction between the process of sanctification and the immediacy of justifying faith."[77] Rack is clearer of the importance Wesley placed on love for God, as the key

---

75. Appendix 12: Directions to the band societies.
76. Wesley, *Works [BE]*, Vol. 25, 487.
77. Watson, *The Early Methodist Class Meeting*, 68.

to being perfect. "To be a "perfect" Christian is to love God with one's whole heart, mind, soul and strength."[78]

Perfection could be achieved, and the *Directions* and the earlier *Rules of the Band Societies* were intended to help Methodists achieve this state. If this doctrine of perfection, which often found Wesley embroiled in controversy with his opponents, seems impossible to achieve, Wesley's understanding of sin helps to illuminate how a believer might achieve it. Perfection for Wesley was not to be entirely sinless. Certainly voluntary transgressions (as Wesley termed sin) would mean a believer was not perfect; however, committing involuntary transgressions (breaking a divine law) did not mean a person was not perfect in this life. For that reason Wesley shied away from the term "sinless perfection," for that would mean that neither voluntary nor involuntary sins were committed. Wesley justified his position in *A Plain Account*. He did not accept that involuntary transgressions were sin in the sense that voluntary transgressions were.[79]

Perfection was more than freedom from voluntary sin; it was the whole of the Christian life. In *A Plain Account*, Wesley refused to allow that those who do not attend the means of grace could claim perfection:

> We not only allow, but earnestly contend, that there is no perfection in this life which implies any dispensation from attending all the ordinances of God; or from doing good unto all men while we have time though "especially unto the household of faith."[80]

The societies, classes, and bands also acted as collegial bodies where one learned from his or her peers how to live the Christian life, and journey toward perfection. This learning and experience could be found in attending all the means of grace:

> We believe that not only the babes in Christ, who have newly found redemption in His blood, but those also who are "grown up into perfect men," and indispensably obliged, as often as they have opportunity, to "eat bread and drink wine in remembrance of Him," and to "search the Scriptures," by fasting, as well as temperance, "to keep their bodies under, and bring them into

---

78. Rack, *Reasonable Enthusiast*, 397.
79. Wesley, *A Plain Account*, 45.
80. Ibid., 28.

subjection"; and, above all, to pour out their souls in prayer, both secretly, and in the great congregation.[81]

A Plain Account, written in 1766, is a retrospective of Wesley's views and there was an element of personal experience for Wesley had traveled the societies and witnessed the Christian growth of others. Equally, he was offering an apologia for perfection following the perfection controversies of that decade.

Throughout the *Plain Account* he refers to his sermon on *The Circumcision of the Heart*. In it, Wesley sets out his understanding of Christian living. At an early point in the sermon he writes that circumcision of the heart is "a right state of soul, a mind and spirit renewed after the image of him that created it."[82] This is evidenced for Wesley by only one thing: love. It is love to God and to neighbor which led an individual to perfection, and as Wesley wrote in conclusion of the sermon: "Here, then, is the sum of the perfect law; this is the true circumcision of the heart."[83] In the Methodist societies, this love could be expressed in a community of faith. This ideal of love, coupled with his understanding of the doctrine of perfection, gave to the bands in particular, but to the whole societal structure, a dynamic which was interconnected in a way that no other society could achieve.

THE CLASS MEETING AND BAND MEETING COMPARED

The class and band need some differentiation to understand fully their relationship. As a continuation of Moravian practice, the band was used in Methodism from 1740. The bands were small groups for earnest Christians. This meant that inquirers after faith joined a society, and later were allocated to a band.

From 1742, the class became a compulsory group, relegating the band to a meeting for serious believers, and continuing to receive members who were justified. The class, however, welcomed inquirers, and class members were placed "on trial" for a period of three months before membership of the society was offered. The sole condition of membership of the class was the desire to flee from the wrath to come, and actively seek faith.

---

81. Ibid., 28.
82. Wesley, *Sermons on Several Occasions, First Series*, 152. See paragraph 3.
83. Wesley, *Sermons*, 161. See paragraph 10.

The emphasis of the movement changed from society-focused to class-focused. Every society consisted of the total class membership, and every society began as a class. The band took on significance as the group for those pressing after perfection, with the class acting as an introductory and discipling group. The band was further subdivided into select bands, for those who had attained perfection, and penitential bands, for those who had slipped from the state of perfection.

THE FORMATION OF THE CLASS MEETING

The class began in Bristol, as a means of settling the outstanding debt on the "New Room" which stood at £150.[84] Wesley carried this debt personally from 1739 to February 1742. At a meeting specifically called to discuss means of discharging it, the suggestion was put forward to divide the society into groups, and make each member responsible for a penny each week toward settling the debt. A leader was put over each class, charged to visit house to house to collect the money and deliver it to the stewards.[85]

The person responsible for this revolutionary suggestion was Captain Foy, thought to be a mariner from Bristol, whom Wesley mentions only once by name in his *Thoughts upon Methodism* of 1786:

> A year or two after Mr. Wesley met the chief of the society in Bristol, and inquired, "How shall we pay the debt upon the preaching-house?" Captain Foy stood up and said, "Let everyone in the society give a penny a week and it will easily be done."[86]

Foy was unwittingly responsible for the close and careful system of accountability that was to sweep through the Methodist movement, replacing the band as the primary small group meeting, and becoming the place at which every Methodist began their Christian life in fellowship.

Captain Foy might properly be described as "elusive." He received little credit from Wesley for his idea and has become a footnote in Methodist folklore. The most detailed investigation into Foy's background can be found in a 1902 article of the *Proceedings*, although that

---

84. Wesley, *Works [BE]*, Vol. 19, 56.
85. Ibid., 251.
86. Wesley, *Works [BE]*, Vol. 9, 528.

article is entirely inconclusive.[87] My own attempt at tracing him using a maritime researcher[88] proved equally inconclusive.

Frank Baker stated that the class filled a position of pastoral oversight within the Methodist framework, an oversight that was not possible with the system of bands and society alone:

> With very large societies such as those at Bristol and London adequate pastoral oversight by visiting necessitated some delegation of responsibility, and something much more definite than expecting the band members in general to keep their eye on the peripheral members of the society.[89]

Wesley related the development of the class in his *Thoughts*,[90] and in a letter of 1748 to Vincent Perronet, commonly called, *A Plain Account of the People Called Methodists*. In short, the leaders found visiting from house to house onerous[91] and also discovered that Methodists were not behaving as if they were indeed on the path to perfection: "In a while, some of these informed me, they found such and such an one did not live as he ought."[92]

From Wesley's viewpoint, at this early stage it appears the class was a disciplinary tool. Those who were disorderly, or failed to live out their faith, could be disciplined more simply if there was a means of closely following members' behavior. Some would be put out of the society, others reproved, and the remainder of the class were no doubt suitably chastened, and urged to pray for their erring brothers and sisters.

Although the class quickly became the point of entry for all Methodists, John Evans a soldier under the command of Captain Desaguiler in Brussels, was not aware of the class in 1744. He belonged to a society of soldiers:

> (the) United Society is divided into Bands. Our manner of meeting at Ghent is this: we hired two rooms, one a small one, wherein the bands do meet every day, at One o'Clock; and another large

---

87. Foster, "Bristol Methodist Notes. V.-Who Was Captain Foy?," 64–65.
88. The firm were Tim Hughes & Associates of Twickenham.
89. Baker, "The People Called Methodists 3: Polity," 222.
90. Wesley, *Works [BE]*, Vol. 9, 528–29.
91. Ibid., 261.
92. Ibid., 260–1.

one for Public Meeting, where we meet twice a day, at Nine in the Morning, and Four in the Afternoon.[93]

Baker, however, notes that once classes "were established there was a strong tendency for the classes to oust the bands from their key position."[94]

Once the class became the entry point, possession of a class ticket enabled entry to the society meeting. Entry restrictions were carefully maintained, as Thomas Olivers discovered. Despite attending the public service, he was ejected before the society meeting began: "When the public preaching was over on a Sunday evening, and I, along with the multitude, was shut out from the society, I used to go to a field at the back of the preaching-house, and listen while they sang the praises of God."[95] Sarah Perrin, who had been a follower of the Wesleys since 1740, found herself in the same position in 1743 as she had not been baptized, and was therefore excluded from membership, but not the open meeting:

> My trouble is deepened since I spoke to thy brother (Charles Wesley) for I had let it into my mind from the Rules you Publish'd that I was to be excluded the Society but he tells me we that do not think the same way may be of the united society and so far as you will admit me so far will I join with you.[96]

The class was not universally well received. Wesley noted that some felt the class was simply a means of regulation and restraint, others that it was something new in the Methodist system and others that there was no scriptural warrant to allow for it.[97] For Wesley the class was a prudential[98] means of grace: that is a tool which assists Christians in their journey toward sanctification. In the *Large Minutes*, the following question is asked: "Q. Do we sufficiently watch over our helpers?" In the response, a discussion of instituted and prudential means, the answer is

---

93. Letter: John Evans to John Wesley, 12th November 1744, in *Arminian Magazine*, Vol. I, 277. Evans was killed at the battle of Fontenoy (word in italics mine).

94. Baker, "The People Called Methodists 3: Polity," 223.

95. Olivers, "The Life of Thomas Olivers," 85.

96. Letter: Sarah Perrin to John Wesley. June 9th 1743. From: *Letters Chiefly to the Wesley's Volume II*. JRULM (words in brackets mine).

97. Wesley, *Works [BE]*, Vol. 9, 262–63.

98. See Wesley, *Minutes of the Methodist Conference, volume I*, 548–54. The questions and answers in relation to the means of grace first appeared in the *Large Minutes* of 1763.

made under the prudential means: "*Prudential* Means we may use, either as common Christians, as Methodists, as Preachers, or as Assistants... 2. As Methodists, do you never miss any meeting of the Society? Neither your Class or Band?"[99]

Objections were raised to the suitability of the class leaders, as none were specifically trained for the role. In *A Plain Account of the People Called Methodists*,[100] Wesley displays something of his pragmatism, accepting the criticism. However, he argued that God would give leaders the grace and abilities they need; that meeting regularly with the minister would enable them to improve; and any who were unsuitable could be removed.[101]

Finding sufficient class leaders must have been difficult for Wesley. Grace Murray, at one time matron at the Orphan House in Newcastle led extremely large classes: "I had a full hundred in classes, whom I met in two separate meetings; and a Band for each day of the week."[102] Leaders also had care of more than one class, as Benjamin Rhodes accounted. "I was desired to lead several classes."[103] Youth was not a bar to leading classes. Mary Bosanquet[104] and Judith Land became class leaders at only 18.[105] Mary Bosanquet was appointed by Wesley.[106]

In March 1742 classes were introduced in London, and Wesley proposed an alternative purpose:

> I appointed several earnest and sensible men to meet me, to whom I showed the great difficulty I had long found of knowing the people who desired to be under my care. After much discourse, they all agreed there could be no better way to come to a sure, thorough knowledge of each person, than to divide them

---

99. Ibid., 552.

100. See Wesley, *Works [BE]*, Vol. 9, 254–80.

101. Ibid., 263–64.

102. Valentine, *John Bennet and the Origins of Methodism and the Evangelical Revival in England*, 207.

103. Rhodes, "An Account of Benjamin Rhodes," 364.

104. Taft, *Biographical Sketches of the Lives and Public Ministry of Various Holy Women, Whose Eminent Usefulness and Successful labours in the Church of Christ, Have Entitled them to be Enrolled among the great Benefactors of Mankind: In Which are Included Several Letters from the Rev J. Wesley never before Published: Volume I*, 19.

105. Ibid., 201.

106. Ibid., 19.

into classes like those at Bristol, under the inspection of those in whom I could most confide.[107]

Appointed leaders acted as Wesley's "deputies," reporting on the spiritual state of class members to allow progress and discipline to be noted. As Methodism developed, Wesley's role was taken over by the assistant. Baker argues that all others in the society were under the authority of the assistant in Wesley's place.[108]

Further development came as class leaders began to meet their class together and the introduction of rules for class leaders and members set the pattern for their meetings. These rules were made known to prospective members: "I took an opportunity of asking one of them, Robert Anderton, "What were the terms of admission among them?" He told me, "These:" putting the rules of the Society into my hands, and desiring me to read and consider them."[109] The rules were mass-produced and made available to the societies for prospective members: "Pray send with the next magazines, 100 *Rules of the Society* and 6 *Spiritual Hymn Books*."[110]

The class itself was regulated by the leader through weekly meeting of the class, weekly meeting with the society leaders, and quarterly visitation by John or Charles Wesley, or in later years the assistant. At any point in the weekly visitation process a person could be received into the class on trial, and then received as a member at the quarterly visitation. It was at this time that lapsed or "disorderly walkers" were removed.[111] Richard Viney's *Diary* records meeting Wesley with the Foundery class leaders in 1744 from which he understood the meeting's primary functions were fund raising and poor relief:

> Mr. Westley had a meeting with ye leaders of ye classes, men and women, who bring in every Monday ye money collected in each

---

107. J. Wesley, *Works [BE]*, Vol. 19, 258.

108. See Baker, "The People Called Methodists 3: Polity," 225–26.

109. Oliver, "An Account of Mr. John Oliver," 419.

110. Bowmer and Vickers, *The Letters of John Pawson (Methodist Itinerant, 1762–1806), Volume I: To the Conference of 1794*, 28.

111. Wesley, *Letters [SE]*, Vol. VI, 208. John Wesley to Joseph Benson February 22nd 1776. See also Wesley, *Letters [SE]*, Vol. IV, 273. John Wesley to the Bristol Society October 1764.

class for ye poor, and at ye same time as much of it as is found needfull by ye majority present is given to such who want it.[112]

The disciplinary function of the class through visitation can be seen in a letter from Joseph Sanderson, then in Scotland to Samuel Bardsley in Berwick. In 1782, attendance was far from universal, and gave cause for concern. "There are numbers of them meet their Class once or twice a quarter. I told them the other day I would have no such Members amongst us."[113] He believed that the use of discipline had been lax, and he had decided to "put our rules in execution here more than usual."[114] The system of class paper notation was enough to cause him little short of heartache.[115] In reading these papers, he was aware that class attendance was poor, and that instituting more strongly the known discipline, would reduce numbers making "our small number still smaller."[116]

Wesley was asked to regulate the Newcastle Society by letter. "Through the earnest requests of Brother *Nelson*, I am constrained to stay, and visit the Classes with him. By the return of the Post, we should be glad of your Advice, whom to put out and whom to take in."[117] Sarah Perrin invited the Wesleys to Bristol in 1744 to regulate the classes there. She thought that this would be an "unspeakable blessing." "I am fully persuaded we have many choice members amongst us but believe if you could spend some time with us they w^d increase in number and stature."[118]

A simple system of annotating class papers was devised to denote the state of each member, and this annotation could be altered by the class leader. These papers became a method for the quarterly visitor to assess a member's progress.[119] Some of these shorthand codes[120] are un-

---

112. Riggall, "Richard Viney's Diary. 1744," 52.
113. Simon, "The Letters of Joseph Sanderson," 148.
114. Ibid.
115. Ibid.
116. Ibid.
117. Wesley, *Works [BE]*, Vol. 26, 121.
118. Sarah Perrin to John Wesley: June 1744. *Letters chiefly to the Wesley's*: Volume II, JRULM.
119. Simon, 'The Letters of Joseph Sanderson," 148.
120. For a list of these coded letters see Baker, "The People Called Methodists 3: Polity," 224. See also Crowther, *A True and Complete Portraiture of Methodism*, 228. Crowther reprints the form that class papers took.

decipherable, but no doubt allowed a means of assessing an individual's spiritual state while retaining the confidence of the class.[121]

As the title of this book suggests, I am arguing that the class meeting, which became a cross to Methodism within Wesley's lifetime, was also the crown of the scheme of salvation that Wesley gave to the Methodist Movement. As the introduction stated, the Wesleyan *movement* existed until 1749 when the first quarterly meetings were held. After that date, Wesleyan Methodism was established as an *organization* that would not be altered until after Wesley's death.

THE CLASS MEETING: THE CROWN OF METHODISM

The class as a "crown" was established in four distinct, yet interrelated aspects of operation. These were fellowship, conversion and discipleship, financial accountability, and discipline. This chapter will now turn to examine these individually using personal testimony and published work on the class system. The class held a vital function for Methodism's period as a movement and early organization, a function which became outdated before Wesley's death in 1791. Later in this chapter it will be indicated just how different the class was from any earlier small group structures, and the spirituality encapsulated within it.

Fellowship

Class fellowship was of paramount importance to Wesley. In his letter to Edward Perronet, Wesley indicated that once the classes were meeting weekly, fellowship was the vital ingredient that gave them purpose. This was enhanced by class member's "intimate acquaintance" which gave them "more endeared affection for each other."[122] Baker assesses the fellowship of the class to be of a "less searching kind"[123] than the bands, but regulation of both band and class was applied equally to any who were unwilling to be open with their neighbor.

The primary aim of the band was fellowship for those seeking, or who had attained, perfection, while the class member was growing in grace and holiness, with perfection as a long-term rather than imme-

---

121. See Sugden, "A Wesley Class," 75–77. See also Bretherton, "Mrs Fletcher's Class Paper," 197–98.
122. Wesley, *Works [BE]*, Vol. 9, 262.
123. Baker, *John Wesley and the Church of England*, 78.

diate goal. The nearest that one can come to accept Baker's argument is through a careful examination of the *Directions Given to the Band Societies* in 1744. However, while these rules are clearly intended to guide the band member through life, it should also be noted that there was a need to differentiate the band from the class in purpose. These rules accomplish this aim.

Fellowship was engendered because as Watson suggests class members were on "a common journey."[124] Watson argues that fellowship was born from a mutual accountability to each other through the discipleship process. A detailed study of fellowship in early Methodism was made by Leslie Church who unfortunately affords the class a rather homely "fireside"[125] setting, although he does consider the class to be Methodism's crowning glory. To restrict the class to this level of operation romanticizes the class and its purpose.

Church asserts that the purpose of the class was fulfilled when the leaders took their position seriously as a charge over the souls of others in their care, and recognized that they too were accountable. Wesley encountered slack leaders[126] and removed them from command of the souls of a class. John Bennet noted in 1744 that leaders were not always reliable:

> In my way called of Thomas Hallom a young man at Smalldale who had for sometime seemed slack in meeting and was a leader of that Class. He went with me, but alas! He was drowned with the pleasures of this world etc.[127]

Not all leaders were slack, and Church cites instances of leaders who faithfully carried out their duties, imbuing their class members with a desire to seek fellowship with them. James Field, who in old age reduced his classes from five to four, (effectively 84 people), continued to visit and meet with his classes.[128]

The leaders facilitated or damaged the opportunity for fellowship. Joseph Barker's experience at a class meeting in 1822 shows how a lead-

124. Watson, *The Early Methodist Class Meeting*, 116.
125. Church, *The Early Methodist People*, 149–50.
126. Wesley, *Letters [SE]*, Vol. VI, 208. John Wesley to Joseph Benson, February 22nd 1776.
127. Valentine, *Mirror of the Soul. The Diary of an Early Methodist Preacher, John Bennet: 1714–1754*, 82.
128. Church, *The Early Methodist People*, 167.

er's obsequiousness toward the rich, and contempt of the poor prevented any form of fellowship. Barker concludes his bitter attack: "I wonder how we could bear with such a shallow worthless person for a leader; but we knew no better, I suppose, then?"[129]

Close fellowship was occasioned by the routine of the meeting, offering order, and familiarity. Meetings began with a hymn and prayer followed by interrogation of each member with appropriate advice and admonition, concluding with a prayer and hymn. James Lackington described in his *Memoirs* the proceedings of a class meeting:

> When they met together, the Leader first gave out and hymn, which they all sang: after the hymn they all kneeled down, and their leader made an extempore prayer: after which they were seated, and when the leader had informed them of the state of his own mind, he inquired of all present, one after another, how they found the state of their souls. They then sang and prayed again. This lasted about one hour.[130]

Within the regular pattern of meeting, new members could experience the same careful examination as more experienced peers in a regulated but supportive group.

As the class was a private group, there is little extant material pertaining to the interrogation and responses of members. Usually, a biography or diary will simply refer to class membership. However, there are clear examples of the effect that fellowship had on individuals, and some of the most expressive can be found in the period of the early bands. Prior to the classes, the band's function was the closest parallel, and therefore any band material provides helpful information about the close functioning of the small group. Elizabeth Baddiley had ceased to meet because she found the interrogation intolerable.[131] Her experience of such questioning took place prior to the removal of the bands to a meeting for those pressing toward perfection after the creation of the class meeting:

---

129. Thompson, *Nonconformity in the Nineteenth Century*, 48–50.

130. Lackington, *Memoirs of the first forty-five years of the Life of James Lackington*, 62–63. See also Alexander, *Reasons for Methodism Briefly Stated in Three Letters to a Friend*, 39–40. Contained in Polemical Tracts: Methodist Apology Volume II, Wesley College Archives, IC3?D6/5.

131. See Appendix 11. The close questioning of each band member was set out in the *Rules of the Band Societies* drawn up in 1738.

I do not meet my band the reason is this time after time being told I had not a spark of sincerity in me which was the truth tho I could not bear it thus far for it stopt my mouth that I could not speak my mind then I was charged with not never being open.[132]

The reception of the assurance of faith was a common experience in the class as was a deeper feeling of personal faith. Samuel Webb received the witness of the Spirit and declared that openly in band.[133] Sarah Barber found comfort from band membership, and waited for faith: "I was admitted upon tryall and then I was most time in great doubts but then hearing the Lord justifieth the ungodly then I knew I was ungodly . . . then I hoped and found great comfort and indeed the band was of great service to me for I was never sent away without some comforts."[134]

Elizabeth Collett's biography shows just how deeply the fellowship experience could be felt.

When she was about sixteen, her circumspect walk attracted the attention of some members of the Methodist Society, who invited her to attend a class-meeting; this she accordingly did, and was most agreeably surpized (sic) to hear others speaking of religious enjoyments, similar to thos she had experienced for the last two years . . . She now began to experience the great benefit arising from the fellowship of saints, having that eminent Christian, the late Mrs. Ann Gilbert for her class leader.[135]

The openness of the fellowship was exhibited in the manner in which members spoke to each other. Margaret Austin[136] was accused of "self" by a band sister for meeting Charles Wesley privately after he preached. Elizabeth Sayce was interrogated in her band by Charles Wesley, an experience that was shared by her band sisters in their close fellowship.[137]

---

132. Letter: Elizabeth Baddiley to John Wesley. Bristol, December 31st 1741. Wesley College Archives: D5/69/2.

133. Letter: Samuel Webb to Charles Wesley. 20th November 1741. *Early Methodist Volume*.

134. Letter: Sarah Barber to Charles Wesley. May 1740. *Early Methodist Volume*.

135. Taft, *Biographical Sketches of the Lives and Public Ministry of Various Holy Women, Whose Eminent Usefulness and Successful Labours in the Church of Christ, Have entitled them to be enrolled among the great benefactors of Mankind: In which are included Several Letters from the Rev J. Wesley never before published: Volume II*, 120–21.

136. Letter: Margaret Austen to Charles Wesley. 19th May 1740. *Early Methodist Volume*.

137. Morgan, "Methodist Testimonials for Bristol Collected by Charles Wesley in

Personal accounts are early relative to Methodism and the class meeting. It appears that as time progressed, and the meeting's business became confidential, little was written about what was actually said. Later testimonials and biographies of local or itinerant preachers concentrate on a broader life and ministry. However, in some accounts, the activities of the classes are noted, as is the depth of feeling between members. Mary Holder was distressed to leave her class after her marriage to an itinerant preacher: "I felt *much* at leaving a large *class of young women*, whom I had met ten years or more–with my *band sisters*. We had been united in bonds of love, ever glad to meet—but not very willing to part—though sure we were one in heart."[138]

Conversion and discipleship

The class became the center of Methodist life, the group into which searching or awakened individuals were introduced. Membership on trial for three months preceded admission to the society. During that time, it was expected that some growth in understanding or faith was made plain to the class leader. Part of the on trial period was to readjust to a new manner of living.

William Green's biography shows how joining a class and entering the process of conversion meant leaving former friends behind. "My dear mother, by much persuasion, prevailed upon me to meet in a Class. From this time my chains began to fall off. I think I had not met above three times, before all my outward sins left me, and I shook off all my old companions."[139] In a space of three weeks, Green not only re-orientated his spiritual direction, but he gave up his previous lifestyle. John Atlay also gave up his previous "trifling company"[140] following his religious awakening.

Ann Whitfield was justified at a class meeting. "I went to a class-meeting at my father's house, and there the Lord pardoned all my sins."[141] Commonly, personal accounts describe a period of searching, or mourn-

---

1742," 97.

138. Taft, *Biographical Sketches*, Vol. I, 19.

139. Green, 'An Account of the life of Mr. William Green,' in *Arminian Magazine*, Vol. III, 252.

140. Atlay, 'Account of the life of Mr. John Atlay,' in *Arminian Magazine*, Vol. I, 577.

141. Taft, *Biographical Sketches*, Vol. I, 266.

ing, which is brought to a conclusion by a momentous or instantaneous revelation. Sarah Cox's biography shows this to be her experience. Her soul was "sinking beneath the pressure of unpardoned guilt," and after meeting in class two or three times, she heard Jesus speak to her, and was "presently filled with love to God and all mankind."[142] Further, she recounted this heartfelt moment through Charles Wesley's hymn, *Let earth and heaven agree*.[143] This experience became a personal testimony to share and encourage others. Robert Wilkinson also found faith while a hymn was being sung. For Wilkinson, the hymn "All ye that pass by" led to a decisive moment of forgiveness:

> Then, all within me cried out,
> The sinner am I
> Who on Jesus rely,
> And come for the pardon, God cannot deny.[144]

John Atlay[145] was moved at the singing of "Come, Lord! The Drooping sinner cheer." Over time, his sense of being awakened was challenged, until walking alone he heard a voice speaking to him. This turned his awakening into assurance. Atlay used that experience as a testimony to his class:

> From this Time, I was exhorting every Company wherein I was; and God continually confirmed what was spoken: but especially to the Class whereof I was Leader, most of whom were justified in a few months.[146]

The distress and searching of others affected class members so deeply that they were justified, as Sarah Ryan's biography shows:

> Being one night at class, with my sister, who was in great distress, I felt the burden of her soul laid upon mine in an inexpressible manner: and while I was exhorting her to believe, the power of God overwhelmed my soul, so that I fell back in my chair, and my eye-sight was taken from me: but in the same moment the

---

142. Ibid., 71.

143. This hymn was published in 1742 in *Hymns on God's Everlasting Love* (2d series). See J. Wesley, *Works [BE]*, Vol. 7, 121–23.

144. Wilkinson, "A Short Account of Mr. Robert Wilkinson," 182. The hymn appeared in *Hymns and Sacred Poems* in 1749 in the section *Invitation to Sinners*.

145. Atlay, "Account of the life of Mr. John Atlay," 577–78. The person exhorting in the society was Hannah Harrison.

146. Ibid., 579.

> Lord Jesus appeared to my inward sight . . . a little after, my leader asked me, "Do you now believe?" I faintly answered, "Yes."[147]

Benjamin Rhodes' careful leadership of several classes brought members to faith or to a "stirring up,"[148] (presumably awakening or questioning). The support of a class leader could assist the searching individual in the quest for belief, as Robert Wilkinson testified, who felt there was no hope of mercy for him. His leader's response that his attendance to the means of grace meant his hope was not unfounded gave him encouragement.[149]

The public confession of an individual's spiritual state could adversely affect another class member, with potentially fatal results. John Oliver recounted how another's testimony caused him to become suicidal. He had experienced assurance, but the open testimony of one who felt wicked caused him to reflect on his state and he threw himself into a river and almost drowned.[150] This uncertainty extended to class leaders. John Mason felt leadership of a class was a great trial, but the experience itself confirmed his own faith as he encouraged others. "While I prayed for my brethren, and laboured to help them forward in the way to the kingdom, he gave me great consolation in my own soul."[151]

The class was not the meeting for those who were explicitly pressing toward perfection, although Lackington[152] noted that those in a state of perfection continued to meet in class. Perfection was not easily achieved or maintained, and as early as 1744, Wesley was cautioning his preachers in regard to the acceptance of a believer's claim to this spiritual state.[153] When this book considers reasons for the decline of the class as the central constituent of Wesleyan ecclesiology, the decline of the band with its central tenet of perfection will also be briefly noted.

---

147. Ryan, "Account of the life of Sarah Ryan," 302.
148. Rhodes, "An Account of Benjamin Rhodes," 364.
149. Wilkinson, "A Short Account of Mr. Robert Wilkinson," 181.
150. Oliver, "An Account of Mr. John Oliver," 420.
151. Mason, 'Short Account of the life of Mr. John Mason,' 653.
152. Lackington, *Memoirs*, 63–64.
153. Myles, *A Chronological History of the People Called Methodist of the Connexion of the Late John Wesley from their rise on 1729 to their Last Conference in 1802*, 28–29. This is the question and answer on the subject of sanctification from the Conference of 1744.

Before leaving this section, some account of the place of hymnody in Methodism must be given. From the outset, hymns played an important part in the spiritual devotion of every Methodist. Charles Wesley's hymns were used in every small group meeting, at the preaching service, and society meeting, as well as field preaching. Thomas Langford asserted that "hymns were to eighteenth century England what stained glass windows were to medieval Europe—a medium for teaching."[154]

Through hymnody, Methodists learned their theology as they sang publicly and meditated on their hymn books privately. This gave rise to the Wesleyan tradition, a warm-hearted Arminianism, which encompassed both social and personal piety and the rigors of regular meetings and the observance of the means of grace. The usefulness of the group was enhanced by hymns which identified a common experience of awakening, conversion, and discipleship. Tore Meistad recognized the purpose of hymns. "Charles Wesley's hymns popularised Methodist ideas and probably spread them more widely than the preaching did."[155]

John Wesley recognized the value of hymnody in the preface to the 1780 collection of hymns, as a means of increasing devotion, confirming faith, and enabling a deeper love for God and neighbor.[156]

Joseph Nightingale's *Portraiture of Methodism* indicates there were hymns, which were of importance to the class, reproducing five specimen hymns.[157] They are revealing: praying for repentance; a mourner convinced of sin; a mourner brought to the birth; rejoicing; a believer groaning for full redemption. The hymn for rejoicing overflows with superlatives and offered to the assembled class hope and potentially assurance. Any within the class might experience these sentiments in an instant and declare them to his or her peers:

> True pleasures abound in the rapturous sound;
> And whoever hath found it hath paradise found:
> My Jesus to know, and feel his blood flow,
> 'Tis life everlasting, 'tis heaven below![158]

154. Langford, "Charles Wesley as Theologian," 98.

155. Meistad, "The Missiology of Charles Wesley and its Links to the Eastern Church," 205.

156. Wesley, *Works [BE]*, Vol. 7, 75.

157. Nightingale, *A Portraiture of Methodism being an Impartial View of the Rise, Progress, Doctrines, Discipline and Manners of the Wesleyan Methodists in a Series of Letter Addressed to a Lady*, 185–88.

158. Ibid., 187. This hymn is also contained in Wesley, *Works [BE]*, Vol. 7, 328. This

The word "feel" is used to mean "experienced." What is "felt" (experienced) through faith is explained in the following line: eternal life in heaven, and the practice of heaven now.

The use of Wesleyan hymns changed over time. The hymn "Come wisdom, power and grace divine!" is a useful example of this. In 1814 it was allocated to a section for use in band, class or society meetings. However, it first appeared in 1767 in "Family Hymns," and in 1780 appeared in the section "For the Society, Praying." Over time, its place and purpose were reassigned as its use was more specifically identified.

Financial accountability

The class functioned as a body of people accountable to each other both spiritually and financially. The spiritual element of this accountability has been noted under fellowship, and will be further discussed in relation to discipline.

Financially, the class began as a means of paying a building debt, and there can be little doubt that had the class remained only a means of paying building debts,[159] it would not have survived at all. Further class leaders would have to have been drawn from a relatively wealthy section of the movement. If Captain Foy's suggestion had been followed strictly, leadership would have been limited to those who were able to make up any weekly financial shortfall.

Class monies continued to be paid by members after the class had become distinctly pastoral, and this financial accountability between members gave the class the means through each society to support the poor[160] and discharge building debts. Wesley noted in his *Journal* for October 15th 1743 that the monies collected to that date had paid the New Room debt.[161] This fund later supported the work of the itinerant preachers and other expenses.[162] Lackington offers an insight into the financial life of the class:

---

hymn is number 197 and entered in the section 'For Believers Rejoicing.'

159. Until the Conference of 1779, some Class monies were used towards the cost of building new preaching houses. See Myles, *A Chronological History*, 138.

160. See Appendix 10: Rule 3(1).

161. Wesley, *Works [BE]*, Vol. 19, 343.

162. See Crowther, *A True and Complete Portraiture of Methodism*, 256.

> In these classes each made a weekly contribution towards the general support of the preachers &c. Such as were very poor contributed a penny a week, others two-pence, and some who could afford it sixpence. This money was entered in a book kept for that purpose, and one in every class called the Steward, had the care of the cash.[163]

He also gives some vital detail about the social structure of each class. Each class consisted of a disparate group of people, who in the social order of the period would have the minimum of dealings with each other. In the class, social divisions were set aside and equality in faith was raised up. The fact that some could afford more than others meant that a mutual accountability in matters of finance was shared across the individual class and indeed all classes so that no intolerable burden fell upon the poorest members.

Discipline

William Dean's 1985 thesis[164] held discipline to be the primary function of the class meeting. Dean asserted that this function had a higher priority than fellowship, and was a character of life modeled by Wesley himself:

> Discipline was a hallmark of Methodism. Eighteenth-century Methodists were expected to live carefully, frugally, and in accordance with strict rules of conduct. The source of these expectations was John Wesley himself, who assumed that the rigorous discipline which marked his own lifestyle should be copied by those around him.[165]

Dean understood discipline to be a means of cohesion as well as control; that group experience gave rise to a sense of belonging as well as a particular pattern of behavior. More will be written about the nature of group experience below in relation to the success of the class.

For Dean, fellowship was a by-product of discipline, for only discipline enabled the conditions to create a sense of fellowship. This demeans the class meeting's purpose as the crown of the Methodist movement; for if fellowship, conversion, commitment, and accountability arise only

---

163. Lackington, *Memoirs*, 63.

164. Dean, "Disciplined Fellowship: The Rise and Decline of Cell Groups in British Methodism."

165. Ibid., 51.

from a disciplined group then the purpose of the group itself was merely as a form of policing.

Dean is right to maintain that discipline was an important element of class membership, but wrong in his singular application. Wesley realized that to meet together in a regular pattern broke old habits, and cultivated a new outlook on living that was shared by the whole local Methodist body. Discipline was also important to maintain a specifically Methodist identity. Perhaps, too, aware of the problems the doctrine of stillness had caused in Fetter Lane, Wesley was keen to ensure that only his doctrines were espoused in any meeting. However, as an itinerant leader, there were moments when his disciplinary leadership was exercised after damage had been caused, as was the case in Wednesbury. "Wed. 3 I made an end of visiting the classes, miserably shattered by the sowers of strange doctrines."[166]

Dean understands "discipline" predominantly in the form of a rule for corporate shared living, stemming from Wesley's own disciplined lifestyle. Discipline in this form was by no means unique to Methodism. The earliest Anglican Unitary societies were disciplined units which met together under a rule[167] of living intended to promote a model of holiness, and an allegiance to the Anglican Church. Fetter Lane also had stringent disciplinary processes.

Local class leaders acted on behalf of John Wesley once Methodism became too large for him to easily itinerate, and, when meeting together weekly, exercised a "collegiate episcopacy" over the entire society, as it was divided into classes. Class leaders were responsible for ensuring that discipline within the classes was adequately maintained, and this was done by reproof, encouragement, or dismissal. Reproof or encouragement always took place within the hearing of others. This ensured that the discipline of life could be regulated. It also ensured that good order, using discipline in its active sense could be maintained. An example of this is shown by John Bennet's *Diary*. In 1747,[168] Bennet reproved a male class leader and band member who was unmarried but living with a woman as husband and wife. He had infringed Methodist discipline as a rule for holy living, breaching the disciplinary code.

---

166. See Wesley, *Works [BE]*, Vol. 20, 382.
167. Examples of these rules can be found at Appendices 1 to 5.
168. Valentine, *Mirror of the Soul*, 133–34.

At leaders' meetings, or when Wesley or an itinerant preacher regulated the classes, expulsion was always a disciplinary option. In Norwich in 1759, despite the society numbering 500 people, 150 did not meet in class. These Wesley stated "hang on but a single thread."[169] Such a *Journal* entry was made after he had declared to the entire society the purpose of the class, that is, as part of the Wesleyan schema of holy living. To those who were wavering over society membership Wesley wrote an open letter in 1764, answering many common objections. He makes plain that to belong to a class is to enter into a disciplinary arrangement: that there is a discipline in meeting, and that discipline may be exercised within it.[170]

Discipline was exercised through regulation even if it meant the local society was severely depleted. In Newcastle in 1743,[171] Wesley noted that 64 members had been expelled because their lifestyle did not match that required by Wesley. Almost 40 years later, he wrote to John Valton,[172] expelling a class leader whose behavior was clearly not acceptable. Wesley allowed that 20 of his class might leave with him, but that such loss maintained the proper regulation of the whole. This use of discipline was intended to ensure classes remained lively places where Christian growth could be nurtured, and ensured the society as a whole was not brought into disrepute.

At the earliest point of the Methodist movement, any possible reason for the authorities to arrest preachers or disrupt meetings was seized upon, and the need for a disciplined and organized meeting became all the more vital. Later, disaffected Methodists caused problems for Methodism as John Pawson's letter to Matthew Mayer indicates. Mr.Requit, a former Bristol Methodist, was preaching at the Foundery and abusing the Bristol Society "by telling the whole (Foundery) congregation that he knew there were whores and Baudes, even in the Bands."[173] Pawson was clear; more discipline amongst them might prevent others from having such accounts to pass on. Discipline was a tool for personnel regulation, and was useful to ensure the smooth running of Methodism, especially after its expansion across England. It was not,

169. See Wesley, *Works [BE]*, Vol. 21, 226.
170. Ibid., 478–79.
171. Wesley, *Works [BE]*, Vol. 19, 318.
172. Wesley, *Journal [SE]*, Vol. VII, 100–101.
173. Bowmer and Vickers, *The Letters of John Pawson: volume 1*, 15. Baudes is an obsolete form of "bawd." Word in brackets mine.

however, in my view, the tool that Dean suggests, overarching all other aspects of organization life.

THE CLASS MEETING REVIEWED

The regulated and holy life that Wesley envisaged through the class system reflected his personal theology detailed in previous chapters. I will now examine how this theology was expressed through the class, using the four areas of class life mentioned above, and then consider the nature of the group experience. Through this, I will contend that the class meeting is the crown of Methodism's organization.

I have already mentioned that John Wesley synthesized disparate Christian doctrine and theology. Ted Campbell has skillfully shown how the seventeenth-century desire for an affective faith spread through Protestant, Catholic, and Orthodox traditions, and I argue that its most affective form was through the warm-hearted Pietsm of the class meeting.

Wesley's rather unusual hybrid of doctrine flourished, as he was able to encourage his people to accept Non-Juring teachings, just as easily as he could command their allegiance to the Church of England. Thus he was able to encourage a lifestyle for the classes that broadly reflected his own. As Wesley held a high regard for the means of grace, so too did his people, and as often as the sacrament was celebrated at the parish church, Methodists were to receive it, and when the Sunday service was morning prayer, they were to attend the parish service. Charles Wesley, meeting three classes in Manchester in 1756, had to persuade the members to attend the parish services, and receive the sacrament. They had ceased as the preachers were not recommending attendance, and were not attending themselves. All but the Dissenters among the classes agreed to go.[174]

The class had four distinctive aspects, and these were affective in the lives of the Methodists. To share fellowship was to continue something of the Holy Club and the bands of Fetter Lane; to experience conversion and continue discipleship was a distinctly Moravian practice, but Wesley ensured this was channelled through a regulated group, similar to that of the Unitary societies. To be accountable to one another, personally and financially, maintained the tradition of the Unitary societies in their

---

174. Wesley, *Journal*, Vol. II, 134.

regular collections and also picked up something of work of the Halle Pietists who engaged in social action.

Most importantly for Wesley, the meeting of individuals in class was an opportunity to continue together the path to entire sanctification and the journey of a holy life. Here there are overtones of Bishop Jeremy Taylor's works, *Holy Living* and *Holy Dying*, which set out for the earnest Christian a pattern for living well and ultimately dying a good death. The difference in Wesley's life, and the Methodist experience was that such a life was experienced corporately, not individually as Taylor expected. There are also nuances of an earlier Puritanism which urged the Christian toward holiness, centered in a personal relationship with God.

A "background" Puritanism can be sensed through the Wesleyan reliance on using time wisely, part of which was shown through the class and other Methodist meetings, and through living a careful, even frugal, life in society. The detailed instructions of the 1743 rules[175] show how important the use of time was. While these rules are laid out for the societies, each class member was expected to adhere to them, and failure to do so could result in expulsion, as occurred in Newcastle in the same year. Abraham Jones wrote to Wesley in 1742, shortly after the classes were introduced, and noted that his role as a class leader was to ensure they all "walk orderly, and keep close to the Word, and the means of grace."[176] Charles Wesley also noted that personal life was to include good works.[177]

Another mark of Methodism, which made the class a crowning point of Methodism, was Wesley's Arminianism. This set Wesley apart from the majority of his evangelical contemporaries in England, and gave him an unrivaled platform from which to begin his ministry. Through field preaching, Wesley was able to declare the nature of the gospel as he interpreted it. Those hearers who filtered from the open air to the public preaching services, and from there to the society meeting and class meeting, would become immersed in a teaching which offered, through God's prevenient grace, the opportunity to become Christians, not by works, nor by election, but through faith alone.

In the class the first stirrings of faith, which were often dramatic and accompanied by emotional or ecstatic experiences could be nur-

---

175. Appendix 10: Rules 5, 6 &7.
176. Wesley, *Works [BE]*, Vol. 26, 94–95.
177. Ibid., 96.

tured, secure in the Wesleyan understanding that any who professed faith through justification had received faith. In the class, faith was not uncertain and reliant upon election but open to all. This Arminianism led to the continuing path of holy living toward perfection. In this Wesley was picking up the tolerant Puritan piety of Richard Baxter, and the teaching of his parental High Church background.

Arminianism meant a Methodist could feel the assurance of salvation, free from the uncertainty of Calvinism's election only for the few. Such a doctrine appealed to those classes of society otherwise excluded from society. What was denied in life—acceptance—was available in the society and made perfect in death.

The class was the central feature of the Wesleyan movement, and remained so when the movement became a distinct organization, with a carefully structured ecclesiology of its own after 1749. Wesley declared that Methodism was a rediscovery of primitive religion, a religion he had traveled to Georgia to find. In the class the primitive nature of that religion was most clearly expressed as small groups met to learn, grow, and develop a Christian faith that could be lived effectively in society.

The class meeting created a distinct identity amongst the Methodist people ensuring the class was the crown of Methodism. This book will now consider some of the issues surrounding small group purpose and identity.

THE CLASS MEETING: SOCIAL IDENTITY AND GROUP PROCESSES

Social psychologists have developed social identity and group process theories, and these can inform our understanding of the eighteenth-century class meeting, and elucidate reasons for its success as a group. Simply put, groups are fundamental to human identity as people, consisting of "people in *face-to-face interaction* with one another."[178] Groups are essentially public entities and belonging means that a person's social identity becomes bound up with that group in the understanding of others. An individual will join a group having reconnoitered it prior to making a commitment to it. Questions asked of the new group include the benefits group membership will offer, and commitment level demanded

---

178. Brown, *Group Processes*, 3.

by the group. Through this process a redefinition of the personal identity occurs, and an initiation takes place.

A common dependence is formed between members and any common goals are shared interdependently. Tensions that arise in the achievement of those goals must be addressed and released, and emotions fully dealt with. Group norms are created; values that are held corporately and developed. These norms give the individual and the group a particular way to view and respond to the world. Such normative values offer a frame of reference for acceptable behavior and set apart those who *do not belong.*

Understandably, individuals compare themselves socially, and through that process evaluate how good they are as individuals, and who they are in the group. This takes place by assessing peers within the group. As Brown states, "the achievements of others who are similar to us in ability act as a guide to our own likely achievements."[179]

Within every group certain distinctive features can be seen: language, ethics, dress, for example. These features offer a social categorization, as well as a social identity. Some distinctive features may be described by those outside the group, a process known as "priming." This leads to homogeneity within the group through the sharing of common ideals and values.

Social identity is that which gives an individual an identity amongst others through the groups to which he or she belongs. There are three characteristics of this: cognitive, evaluative, and emotional or affective.[180] A means of assessing self-worth is to compare the group(s) to which an individual may belong with other groups. To feel that "my" group is superior to another adds to self-esteem. If, however, "my" group is inferior to another, an attempt may be made to become upwardly mobile, and to join the "better group."

The eighteenth century was a period of association. Clubs and organizations were formed that gave rise to modern political parties, drinking clubs, societies for the reformation of public morals, and religious groups added to the diversity of an associational age. In each of these clubs and groups social identities and categorizations were created.

---

179. Ibid., 79.

180. The use of 'affective' comes from Hogg, and Terry, *Social Identity Processes in Organizational Contexts*, 104.

The Methodist class was a relative latecomer to this associational age, but was born out of Wesley's previous personal experience with the Holy Club, Unitary societies, and Fetter Lane. Throughout his adult life, Wesley constantly fought to be recognized as an Anglican and a clergyman against those who argued he had abandoned the Church of England. For him, his social identity and social category was that of an Anglican. He fought with equal strength to ensure that his own Methodists were understood to be Anglicans too, despite the fact that they would also identify quite distinctly as Methodists.

He achieved the former by insisting that those who belonged to his societies regularly attended the parish church, and were communicant members of it. He would not allow Dissenters to belong fully to a society unless they were baptized according to the rubric of the Church of England.[181] The latter was achieved by the distinctive groups of Methodism to which every Methodist belonged, the society and the class.

For those who came to join the class, the realignment of the individual in relation to society was not as great as it would be in the twenty-first century. Individuals did not have a developed sense of personal social identity, so the group would have an added importance for those persons in their own eyes, and the eyes of those outside the class. Joining the class was a vital period of assessment as to whether what was offered was worthwhile. The "on trial" period of Methodism which demanded some personal change was the point at which evaluation of the class occurred, and those who found the class too demanding did not join. In the same vein, the leaders of the society also had the ability to refuse to admit the individual who had not accepted the discipline and rigor of the class.

John Wesley's *Journal* entry for 12th March 1743 gives a clear early picture of the cost of membership. The evaluative process led one individual to leave because those who were not Methodists were rude in the street, nine people to leave because they were laughed at and a further five because uncomplimentary remarks were made of the society.[182]

---

181. See the correspondence between Sarah Perrin and Charles Wesley in *Letters Chiefly to Wesley's*, Volume II. See also Wesley, *Works [BE]*, Vol. 19, 318. Here Dissenters had left the society as their own ministers refused them communion. The corollary to this is that Wesley would not allow them to fully participate while they remained Dissenters.

182. Wesley, *Works [BE]*, Vol. 19, 318.

For those who became and remained Methodists, the admission to membership and receipt of a class ticket was the recognition of membership of a group which offered a distinct identity. Every potential class member had to be aware of what was demanded, evaluate whether that was worthwhile, and emotionally or affectively attach to the group. This cohesion gave to the class a shared purpose and shared values.

Each justified class member was in community on the path toward entire sanctification; each person could be made perfect. This gave a distinct social categorization, and along with behavior, dress, and language made the class unlike any other religious group. The printed rules show just how a Methodist was to dress and behave, socially and in business. The distinct language of Methodism can be seen in testimony and biography associated with the language of Charles Wesley's hymns, and Wesleyan Pietstic phraseology usually used to describe the pre- and post-conversion state. One woman described herself as a "publican."[183] Another, after receiving faith testified, "I was a brand plucked from the fire."[184]

The distinctive features of being a Methodist—fellowship, conversion and discipleship, financial accountability and discipline—offered to the Methodist in the class a structure for social identity and a social category that marked him or her out within any community. These features were also lived outside the group's regular meetings, making the Methodist recognizable in the street, in business or in the social context. This stands in contrast to the Anglican Unitary societies which, while giving to young single men a form of piety, did not have such a strong or distinctive ethos about their regulations. The primary aim of the Unitary societies was retention of young men within the Anglican Church. The primary aim of class membership was growth in grace and holiness.

Membership of a class was not segregated by sex or status as the Moravian style bands of Fetter Lane were, or the Unitary societies, which were open only to young men. This gave to the class a unique dimension in that the business and purpose of each meeting was shared with people with whom an individual might not usually frequent, owing to social status or sex. For the women especially this gave a social categorization that was inclusive, and also admitted them to class leadership, even over men. Only the Methodist bands retained the earlier segregation.

183. Letter: Sarah Barber to Charles Wesley. May 1740. *Early Methodist Volume*.

184. Letter: Margaret Austen to Charles Wesley. 19th May 1740. *Early Methodist Volume*.

After Methodism's model, Anglican clergymen attempted a similar organizational structure for their parishioners, particularly Henry Venn, vicar of Huddersfield, who was sympathetic to Wesley's aims, and Samuel Walker who began a religious society with bands in Truro with the aim of outwitting the Methodists. Both Venn and Walker intended their small groups to remain under the clear authority of the parish Minister. Methodists had no parish affinity, despite Wesley's insistence on regular attendance at the parish church. This allowed Methodists, one step removed from Anglican parochial authority, to compare their group, the class with their nearest rival, the parish, and consider their self-esteem in the light of that comparison. Over time a sense of self-esteem that gave rise to self-worth was created. I will discuss this more fully in following chapters.

Overall then, the use of social identity and social categorization theories have assisted in understanding the process of joining and belonging to the class. These theories explain the manner in which disparate individuals became united with a common purpose, sharing attributes and goals and beliefs that tended in varying degrees to mark them out with a distinctive identity. W. Ferguson's experience led him to note, in his *Account* in the *Arminian Magazine* of 1782, that Methodists were markedly different in their demeanor: "I saw an abundance of people going along who seemed remarkably serious. I asked a man, 'Pray, who are all these?' He answered, 'these are all Wesleyites; they are coming from the preaching.' This was the first time I saw or heard of them."[185] Ferguson's *Account* also indicates they used distinctinctive terms of address, "the sailors that came into our shop, did not curse or swear at all. But several of them took my Master by the hand, and said, 'How do you do, Brother?' I asked, 'Pray, Sir, are all these your Brothers?' He said, 'We are all brethren in Christ.'"[186] John Valton,[187] who returned to a former society in Purfleet[188] in 1775, met with an officer who remarked that his dress had altered since his initial time in the Purfleet area. The officer, noting Valton's plain black attire remarked. "What, is

---

185. Ferguson, "Account of the Life of Mr. W. Ferguson," 298.

186. Ibid., 298.

187. See Myles, *A Chronological Account*, 305. Valton began his itinerancy in 1775. He is numbered by Myles amongst "the Second Race of Methodist Preachers."

188. Valton, "The Life of Mr. John Valton," 10–12. Valton, a clerk in the Office of Ordinance, was in Purfleet from December 1763 onwards.

this the little gentleman that came to us in a cocked hat, and gold-laced waistcoat?"[189] Valton's changed style of dress signaled the difference that accepting Christ and subsequently joining the Methodist itinerancy had made in his life. In response to the officer, Valton stated, "It is, sir . . . But the Lord, since that time, has done something under the waistcoat."[190] Valton's change of dress style reflected the rules of the Methodists,[191] and indicated his choice to identify himself as a Methodist.[192] In early 1764, Valton had written to Wesley an anonymous letter concerning his state of mind. Wesley replied to this, but also dispatched a Methodist, who was a carpenter, to find him. Valton's reaction to the Methodist was to shame him, but he also noted that accepting the carpenter's message would mean that he would "apply his chisel and mallet to cut off my ruffles, and hair that was tied back."[193]

The class gave identity, purpose, and meaning within the context of a close Christian fellowship, and enabled Wesley's affective Pietsm to become deeply rooted in the Methodist psyche. When a new member was received on trial into the class, a process began toward entire sanctification. This process could only fully be possible if it was shared with like-minded Christians.

CHAPTER SUMMARY

The class was the crown of Methodism, as it was only in the small, regulated, and sometimes highly charged group that the Methodist identity was really forged. The class meeting was the zenith of eighteenth-century piety, unlike anything that preceded it.

Unlike the mystics, whose quest for piety would often lead to an annihilation of the will, the class enabled the will to be subjected to God,

---

189. Ibid., 96.

190. Ibid.

191. See Appendices 10 and 11. See also Wesley, *Minutes of the Methodist Conferences, from the First, Held in London by the Late Rev. John Wesley A.M. in the Year 1744, Volume I*, 12.

192. See also Olivers, "The Life of Mr. Thomas Olivers," 53–54. Although aquainted with Methodism, while in Bridgenorth with a companion, he lodged with a woman who was a Methodist. This was "soon discovered by her conversation" p. 53. Olivers *Life* first appeared in the *Arminian Magazine* for 1779. See Olivers, "The Life of Mr. Thomas Olivers," 77–89.

193. Valton, *The Christian Experience of the Late Rev. John Valton*, volume 1, 28. (Undated entry.) MA 1977/293.

yet turned toward works of mercy in community: unlike the Puritans who used the diary as a means of personal confessional, the class engendered a shared confessional, and made the class leader a spiritual director: unlike the Unitary societies that offered advancement in trade as much as a tie to the Anglican Church, the class offered the opportunity to quest for a Christian life, regardless of age, sex, or marital status: unlike the Moravians, who were concerned with stillness and refused to engage in works of mercy, the class actively encouraged each member to participate fully in the means of grace, alone and corporately, and to be actively concerned with the well-being of neighbors.

The class was the Methodist incarnation of Wesley's spirituality, Wesley's quest to find faith and then systematize that into a personal piety woven through many traditions, from which he took those elements that appealed to him, or which offered him some means of reviewing and disciplining his life. The class is representational of a personal piety, yet expressed within a group. Wesley could never have hoped to impose the model of faith he had created for himself on individual men and women, but he was able to do so with a carefully regulated group, that was subject to inspection and discipline.

Methodism was a reflection of Wesley's own journey to, and discipleship in, faith. Ted Campbell describes this as "an epistemology of religious experience."[194] Everything that John and Charles Wesley considered relevant, they passed on to the body of people known as Methodists, who met in classes. Wesley expressed this epistemology in *An Earnest Appeal to Men of Reason and Religion*[195] of 1743. Through the *Appeal*, Wesley sets out the way of awakening, justification, and sanctification in the Methodist pattern. As Heitzenrater notes for Wesley, "Methodism moves beyond a lifeless, formal religion to one worthy of God, and that is love–love of God and love of neighbour, seated in the heart and showing its fruits in virtue and happiness."[196]

Part Two has discussed in an original manner why the class became vital to the success of the early Methodists, and why the earliest Methodist people found their spiritual needs met within a small interrogatory group that placed responsibility on each class member for their own, and their peers' spiritual development.

---

194. Campbell, *The Religion of the Heart*, 121.
195. Wesley, *Works [BE]*, Vol. 11, 45–94.
196. Heitzenrater, *Wesley and the People Called Methodists*, 130.

I now turn in the following chapters to the reasons for the decline of the class meeting. I will argue that decline began before Wesley's death, and indeed the class contained the seeds of decline from the outset. The class meeting, in every way the crown of Methodism, was unable to survive over time as the religious experience and system of faith on which it thrived passed from Methodism's way of being (despite the retention of distinctive language). The group-experience model which the class relied upon was unsustainable. The homogenous group, who chose to be different from the rest of society, eventually came to be respected within society and group purpose radically changed.

Part Three

Introductory Comments

THE FOLLOWING THREE CHAPTERS examine reasons for the decline of the class meeting, moving the book to consider the class as a "cross." The crowning aspects of the class have been fully discussed above, and I have described how Wesley's spirituality was literally lived in the class meeting in the earliest years of Methodism. All that Wesley took into his system of belief—assurance; good works; perfection; godliness; holiness; the means of grace; primitive Christianity; the need for regular supportive meetings—was found in the class meeting.

As a crown, the relationship between faith and life was a dynamic that was attractive and made a difference to a social class of men and women previously excluded from the activity of Christian life. Within the class, people found and exercised leadership, and for men, leadership could increase to local preacher, helper, or assistant. Some women preached, and some notable women, such as Grace Murray, Sarah Perrin, Mary Bosanquet, and Sarah Mallet[1] were clearly in leadership roles.

The class meeting also offered a sense of shared purpose within a disciplined, accountable, discipling context. At its best the class offered a new way of being in relationship with others. Neither Methodism, nor the class itself, was a solitary existence, and that relationship gave to those who belonged a way of relating to others in a faith context, and the opportunity to behave differently within society. As a model for the amendment of life, Methodism was unsurpassed.

With those superlatives, it is easy to avoid the reasons for the decline of the class. Indeed, as some authors, like Henderson,[2] and Matthaei[3] maintain, the class can become a means for discipling new genera-

---

1. Grace Murray and Sarah Perrin were Housekeepers for Wesley's early properties. Murray at the Orphan House, Perrin at Kingswood. Mary Bosanquet (Fletcher) was active in Madeley. Sarah Mallet was a preacher in the Norfolk area, with Wesley's knowledge. See East, *My Dear Sally: The Life of Sarah Mallet One of John Wesley's Preachers*.

2. Henderson, *John Wesley's Class Meeting*.

3. Matthaei, *Making Disciples Faith Formation in the Wesleyan Tradition*.

tions, or at least be an element of a new "Wesleyan Economy of Faith Formation."[4] These authors assume that the class meeting can be as effective today as an element of faith formation as it was in the eighteenth century. However, none of these assumptions consider why the class meeting is not now the bedrock or center of the Methodist system.

Others, notably Watson and Hardt, who discuss the class meeting, (Watson concentrating on the classes in England, and Hardt on New York classes), spend little time discussing the decline of the class. Watson views the transformation of Methodism from Society to Church as a symptom of this decline.[5] He also saw formalism and a loss of accountability as significant aspects of the class's decline.[6] Hardt's introduction to his study of early New York Methodism concludes briefly that early British Methodism's classes declined because:

> In the early nineteenth century, after the Methodist "societies" had become the Wesleyan Methodist Church, declining class attendance, the higher expectations placed upon the role of the class leader, and the growing tensions between class leaders and traveling preachers all combined to weaken its earlier dynamism.[7]

Although the Wesleyan Methodists did not style themselves as a church until the later nineteenth century, his single sentence does not address the reasons for class decline. Snyder, in his discussion of patterns of church renewal, addresses class decline. "Well before 1900 the class system had lost its vitality, however, in most of Methodism. Where it survived, the classes often became legalistic or moralistic; the life had long since departed."[8] Again, this does not address the reasons for the decline. If the class became legalistic or moralistic, why had this happened? If the life had departed what factors caused this?

Laceye Warner spends one paragraph on the decline of the class, primarily from a North American perspective. His comment however is perceptive and I pick up something of his statement in chapter 8. Warner writes: "During the nineteenth century, class meetings in British

---

4. Ibid., 166–83.
5. Watson, *The Early Methodist Class Meeting*, 136–37.
6. Ibid., 145–47.
7. Hardt, *The Soul of Methodism*, 23–24.
8. Snyder, *The Radical Wesley and Patterns for Church Renewal*, 62.

and North American Methodism steadily declined as a result of several cultural and ecclesiological dynamics."[9]

William Dean's thesis concluded that the class declined because there was a change in its fundamental tasks. This is picked up by Watson in his consideration of the class's decline. The difference between Wesley's understanding of the class meeting and its reality must be distinguished. During Wesley's lifetime the class's purpose was "recruitment and assimilation of new members."[10] Beyond that, these functions changed as society changed. Again, I pick this theme up in chapter 7 and assert that the changes which Dean ascribes to the nineteenth century occurred during Wesley's lifetime.

A useful argument from Dean's thesis, relating to the loss of the bands and classes, assists the purpose of this final section, and the importance of assessing why the class meeting ceased to be an effective element of Methodist ecclesiology:

> The bands were based on the interaction of disciplined Christians, and had no rationale for existence apart from the quality of the relationships created. As religious fervour cooled and the vision of perfection dimmed and became less urgent, the bands disintegrated. In the class system, where the rationale was disciplinary, the distinction between the "Methodist" and the "world" was a shared value, and the class meeting when faced with declining fervour, simply became an institutionalized ritual which continued to function until the disciplinary rationale faded.[11]

I disagree with Dean's assertion that discipline as a functionary element of the class was as all-pervading as he holds it to be, but he picks up a very important factor in the distinction the class engendered between being a Methodist and being in the world. This process, known as homogenization, is discussed in chapter 8, and assists in understanding the theme of that chapter which is outlined below.

In articles published in the *Proceedings*, Rack and Dean discuss class decline in the nineteenth century. Rack assesses decline around the period when class meeting membership was removed as the basis of

---

9. Warner, "Offer Them Christ: Characteristics of Wesleyan Paradigm for Evangelism," 171.

10. Watson, *The Early Methodist Class Meeting*, 137.

11. Dean, "Disciplined Fellowship," 180.

Methodist society membership.[12] Dean's article discusses class decline in the first half of the nineteenth century.[13]

For Rack, the major problems for the class in the second half of the nineteenth century were "the unpopularity of the class as an institution; and the problem of the relationship between class-membership and membership of the church."[14] Dean remarked that the classes became "silent" from the 1830s onwards. "A startling and general feature shared by many of these (Methodist autobiographies) accounts is that during the 1830s references to class meetings seem to decline almost to zero."[15] He suggested that decline occurred because "the web of circumstances that gave the class meeting functional significance in the eighteenth century eroded, leaving an institutional shell without a clearly manifest purpose, except that attendance was the door to membership."[16]

Through the following section, I will argue that the decline of which Rack and Dean write began during Wesley's lifetime. After Wesley's death, this was discussed openly, and pamphlets and articles were published urging Methodists to continue meeting for the edification and growth of Methodism. In 1797, the anonymous publication *An Address to the Heads of Families on the Necessity of Family Religion*[17] contained the appendix *An interesting Discourse on Weekly Class Meetings*.[18] This appendix quoted Perronet's *Right Method*,[19] and exhorted the reader to rediscover the duty imposed on all Methodists to meet. The author stated:

> where the people are wanting in *piety, simplicity,* and *freedom,* the true end of these special means is wholly subverted, and the devotion rendered both tedious and unprofitable.[20]

---

12. Rack, "The Decline of the Class-Meeting and the Problem of Church-Membership in Nineteenth-Century Wesleyanism," 12–21.

13. Dean, "The Methodist Class Meeting. The Significance of its Decline," 41–48.

14. Rack, "The Decline of the Class-Meeting and the Problem of Church-Membership in Nineteenth-Century Wesleyanism," 12–13.

15. Dean, "The Methodist Class Meeting. The Significance of its Decline," 42. Words in brackets mine.

16. Ibid., 43.

17. Anonymous, *An Address to the Heads of Families on the Necessity of Family Religion. Also, an Interesting Discourse on Weekly Class Meetings.*

18. Anon, *An Address to the Heads of Families*, 13–16.

19. Appendix 13.

20. Anon, *An Address to the Heads of Families*, 13–14.

The pamphlet is primarily directed toward leaders, whom the author cited should be "properly qualified,"[21] but who appeared to be unable to work according to Perronet's *Method*. The writer noted, "this is a *duty* to which I am afraid not more than one half of our leaders are equal."[22] The remedy to this was to read edifying books, especially Scripture. The need for leaders, who might be described as qualified, was a radical shift from Wesley's original appointment of people whom he believed suitable, if not educated or qualified, to be leaders.

Of the class member, the author required that they should be "open, lively, and affectionate."[23] In the opinion of the writer, such a demeanor would resolve the problems that were serious enough to warrant publication of the pamphlet. The concluding paragraph is written in terms that indicate the benefits of the right conduct that would rebuild the individuals' state with God, and enliven the class to which those persons belonged. "Those who live, or endeavour to live in this happy state, have always something to speak in their class which is animating and instructive, and the people hang on their lips for edification and comfort."[24]

This addendum to *An Address to the Heads of Families* was published six years after Wesley's death, and is an indication that the class was not functioning well. As Wesley had maintained a tight rein on all publications during his lifetime,[25] this may be the first private pamphlet offering a view of the class which would have otherwise been prevented from publication while Wesley lived owing to its contents.

Thomas Jackson, whose *Recollections* were published in 1873,[26] wrote in relation to articles encouraging attendance at class meetings that:

> Pamphlets and tracts may be written and circulated without end in favour of these weekly meetings . . . but if the people have no

21. Ibid., 13.
22. Ibid., 15.
23. Ibid., Ibid., 16.
24. Ibid.
25. Wesley, *Minutes of Several Conversations between the Reverend Mr John and Charles Wesley and Others from the Year 1744, to the Year 1780*, 26. 'Q. 39, Ought we to insist upon our Rule, that no Preacher print any Thing without your approbation? A. Undoubtedly. And whoever does it for the time to come, cannot take it ill, if he is excluded from our connection. Let every one take this warning, and afterwards blame not but himself.' See also Myles, *A Chronological History*, 279–82.
26. Jackson, *Recollections of My Own Life and Times*.

religious experience to communicate, they will be urged in vain to meet together for any such purpose. If they feel no sorrowful conviction of sin, they will never seek the sympathy and prayers of those who have passed through the same painful process to the joys of pardon.[27]

The anonymous author of the appendix to *An Address to the Heads of Families* appeared to pre-empt Jackson by almost 80 years in his appeal to leaders and class members to lead and attend their class with the spirit that Wesley envisaged in his *General Rules*.

In the following chapters, considering the decline of the class from its place as the crown of the Methodist schema, the picture of decline must not be understood to be a "blanket decline." While the three approaches I outline below are models of understanding the decline that began during Wesley's lifetime, it must be recognized that other classes continued to be formed and functioned well. John Goodfellow's own experience of class membership in 1784 led him to write warmly of it in his diary.[28] However, within three years his experience in his own class and that of a fellow class leader was dissension.[29] In the discussion of the class as a one generational model, I shall draw on John Kent's use of primary and secondary periods of Methodism.[30] In the primary period, Methodist life was experiential and immediate. In the secondary period, stated by Kent to begin in the 1760s, Methodist life became more routine, and less experiential. I will show that in part this change occurred because Methodism became more accepted within English religious life. Although writing in the middle years of the 1780s, through his conversion narrative, Goodfellow clearly had a primary experience of Methodism. However, those whom he led in classes had a secondary understanding of Methodist life, in which the close unity and fundamentally experiential nature of the class had declined.

Dean noted in his article that in 1791, the year of Wesley's death, Mary Lomas felt herself under the burden of sin, and "found her way to a Methodist class meeting, having a desire to 'flee from the wrath to come.'"[31] Thomas Jackson's *Recollections* contain a description of Methodism's

27. Ibid., 496.
28. Goodfellow, *The Diary of John Goodfellow*, after April 1784. MA 1977/236.
29. Ibid., entries for the 2nd August 1786 and 25th April 1787.
30. Kent, *Wesley and the Wesleyans*.
31. Dean, "The Methodist Class Meeting. The Significance of its Decline," 44.

arrival in his home village of Sancton, East Yorkshire. Until the Reverend George Holder was invited to preach in a cottage in the village in 1786, there was no Methodist cause locally. As a result of his preaching a "Class was formed, of which she (Jackson's mother) became one of the earliest members; and was soon made happy in the enjoyment of God's pardoning mercy and renewing grace, as was her sister, Elizabeth."[32]

Through the following chapters, evidence will be drawn from Wesley's letters, journal, publications through tracts and pamphlets, letters to friends and leaders, and an open letter of the need to maintain, improve, and regulate the classes appropriately. In each of these situations Wesley was addressing a situation before him at that point. This book does not set out to prove that Wesley had a sense of the class failing or its basic functions ceasing to be effective for the leaders or membership.

The following three chapters address three distinct patterns that emerged within Wesley's lifetime and led to the decline of the class meeting. Using the writings of sociologists of religion, these indicate ways in which the exuberant and experiential class meeting ceased to be so. Each of the chapters takes a key theme associated with the writings of one particular sociologist. It is in this context that each aspect of decline is set. I am taking each idea, as a general theme, and discussing how the decline of Methodism fits within this theme.

Using Weber's, Durkheim's, and Troeltsch's theories from the school of the sociology of religion, I will indicate that Methodism could not escape Weber's routinization, Durkheim's totemism, or Troeltsch's mysticism/sect models. I use Troeltsch to show that the class meeting was a "one generational" model.

Where appropriate, parallels are drawn to assist the understanding of these themes. Chapter 6 opens with an example of an American evangelistic meeting which continues to use an approach from some 30 years before. I shall also use the layout of a small Methodist Church building in East Anglia to show how totemism led to the inclusion of a tiny "Class Room" which was wholly unsuited to the needs of a class in chapter 7. Within that same chapter, a contemporary example of totemism from North Korea will be described.

In chapter 8, Lester Ruth's descriptive account of the early American quarterly meeting's love feasts, offers a picture of the manner in which

32. Jackson, *Recollections*, 24. (Words in brackets mine.)

only one generation find the real depth of a meeting's purpose. In Troeltsch's mystic/sect descriptor, the transition from mysticism to sect means that those who attach themselves to an organization or group at a later stage than its inception do not do so for the same reasons as the first generation. This draws on the group processes described in chapter 5. John Kent offers Troeltsch's model (without specifically referring to it) as Primary and Secondary religion.[33] Most helpfully, he sets these models specifically within the context of Methodism.

With the growth of Methodism, classes became difficult to police. Wesley relied on his class leaders, society leaders and ultimately the assistants to act with his authority. These leaders did not possess Wesley's charisma, or gravity, and ultimately, Wesley became distanced from the people he led.

I have already stated that Wesley believed the class to be prudentially ordained.[34] I would also suggest he saw it as the expression of early church community, or primitive Christianity. Those means which are prudential may be used by Christians to assist the Christian journey as each individual saw fit. In the Methodist schema the class, although a prudential means, was by no means merely a meeting that was to be used as and when a person felt it necessary. The class was obligatory for all the Methodist people. In effect, for Methodists the class was the sole means of grace that was "instituted," not by divine command but by John Wesley. Within this section I will show that throughout Wesley's leadership of the Methodists, his letters and publications contained requests and pleas to the Methodist people to continue meeting, or resume meeting within the class.

To conclude these comments, I quote below a letter Wesley wrote shortly before his death. This letter to Ann (Nancy) Bolton[35] a class

---

33. Kent, *Wesley and the Wesleyans*.

34. Wesley began to use the term 'prudential' while under the influence of the Nonjurors. Such prudential means were those that were not laid down by the canons of the church, but which were nonetheless useful to Christian life and practice. See Bowmer, *The Sacrament of the Lord's Supper in Early Methodism*, 233–37. Wesley annoted his handwritten manuscripts of *The Apostolic Canons*, indicating those which were observed by duty, and those observed prudentially. These manuscripts date to around 1736. See 234. Wesley used the term 'prudential regulation' in reference to the class in *A Plain Account of the People Called Methodists*. See Wesley, *Works [BE]*, Vol. 9, 262.

35. Batstone, "Bolton, Ann (Nancy)," 35–36.

leader and friend for some 30 years, indicates that even those who knew Wesley well found the class difficult, if not burdensome. Wesley wrote with feeling and clearly out of concern for her:

> From the time you omitted meeting your class or band you grieved the Holy Spirit of God, and He gave a commission to Satan to buffet you; nor will that commission ever be revoked till you begin to meet again . . . I exhort you for my sake (who tenderly love you), for God's sake, for the sake of your own soul, begin again without delay. The day after you receive this go and meet a class or a band. Sick or well, go! If you cannot speak a word, go; and God will go with you. You sink under the sin of omission! My friend, my sister, go! Go, whether you can or not.[36]

This quotation reflects Wesley's continuing conviction that the class meeting was vital for Methodist spiritual health. The letter also shows Wesley's strong sense of divine and diabolical intervention. Classes and bands were seen as vehicles for God's gracious action while omitting to use them left one open to Satan's influence. In chapter 8 I will show that he retained this supernatural understanding of the fluctuations of Christian experience to the end of his life.

---

36. Wesley, *Letters [SE]*, Vol. VIII, 246. John Wesley to Ann Bolton, November 4th 1790.

6

Routinization

Randall Balmer's analysis of American Evangelicalism[37] briefly discusses routinization in the context of a study of the work of Calvary Chapel in Santa Ana, California. Balmer notes that at the outset, a voluntary association, in his study a church, will gather around a 'charismatic leader, who defines the group largely through the force of his personality.'[38] Over time, the force of charisma gives way to a process of routinization. leading to institutionalization, and set patterns of behavior.

The example Balmer uses is an 'Outreach Night.'[39] These evenings for young people end with an opportunity to witness at Balboa Pier in Newport Beach. In the 1970s at Pirate's Cove, a short distance from the pier, hippies, drug users, and others came to hear preaching organized by Chuck Smith, pastor of Calvary Chapel, and to be baptized. The scene of thousands of otherwise unreached people touched by the preaching of Smith was an indication of the charisma he possessed to lead such a large and inspiring gathering. By the time Balmer undertook his study, the scene at Balboa Pier, while reminiscent of Smith's outreach, was a pale imitation of its forebear. Pastor Smith's charisma could not be emulated by a young preacher following a tried and trusted approach to evangelism. Such was his methodology that he told those willing to accompany him:

> it's very important that you all pay close attention, that you look at me as if you've never seen me before. That's the key, because

---

37. Balmer, *Mines Eyes Have Seen the Glory: A Journey into the Evangelical Subculture in America*, 12–30. See especially 26–29.

38. Ibid., 26.

39. Ibid., 26.

people walking by will look at the audience and see how interested they are before deciding whether or not to stop and listen.[40]

Balmer outlined two key elements of the routinization process: first, that the charisma of the original leader led to the initial success of the enterprise. In this instance, Pastor Smith picked up on the felt disquiet of many young people and channelled his energy into reaching them appropriately.[41] Second, that the continuation of the enterprise does not possess the leader's charisma and therefore relies on tried and trusted models of work. This is routinization. The outward form remains, the internal charisma has gone.

I will argue that the class meeting became routinized both within the broader organization of Methodism, and within its own milieu. It will be argued that, like Balmer's example above, routinization becomes identifiable within a short period of time. In the case of Calvary Chapel's outreach it was some 15 to 20 years.[42]

The theory of routinization was first evinced by Max Weber,[43] who was amongst the first wave of sociologists of religion who sought explanations through social sciences for the manner in which religions operated. His theory, *The Routinization of Charisma*, stressed the decline in an organization's initial appeal under a charismatic leader toward an institution which exists to promote the material interests of the members of the organization.

Käsler marks this process through the need to maintain an organization financially. Once this form of routinization occurs, then the organization itself exists because of the need to financially maintain it.[44] David Bosch, the South African theologian, offers this critique of routinization:

> Either a movement disintegrates or it becomes an institution–this is simply a sociological law. Every religious group that started out as a movement and managed to survive did so because it was

---

40. Ibid., 27.
41. Ibid., 23–25.
42. Randall Balmer published the first edition in 1989
43. A comprehensive biography of Max Weber can be found in Käsler, *Max Weber An Introduction to his Life and Work*, 1–23.
44. Käsler, *Max Weber*, 165.

gradually institutionalized: the Waldensians, the Quakers, the Moravians, the Pentecostals . . .[45]

This is true of Methodism through the shift from movement to organization over the first ten years of Methodism, and through the class meeting, the primary element of the emerging organization to 1791. The latter will be evidenced by testimony from class members, diaries, and publications.

Weber noted that charismatic leadership is unstable, and routinization acts to stabilize this:

> The pure type of charismatic rulership is in a very specific sense unstable, and all its modifications have basically one and the same cause: the desire to transform charisma and charismatic blessing from a unique, transitory gift of grace . . . into a permanent possession of everyday life.[46]

Weber stated this desire was to capture the transitory charisma of the leader and turn it into a permanent possession of the organization. This "is desired usually by the master, always by disciples, and most of all by his charismatic subjects. Inevitably, however, this changes the nature of the charismatic structure."[47] This adds insight into the experience of Calvary Chapel's outreach team, who longed for the same charisma as Pastor Smith, and his success, yet who clearly could not emulate this when Balmer witnessed their efforts.

The administrative staff offers insight into the process of routinization. This level of leadership, subject to the charismatic leader, organizes around their own material, or ideal interests: one such interest being the continuation of the organization:

> the great majority of disciples and followers will in the long run "make their living" out of their "calling" in a material sense as well. Indeed this must be the case if the movement is not to disintegrate.[48]

This is not necessarily paid employment, but is a bureaucratic office. Staff are not trained but appointed by the leader who notices their own

45. Bosch, *Transforming Mission*, 52.
46. Weber, *Economy and Society an Outline of Interpretive Sociology*: volume 2, 1121.
47. Ibid., 1121.
48. Ibid., *Volume I*, 249.

charismatic qualities, yet they are limited in their functions. These staff may be friends of the leader, who are gathered to offer support, friendship, and the execution of the leader's ideas.[49] William Dean addressed this point: "These men (class leaders) were literally physical extensions of his (Wesley's) own ministry and purpose. Their authority was held by delegation from him and they were personally responsible to him in the exercise of it."[50] White, in his discussion of class decline, noted how Wesley's personal appointment of class leaders was frequently delegated to others as Methodism grew.[51] In the early years of Methodism, as Wesley was visiting the classes of Gateshead, he recognized that meeting with the leader of each class rather than each member could achieve the aim of regulating the class. In visiting Robert Peacock, a class leader, the close questioning Wesley made of him about each member of his class would enable a previously "one-to-one" regulatory process to be undertaken through the individual who represented Wesley's authority, and who would have to remove any disorderly walkers on Wesley's behalf.[52] Through this method, a society of 800 was halved.

However, as Methodism grew, Wesley had little control over the appointment of local leaders. Samuel Bradburn's *Memorandum Book*[53] indicates that in some places there were no society leaders and by implication no class leaders. In Dublin in 1771, Wesley had to deal with problems in the society which affected preachers, stewards, and leaders. After meeting with them, Wesley addressed the society and laid before them in strong terms the purpose and authority of those in leadership of the society. Amongst those leaders were the class leaders, whose position is the first to be addressed by Wesley. In his exhortation, Wesley had to reintroduce their authority, along with the authority of other leaders. The people of the Dublin society had for some time not recognized the class leader's authority as stemming from Wesley personally.[54] Similarly, in a letter to Joseph Benson in 1776, Wesley advised Benson to remove

49. Finney, *Fading Splendour? A New Model of Renewal*, 31.
50. Dean, "Disciplined Fellowship," 227. (Words in brackets mine.)
51. White, "The Decline of the Class Meeting," 259.
52. Wesley, *Works [BE]*, Vol. 20, 162–3.
53. See Bradburn, *A Memorandum Book Containing a List of the Places I Have Been in and the Texts of Scripture I Have Preached on, With the Times of Preaching in Each Place: Since May 31 1774* (Handwritten, unpublished diary), MA 1977/296.
54. Wesley, *Works [BE]*, Vol. 22, 267–69.

any class leader who failed to "watch over the souls committed to their care."[55] At that point in Methodism's existence, some class leaders were not exercising their role as if their authority was from Wesley himself. This raises questions in relation to Dean's strong assertion.

Finally, elective affinity needs discussion. Weber examined a link between Calvinism and capitalism to show this affinity. Essentially, Weber argued that Calvinists became drawn toward social achievement to counter any uncertainty felt by the doctrine of election. This tension arising from predestination "results in the 'interests' of Calvinists in *knowing* whether or not they are among the elect."[56] Thus capitalism arose as Calvinists sought to effect their salvation through work. Elective affinity is the appropriation (or election) of those points of the original idea with which there is affinity. As Hill points out, once a religious movement begins, its adherents begin to select those parts of the core message that have greatest relevance.[57]

In Methodist terms some of those parts related to the change in an individual's life leading toward holiness, which might also mean an improvement in social status, and the acquisition of wealth, while maintaining a policy of giving to the poor. Noting that Wesley saw Methodists becoming rich as early as 1760 Henry Rack writes of Methodism and capitalism:

> Methodism appealed to the industrious middling and artisan classes. It certainly taught an industrious and frugal life, and its rules strongly discouraged conspicuous consumption or adornment.[58]

Weber noted that the acquisition of wealth occurred in Methodism. Although his theory of the rise of capitalism applied to Calvinism, he wrote of Methodism:

> The mighty "revival" of Methodism, which preceded the rapid development of English industry . . . can,—if the comparison is taken with a pinch of salt!—be very aptly likened to such a reform of the monasteries. Those mighty religious movements, whose significance for the economic development lay primarily

---

55. Wesley, *Letters [SE]*, Vol VI, 208.
56. Hill, *A Sociology of Religion*, 121.
57. See Hill, *A Sociology of Religion*, 108.
58. Rack, *Reasonable Enthusiast*, 366.

in the ascetic *education* they provided, only developed their full *economic* effect after the pinnacle of purely religious enthusiasm had been left behind . . . (when) religious roots were beginning to die and give way to utilitarian earthly concerns.[59]

Rack asserts that by 1760 Wesley noticed the tendency for those Methodists who lived regulated and frugal lives to become financially better off.[60] In his journal for October 1760, Wesley wrote, "As many of them increase in worldly goods, the great danger I apprehend now is their relapsing into the spirit of the world. And then their religion is but a dream."[61]

One other point needs attention, arising from the study of group processes in the previous chapter: homogeneity. This is discussed by Rupert Brown,[62] and has two strands to it: first, the homogeneity of those outside a group—that the group perceives those who do not belong as having the same description; and secondly, the homogeneity of the group itself—that those within the group possess common values, attributes, and goals. This is made more complex when the group studied is small. In this instance a greater degree of homogeneity is apparent.

A homogenous unit is as liable to routinization as any other, and the class meeting of around 12 people falls directly into the category of small units whose homogeneity is more easily identifiable, and therefore a barrier to new members. John Munsey Turner admirably describes homogeneity among the nineteenth-century Primitive Methodists. In this period, rural villages and recently industrialized centres became a boom area of growth, with the majority of the congregation "composed of labourers with the leading lay man often enough a shopkeeper."[63] This homogenous unit of Methodists stood against the prevailing changing world, which was in turn seen by them as homogenous in itself.

---

59. Weber, *The Protestant Ethic and the "Spirit" of Capitalism*, 118. (Word in brackets mine.)

60. See Rack, *Reasonable Enthusiast*, 366. Rack suggests that Wesley adopts a 'Weberian strain' in some of his later sermons. See note 113 to 366.

61. Wesley, *Works [BE]*, Vol. 21, 284.

62. Brown, *Group Processes*, 287ff.

63. Turner, *Conflict and Reconciliation*, 85.

William Dean is dismissive on the matter of routinization. Quoting from an unpublished PhD thesis,[64] and recognizing the strength of the argument, he dismissed it:

> The weakness of the routinization hypothesis is that once the change has been described, the description itself becomes the explanation of the change. The logic runs thus: This is what happened; it happened because it happened. To describe a situation, however, is very different from explaining it; to confuse explanation with description is to introduce an element of determinism. Such a hypothesis seems to postulate some sort of hidden natural law which determined the course of change. I accept the description as valid, but I reject the determinism. We are not dealing with an irresistible (or in this context, psychological) process. There is evidence in the history of American denominations which suggests that such routinization can be addressed and overcome.[65]

I disagree with Dean. It is true that describing routinization is not the same as explaining it, but the experience of early Methodism supports the theory. Dean's assertion that routinization might be overcome does not in this instance negate the point I am making through this chapter. I am offering an explanation as to why the class meeting began to decline within a relatively short space of time.

A useful place to begin is the diaries of early Methodist leaders. These diaries record widely varying spiritual temperatures. Authors describe experiencing the buffets of Satan just as frequently as hearts enlarged after holiness. From one day to the next, or even within the same day's entries it is not unusual to note that a writer swings from extreme contentment to a deep sense of sinfulness:

> This morning I was exceeding happy and more and more confirmed in the truth of my experience: yet afterwards was very much striped and stripped exceedingly; Satan casting his fiery darts like a flood into my soul.[66]

---

64. The thesis referred to is Turner, "The Decline of Methodism: An analysis of Religious Commitment and Organisation," 25–26.

65. Dean, "Disciplined Fellowship," 363.

66. Holder, *The Diary of William Holder, who was Born in Painswick (Glos) and Died in London January 17th 1810 aged 70*, entry for 25th October 1768. MA 1977/238.

This careful personal searching extended to the company one kept:

> I feel my heart too easily affected by the company I happen to be in. Hence lightness of spirit often carries me I know not whither, and makes me ashamed to go to prayer.[67]

These diaries share the same purpose as John Wesley's exacting *Diary*, and earlier Puritan diaries. According to Ted Campbell, journals and diaries served in a similar manner to the Catholic confessional, and the earlier practice of spiritual direction in that they were not solely private documents, but were read to family, friends, and the minister.[68] This practice continued within Methodism as William Holder used extracts of his diary to encourage others. "After breakfast I read some things of my *Journal* to them, particularly how I was before, at the time, and after my deliverance."[69] One might properly expect that the class was a mutual confessional and it was so, but not a confessional of temptation and sinfulness as much as an opportunity to describe the previous week's experience of daily life.

The diary records of class meetings are numerous, but rarely give detailed information of a meeting's events. John Goodfellow allows an insight on the 28th September 1784: "At Class, but discomforted by the actions of a person making much ado there: O God grant I pray that I may not judge rashly or condemn others."[70] It is more common to read of the reproof or encouragement of a class member outside the class meeting, as in William Holder's[71] and John Goodfellow's diaries.[72]

The manner in which diarist's refer to the effects of the class meeting upon themselves, and by extension to other members, is difficult to assess. Whether the language used by these leaders to describe a class meeting was routinized is difficult to claim definitively. If it is, then the

---

67. Bradburn, *A Memorandum Book: volume 1*, entry for May 1775. MA 1977/296.

68. Campbell, *The Religion of the Heart*, 49.

69. Holder, *The Diary of William Holder*, entry for 29th September 1768. MA 1977/238.

70. Goodfellow, *The Diary of John Goodfellow*, entry for 28th September 1784. MA 1977/236.

71. Holder, *The Diary of William Holder*, entry for 15th November 1768. MA 1977/238.

72. Goodfellow, *The Diary of John Goodfellow*, Entries for the 19th September and 27th December 1787. MA 1977/236.

terms used may have been understood or accepted by others who may have read or heard extracts of the leader's diaries, as representing an experience expressed in recognized or common terms. If not, then these terms must be allowed to stand alone as representative of the felt need met at the meeting.

The language or terminology used in the diaries of William Holder, John Goodfellow, Bennet Dugdale, and Samuel Bradburn ranges from "sweet opportunity," "found it very good," "peace in my own soul," "peace flowed as a river," "greatly blessed," "I find my spirit greatly united," "abundantly strengthened and refreshed" and "melting time." Goodfellow used the phrase "melting time"[73] twice. This term, or variations of it, was not uncommon in the period covered by his diary. George Whitefield recorded in his journal that his "heart was melted down"[74] at his ordination by the Bishop of Gloucester in 1736. Charles Wesley described himself "melted down" after preaching at Newgate in November 1738.[75] John Valton considered that those who heard him exhort and pray "melt and weep" as he spoke.[76] He also wrote on the 14th April 1766, that while at breakfast he felt that his soul "melted into tears of joy."[77] John Wesley used the term "melted down" in his journal having met the society in Norwich. On meeting them at seven, he informed them that they were "the most ignorant, self-conceited, self-willed, fickle, untractable, disorderly, disjointed society."[78] In speaking to the society in these terms, he was by default chastising the classes and leaders for not functioning in a manner which would prevent the need for such an address. On the same day (9th September 1759) he met them again at ten, and this time, following his earlier discourse, "many stubborn hearts were melted down."[79] There may therefore be a mimetic quality to these phrases, used

73. Ibid., entries for the 2nd December 1785 and 11th May 1787. MA 1977/236.

74. Whitefield, *George Whitefield's Journals*, 69.

75. Wesley, *Journal*, Vol. I, 134. Entry for the 7th November 1738.

76. Valton, "The Life of John Valton," 28. (21st November 1764.) See also Hindmarsh, *The Evangelical Conversion Narrative*, 83. Hindmarsh writes of the experience of Joseph Humphreys, an early associate of the Wesley's. In his personal diary, he too writes of being "melted down."

77. Valton, "The Life of John Valton," in *Preachers*, 50.

78. Wesley, *Works [BE]*, Vol. 21, 227. For an interesting discourse on Wesley's use of English, through his writing, both private, and public, see Lawton, *John Wesley's English A Study of His Literary Style*.

79. Ibid.

by leaders in a manner which was representative of their felt experience, and which would be understood by others. This usage of language may therefore be "routine," but not without depth.

Of the four diarists, three frequently took a common diary style when writing of meeting a class. Dugdale,[80] Goodfellow,[81] and Holder[82] each described his feelings or emotional state during the course of the day, and carried those feelings to the meeting. Thus, Dugdale wrote on the 2nd April 1786, "the greater part of the day felt much heaviness and inactivity accompanied with heaviness so that I would have shunned meeting my class."[83] He attempted to find a person to take his place, but failed. Having to lead the class, his record of the meeting exceeded his expectation "glory be to God who was better than my hopes and greater than my fear."[84] William Holder was similarly exercised. "I have been much buffetted (sic) all this day by the enemy."[85] In the evening, after meeting his class his emotional state changed: "I met my Class, & was exceedingly strengthened thereby. I believe it was a time of refreshing to all."[86] The same prose style was used by John Valton to indicate to the reader of his biography that despite his feeling lifeless and forlorn, and his resolution not to go to his class, his subsequent attendance resulted in a "refreshing time."[87]

Unlike his fellow diarists, Samuel Bradburn wrote sparingly of the class meeting. Traveling from 1774[88] and stationed in Pembroke, Wales,

---

80. Dugdale, *The Diary of Bennet Dugdale*, see the entries for the 2nd April 1786, 21st May 1786, and 13th August 1786. MA 1977/216.

81. Goodfellow, *The Diary of John Goodfellow*, see the entries for 2nd December 1785, 2nd June 1786, and 23rd November 1787. MA 1977/236.

82. Holder, *The Diary of William Holder*, see the entries for 13th October 1768, 17th November 1768, 23rd February 1769, 2nd March 1769, 23rd March 1769, 25th May 1769, 29th June 1769, 20th July 1769, 17th August 1769, 31st August 1769, 21st September 1769, 7th December 1769. MA 1977/238.

83. Dugdale, *The Diary of Bennet Dugdale*, entry for the 2nd April 1786. MA 1977/216.

84. Ibid.

85. Holder, *The Diary of William Holder*, entry for the 29th June 1769. MA 1977/238.

86. Ibid.

87. Valton, "The Life of John Valton," in *Preachers*, 37. This is the entry for the 19th May 1765.

88. Myles, *A Chronological History*, 299. Myles places Bradburn in the "second race of Methodist Preachers."

in 1775, he noted in his first month that meeting the classes was useful for his preaching: "by frequently meeting the Classes, I find my Spirit greatly united to the people. It likewise furnishes me with many useful hints for preaching."[89] However in a reflective moment, he noted that he had not grown in grace and had a tendency to self-sufficiency.[90] Bradburn did not write about the classes again until he was stationed in London in 1786, when he was contemptuous of their state.[91]

As I have indicated already and will show elsewhere, the diaries and journals of class leaders were not intended as wholly private documents. These entries were therefore of assistance in convincing, or encouraging others to meet, or continue meeting in class, particularly if the reluctant individual was expressing a similar emotive state prior to the regular scheduled class meeting. These diarists, rather like other firsthand accounts illustrate that there was not an even picture of class life. Elsewhere in this book I have used these diarists as they write of the class failing to operate as the Methodist system required. As I noted in the introduction to this section, the class functioned well in some places, while proving to be a cross in others.

The process of routinization meant that following the same routine of prayer, hymn, inquisition with response, and prayer had led to a routine language and perhaps expectation of experience that is codified by the descriptive language of the class meeting's events.

In the earliest period Wesley's own providential phrase, "a brand plucked from the burning" was used by early Methodists of their conversion experience. Catharine Gilbert[92] and Margaret Austin[93] both use the term, albeit with their own phraseology. Elizabeth Sayce used the phrase "my chains fell off,"[94] reminiscient of Charles Wesley's hymn, "And can it be?" to describe her assurance. These phrases may have been used in testimony to Charles Wesley as they had heard the term in preaching or

89. Bradburn, *A Memorandum Book*, entry for September 1775. MA 1977/296.

90. Ibid.

91. Bradburn, *A Memorandum Book*, entries for December 7th, 8th, 9th 1786. In London he filled his role as an Assistant, and was responsible for regulating the classes. MA 1977/296.

92. Catharine Gilbert to Charles Wesley, 19th May 1740, 1. *Early Methodist Volume*.

93. Margaret Austin to Charles Wesley, 1740, 6. *Early Methodist Volume*.

94. Testimonial of Elizabeth Sayce to Charles Wesley from Morgan, "Methodist Testimonials for Bristol Collected by Charles Wesley in 1742," 97.

band meetings, or through singing and in order to describe their movement from sin to faith; this term aptly described their present state. The language was borrowed, and in some way routine for a description of the journey to faith, a journey that was often tortuous.

Similarly, the experiences of seeing Christ at the sacrament or hearing voices giving an assurance of forgiveness are remarkably similar.[95] A note of caution, however, should be added in that the earliest testimonials were written around the period of the stillness controversy, which was not confined to Fetter Lane. The highly charged visions of Christ at the sacrament may have been elicited by Charles Wesley to counter the exponents of stillness.

Routinization of language occurred in the class meeting as those who maintained journals were unable to give particular detail, and wanted to express something of the meetings events, as they understood them. The early testimonials had a similarity of language, which is to be expected, but described an individual's personal experience. The later journals described the meetings of later Methodists for whom the ecstatic experience of the early testimonies was predominantly historical and reported the communal experience of the class meeting which no longer held the ecstatic as a common occurrence.

Hindmarsh skillfully relates the place of testimony and autobiography as a means of expressing the experiences of the individual. Early testimony was written to Wesley, later autobiography was written for the Methodists. The accounts published in the *Arminian Magazine* were drawn from personal journals and diaries and offer a less personal account of the routine of life than the testimonies. The journals and diaries from which the above accounts of class meeting business are drawn represent the firsthand, contemporary journaling of leaders whose language is, to say the least, not highly expressive of personal experience, but rather fettered.

John Atlay's life, recorded in the *Arminian Magazine* of 1778, stands sharply against this. Atlay, drawing on his own conversion experience to

---

95. See Cowper to Charles Wesley, 1741, 16. Sarah Middleton to Charles Wesley, May 1740, 5. Both letters are from the *Early Methodist Volume*. See also Morgan, "Methodist Testimonials for Bristol Collected by Charles Wesley in 1742," in *Reformation and Revival in Eighteenth-Century Bristol*, testimonial of Eliazabeth Downs 13th April 1742, 87. In addition see the undated testimonial of Elizabeth Sayce, 98.

encourage his class, is able to write that his fellow class members came to the same experience in a short time:

> from that hour I never had a moment's doubt of God's love to me ... God continually confirmed what was spoken: but especially to the Class whereof I was Leader, most of whom were justified in a few months.[96]

A similar account is given by Benjamin Rhodes, who became a class leader in the early 1760s. He led several classes, and recounted in his autobiography, "I found those meetings were both solemn and profitable to my self and others. The first quarter several found a sense of forgiveness; and others were greatly stirred up."[97] Likewise, the *Account* of Robert Wilkinson, a class member in 1767, shows that at that point the class was functioning sufficiently well to enable him to receive verbal assurance from his leader that his Christian life was not without merit. Wilkinson's *Account* is rare in that he gives a brief, but vital insight into the inquisitorial nature of the class:

> After the first prayer was over, it was with difficulty I rose from my knees. When the Leader asked how I found the state of my soul, I answered, I am left without one spark of hope that God will ever have mercy on me. No, he said, you are not; for if you were, you would not now be using the means of grace.[98]

John Wesley, in a letter written to Charles in 1748, reported the experience of two individuals who openly pronounced their state. Tellingly, Wesley comments of one. "Had it been desired, he would have explained before them all."[99] This indicates that the classes in Dublin were functioning as experiential confessionals, with the added function of small communities for faith development.

Wesley's letter to his brother was intended to encourage the Methodists in England. The letter, written on April 16th 1748, is an ex-

---

96. Atlay, "Account of Mr John Atlay," 579. In the 1780s Atlay was in dispute with John Wesley, and left the Connexion having attempted to begin his own circuit. Hindmarsh notes that from that point he was expunged from the Methodist memory. See Hindmarsh, *The Evangelical Conversion Narrative*, 239.

97. Rhodes, "Account of Benjamin Rhodes," 364. See also Mason, "A Short Account of the Life of John Mason," 653.

98. Wilkinson, "A Short Account of Mr. Robert Wilkinson," 181.

99. Wesley, *Works [BE]*, Vol. 26, 306.

tract from the *Journal*.[100] I contend the letter would have been read out publicly by Methodists and non-Methodists alike. This contrasts sharply with later accounts and diaries that leave the reader with little doubt that the class was a routine element of the Methodist pattern, rather than a foundation of the path to faith.

Samuel Bradburn offers a personal insight into the malaise of the classes in London in 1786. Appointed by Conference to London, his first attempt at regulating the classes occasioned this entry: "Regulating the Classes, which I seriously think is mere loss of time, as people will not meet but where they profit. Why should they?"[101] He had previously been in Wales (1775) where there were no classes. He began his own "divisions" which later became classes.

Bradburn also highlights another possible cause for routinization: the transition to society consciousness. In this the rule of John Wesley himself was diminished, and the leaders of the society took greater power to themselves. In 1779, while in Ireland, Bradburn noted that members with money considered they should have precedence in the society. Bradburn remarked, "Owing to two or three persons, who think to rule everybody in the Society, because they have got money."[102] It was no longer possible to control the leaders from a distance as it had been. Bradburn had been told by Wesley himself to dismiss one of the leaders. The leader refused to leave his post, or hand back the money or books he held.[103] Disaffection from the society also plagued his work in Ireland.[104]

These changes in societal understanding were a form of routinization as local leaders took responsibility for that which was previously under the direct authority of John Wesley, the charismatic leader. This routinization permeated throughout the society's groups, including the class, moving the group away from its experiential, accountable, disciplinary, close Pietstic fellowship of the early years of Methodism. Gareth Lloyd, writing about the place of early female preachers after Wesley's, succinctly evidenced the progression of routinization as the male leader-

100. See Wesley, *Works [BE]*, Vol. 20, 217.
101. S. Bradburn, *A Memorandum Book, volume 1*, entry for December 1786. MA 1977/296.
102. Ibid.,Vol. I, entry for July 1779. MA 1977/296.
103. Ibid., entry for December 1779. MA 1977/296.
104. Ibid., entry for January 1780. MA 1977/296.

ship actively assisted the Methodists to leave their more distinctive early characteristics in their history:

> As the Methodists completed this transition from revival movement to denomination, they quietly shed important aspects of their early identity. Open-air preaching for example had largely died out even before Wesley passed from the scene, while the more charismatic brand of Christianity that had once been so distinctively Wesleyan was fast losing favour with the national leadership.[105]

A similar situation can be seen in the first American quarterly meetings. These meetings were entirely different to the British meeting founded by John Bennet in 1748 at Todmorden.[106] The American model was a weekend camp, at which preaching, teaching, and liturgical services, including, baptisms, weddings, and funerals were shared, and business transacted. They attracted large crowds of members and adherents and the itinerant preachers of the locality. In *A Little Heaven Below* Lester Ruth discusses these meetings and notes that in the late eighteenth century crowds of six to ten thousand people were recorded.[107]

By the middle years of the nineteenth century the crowds had died away and worship, revivalist preaching, and liturgy had been replaced by a shortened weekend dominated by business. The American Methodist way of worship had graduated to the local church and the needs of a settled "churchy" congregation were now met by a settled ministry. This change led those who recalled the earlier revivalist period to lament the loss of what they saw as a fundamental building block of American Methodism. Lester Ruth quotes an itinerant preacher, David Lewis:

> Methodists would go forty and fifty miles to quarterly meetings. These were our great festivals. Here we renewed our covenants with God and his people, obtained encouragement and strength in our souls, and rejoiced together in the salvation of God . . . Truly our fellowship was with the Father, and with his Son Jesus Christ.[108]

105. Lloyd, "Repression and Resistance: Wesleyan Female Public Ministry in the Generation after 1791," 102.

106. Valentine, *Mirror of the Soul*, 179. See the entry for October 18th 1748. The Reverend William Grimshaw presided at the meeting.

107. Ruth, *A Little Heaven Below. Worship at Early Methodist Quarterly Meetings*, 32.

108. Ibid., 183.

Ruth states that for Lewis this reminiscence contains "a note of sadness... quarterly meetings *were* great festivals, but they are no longer."[109] Ruth continues his account of the decline of the quarterly meeting, and quotes Henry Boehm, who had traveled with Francis Asbury. "What would we do if we could witness such a scene (of revival) at a modern quarterly meeting?"[110] Time engendered a shift in emphasis in the priorities of the American Methodists and the quarterly meeting's role was subsumed by other meetings for worship and business as the revival died away, and the routine life of discipleship took over.

The class could be revitalized by some outside events causing the membership to seek strength in their meeting together. In 1786, John Goodfellow noted that two Calvinist preachers were decimating his society, such that "they are so pleased with this novelty, that they cannot be happy in our meetings, nor can they endure the class meeting!"[111] Their preaching led him to conclude: "This doctrine mightilly (sic) please many of our lukewarm brethren, who are so safe that they have no need of class meetings."[112] The problem became so severe that neither band nor class members were attending their meetings.

The remaining class members regrouped and found within themselves another gust of charisma, and within a year, Goodfellow's account of class meetings had changed, such that there was a sense of purpose that his previous *Journal* entries did not posses:

> I met my Class, it was a melting time to all, one who came with the determination to give up her tickett (sic), & be struck out of the paper, was so melted down by the power of God, that she publicly declared her intention in coming this evening; but departed with . . . a determination to live more to God than ever, and never to forsake his cause, or people.[113]

The routinization and comfort of the class was shaken by an alternative doctrine, thus causing over time a rediscovery of the charisma of Wesley's purpose of the class as a body for mutual edification and perseverance.

109. Ibid.
110. Ibid., 184.
111. Goodfellow, *The Diary of John Goodfellow*, entry for 20th March 1786. MA 1977/236.
112. Ibid., entry for 21st May 1786. MA 1977/236.
113. Ibid., entry for 11th May 1787. MA 1977/236.

Low attendance also occurred simply because people did not meet; a problem Wesley was to regularly exhort the Methodists to overcome in his later life. William Holder, who otherwise seldom gave much detail of his class meetings, noted in his *Diary* two occasions of poor attendance, "in the evening I met my Class, we was (sic) but few but it was a good opportunity."[114] Likewise he wrote, "I met my Class, we were but few, but I believe it was a time of good things to all."[115]

Low attendance broke the rule that class attendance was a vital sign of acceptance of the Wesleyan system of organization. If the *General Rules* had any force, the leader's duty was to see members in class weekly,[116] and this was not happening within Holder's class. Other diaries omit non-attendance, possibly for fear of being considered a poor leader.

By 1764, Wesley was clearly contending with non-attendance, just 22 years after the inception of the class. His correspondence begins to be peppered with exhortations to ensure class attendance is maintained:

> Whoever misses his class thrice together thereby excludes himself, and the preacher that comes next ought to put out his name ... Meet the brethren or leave them ... Never miss your class till you miss it for good and all.[117]

In 1788, Wesley wrote to Edward Jackson commending him for denying tickets to all who failed to attend class, as a means of encouraging others to attend regularly. Vitally, Wesley suggests, however unknowingly, that the class might not have the same evangelistic appeal that it did: "the grand means of revival of the work of God in Sheffield was the prayer-meetings. There were then twelve of them in various parts of the town every Sunday night. Keep up these, and you will keep up the flame."[118] While Wesley did not explicitly state the class no longer held pre-eminence, he recognized the value that the prayer meeting developed in Methodisms economy. Routinization had affected the class meeting's status and vitality. Certainly the prayer meeting was being used in other places; John Pawson, who was himself converted at a prayer meeting,[119]

114. Holder, *The Diary of William Holder*, entry for 2nd November 1769. MA 1977/238.

115. Ibid., entry for 11th January 1770. MA 1977/238.

116. See Appendix 10: Rule 3(1).

117. Wesley, *Letters [SE]*, Vol. IV, 273.

118. Wesley, *Letters [SE]*, Vol. VIII, 98–99.

119. Pawson, "The Life of Mr John Pawson," 20. His conversion took place on the

was clear about its benefits in his Birstall appointment.[120] James Rogers[121] also felt the prayer meeting useful, as did John Mason.[122]

At Darlaston in 1759, Alexander Mather discovered that the prayer meeting was bringing people to faith. "Some of these coming over to the prayer-meetings at Wednesbury, and hearing (what they thought they had never heard before) that they were to believe now; that they might come to Christ now, without any other qualification than a sense of their own sinfulness and helplessness . . . Presently a prayer-meeting was set up at Darlaston. And in a little time many souls were set at liberty."[123]

The prayer meeting was a recent innovation, and there was opposition to the move, such that Mather eventually ceased holding them. Whether this was because Mather's wife was leading them or because it was simply a novel move is not clear. However, the cessation of these meetings meant that "immediately the work began to decay, both as to its swiftness and extensiveness. And though I continued to insist as strongly as ever upon the same points, yet there was not the same effect, for want of seconding by prayer-meetings the blow which was given in preaching."[124] Preaching followed by attendance at a prayer meeting was at best unusual. Under Methodist polity, it was the class, portal to the society, in which a searching individual heard the call to faith through experiential testimony of his or her peers.[125]

In a letter to Hannah Ball on the 13th April 1786, Wesley commended her society, and indicated that it would prosper as long as "the prayer meetings are kept up."[126] He then issued a caveat, "without interfering with the classes and bands."[127] Writing on the decline of the class in the nineteenth century, William Dean noted the class was the single group in which people were recruited and assimilated into Methodism. Yet this role was lost to the prayer meeting. "It was during the first generation of

---

16th March 1760.

120. Ibid., 47.

121. Rogers, "The Life of James Rogers," 321.

122. Mason, "The Life of John Mason," 310.

123. Mather, "The Life of Alexander Mather," 178–79.

124. A. Mather, "The Life of Alexander Mather," 181.

125. See also Rack, *Reasonable Enthusiast*, 492. Rack discusses the prayer meetings associated with the revivals in the 1780s.

126. J. Wesley, *Letters [SE]*, Vol. VII, 324.

127. Ibid.

the nineteenth century that the evangelistic function of the class meeting was lost to the prayer meeting."[128] The examples above, point toward an earlier date for the decline of the class as the place in which people were awakened, or converted.

In part this must be related to the activities of the classes as the class leaders recorded them. Each diary is as much a record of personal spirituality as it is a record of events. The events of the past week were shared in class, and with such a variation in temperature and state this must have given the class a very complex milieu. Many Methodists were unable, or unwilling, to unburden themselves in this manner, and as the class was a mutual confessional it is not surprising that the proceedings of the class became routine. Bennet Dugdale wrote on visiting a dying class member that his death was a "sifting"[129] as he had "stayed away a few times and then was ashamed to come."[130] Could it rather be that the class no longer had any elective affinity for him, or that he found the routine too irksome to attend? When John Goodfellow met the members of another leader's class, he discovered little harmony, and ready blame of neighbor by neighbor for the situation.[131]

Charles Perronet's long document relating how class leaders should operate details the manner of running either a class or band and was roundly endorsed by Wesley as an acceptable method for running class business. Perronet's document is more than merely a support to leaders: it is prescriptive, detailed, and routine.

Mary Tooth left no room for spontaneity in her classes as she prepared a catechism for class members with sufficient material for 124 meetings.[132] Another paper in the Fletcher Tooth Collection is a children's catechism, again intended to leave little or no room for personal testimony.[133] These routinized meetings bear no resemblance to the ideal of Wesley's meeting of early Methodism.

---

128. Dean, "The Methodist Class Meeting: The Significance of its Decline," 43.

129. Dugdale, *The Diary of Bennet Dugdale*, entry for 16th May 1786. MA 1977/216.

130. Ibid.

131. Goodfellow, *The Diary of John Goodfellow*, entry for 25th April 1787. MA 1977/236.

132. JRULM: *Fletcher Tooth Collection*. MA Fl 38.1

133. Ibid.

In Perronet's document, routinisation is obvious. The work of the class leader is simply to maintain the status quo, rather than to be open to the Holy Spirit's sifting and encouraging. The paper relates to behavior within and without the society, and sets a standard of behavior that veered toward respectability (or godliness) rather than developing spirituality (holiness). In many ways, it reflects an organization that had become homogenous, as the piece understands that all Methodists will believe and behave in a manner different to the world.

Perronet's article reflects the discussion relating to group processes of chapter 5, especially the section considering homogeneity. I consider homogeneity to have parallels with Weber's consideration of elective affinity mentioned earlier in this chapter. Michael Hill helpfully describes this elective affinity:

> As soon as a group of adherents is attracted to a particular idea or ethical system, which in origin is purely concerned with problems of salvation and ultimate meaning, they will begin to "elect" those features of the original idea with which they have "affinity" or "point of coincidence." Thus there is the paradox that as soon as a new religious idea gets under way in the form of a religious movement, its members will have already begun the process of selection from the core of the message of those elements that are particularly relevant to the social location of those who have joined the movement.[134]

If it is shared values and understanding, including modes of dress, language and behavior that make a group homogenous, and it is the appropriation of points from the founder's teaching, or doctrine (including dress, language and behavior) that assist elective affinity, then there is a clear parallel between the two models.

Idealist and material interests also merge through elective affinity. On the surface there is divergence between the homogenous unit principle and elective affinity, as homogeneity does not require a merging of material interests into the ideals held by the group. In Methodism, however, it is fair to state that material interests became an element of the organization's *raison d'être*, and were so from the outset, as seen through the *General Rules* of 1743.[135]

---

134. Hill, *A Sociology of Religion*, 108.
135. See Appendix 10.

Perronet's *Right Method* was written 34 years after the classes first appeared, and published 39 years after. In that period, the initial charisma and excitement of belonging to a class had given way to the set routine and practice of meeting a class as the gateway into society membership. It is unsurprising that homogeneity and elective affinity can be discerned in his writing.

A brief comparison of the 1743 *General Rules* and the later *Right Method* of 1776 highlights the effect of homogeneity and elective affinity as elements of routinization. Wesley's rule required the class leader to visit the class weekly, receive financial contributions and act as a spiritual director.[136] Perronet, however, is highly prescriptive in the expectation placed on the class leader.[137] The expectancy ranged from knowing who was a member of the society to knowledge of each member's spiritual understanding and personal development.

That a process of elective affinity and homogenization had occurred within the process of routinization is indicated by Wesley's own endorsement: "I earnestly exhort all Leaders of classes and bands to consider the preceding Observations, and to put them in execution."[138] By the second half of the 1770s, a more prescriptive stance was required to ensure that the classes functioned in a manner that was helpful and effective to the class members. From the discussion above, using class leaders' diaries and journals, rules, such as these written by Charles Perronet, would have been useful regulatory tools.

To assist in understanding the place of homogeneity and elective affinity in early Methodism, the experience of John Goodfellow's Society, after the conviction for theft of one of their number, shows that each society member was brought into disrepute through one person's behavior:

> May 12th This was a day of great trial; one of our Society was convicted of theft, so that the name of ~ Methodist is in everyones mouth as a reproach to us all, because one has been overcome by the enemy of souls, in an unwatchful moment.[139]

---

136. Appendix 10: Paragraph 3(1).
137. Appendix 13.
138. Ibid.
139. Goodfellow, *The Diary of John Goodfellow*, entry for May 12th 1786. MA 1977/236.

This disrepute was shared as the *whole* were disgraced by one person. The shared values and even material interests of the society had been severely tried as their homogeneity; that which they shared in common, and their elective affinity; those primary material and spiritual interests within their collective life, were laid open to ridicule by people who were in their terms outside the group, and who were by definition spiritually inferior.

Though Goodfellow does not describe how his society and classes dealt with the situation, this event may have temporarily broken the routinization process while members searched themselves once more and rebuilt their society's reputation, putting life into otherwise moribund classes. If a Methodist could be convicted of theft the class was not fulfilling its role in the believer's life.

Samuel Bradburn offers a sign of the types of people who were joining the Methodist classes by 1787:

> There are three sorts of people among them:- the Truly spiritual:- the regularly sincere, who live much below their privileges:- and the scarcely awakened outward court worshippers, who just conform to the rules enough to be kept in connexion.[140]

It can barely be imagined that there could be such a definition of the Methodist people in the earliest period of Methodism when to belong to the Methodists brought scorn, ridicule, and even personal danger. This description leads to the tentative conclusion that Methodism was far more respectable than it had been, and the deeply experiential process of belonging to a class had faded to a routine of weekly meeting with little purpose.

This is a cross to Methodism, which required the class to act as a life-changing portal into the full life of the society, yet obviously served only to function as a custom of the Methodists, somewhat as a totem, which will be discussed in the next chapter. The experience of the work of Calvary Chapel, Santa Ana, and the early American quarterly meetings, shows that routinization was not confined to the experience of the Methodist class meeting from 1742.

In the previous chapter, the place of the class as a crown to Methodism was discussed, and I showed how the class required a par-

---

140. Bradburn, *A Memorandum Book, volume 1*, entry for May 1787. MA 1977/296.

ticular type of religious experience to enable it to function. The class operated as a confessional and was only functional when the group was prepared to engage fully in the experiential life of the meeting. The early entry requirement of Methodism, a desire "to flee from the wrath to come," lost its urgency over the years of Methodist development, and as will be shown in chapter 8, second-generation Methodists did not feel this burning desire. It was inevitable that the class would suffer a form of routinization which left the appearance of the experiential class in place, but in reality operated as a shell of its former being.

To have maintained a high spiritual temperature amongst the classes, Wesley, or an appointed person with his authority, would have been needed to constantly visit the classes around the emerging Connexion and purge them. This purging, however, would then need new recruits who had recently been awakened or converted. The class routinized, not because of a failing on Wesley's part, nor because of the quality of the leaders, but because of familiarity with other members, and a deepening sense of religious consciousness as a Methodist identity beyond the Anglican Church grew.

The decline of the class meant that the four "pillars" that underpinned the classes—fellowship, conversion and discipleship, financial accountability, and discipline—declined too. Likewise the life of the class as a center for spiritual growth and development as a "Methodist" declined too. The life of the Methodist people centered more on the society meeting and the settled Ministry which provided the entire spiritual needs of the people.

From routinization, I shall discuss the class as a totem in Methodism. Totemism meant that when the class may have required reformation, even in Wesley's lifetime, it was impossible to amend or alter it, as it embodied all that Wesley desired for his people. The class as a totem meant that its purpose could not be altered or its function changed. Once the earliest generation, who required a wholly experiential group meeting, moved into leadership as class leaders, preachers or assistants, then they became a part of the reason for its totemism, as much as Wesley's view that the class was immutable.

7

Totemism

In 1886, the Wesleyan Methodists in Caister-on-Sea, Norfolk, opened their new chapel in Beach Road, just a few hundred yards from the sea. Facing the chapel, and looking at the façade, it is possible to see the foundation stones, and date stone above the door bearing the year 1886. Inside the chapel today, even though the original high central pulpit has been replaced by a large, low platform, the interior still bears many of the original features.

Looking toward the front, to either side of the recent platform, are two doors, both original to the construction which lead the visitor to the rear rooms of the small complex. One, to the left, bears the word "Vestry," and leads into a room intended for the preacher or minister prior to the service. To the right, the door bears the words "Class Room" and leads visitors into a tiny room, measuring 8 feet 10 inches by 5 feet 7 inches,[1] hardly large enough to hold a meeting of two or three people, and certainly not of a sufficient size to hold class meetings of ten to twelve people. The class meetings at Caister-on-Sea Wesleyan Methodist Chapel were unlikely to be held in the designated class Room. This small village Methodist Chapel was experiencing a phenomenon by then common across the Connexion and which from 1887 onwards was exercising the minds of those at Conference. By 1889, the link between class attendance and society membership, a link that had been maintained since 1742, was de facto severed.

This pressure for detaching class attendance from membership which had become evident in debates and pamphlet controversies during the nineteenth century was now openly recognized.[2] When the issue

---

1. In metric dimensions the room measures 2.7metres by 1.7metres.

2. See Rack, "The Decline of the Class-Meeting and the Problem of Church-Membership in Nineteenth-Century Methodism," 12–21. See also Dean, "The Methodist

of the separating class attendance from membership was put forward at the Wesleyan Methodist Conference in 1887, the idea was commuted to a Conference appointed committee. A. J. French, author of a paper initially read to the 1889 Liverpool ministers' meeting, noted that the committee given the task to examine the issue of class attendance and membership, did so because of a "decrease in our societies; and also, generally, into our mode of Church-membership."[3] The major point of disagreement was a recommendation to introduce a "communicant's ticket, for those who were regular in worship, but did not go to class meeting."[4] When the Conference committee report was presented to the 1888 Conference, "a warm debate ensued, more particularly with reference to Recommendation X. Ultimately the whole business was sent down to the May district meetings, whose suggestions were to be considered by the Committee and reported to the Conference of 1889."[5]

The Conference committee report recognized the difficulties experienced by local societies in ensuring class attendance, thus fulfilling the sole duty for membership. However, the report equally reads as a document that shows the unwillingness of the committee members who compiled the report to allow this long-standing conjunction of attendance and membership to be separated. Much of the language of the report indicated a totemic understanding of the class' purpose, and place in the Methodist schema:

> It is not merely a gateway of entrance into membership; it is not merely a gauge by which fitness for continuing in membership with a living and spiritual Church may be tested. It is all this, but it is more . . . It is an organized form of Christian fellowship which is enjoined by the New Testament upon all believers . . .

Class Meeting, The Significance of its Decline," 41–48. I have addressed the manner in which Rack and Dean discuss class attendance and society membership in the introduction to Part Three in this book.

3. French, *The World in the Church; A Contribution to the Class-Meeting Question*, 3. The contentious proposal of the Conference committee was contained in Recommendation X.

4. Ibid., 4. This was the main point of recommendation X.

5. Ibid.,4. At the time the Wesleyan Methodists were considering this change, the United Methodist Free Church Conference directed that each church should decide whether to adopt the communicant or class meeting system. The result, French noted, quoting Dr. Rigg was that, "In some circuits they are completely gone, and in many others they are slowly dying." 9. The Primitive Methodist Church retained the condition of class attendance to membership. See the Footnote on 24.

> Such a system, moulded for us by the hand of providence, hallowed and sanctioned during a century and a half by the manifest and abundant blessing of God upon its continual use.[6]

However, the report accepted that the reality of Methodist experience was rather different to the ideal expressed above:

> It has indeed been said by some that this vital and essential element of Methodism has lost its former hold upon the attachment of our people. In some parts of the country this is lamentably true. Too many persons attend the Class-meeting very irregularly. In other cases, membership is very lightly estimated, so that absence for any reason during a few weeks leads to a quiet abandonment of it. Often through carelessness, sometimes of set purpose, removal to another place becomes the occasion of ceasing to meet.[7]

The report recognized that these motives were not confined to the last quarter of the nineteenth century, but had an earlier origin. "Complaints of this character are by no means new in Methodism. They are indeed as old as the days of Wesley."[8]

The report also noted that for some time the reality across the connexion had been to allow that non-attendance at a class did not constitute grounds for exclusion from the society. In effect, the system instituted by Wesley was amended to permit a nominal class membership for Methodists who were actively engaged in the life of Methodism, but not the class.[9] This recognition was noted, but it was recommended by the committee that the traditional basis of membership—attendance at class—was to remain.[10]

By the final quarter of the nineteenth century, that which Wesley had responded to publicly and privately was more openly debated. This led the Wesleyans to consider carefully the relationship between class at-

---

6. See the "Report of the Committee On Church-Membership, as Adopted by the Conference of 1889, Having Special Reference to the Class-Meeting," 405–6.

7. Ibid., 406–8.

8. Ibid., 408.

9. See beginning of chapter 7, including footnote 2. Here I show that during Wesley's lifetime there were those who received class tickets and yet did not attend class.

10. See Rack, "The Decline of the Class Meeting," 20. See also "Report of the Committee on Church-Membership, as Adopted by the Conference of 1889, Having Special Reference to the Class-Meeting," 412–13. Those who were not members by class attendance could seek a "special note of admission" or Communicant's Ticket to the Lord's Supper, love feasts, and covenant services.

tendance as the condition of membership and regular attendance at the public preaching with a desire to receive the sacrament without attending a class. Undoubtedly the situation facing the Wesleyan Methodists was different to that of Wesley's era. For Wesley, the Methodist people were subordinate to the Church of England; the later Methodists owed no allegiance to Anglicanism and sought to define their membership status as a church.[11] Whether such status was to remain firmly locked to a revivalist meeting or hold to a moment of public recognition was the issue that exercised the mind of Conference.

The theory of totemism was advanced by Emile Durkheim. His major work *The Elementary Forms of the Religious Life*, exploring totemism was written in 1913. Durkheim viewed all religion as a human construct which existed to understand the human need at the root of the religion or belief system. Religion in Durkheim's opinion was fundamental to the prevailing conditions of civilization, and should be seen by sociologists as a priority in the study of society.[12] Durkheim made no value judgment upon religion, considering no religion to be false. For Durkheim, religion was a distinction between the sacred and the profane:

> The division of the world into two comprehensive domains, one sacred, the other profane, is the hallmark of religious thought; Beliefs, myths, gnomic[13] spirits and legends are either representations or systems of representation that express the nature of sacred things, the virtues and powers attributed to them, their history, their relations with each other and with profane things.[14]

Every society imbues objects with a sacred status, known to the members of that society, with an appropriate manner of approaching and treating those objects. Durkheim assessed the gathering of people around the sacred to be "one single moral community called a Church."[15]

---

11. By the time this report was adopted, Methodism considered itself a church, separate from any other ecclesiastical body. This is shown in the issue of exclusion. See the "Report of the Committee On Church-Membership, as Adopted by the Conference of 1889, Having Special Reference to the Class-Meeting," 409. The report stated "in the independent ecclesiastical position into which Methodism has been led by the Providence of God since the death of Wesley, exclusion from membership in the Class-Meeting involves, for the time being, excommunication from the visible Church."

12. See La Capra, *Emile Durkheim Sociologist and Philosopher*, 246–47.

13. A definition of gnomic can be found in Pearsall, "Gnomic," 606. Gnomic is defined thus, "1. in the form of short, pithy maxims or aphorisms, 2 enigmatic, ambiguous. It is the second of these definitions that is relevant to Durkheim''s description.

14. Durkheim, *The Elementary Forms of the Religious Life*, 36.

15. Ibid., 46. This phrase is drawn from Durkheim's definition of religion.

Durkheim's example of this collective experience rested on primitive Aboriginal Australian society. In indigenous Aboriginal society the use of symbol as a totem is highly developed, and objects which are crafted or painted, or even natural formations, are separated from the profane (world) by a sacred significance. The totem, however, is more than mere symbol for it is recognized by the society and reflects "that group in the religion it creates."[16] From this Durkheim reasserted his view that all religion was a social phenomenon. In addition to the totem, a god or gods are created over time which become representative of the sacred. Allied to the separation of the sacred totem from the profane world and the development of a deistic system is the development of rituals which enhance the "solidarity of the group."[17] These rituals form a regular element of the process of collective belief.

This development of totem, god, and ritual is well described, although unknowingly, in an article in *The Independent* of the 17th September 2004, in a discussion by Anne Penketh of the deific status accorded to Kim Il Sung, President of North Korea until 1994. The article describes how Sung's person has become a totem through the erection of statues and portraits as well as representations of him in murals as the rising sun. This former leader, now a totem to the North Koreans of the embodiment of the state, has recently become godlike as he has been incorporated into a trinity comprising his mother, Kim Jung Sook, and his son, Kim Jong Il, referred to as Juche ("self-reliance").

As part of the respect shown to Kim Il Sung, in a park in Pyongyang, a statue of the president is revered as a totem might be by Aboriginal Australians. "Throngs of young couples made their way to the statue on the way to their weddings."[18] This reverence even extends to folding his image so that no crease falls across the face:

> "You must not fold the Great Leader's face." The stewardess was not joking when she sternly addressed the passenger on the Air Koryo flight out of Pyongyang, as he creased a special issue of a magazine devoted to the achievements of the late leader of North Korea, Kim Il Sung, to place it in his bag.[19]

---

16. Bierstedt, *Émile Durkheim*, 201.
17. See Giddens, *Durkheim*, 95.
18. Penketh, 'God is dead. Long live Kim Il Sung," 32.
19. Penketh, "God is dead. Long live Kim Il Sung," 32.

Rituals have emerged, including the placing of wreaths at the foot of statues to the Great Leader. This chapter outlines the manner in which the class became a totem for the Methodist people, and particularly for John Wesley, and the way in which the interrogative nature of the class became ritualistic.

As totemism is a theme in this chapter, I shall concentrate on the two most relevant points to this book: the class and its activity. Allied to this, however, is the place of the class ticket as a symbol of the totem (class meeting) and indeed perhaps in its own right a totem, allowing as it did entry into the society meeting. There was also ritual associated with the ticket in that the offering or withdrawal of the same afforded either status or exclusion from the intimate meetings of the Methodists. In part I shall use the Minutes of Conference from 1744 to show Wesley's view of the class meeting, and also his writings in which aspects of Methodist organization are defended— among them, the class meeting.

The class was an "accident" of invention, arising out of a suggestion to settle the debt on the building of the New Room in Bristol. Each Methodist was expected under the scheme put forward by Captain Foy to pay one penny per week in order that the building debt could be paid off. Foy, however, offered to have the eleven poorest in his group so that any who could not pay would have their subscription met by him. The society was divided into classes, each with a leader who went from home to home collecting the money.

John Wesley saw the benefit that could be gained in collecting pastoral information on each member, and over time classes began to meet together under the leadership of one of the members, ostensibly to hear personal testimony, regulate wrongdoers and receive new members. Wesley's *Journal* gives the nearest contemporary personal account of the creation of the class System.[20] This account is short and matter-of-fact, simply describing what was agreed. The same system was quickly introduced to the Foundery. In 1786, however, Wesley's recollection of the class meeting's foundation is far more descriptive and offers the reader of *Thoughts upon Methodism* the sense that the class was divinely inspired,[21] and from that inspiration, the class became the most effective long term means of pastoral care and discipline.

---

20. Wesley, *Works [BE]*, Vol. 19, 251.
21. Wesley, *Works [BE]*, Vol. 9, 528–29.

Given the lapse of time between those two accounts, some reflection of the circumstances is to be expected. However, only six years after they began, Wesley wrote of them in a similar manner to his 1786 description. In *A Plain Account*, his open letter to the Reverend Vincent Perronet, Anglican Priest, and Methodist supporter, the rise and development of Methodism to that date is laid out.

Commenting on the rise of the class meeting he wrote: "While we were thinking of quite another thing, we struck upon a method for which we have cause to bless God ever since."[22] Omitting the original purpose of raising monies, Wesley described their purpose, and he wrote of the class as a tool for spiritual growth and discipline. Wesley's account of the class's purpose and rise is glowing.

Allowing that the open letter to Perronet was a form of propaganda for the Methodist cause, it remains obvious that Wesley is imbuing the class meeting *per se* with a degree of importance that he does not attach to any other aspect of Methodism. Indeed he described the class as a "prudential means of grace," that is, a method of Christian growth and improvement that was not "instituted," such as prayer or communion. This term was allowed of the classes in the *Large Minutes* and Wesley exhorted every Methodist not to miss the class meeting.

Wesley was careful to outline and refute the arguments raised against the class meeting, ranging from being a new meeting imposed upon the people, to a lack of leaders to run the classes.[23] It is impressive that Wesley has such an ability to handle opposition in relation to the class. Perhaps from the outset, Wesley's opinion of the class was such that his refutation of the objections raised meant he could not recognize the usefulness and vitality of the class would not stand the test of time.

The class fulfilled a number of tasks in a small and close meeting that did indeed enable it to be a crown to a new and emerging movement. That said, however, for Wesley the class quickly became an immutable and unchanging element of Methodist organization that he believed would give everyone the same experience of awakening, conversion, and potentially sanctification. His letter to Vincent Perronet shows this belief:

> It can scarce be conceived what advantages have been reaped from this little prudential regulation. Many now happily experienced that Christian fellowship of which they had not so much

---

22. Ibid., 260.
23. Ibid., 262–64.

as an idea before. They began to "bear one another's burdens," and "naturally" to "care for each other." As they had daily a more intimate acquaintance with, so they had a more endeared affection for each other.[24]

If that is indeed the case, within 25 years others did not find the class as attractive a meeting. Bearing in mind that class attendance was compulsory, William Holder, a class leader, wrote in his diary more than once that attendance at meetings was poor. By 1764 Wesley was himself writing that those who failed to attend their class three times should be removed from membership.[25] Samuel Bradburn also noted that Methodists did not meet in class when there was no profit to meeting.[26]

The Methodist Conference first met in 1744, and from that meeting onwards, minutes were kept of issues discussed, decisions made and appointments ratified. To all intents and purposes Conference during Wesley's life was a body that met to hear Wesley's opinions, and as Methodism grew, to undertake matters of organizational necessity such as the stationing of assistants.

Wesley's portrayal of the class in Methodism in the Conference *Minutes* is strikingly different from that in his *Journal*, letters or other writings. In Conference, the class is an element of the total organization. In 1744, the class did not merit mention when the structure of Methodism was reported, showing only "the United Societies, the bands, the Select Societies, and the Penitents."[27] If at that point of the class's existence, Wesley was still formulating the later important role the class would take on this is not too strange an omission.

The assistants were permitted to visit the classes monthly if they were stationed away from London or Bristol, where John or Charles Wesley undertook visitation. Their function was formally to receive members on trial for the bands and classes. As early as 1753 Conference laid down clear guidance to those responsible for admission to the society. The extract below shows the manner in which prospective Methodists were to be "screened" prior to full admission into the society:

24. Ibid., 262.
25. Wesley, *Letters [SE]*, Vol. IV, 273.
26. Bradburn, *A Memorandum Book, volume 1*, entry for December 1786. MA 1977/296.
27. Publications of the Wesley Historical Society, *John Bennet's Copy of the Minutes of the Conferences of 1744, 1745, 1747 and 1748; with Wesley's Copy for those for 1746*, 14.

> Q.14. How shall we prevent improper persons from insinuating into the Society?
> A. (1.) Give tickets to none till they are recommended by a Leader, with whom they have met at least two months on trial.
> (2.) Give notes to none but those who are recommended by one you know, or till they have met three or four times in a class.
> (3.) Give them the Rules the first time they meet. See that this be never neglected.[28]

Although there is no record of why this decision was taken, the inference is that men and women who were not serious in joining a society, which meant entering into the life of a class, were seeking admission and either failing to attend class or reorientate their lives. Prior to this Conference decision, admission was regulated solely by the *Band Rules*, the *General Rules* and from December 1744 the *Directions given to the Band Societies*.[29] These written regulations detailed the behavior, dress, and spiritual growth expected from each new society member on entry into a class or band on trial. Wesley insisted through Conference that his *Thoughts upon Dress* should be read to each society, and class members were urged to dress modestly. Failure to do so could lead to expulsion. Wesley directed that the assistants, a group of trusted men who increasingly took an *Episkope* role within the emerging circuits should be the class visitor, responsible for regulating them and deciding who should receive tickets and who should be excluded from the society. The helpers, a group of men subordinate to the assistants, took responsibility for meeting weekly with the class leaders.

Throughout Wesley's life, the classes functioned with varying degrees of success. It is likely that the classes remained active because of the insistence from Wesley that entry to the society could only be effected as a class member. By 1786, however, Conference was appealing to the societies to revive the bands and select bands as these had fallen into neglect.[30] Had the class not been so closely allied to the society at an early point, as the necessary condition of membership, it too might have been on this list in 1786.

---

28. Wesley, *The Minutes of The Methodist Conferences from the First*, volume 1, 478. The *Large Minutes* from which this is reproduced first appeared in 1753.

29. For these three documents see chapter 8, Appendices 10, 11 and 12.

30. Wesleyan Methodist Conference, *The Minutes of some late Conversations Between the Rev Messrs. Wesley and Others*, 22.

These two strands effectively created the totem of the class meeting. On the one hand, Wesley's polemic created an element of the organization that was "prudential," indeed divinely inspired, and this was enhanced by its becoming a mandatory aspect of belonging to the Methodists. On the other hand, the decisions made in Conference actively directed the work of the class meeting as a life changing experience, both spiritually, and socially, through dress and manner. These decisions were reinforced by the publication of specific directions or rules that could be enforced by class leaders.

Wesley also published for the Methodists, *The Character of a Methodist*,[31] and *The Principles of a Methodist*,[32] both published in 1742, set out how a Methodist behaved on the path to perfection, and what a Methodist believed. The latter tract was written to refute anti-Methodist polemic.

According to Hempton, Wesley's publishing enterprise was "one of the most striking features of Methodism . . . Wesley tried to secure control over the discourse of the movement . . . He edited hymnbooks, published tracts, and distributed a connectional magazine."[33] In chapter 8 I shall offer more detail about the use of publications as a means to encourage Methodists to rediscover their early class meeting heritage.

These tracts idealized Methodism to her own people, and are reminiscent of another of Durkheim's concepts: the idealization of religion. This supports the theory of totemism by creating the ideal toward which all should strive. Wesley set before his people the ideal of what a Methodist should experience and how a Methodist should behave. For Durkheim idealization was inevitable. He argued that to sustain the required intensity to create the ideal, individuals had to be brought together in "sufficient concentration."[34] This concentration then enabled "an exaltation of moral life that is expressed by a set of ideal conceptions in which the new life thus awakened is portrayed."[35]

As idealization was unavoidable, Durkheim stated that humankind added the ideal to the reality. John Wesley did this through his writing, both for Methodism's supporters and opponents. Durkheim writes:

31. Wesley, *Works [BE]*, Vol. 9, 31–46.
32. Wesley, *Works [BE]*, Vol. 9, 47–66.
33. Hempton, *Methodism*, 58.
34. Durkheim, *The Elementary Forms of the Religious Life*, 317.
35. Ibid.

> We have seen that when collective life reaches a certain degree of intensity it awakens religious thought, because it determines a state of effervescence that changes the conditions of psychic activity... Man does not recognize himself; he feels he is transformed, and so he transforms his surroundings. To account for the very specific impressions he feels, he endows things with which he is mostly in contact with properties that they do not have, exceptional powers, virtues that the objects of ordinary experience do not possess. In a word, on the real world in which his profane life unfolds he superimposes another one that, in a sense exists only in his thought, but to which he ascribes a kind of higher dignity in relation to the first.[36]

Through his publications, letters, and Conference decisions, Wesley created an idealized "world" for the Methodist people, accessed not through a large society meeting, but a smaller, more intimate class meeting. This idealized understanding of conversion, faith development and the reorienting of life came through Wesley's long journey to faith up to his moment of the warned heart in 1738, and the almost tortured manner in which he finally came to an evangelical "conversion" state on May 24th 1738. Wesley searched for a meaningful experience of faith from his university days, even traveling to America to find "primitive Christianity"; yet until his meeting with the Moravians and the beginning of the Fetter Lane meeting, every effort seemed vain.

The class meeting was a totem, because Wesley's own "warmed heart" experience was in a small group, and when the opportunity came along for a group meeting that was pastoral and educational as well as a catalyst to conversion and sanctification, it was hard for Wesley to admit that the class meeting could outlive its usefulness, and might need to be replaced or supplemented by other organizations.

This can in part be understood by standing Durkheim's writing on idealization alongside totemism. The class meeting was a totem for Wesley of all that Methodism embodied: its social conscience, its moral reorientation, its religious development, and its personal and corporate discipline. It is not, therefore, strange to see how the class was also an "ideal" or perfect form of Methodism. Here Wesley created his ideal, recognizing the reality of life, but wanting through the class to offer Methodists an ideal superimposed on society.

---

36. Durkheim, *The Elementary Forms of the Religious Life*, 37.

But this idealized understanding of what happens within a small group also stretches back to Wesley's reading and his personal experience. His early and influential reading included the life of the Marquis de Renty. Wesley began abridging de Renty's biography (written by Saint-Jure) on the journey back from Georgia in 1738. De Renty's small group structure, the *Company of the Holy Sacrament*, was a model for Wesley in its aim of personal Christian development, philanthropic life, and mystical union with God. It is not hard to see how even as a concept the small group was idealized by Wesley. Although the class did not hold perfection as its imperative, it was nonetheless the place in which awakening could lead to justification, and the deepening Christian life shared amongst peers.

On a practical level, Wesley had personal experiences of small group meetings. The small, earnest Holy Club, which met regularly, prayed, talked, and engaged in practical piety, was an embryonic form of the class. His first attempt at a "class" in Georgia was modeled on the lines of his reading and early experience, but it was his subsequent experience with the Moravians, and their regular small band meetings, disciplined and lay led, that laid the final foundation for the Methodist class. The class was idealized by John Wesley because of the influence that small groups had in his Christian formation. It is not surprising that this led to the conception by him of the class as a totem of all that it had done for him, and as he understood it would do for others.

John Wesley understood the class to be a microcosm of a really Christian society, and therefore worthy of totemic status. As previously discussed, gathering individuals who share common aims and ideals, leads to an homogenous group. This creates a "them and us" mindset, in which the homogenous unit is separate *from* and different *to* those outside the unit. In Wesley's idealized and totemic understanding of the class the "us" of the homogenous unit were expressing what it meant to *be* a Methodist within the class meeting. Those outside the unit might be influenced by the change that belonging to a class had made to friends, relatives, and co-workers and want to join and share in the same experience.

However, unless those beyond the homogenous unit entered the unit (the class) by the same experiential method (the process of conviction of sin and conversion) the class would be changed from its original purpose. The class functioned successfully only when every member shared not only common aims and ideals, but had undergone the same initiation that led to the common cause expressed through membership of the class; the path of discipleship and potentially perfection.

Thus far, I have focused on Wesley's personal view of the class meeting, and the importance he attached to it and attendance at it. As I have previously indicated, there is little evidence for the opinions of the people who became Methodists. Primarily, the available views were written by class leaders, who possessed a degree of literacy. Their vocabulary is limited and it is difficult to fully ascertain what feeling or attachment to the class lies behind a single word or phrase.

Bennet Dugdale refers to feeling that meeting his class could be a "great cross"[37] or by contrast a "sweet season."[38] Dugdale also met with a class member who had "stayed away a few times and then was ashamed to come."[39] Samuel Bradburn is scathing after his three days of meeting the classes attached to City Road Chapel, "Regulating the Classes, which I seriously think is mere loss of time, as people will not meet but where they profit. Why should they?"[40] John Goodfellow found in July 1786 that he was hindered from meeting his class, and in the August discovered that many of his class had resolved to cease meeting: "I met a few of my Class in the evening, but Oh how lifeless & cold do they seem! Many of them that used to meet do not intend coming any more."[41] Samuel Bradburn commented in his diary in 1780 that many of the people in his Bradford circuit were loving, but that "the generality of the hearers, as well as others, and too many of the Society are much more affected by the world than they are by religion."[42] While Bradburn does not refer directly to the classes which he led, or which were in his society, his entry suggests that for some of those attached to the society, the classes aims of reorienting life and offering mutual discipleship were not effective.

---

37. Dugdale, *The Diary of Bennet Dugdale*, entry for 13th August 1786. MA 1977/216.

38. Ibid., entry for 25th September 1786. MA 1977/216.

39. Ibid., entry for 16th May 1786. MA 1977/216.

40. Bradburn, *A Memorandum Book, volume 1*, entry for December 1786. He met the classes over three days from the 7th to 9th December. MA 1977/296.

41. Goodfellow, *the Diary of John Goodfellow*, entry for 2nd August 1786. MA 1977/236.

42. Bradburn, *A Memorandum Book, volme 1*, entry for November 1780. MA 1977/296.

John Goodfellow first met with the Methodists in 1783, and received assurance on the 10th April 1784, characteristically while at the sacrament. Unusually, he was not invited to join a class until after his conversion. "I had not yet joined the society, or been at a class-meeting, but having been pressed by Letter and otherwise: I now went."[43] Goodfellow's diary begins with a retrospective of his life from his birth in 1755. This element of his diary is not written by dated daily entry, but as a continuous record of his life, with the date of his conversion included. Within this element of the diary is the undated entry below, added after the account of conversion and joining the Methodists. This is followed by a daily diary. This fits into the accepted model of journaling of the period. Bruce Hindmarsh has indicated how personal biographies were written in *The Evangelical Conversion Narrative*.[44] Goodfellow's account of the usefulness of the class stands as a testament to the totem:

> I found likewise that my soul was constantly in need of spiritual food, and that for want of using this means, I had hitherto been ignorant of the devices of the Devil, and easily drawn aside by temptation, which I was after this more aware of, and by looking to Jesus at the first approach of the enemy, I was kept from the snare and enabled to overcome: upon the whole I think this to be the most useful means (except preaching) that we (Methodists) enjoy: it is instructive; it unites together; it stirs us up to press forward; the enemy's schemes are brought to light and defeated; and our souls in general, abundantly comforted, and strengthened.[45]

John Goodfellow related both the class, and preaching as "means." If this entry was written in 1784, then Goodfellow is using language to describe an aspect of Methodism with which he had become familiar

---

43. Holder, *The Diary of William Holder*, entry around August or September 1784. MA 1977/238.

44. See Hindmarsh, *The Evangelical Conversion Narrative*, 83–86. In his discussion of Joseph Humphries conversion narrative, Hindmarsh shows how this early Methodist convert wrote of his awakening, conversion and justification. Humphries later became a Dissenting minister, and eventually an Anglican clergyman. See also 226 and 228. Here Hindmarsh offers his view of John Pawson's narrative autobiography, written with the benefit of a long retrospective review. On 228 Hindmarsh notes that Pawson's autobiography was the 'syntax of a retrospective consciousness, and it differs markedly from the punctual identity of the lay converts in the 1740s or the serial identity of the Methodist leaders who continued to publish and revise their journals over time.'

45. Goodfellow, *The Diary of John Goodfellow*, entry after April 1784, otherwise undated. MA 1977/236.

only after April 1784. This language would have come from reading, or hearing others describe the class, the preaching and other aspects of Methodist organization. If he maintained a daily record which he later wrote up into the surviving diary, he may have written the entry at a later point in his life than 1784.[46] However, as I have indicated above, he also wrote of his distraction while attending a class,[47] and within two years, he wrote despairingly of leading classes. John Valton wrote about the class in his diary in a similar manner to Goodfellow in June 1765. He had been with the Methodists for more than a year, and had already noted on two occasions that his experience of class was difficult.[48] However, on the 26th June he wrote, "O what blessings these are, hearing the word of God expounded, meeting class and Band, and Christian Fellowship."[49]

For both Goodfellow and Valton, the reality class experience is at variance with the entries relating the benefits of the class meeting. These entries then have a totemic feel to them, drawing on their place within the Methodist system as a means of grace.

The totemic nature of the class was no doubt aided by the ridicule of former friends and neighbors. Elizabeth Collett faced derision. "Being the only young person then in those parts, who manifested any concern for eternal things, she was subject to much reproach and ridicule, from her ungodly neighbours: but the benefit and comfort she derived from communion with the people of God, far outweighed her toil and suffering."[50] John Oliver faced a similar trial from his father, who was violent toward him.[51] Mary Bosanquet, who later married John Fletcher, was put out of her family at 21,[52] and William Green made the choice to forsake his friends after joining a class.[53]

---

46. Again Hindmarsh is helpful here. In writing of the early Methodist testimonial writers, he notes that what was heard and experienced within a community offered a "sense of narrative convention." See Hindmarsh, *The Evangelical Conversion Narrative*, 157.

47. Goodfellow, *The Diary of John Goodfellow*, entry for 28th September 1784. MA 1977/236.

48. Valton, *The Christian Experience of the Late Rev. John Valton*, volume 1, 130–1. (25th September 1764.) Volume II, 66–67. (20th May 1765.) MA 1977/293.

49. Valton, *The Christian Experience of the Late Rev. John Valton*, volume II, 79. (26th June 1765.) MA 1977/293.

50. Taft, *Biographical Sketches*, volume II, 121.

51. Oliver, "The Life of John Oliver," 418–22.

52. Taft, *Biographical Sketches*, Vol. I, 19.

53. Green, "An Account of the life of Mr William Green," 252.

Itinerant preachers were also badly treated, no doubt adding to the sense of "us and them" which arises through homogeneity. Thomas Hanby's *Life* relates the following treatment being meted out to the preachers: "(they) often preached to us while the blood run down their faces, by the blows and pointed arrows thrown at them, while they were preaching."[54] Wesley himself was subject to similar treatment: "Soon after you, Sir, paid us a visit, but we were interrupted by the fire-engine being played on the audience."[55]

Added to personal experience, poor treatment from neighbors and families, and the sense of being "different" through adhering to the Methodist cause, is the singular experience of *joining* a class. Whether an individual became a class leader, local preacher, or assistant, each personal account has a common thread, namely an ecstatic or experiential awakening and conversion that gave to each class member a shared foundation on which to build a Christian, discipled, accountable, and disciplined life.

Robert Wilkinson joined the Methodists in 1767, and was admitted to a class. His spiritual state was disturbed, but in the class he was able to discuss this, and found encouragment. Eventually he was converted, but it was his spiritual trials and ecstasies that lent the class a special importance.[56] W. Ferguson also found the class vital to his Christian journey. He was from a Scottish Presbyterian background and wanted to join a class to testify of the work of God in his life. At Whitfield's Tabernacle he asked two leaders whether he might join a class:

> I went into the Vestry and two Gentlemen I found there, "I should be glad to meet in a Class, that I may speak my experience, and tell of the work of God which I have found upon my heart." One of them said, "What Class shall we put him into?" The other answered, "Indeed I cannot tell, Mr. Wesley's Classes are far more strictly looked after than ours." If you please then, said I, I will go and meet in one of his Classes. He looked at me and said, "Really young man, I cannot blame you."[57]

The ecstatic conversion is related in a number of the testimonials and biographies and these experiences no doubt colored the understand-

54. Hanby, "The Life of Thomas Hanby," 511.
55. Hanby, "The Life of Thomas Hanby," 511.
56. Wilkinson, "A Short Account of Mr. Robert Wilkinson," 181–82.
57. Ferguson, "An Account of the life of Mr W. Ferguson," 296–97.

ing and aided the journey of other members. Ann Gilbert's exhorting in class had a profound effect on the membership:

> I admonished the young people, and while I was speaking to them was so filled with peace and love of God, that I could not but exhort and entreat them to repent. Presently their laughter was turned to weeping, and one person who had been a backslider for twenty-three years, cried aloud for the disquietude of her soul, and the Lord healed her wounded mind before the conclusion of the meeting.[58]

This would surely have had a profound effect on all present. For those whose faith was rekindled (especially the backslider) and those who were rebuked, shared intimate moments gave mutual purpose, setting them apart from any who had not been party to the meeting, and preventing any new attendees from fully sharing in the mutuality of the group's experience. Perhaps, from that moment, to the members, that class became a totem of God's work amongst them.

Here, then, is the totemic theme outlined in this chapter found in the practice and ideals of the Methodist people and John Wesley. The totem that the class became was linked to the idealization process that meant that for each class member who had undergone the same or at least similar entry process into a class meeting, an ideal was created that could not be diluted or altered without irrevocably changing the very nature of the class itself.

Allied to this is the process of homogenization. When linked with the idealization process, the members of the class share more than a common interest; they are joined together in a shared, experiential group that demands much in terms of time, personal development, public accountability, and social behavior. All of these characteristics were regulated by rules.[59]

With John Wesley's continual insistence on the value of the class meeting, and the unquestionable value that the meeting had for the early Methodists, especially when a society was recently formed and local opposition was at its height, the class attained a sacred status that developed into a totem.

---

58. Taft, *Biographical Sketches, volume I*, 49.

59. Appendix 10 expresses this admirably, but the same close observance to regulation can be found in Appendices 11 and 12.

Throughout Wesley's life, the class meeting stood as the portal for an experiential change of every aspect of individual life. As discussed in chapter 5, the class was the crown of Methodism, because it offered so much to men and women who previously found themselves excluded from an affective Christian life.[60]

In opposition to that is the cross that the class became, and that is seen not only in routinization, but also in totemism. Having used Durkheim's theory as a theme, I have shown how the class fossilized into a totem as it was unable to change from its useful fundamental purpose at the point of creation of a new society, or at a time when a society was under crisis, such as that described in chapter 6 when Calvinist preachers threatened the viability of the Methodist society.

Totemism occurred when for Wesley, and for other Methodists, the class became idealized. The Methodist people came to believe the class was sacred and rather like the North Koreans, who are now urged to give totemic status to the *Great Leader* and imbue his image with meaning, so the Methodist people attached significance to what it meant to be a class member. Just as for the indigenous people of Australia who imbue significant meaning to the natural world, and worship it, so the Methodists came to hold that the class was a significant step in the journey of faith because of the testimonial, biographical, and sometimes idealized accounts of belonging to a class.

In the following chapter, I shall consider the class meeting as a model useful to only one generation of Methodists. Here elements of routinization, totemism, and homogeneity will surface. I will show that the model of class which became fixed under totemism was not helpful to a generation of Methodists who grew up within the Methodist society from childhood.

The classic rule for entry to the class was a desire to flee from the wrath to come. Such a rule has authority only for those who sense a need to flee. Later generations of Methodists joined not because there was a present sense of wrath from which there was a need to flee, but because the Methodists became respectable, contributing members of society who were no longer ridiculed, and needed to gather into the class to share the week's burdens and receive comfort and encouragement.

---

60. This level of exclusion, affects those for whom the "middle level" needs of life are not met. These needs are present and may be subject to crises. Within this level, folk religion operates. See Hunter, *The Celtic Way of Evangelism*, 30–32.

Although beyond the conclusion date of this book, a fair example of the acceptance of Methodists in English life can be seen in the employment by Sir Robert Peel Sr. who "boasted that he left his mills in the hands of Methodists and they served him 'excellently well' . . . the Methodist virtues of honesty, sobriety and discipline . . . Made for success in business."[61]

The "one generational" model then is a method of reviewing the early years of Wesley's Methodism, prior to his death, in which the Methodist people traveled a road that did not have the same starting point, nor was co-terminous with Wesley himself.

---

61. Turner, *John Wesley. The Evangelical Revival and the Rise of Methodism in England*, 140.

8

The One-Generational Meeting

THE CLASS MEETING UNDERWENT significant changes in its core functions within a relatively short period of time. Certainly, prior to Wesley's death in 1791, the class meeting had evolved from the first small group meeting in Bristol. Routinization led the class into a settled and ongoing life without the dynamic drive which initially gave it impetus. Over time, organization replaced charisma. The larger society took precedence over the smaller class. The society's aim, to hear preaching and exhortation, to pray and to sing communally, and represent the whole gathering of the people called Methodists, became the primary meeting, removing the pre-eminence of the class. Totemism, on the other hand, brought to the class a sacred status that tied members to the small group, despite the membership's unease with its function. Class membership offered entry to the society. In effect, there was no such thing as "society membership."

This is challenged by Henry Durbin's letter to Charles Wesley of 15th October 1784. Durbin, a trustee of the New Room, was placed on trial within the society during wrangling over amendment of the Bristol New Room Model Trust Deed. Durbin is complaining about John Wesley's actions. Intriguingly, he suggests that class membership was not compulsory, and that this had been agreed by Wesley himself:

> He said I had not been in the Society for some time, as I had not met a class, but he forgot, that about three years ago he declared . . . that any serious person might have a ticket & meet in the society without meeting a class & I have always had a ticket.[1]

---

1. Lloyd, "Charles Wesley. A New Evaluation of his Life and Ministry," 273. From *Letters Chiefly to the Wesley's*, 2:73 MCA. See also Baker, *John Wesley and the Church of England*, 223. Baker asserts that Wesley sent Dr. Thomas Coke to act on his behalf in arranging the settlement of the Model Trust Deed.

This is not the norm; rather it is the exception that proves the rule.[2] Evidence points directly at a keen insistence on class membership and attendance. I would suggest that Durbin was a wealthy benefactor to the New Room, and that Wesley may have been more relaxed in applying the rules with him until such time as he wanted the Model Trust amended.

Together, routinization and totemism led to the subject of this chapter. Every class had within itself the ability to survive for one generation alone. Second or third generations, perhaps the children of the first generation, or people drawn to Methodism as it became more acceptable in society, did not have the enthusiastic experience of awakening and conversion, or desire to pursue the journey to entire sanctification through such experience. This does not mean that the pursuit of holiness was lost; rather that such pursuit was drawn into the society. The function of the class was relegated to the role of gateway to the larger meeting.

In 1783, Wesley published his sermon *On Family Religion*.[3] In the sermon, as he addressed the responsibilities of parents toward family and servants, Wesley considered the possible results of resolving to serve God. As he considered the positive consequences, he also gave voice to the possibilities of neglecting family religion. In his opinion, such negation would lead to revival dying away. Wesley quoted Cicero: "will it not be as the historian speaks of the Roman state in its infancy, *Res unius ætatis?* An event that has its beginning and end within the space of one generation?"[4] Wesley continued by stating that the Methodist revival had survived longer than a generation of 30 years, which according to Luther was the period in which a revival lasted.[5]

---

2. See also Mather, "The Life of Alexander Mather," 230. J Wood, in an addendum to Mather's autobiography noted that he regulated a situation in London in which two members held tickets, without attending a class.

3. Wesley, *Works [BE]*, Vol. 3, 334–36.

4. Ibid., 335.

5. Ibid. The editorial introductory comments to the sermon state that Wesley recognised that Methodism had lasted longer than a single generation and that the future lay with those who were a new generation in the organisation. "Wesley was aware that the Methodist Revival had already outlasted the normal life span of such movements, and that its future depended quite crucially on 'family religion,' " "the education of children," "obedience to parents," "obedience to pastors," etc. Hence the sequence of Nos. 94–97." See Wesley, *Works [BE]*, Vol. 3, 333.

As Wesley dated the Wesleyan revival's beginning to 1729,[6] he could properly point to a period longer than one single generation. Using Wesley's idiosyncratic dating for the commencement of the revival, this had indeed lasted 54 years. If 1740 were taken as the revival's start (the point at which John and Charles Wesley separated from the Fetter Lane Society), the revival had lasted 43 years.

However, the quote which Wesley used within this sermon was initially made to the Methodists in Conference in 1768, giving a revival period of either 39 or 28 years, dependent on which year is used for the origin of the revival.

At the Conference of 1768, the question was asked "Q. 23. In many places the work of God seems to stand still."[7] In twelve numbered paragraphs in reply, Wesley outlined methods in which the revival could be given fresh impetus. The tenth paragraph read, "But what shall we do for the rising generation? Unless we take care of this, the present revival will be *res unius ætatis*; it will last only the age of a man."[8] His five numbered subparagraphs under this question state:

1. Where there are ten Children in a Society, meet them at least an hour every week:
2. Talk with them every time you see any at home.
3. Pray in earnest for them:
4. Diligently instruct and vehemently exhort all Parents at their own houses:
5. Preach expressly on Education, particularly when you speak of *Kingswood*.[9]

In this Wesley was showing concern for those who were entering Methodism as a second generation, and whose experience of it had not been that of the previous age, but were children of an earlier generation of Methodists. These exhortations to the preachers are an advice to catechize and teach the children and parents of a settled Methodism.

---

6. Wesley, *Works [BE]*, Vol. 3, 335.
7. Wesley, *Minutes of The Methodist Conferences from the First, volume I*, 79.
8. Ibid., 82.
9. Ibid.

Ernst Troeltsch described three types of Christian gathering, in which it is possible to clearly identify Methodism's development. Troeltsch, writing in the early years of the twentieth century, held that after the death and resurrection of Christ, fledgling Christian communities needed organization. "From the very beginning there appeared the three main types of the sociological development of Christian thought: The Church, the sect, and mysticism."[10]

Troeltsch described the life of each: essentially church is an institution, sect is a voluntary society and mysticism is a "world of ideas."[11] Early Methodism fitted the description of mysticism and sect. The first years of Methodism do not sit with Troeltsch's description of church as an institution. In this chapter, the short useful life span of the class meeting of one generation will show that the mystical aspirations of generation one were short-lived, as a desire for acceptance and respectability led to the institutionalization of the movement by generation two even prior to the creation of the church as an institution within Troeltsch's definition.

Ernst Troelstch and John Kent are used to describe in sociological terms what I am asserting happened within Methodism, and more pertinently, within the class meeting's life. The move from mystical group to sect was a change that saw the Methodist movement settle into an organization which no longer drew upon the immediacy or experientialism of the early period, preferring to observe the characteristics of the sect. I will show later that Wesley himself understood Methodism as primitive religion, a primary aspect in Troeltsch's model of the sect type. In describing the elements of the sect, Troeltsch concludes that "an Appeal to the New Testament and to the Primitive Church"[12] rank among the key features.

While Troeltsch does not mention Methodism (which Kent helpfully concentrates on) writing primarily on the development of Protestantism in the milieu of medieval Catholicism, he asserts that in the Reformation the church/sect issue was always under the surface for the reformers and the organizations they created. To this, Methodism can relate. Wesley

---

10. Birnbaum and Lenzer, *Sociology and Religion: A Book of Readings*, 310. See also Turner, *Conflict and Reconciliation*, 58–59. Turner offers a brief discussion of the sect/church model

11. N. Birnbaum, & G. Lenzer, (eds.), *Sociology and Religion*, 310.

12. Troeltsch, *The Social Teaching of the Christian Churches*, 336.

began a movement that was deeply rooted in the mystical tradition, and the class was central to this. He oversaw Methodism's development into the "sect type," referring for its authority to the primitive church, and sitting uneasily with the state Church.

A simple yet telling definition of both these types can be found in Troeltsch's *Religion in History*. Mystical religion is defined by Troeltsch thus: "mysticism aims at the immediate, present, and inward quality of the religious experience, and the immediate relationship with God that leaps over or complements traditions, cults, and institutions . . . mysticism is concerned strictly with the immediacy of the union with God."[13] Troeltsch defined the purpose of the sect as a community which "seeks to gather mature and personally convinced Christians into a holy community that regards the preaching of the gospel, the sacraments, and the institutional community merely as a means for the implanting and fostering of the religious life, with no miraculous power independent of the subject and subjective achievement."[14]

John Kent's recent book, *Wesley and the Wesleyans*[15] sets Methodism into two distinct periods: primary and secondary. The primary phase lasted from the earliest period into the 1760s. The secondary phase began from the 1760s. Kent sets Troeltsch's theory into the reality of the Methodist movement and organization. In the early, primary period, ecstasy was a common, if not expected experience. In the secondary, "sect phase" the organization of Methodism took precedence over the experiential development of the individual in favor of a more routine journey toward holiness within the context of the organization. Although John

---

13. Troeltsch, *Religion in History*, 326–27.

14. Ibid., 325. Through the writing of H. Richard Niebuhr, this definition has become tendentious. In *Christ and Culture*, Neibuhr postulated that Christianity and culture have become synonymous, and start out to elucidate the manner in which theologians have sought to understand the relationship of Christ to culture. Quoting Troeltsch, Niebuhr wrote "Christianity and Western civilisations are so inextricably intertwined that a Christian can say little about his faith to members of other civilisations, and the latter in turn cannot encounter Christ save as a member of the western world." See Niebuhr, *Christ and Culture*, 30. Neibuhr continued in the chapter "Christ and Culture in Paradox," 149–89, that Troeltsch's "version of the claims of Christ was more akin to the cultural Christian interpretation of the New Testament prevalent in his day than to a more literal and radical teaching of the gospels." Niebuhr, *Christ and Culture*, 183.

15. Kent, *Wesley and the Wesleyans*. Kent uses the themes of primary and secondary religion effectively in his discussion of "Women in Wesleyanism," 104–39.

Kent does not refer to Troeltsch in his model, the parallels are clear and helpfully set in the context of Methodism.

Kent does not continue with his terminology of Methodism's development beyond the secondary stage. However, to extrapolate Kent's model, "the church" would be "Tertiary Religion." This phase of Methodism might be set at the point of Wesleyan Methodism's life when class attendance was divorced from society membership in the later part of the nineteenth century. Troeltsch argued that the church as institution occurred when the church itself mediated salvation, and removed the emphasis on perfection. At this point the church can compromise with society, and recognize those structures that are not Christian, but might be useful for the organization of a sinful world.[16] Methodism's involvement in social issues and political life in the later nineteenth century, the period of "the Non Conformist Conscience," indicates that this step was taken by a more confident church.

The one-generational model can be seen through the work of Mary Fletcher, the wife of the Reverend John William Fletcher, "Fletcher of Madeley." He was an Anglican priest and Swiss national, and a close ally of the Wesley's, and, until his death in 1785, was suggested as a possible successor to John Wesley in the Methodist leadership. Although he has always been linked to Madeley, his only parish, owing to his health, his work in the parish was limited, with considerable time spent in Switzerland, and other parts of England. He was also President of Lady Huntingdon's Trevecka College from 1768 to 1770.

Mary Fletcher, born Mary Bosanquet, became actively involved in Methodism during the London revival of 1761. She founded a community in London with two other women and felt called to preach. The community moved to Leeds in 1768, and in 1781 she married Fletcher.[17] After her husband's death, Mary Fletcher remained in Madeley, with her companion, Mary Tooth, joining in the work amongst the societies and classes.

While catechizing prospective members of the Anglican Church was a common practice at this period, Mary Fletcher was not using the catechetical approach to that end. Her meetings were class meetings, and from a letter printed in her biography, she evinced her Christian life

---

16. Troeltsch, *Religion in History*, 324–25.

17. See Streiff, *Reluctant Saint? A Theological Biography of Fletcher of Madeley*, 265–70.

from the age of 18 within a Methodist context, and in Madeley, describes her leadership of meetings in "my own preaching room, where the congregation increases, and many come from far, and I am, through mercy, at present carried through six or seven meetings in a week."[18]

To a degree the Madeley societies witnessed an unusual conflation of Methodist and Anglican practices. Fletcher maintained a somewhat sketchy parish ministry and had oversight of several local societies from his marriage to his death. Mary Fletcher[19] and Mary Tooth, who wrote the catechetical material, were using it in classes. Both women continued until Mary Fletcher's death in 1815, after which Mary Tooth worked alone.

Amongst the Madeley Society Records are handwritten notes of questions and answers used within class meetings. These notes appear to form a catechumen for the correct manner of Christian living. Unlike the class in its "classic form" which consisted of open questioning and response from the class leader, in the Madeley Society, the leader had a set series of questions which required a specific answer:

> Q Can you tell me who made you?
> A The great God who made all things
> Q Why did God make you?
> A That I might know love and serve him here and being with him forever
> Q What doth God do for you?
> A He keeps me from evil and is always doing me good.[20]

Mary Tooth created a series of catechumenate questions that were sufficient to cover 124 nights of class meetings. Her questions take the catechumen through Scripture from Genesis onwards:

> Night the 7th
> Q Where did we leave off?
> A At the command given to Abram
> Q What did abram do in consequence of it?
> A He left his country directly
> Q How old was Abram? A 75
> What is meant by the souls they had gotten in Haran?

---

18. Taft, *Biographical Sketches*, volume I, 19.

19. For an overview of Female public ministry see Lloyd, "Repression and Resistance: Wesleyan Female Public Ministry in the generation after 1791," 101–14.

20. Madeley Society Business, *Fletcher Tooth Collection*. MA Fl 38.9.

> A Those whom he had persuaded to worship God
> Q Liberty from what?
> A From the Guilt of sin, the Power of sin and the nature of sin.[21]

There is also a set of papers specifically intended for a children's class meeting, "Also the Monday night meeting used for the children in papers of 20 each beginning at Gen 1."[22]

By the latter part of the eighteenth century, in a settled society in Madeley, organized, and overseen by a close Wesleyan supporter, the class was not functioning as it had done in the early period, or indeed, as Wesley frequently reminded the Methodist people it should. These catechumenate classes related more closely to secondary religion or the sect type.

In both Troeltsch's and Kent's models, the emphasis moved from experience to knowledge. In this model holiness can be found through settled Christian growth as a learning process rather than by virtue of a shared experiential life. The highly experiential and "sense of union with God" frequently felt and subsequently described by the first Methodists were unwittingly mystical. The later Methodists sought a more settled and learned community in which to practice a faith.

A parallel will assist in understanding this "settlement phenomena." In *A Little Heaven Below*, Lester Ruth describes the highly charged and experiential love feasts of early American Methodism. Love feasts included testimonial, encouraging others to express "the message of experimental religion."[23] As love feasts were private, those who did not possess the correct ticket of entry would not gain entrance. This made belonging more precious to members, and something to be attained by non-members. Once the American Methodists settled their organization, love feasts like other aspects of the organization became a routine part of Methodist life and no longer had such a valuable purpose.

Essentially second generation Methodists who did not understand the experimental/experiential nature of the previous generation saw little value in belonging. Love feasts, like societies and classes, became part of the organization and not a place in which to share testimony as openly. This is shown by Ruth as he describes testimonies that are anything but experiential:

21. Ibid., MA Fl 38.1.
22. Ibid., MA Fl 38.3.
23. Ruth, *A Little Heaven Below*, 109.

accounts sometimes complain of self-centered boasting masquerading as testimonies, incoherent testimonies, excessively long testimonies, and testimonies by those whose lives contradicted their words.[24]

Once the initial sense of anticipation within the love feast dissipated to routine societal organization, there was no reason to share personal testimony.

Homogeneity is shown in English Methodism through the use of the rules as a precursor to entry into the class → society → band → select band → love feast. The *Large Minutes* directed the leaders to vet prospective members.[25] These Rules were made known to prospective members, as John Oliver discovered when he asked a Methodist leader the requirements for admission.[26] Once rules were published, and made available to those who were not members of the society, an obvious homogeneity is occurring. Attendance and membership is available, not necessarily to those who desire to "flee from the wrath to come," as the rules exhort in the opening paragraph, but to those who are willing to submit to that which all other Methodists submit to: the regulation of the organization, and the reorientation of private, social, and business life.

The publication of rules of admission and behavioral expectations reflect the earlier Anglican religious societies, organized by Horneck and others. These societies published rules to which each member had to assent to on admission, and regularly resubmit to.

The first Methodist generational experience, recounted in highly charged and emotive personal testimony, frequently left a fledgling Christian unsure of salvation, and almost certain of damnation, and was a real living expression of a desire to flee from forthcoming trial. A second generation member must surely have recognized that the wrath to come[27] was not imminent and was rather more likely to settle for a regulated rule orientated Christian life. C. E. White, writing of class decline in the nineteenth century, argued that the doctrine of hell was relaxed

---

24. Ibid., 110.

25. See Wesley, *The Minutes of the Methodist Conferences from the First*, volume I 454–6. See also Bullock, *Voluntary Religious Societies*, 194. This is fully expressed at 282–83.

26. Oliver, "An Account of Mr. John Oliver," 419.

27. See White, "The Decline of the Class Meeting," in *Methodist History*, 265–66.

and class meeting supervision, which provided "one of the chief guards against hell,"[28] waned.

I am not decrying the life or work of the second generation. It is not their devotion to Christian living that is in issue; it is how that devotion was expressed, through a more mature and respectable model of meeting and living that differentiates the mystical (primary) period from the sect (secondary) period. A sense of fresh purpose or re-awakening of the mystical or primary force *could* occur when some upheaval, such as the introduction of Calvinism, or Moravianism (both anathema to Methodism) or the prosecution of a Methodist occurred.

The journals and diaries of Methodist leaders indicate something of the slide into class irrelevance; usually as a frustration that the model of class to which they were working was not effective. I have already indicated Samuel Bradburn's distress at the poor state of the London classes.[29] Around 1773 Thomas Taylor discovered that not one of the class meetings in Birstall, "met well."[30] In the Leeds circuit, Taylor believed that if care were taken with class leaders, then the classes would benefit.[31]

From 1778 the *Arminian Magazine* was intended as a monthly publication for Methodists, those interested in the work of the Methodists, and a polemic against other doctrines. The *Magazine* contained testimonials intended as a means of encouraging a new generation of Methodists to see the process by which a previous generation had come to faith.

Common themes within these accounts are a change of life, a tempestuous discovery of Christ, a regular, though sometimes troubled, Christian life and habitual attendance at Methodist meetings leading to an improvement of life. It was not uncommon within the testimony for reprobates to find new purpose, for voices to be heard and visions to be seen, and for the perseverance to remain faithful to Christ in the face of opposition. The purpose of these autobiographies was encouragement to others that growth in grace and holiness was possible, and that a regulated spiritual life, including works of piety and mercy, paved the way for spiritual growth.

---

28. White, "The Decline of the Class Meeting," 266.

29. Bradburn, *A Memorandum Book, volume I*, see the entry for December 1786 and for May 1788. MA 1977/296.

30. Taylor, "The Life of Thomas Taylor," 44.

31. Ibid., 62.

The later *Lives of the Methodist Preachers* published in the mid nineteenth century offer biographies of men, pioneers of the movement (many of which were previously in the *Arminian Magazine*), to encourage and attempt to recapture the very first Methodist experiences. In the biography of Sampson Staniforth, while the references to awakening are clear, and the spiritual path is not simple, the reader was shown that not only is perseverance through trial of great importance but so was the spiritual experience in the trial. Describing his religious life in the army, Staniforth wrote of going "on my way sorrowing, but bringing forth fruits meet for repentance."[32] Other firsthand accounts recount visions, voices, and ecstatic periods, accounts which Wesley seemed keen to discover and publish.

Hempton offers insight into Wesley's purposes in publishing these biographies. "Here was an attempt to control information, memory, and tradition in a remarkable way . . . he was undoubtedly attempting to define a new tradition whose boundaries of print and access to information were largely drawn by himself."[33]

At the Conference of 1744, Wesley suggested to the assembled preachers that they should maintain personal diaries. This was later codified in his *Rules of an Assistant* of 1753.[34] In later years, Wesley actively sought the biographies of his preachers,[35] and assured them he would edit them as he saw fit.[36] Wesley first addressed the issue of censoring exactly what was published in 1763, and a decision of Conference in 1765 ratified Wesley's right to expel anyone who published without first seeking permission.[37] David Bebbington picks this up in *Evangelicalism*

---

32. Staniforth, "The Life of Sampson Staniforth," 121. The first edition of this series appeared in the 1840s.

33. Hempton, *Methodism*, 59.

34. See Valentine, *Mirror of the Soul*, 1.

35. See Wesley, *Letters [SE]*, Vol VI, 380. This was a letter to John Valton. He wrote to Valton on further occasions. First on the 21st April 1780. See Wesley, *Letters [SE]*, Vol. VII, 17. Secondly, the 1st October 1780, see Wesley, *Works [SE]*, Vol. VII, 35. It is clear from this letter that Valton was unwilling to provide a biographical account. Wesley finally wrote to him on the 19th December 1780. See Wesley, *Letters [SE]*, Vol. VII, 44. In this letter Wesley declared that supplying a biography was a "duty." Wesley also wrote to Christopher Hopper seeking a biography. See Wesley, *Letters [SE]*, Vol. VI, 380.

36. Wesley, *Letters [SE]*, Vol. VII, 100–101. Again this was in correspondence to Valton on the 18th January 1782.

37. See Myles, *A Chronological History*, 279.

in Modern Britain. He asserts that Wesley used the *Arminian Magazine* to disseminate his views and thoughts, and the autobiographies were an important part of this. The *Arminian Magazine* gave him opportunity to redress and perhaps re-establish his hope that Methodists remained an experiential people.

> Wesley tried to maintain a tight control over ideas circulating in the connexion. No preacher, on pain of expulsion, was to go into print without his approval, or, after 1781, without his correction.[38]

Hindmarsh contextualizes the earliest testimonials and later autobiographical material in *The Evangelical Conversion Narrative*. In the early period, the testimonial material described the process of personal conversion within the context of the group meeting,[39] in this period the band. Later autobiographies offer a restrained pattern of pre-awakening, awakening, conversion, and post-conversion life, but within that relate experiential accounts similar to earlier testimonies. Usually the class meeting is related as an experience of grace,[40] but the routine of the meeting is not related.

Hindmarsh's use of Pawson's experiential awakening, which led to the rest of his family accepting Methodism in the late 1750s, evidences that the first generation (Pawson) was able to affect others as deeply as he was affected. An autobiographical letter appeared in the *Arminian Magazine* in 1779,[41] relating his life from the 1760s to that point, followed in 1801 by a fuller autobiography which appeared in *Lives of the Early Methodist Preachers*. As might be expected, shortly after conversion, Pawson was given charge of a class: "Mr. Homer divided our little society into two classes, and made me the leader of one of them."[42] For Pawson, this responsibility was hard, but he recounted that the experience meant that he "was brought into a higher state of grace"[43] and he

---

38. Bebbington, *Evangelicalism*, 68.

39. See Hindmarsh, *The Evangelical Conversion Narrative*, 130–61. Hindmarsh describes the testimonials as offering a sense of individuation within the context of mimesis.

40. Ibid., 228. Hindmarsh used the autobiography of John Pawson to explain the later autobiographical process.

41. Wesley, *Arminian Magazine*, Vol. II, 25–40. As I have shown elsewhere, Wesley edited the submissions of all those who wrote for the *Arminian Magazine*.

42. Pawson, "The Life of John Pawson," 23.

43. Ibid.

knew "the abiding witness of the Spirit."[44] Pawson interestingly was a member of a new society, so small indeed that it could only be made up of a single class. The first taste of leadership for Pawson was at the point of division into two separate classes. As Hindmarsh points out, the earliest years are swiftly given over to the emerging itinerant preacher's ministry.[45]

Pawson, like other early Methodists, was joining the Methodist people in the face of opposition. His uncle believed the Methodists would "murder" the local people,[46] and his father was set against Pawson joining them.[47] For him the reasons for joining the Methodists were that opposition offered a sense of making the Methodists worth joining, and early class experience highlighted the change from sin to salvation.

John Valton,[48] who was asked by Wesley on four occasions to supply a biography, provides further insight into the process of biographical writing. Valton was a prolific diarist, and maintained an annual diary from 1763 onwards. His printed biography in *Lives of the Early Methodist Preachers* fills 136 pages.[49] Prior to Wesley's request in 1780 Valton prepared a journal from his personal diary to send to a friend: "I wrote a long letter to my friend John Watkins who was going to Florida, containing an extract from my journal."[50]

The biography in *Lives of the Early Methodist Preachers* is an edited version of the manuscript diary, omitting those aspects of Valton's experience which he considered unfit to print or unedifying for the Methodist, or non-Methodist reader. Throughout the diary there are words, phrases, sentences, paragraphs, and full pages which have been struck through as this process took place.

---

44. Ibid.
45. Hindmarsh, *The Evangelical Conversion Narrative*, 229.
46. Pawson, "The Life of John Pawson," 7.
47. Ibid., 10.
48. See McGonigle, "Valton, John," 362. Valton was born in 1740 and died in 1794. He maintained his diary from 1763 until his death.
49. See Valton, "The Life of John Valton," in *Preachers*, Vol. VI, 1–136. The biography has additional material added by Joseph Sutcliffe.
50. Valton, *The Christian Experience of the Late Rev. John Valton, volume I*, 79. Entry dated for the 19th June 1764. MA 1977/293.

The biography entry for the 25th September 1764, described Valton's recovery from a fever, during which he felt he might die.[51] However, he expurgated from this printed entry his first account of meeting in class.

> ~~The other evening I was exceedingly tried by one in our Class, who I feared had not a spirit of love. I recommended him to God. After Class the devil roar'd furiously at our Leader's house. Our meeting was forbad, at least our Class Leader my soul's friend was denied the meeting us. I was accused of receiving Stolen Goods and called many bad names.~~[52]

On the 25th May 1765, Valton recorded in his diary a detailed account of his opinion of his fellow class members. Not surprisingly, this is not found in the printed biography,

> ~~Indeed our Class seems to lose both the power and form. Our Class Leader mostly ill, another an elderly person, a Pharisee unwilling to let go her Rage. Another quite lifeless, fell away from what he had received under a dissenting Minister, and another whose pious impressions, like Jonah's Gourd are soon destroyed by levity of spirit and carelessness, and last of all, the unworthiest of all, myself.~~[53]

Valton's diary suggested that a reason for the seeming failure of the class members to meet was the emphases of Methodist teaching. "~~The doctrine seems to be too harsh, to some, and the way too narrow.~~"[54] Further discouraging entries can be found during the period of Valton's working life as an Ordinance Officer in Purfleet. These entries cover minimal attendance,[55] arguments,[56] deadness,[57] and a desire to cease meeting.[58]

51. Valton, "The Life of John Valton," 25.

52. Valton, *The Christian Experience of the Late Rev. John Valton, volume I*, 130. (25th September 1764.) MA 1977/293.

53. Ibid., *volume. II*, 67. (20th May 1765.) MA 1977/293.

54. Ibid., 89. (14th July 1765) MA 1977/293.

55. Ibid., 121. (Sunday 6th October 1765) & 150. (5th December 1765.) *Volume III*, 78. (27th June 1766.) *Volume III*, 85–86. (23rd July 1766.) *Volume III*, 107. (3rd September 1766.) *Volume III*, 113. (10th September 1766.) *Volume III*, 134. (8th October 1766.) *Volume III*, 136. (12th October 1766.) *Volume III*, 138. (16th October 1766.) MA 1977/293.

56. Ibid., 106. (28th August 1765.) *Volume III*, 97. (17th August 1766.) MA 1977/293.

57. Ibid., 119. (4th October 1765.) *Volume III*, 22. (30th January 1766.) MA 1977/293.

58. Ibid., 89. (14th July 1765.) *Volume II*, 106. (28th August 1765.) *Volume II*, 121.

The One-Generational Meeting 257

While the majority of Valton's diary related his daily experience in Purfleet from 1763, he traveled as often as he was able to London to attend the Methodist preaching at Snowsfield, the Foundery, and West Street. While in London he attended a class. "By desire of Mr Windsor, I met his Class without power to speak or pray."[59]

Valton offers an insight into meeting with a sick former class member who had ceased to meet. Thomas Fenis (or Carpenter) had met in class some time before and then left. "Poor Thom*s* Fenis or Carpenter who met with us in Class some time ago, and whom the Lord was convincing of sin, but the Devils servants got him away from us."[60] Valton met Fenis again the next day, but his reaction to Valton was to feel shame. "With extream reluctance I visited the sick Thomas Fenis, was much recovered and seem'd asham'd of me."[61] For Fenis the class was not sufficiently assimilatory or experiential to warrant his remaining amongst the Methodists.

The even picture of the usefulness of the class through his published biography is set in the manuscript diary into the context of Valton's daily life and experience, which is self-critical and sometimes despairing.[62] Valton recorded the class as a helpful meeting on four occasions,[63] and wrote a long account of his class meeting of the 23rd February 1766. This account was written as that evening's experience was unusual to him: "I do not know that we ever had such a night nor, anything like it, when the Lord was so present."[64] However, once home from class his mind was filled with doubt for himself and his friends, and he was afraid he might die.[65] The published biography has a shortened account of this meeting omitting the quotation above, and the disquieting questioning.[66]

(5th October 1765.) MA 1977/293.

59. Ibid., *volume III*, 122. (17th October 1766.) There is no entry under this date in *Preachers*. MA 1977/293.

60. Ibid., 119. (13th September 1776.) MA 1977/293.

61. Ibid., 120. (14th September 1766.) MA 1977/293.

62. Ibid., *volume I*, 29–30. (11th March 1764.) See also Valton, *The Christian Experience of the Late Rev. John Valton*, volume II, 66–67. (20th May 1765.) MA 1977/293.

63. Ibid., *volume I*, 150. (9th December 1764.) *Volume II*, 91. (24th July 1765.) *Volume II*, 92. (31st July 1765.) *Volume III*, 34–36. (23rd February 1766.) MA 1977/293.

64. Ibid., *volume III*, 35. (23rd February 1766.) MA 1977/293.

65. Ibid., 35–36. (23rd February 1766.) MA 1977/293.

66. Valton, "The Life of John Valton," 49.

In the first year of the class's existence, Abraham Jones,[67] a class leader in London, wrote a detailed letter to John Wesley relating his experience of meeting and leading a class. Jones noted. "My class (except Ja[mes] Moss, for I know not how he walks) do all walk orderly, and keep close to the Word, and the means of grace."[68] His personal examination, however, is searching, and self-critical. Although Wesley had appointed him, Jones felt he was still "a worm."[69] Using the imagery of a person learning to swim, he felt that he was "greatly afraid of going out of (his) depth."[70] At this early point, when the class was still used for the collection of monies and the leader visited from house to house, Jones found problems in his class members in persevering in their growth in faith.[71]

In the early period of Methodism Wesley along with his brother shared in the regulation of the classes. I have already stated that in 1747, while in Gateshead, Wesley recognized that questioning the class leader, rather than each class member could reduce the time regulation might take, even if not the number of expulsions.[72] While in Whitehaven in 1751, Wesley remarked that in the society of 240 people, only one person did not meet in class. He described this as a "remarkable circumstance."[73] This appears to be included in the *Journal* as an experience worthy of note, and when placed alongside many of his published remarks upon class attendance is clearly not the norm of class attendance. In 1759, Wesley regulated the Norwich society, noting that 150 of those who held tickets did not "*pretend* to meet at all."[74] At Limerick in 1760, Wesley noted a "considerable decrease"[75] in the classes which he believed was the result of "vice which flows as a torrent."[76] His remedy was to preach in order to quicken the people.

---

67. Wesley, *Works [BE]*, Vol. 26, 94–95.

68. Ibid.

69. Ibid., 95

70. Ibid. (Word in brackets mine.)

71. See Jones comment in relation to E.S. (possibly Eleanor Scholefield), Wesley, *Works [BE]*, Vol. 26. 95.

72. Wesley, *Works [BE]*, Vol. 20, 162–63. By this method Wesley reduced the Newcastle Society from 800 to 400 members.

73. Wesley, *Works [BE]*, Vol. 20, 384.

74. Ibid., Vol. 21, 226.

75. Ibid., 268.

76. Ibid.

At the Conference of 1753, Wesley considered with his preachers how Methodism might make the "Leaders of the Classes more useful."[77] This consideration took place within the context of a general discussion on the scheme of Methodist organization and rules. In response to the question, the following answers were offered:

> Q, How may we make the Leaders of the Classes more useful?–
> A. 1. Let each of them be diligently examined concerning his method of meeting a Class. 2. Let the Leaders converse with all the preachers as frequently and as freely as possible. 3. Let each Leader carefully inquire how every soul in his class prospers? Not only how each person observes the outward rules, but how he grows in the knowledge and love of God. 4. Let the Leaders frequently meet each others Classes.[78]

Although the reason for this review is unknown, the manner of the answers indicated that the leaders were not undertaking their role as effectively as Conference felt appropriate, and therefore needed their task reinforced by a regular interrogation by others of how they ran their class. Conference also required a regular interchange of leaders and classes. Wesley wrote to Adam Clarke in 1790 expressing this same requirement.

From the early 1760s, Wesley published tracts and pamphlets, wrote to friends and leaders, and on one occasion printed an open letter in the *Journal*, all on the issue of class attendance. In 1764, he wrote a general letter to the Bristol societies, and implored them to meet in class. Alongside the encouragement was a "threat" that failing to meet on three occasions brought about self-exclusion from the society and all its associated meetings.

> If you constantly meet your band, I make no doubt that you will constantly meet your class; indeed otherwise you are not of our Society. Whoever misses his class thrice together thereby excludes himself . . . Halt not between the two. Meet the brethren or leave them.[79]

---

77. Wesley, *The Minutes of the Methodist Conferences from the First*, volume I, 454.
78. Ibid.
79. Wesley, *Letters [SE]*, Vol. IV, 273.

Earlier that same year, Wesley wrote a letter to "A Gentleman,"[80] subsequently published in the *Journal* in 1768.[81] In publishing the letter, Wesley signaled that those who chose to remain outside society membership deprived themselves of the benefits that membership brought. Specifically, Wesley addressed the issue of class membership and attendance. Speaking for the "gentleman" addressed in the letter, Wesley wrote: "But I do not care to meet a class; I find no good in it."[82] His response was simple. "Suppose you find a dislike, a loathing of it; may not this be natural, or even diabolical? In spite of this, break through, make a fair trial."[83] In publishing the letter to an anonymous recipient of four years previously, Wesley made available across the connexion and beyond the advice and exhortation to a single person. Wesley's command, to join rather than be a hearer, became available to all those who read the *Journal*, and his advice on the class was therefore open to Methodists and non-Methodists alike to observe.

While in Dublin in 1771, Wesley was faced with a situation that had been "a continual jar, for at least two years past, which had stumbled the people, weakened the hands of the preachers, and greatly hindered."[84] Wesley was explicit in his diagnosis: "if one wheel in a machine gets out of its place, what disorder must ensue!"[85] The leaders had assumed more responsibility than Methodist polity allowed them. These leadership difficulties had led to 100 class members ceasing to meet their class.[86] After meeting the leaders, stewards, and preachers, Wesley met the classes, from which he discerned a "general faintness."[87] Later he met the leaders and read over an amended version of the *General Rules*, setting each position in a society into its place.[88]

During 1776, Wesley wrote twice on the issue of class attendance. In February he wrote to Joseph Benson,[89] stationed in the North East, and

---

80. See Wesley, *Letters [SE]*, Vol. IV, 253–55.
81. Wesley, *Works [BE]*, Vol. 21, 477–79.
82. Ibid., 479.
83. Wesley, *Works [BE]*, Vol. 21, 479.
84. Ibid., Vol. 22, 266.
85. Ibid., 268.
86. White, "The Decline of the Class Meeting," 259–60.
87. Wesley, *Works [BE]*, Vol. 22, 267
88. Ibid., 267–68.
89. See Myles, *A Chronological History*, 299. Benson was amongst the "Second Race

in March to Thomas Rutherford,[90] who was then stationed in Edinburgh. Wesley commented to Benson that he required him to withhold tickets from any who failed to meet a class weekly, and to put out any who had failed to meet twelve times in a quarter without excuse. This instruction was to be enacted in Newcastle and Sunderland.[91] At the beginning of the letter, Wesley appeared to be highlighting a situation that was occurring elsewhere. "We must threaten no longer, but perform."[92] He noted to Benson that he had enacted the same rule in the London Society in the previous November. Wesley also instructed Benson that he should also take care with those appointed class leaders.

> I pray without fear or favour remove the leaders, whether of classes or bands, who do not watch over the souls committed to their care "as those that must give account."[93]

In the following month, in his letter to Rutherford he required three named individuals to be removed from membership for their failure to attend a class. "I require John Campbell, John Laird, and Peter Ferguson to take their choice one way or the other. If they will meet their class weekly, they are with us. If they will not, they put themselves from us."[94] It appeared that Rutherford had written specifically to Wesley seeking advice as to disciplining these three men. Wesley's response left no room for discussion. It is impossible to state what these men had done, other than failed to meet in class, but their refusal to conform to the rules of meeting must have been affecting other members.

The situation in Londonderry, Ireland, in 1783 was even more serious than that in Edinburgh. Wesley wrote to John Cricket,[95] to "reprove strongly their (the people's) unfaithfulness and unfruitfulness";[96] he added, "you must immediately resume the form at least of a Methodist society. I positively forbid you or any preachers to be a leader; rather

---

of Methodist Preachers," and began his itinerancy in 1771.

90. Ibid., 304. Rutherford was amongst the "Second Race of Methodist Preachers," and began his itinerancy in 1772.

91. Wesley, *Letters [SE]*, Vol. VI, 208.

92. Ibid.

93. Ibid.

94. Ibid., 210.

95. See Myles, *A Chronological History*, 300. Cricket was a "Second Race" preacher, beginning his itinerancy in 1780.

96. Wesley, *Letters [SE]*, Vol. VII, 166. (Words in brackets mine.)

put the most insignificant person in each class to be leader of it."[97] In Londonderry the society structure had fallen away, and the classes had ceased to exist. Wesley's express command to put the most insignificant person into leadership of each class was to prevent the leaders taking roles that local Methodists were reluctant to assume. In Londonderry neither the society nor the classes were functioning.

The previous year, (1782) Wesley had visited John and Mary Fletcher. Their complaint to him was that "after all the pains they had taken, they could not prevail on the people to join in society, no, nor even to meet in a class."[98] Wesley's remedy was to preach and issue an invitation to join him and Mr.Fletcher. Wesley recorded. "Ninety-four or ninety-five persons did so; about as many men as women."[99] Earlier that year, Wesley expressly commanded John Valton to put John Sellars out of the society. His desire was clear: "I cannot allow John Sellars to be any longer a leader: and if he will lead the class, whether I will or no, I require you to put him out of our Society. If twenty of his class leave the society too, they must. The first loss is the best. Better forty members should be lost than our discipline lost."[100] Wesley had noted earlier that Sellars "got his own soul much quickened in Macclesfield, he will now be a blessing to many at Chester."[101] It is to be assumed that Wesley meant he had received the Holy Spirit. In less than two weeks his manner of class leadership (of more than the recommended twelve members) had been reported to Wesley. His response was to remove Sellars from the society and accept that some would leave with him.

In 1788, Wesley wrote to Edward Jackson: "I commend you for denying tickets to all that have neglected their classes, unless they seriously promise to meet them for the time to come. You cannot be too exact in this."[102] Wesley wrote to Adam Clarke[103] in Dublin in 1790 that the classes had benefited from a change of leaders. "I am glad our leaders have adopted that excellent method of regularly changing the classes. Wherever this has been done, it has been a means of quickening both the leaders

97. Ibid.
98. Wesley, *Works [BE]*, Vol. 23, 232–33.
99. Ibid., 233.
100. Wesley, *Letters [SE]*, Vol. VII, 101.
101. Ibid., 98. This letter was written to Hester Anne Roe.
102. Wesley, *Letters [SE]*, Vol. VIII, 98–99.
103. Taggart, "Clarke, Dr. Adam," 69. Clarke began itinerating in 1782.

and the people. I wish this custom could be effectually introduced."[104] Wesley's comment to Clarke indicated that the classes had a tendency to become moribund, and the leaders ineffective if left in charge of the same class for any length of time.

Wesley published a tract at the height of the perfection controversy in 1762,[105] entitled *Cautions and Directions given to the Greatest professors in the Methodist societies*.[106] This was subsequently published within *Farther Thoughts on Christian Perfection*,[107] and finally contained in *A Plain Account of Christian Perfection*. This tract addressed the societies when the controversy over the issue of sinless perfection was at its height. Wesley would not allow this particular definition of perfection, always arguing that those made perfect could still be subject to involuntary sin. Some Methodists followed the leaders of the disagreement, Thomas Maxfield and George Bell,[108] to their meetings, and Wesley specifically addressed the schism that he believed this action caused. He insisted within the tract that schism would be avoided if Methodists attended their class or band, as these (along with the public meetings), were "the very sinews of our Society; and whatever weakens, or tends to weaken, our regard for these, or our exactness in attending them, strikes at the very root of our community."[109]

The behavior of the Methodists who chose to follow Maxfield and others was sufficiently important for Wesley to urge his people to maintain the order and rules he had laid out some 20 years before in the *General Rules*. Although Wesley was an advocate of perfection, and was willing to hear accounts of those who claimed to have received it, he was unwilling to allow that perfection meant that discipline and meeting others were unnecessary for those that had attained it. Over a period of time Wesley published this same advice to prevent schism as he understood it, and to encourage meeting in class. These publications were

---

104. Wesley, *Letters [SE]*, Vol. VIII, 244.

105. See Rack, *Reasonable Enthusiast*, 336–42. The leaders of the controversy, Thomas Maxfield and George Bell were based in London, and separated from Wesley over the reception of sinless perfection.

106. Wesley, *Cautions and Directions, Given to the Greatest professors in the Methodist Societies*.

107. Wesley. *Farther Thoughts Upon Christian Perfection* (London: 1763).

108. See Cooney, "Bell, George," 26.

109. Wesley, *A Plain Account*, 94.

available to all those who attended the societies, and was a warning to continue meeting.

I have already shown how Wesley wrote in strong yet affectionate terms to Nancy Bolton in 1790. This letter, written in the last year of his life, is a heartfelt plea to a friend to return to a class meeting. Toward the end of the letter, after his exhortation to her to go to a class, "sick or well," Wesley described the process of meeting as taking up a cross.[110] In this he is stating that the class is not intended to be an easy meeting, but it is clear that Nancy Bolton was unwilling to face the rigors of it.

Rack states clearly the reality of class life. He recognizes that the ideal picture of the class was described by Wesley in the *Plain Account of the People Called Methodists* of 1748.[111] However, as I have shown above from these varied accounts of class difficulties, "there were many casualties from the start."[112] Rack notes that the ideal, laid before Methodists and non-Methodists alike in the *Plain Account*, is tempered by "his records of complaints about members who seldom met and complained that it did them no good when they did; the frequent purges tell their own tale."[113]

Leadership of classes and numbers wishing to belong could in their own way lead to a breakdown of an effective class system. Grace Murray, at one point a possible wife for John Wesley, but who later married John Bennet, wrote in her diary: "I had a full hundred in Classes, whom I met in two separate meetings."[114] Fifty people per class would have led to an ineffective meeting. The class could only operate effectively in an intimate setting, where every member had opportunity to speak, listen, and learn. In a group of 50, the essential intimacy was lost.

At the Conference of 1775, a decision was made to halve any classes containing more than 30 members.[115] The sentence following the decision to reduce class sizes indicates that sizeable classes were not uncommon. "It would be well if this rule were constantly attended to."[116]

---

110. Wesley, *Letters [SE]*, Vol. VIII, 246.
111. Rack, *Reasonable Enthusiast*, 241.
112. Ibid.
113. Rack, *Reasonable Enthusiast*, 241.
114. Valentine, *John Bennet*, 207.
115. Wesley, *Minutes of the Methodist Conferences, from the First, Held in London by the Late Rev. John Wesley A.M. in the year 1744, volume I*, 120.
116. Ibid.

Second generation members would not have found any useful purpose in belonging to a large group. Indeed, even the first generation would rarely have found such a huge meeting helpful.

The rule of class membership as a precondition to society membership meant that each prospective Methodist was assigned a class. A new member, joining a large, settled group, would not have opportunity to experience the close fellowship of the ideal class number, led by an experienced leader. The small group of 10 or 12 could properly lay claim to Troeltsch's model of mysticism. It was intimate, it had access to shared experience, it could respond sensitively to need or admonish sin. The larger classes were in effect more like Troeltsch's Sect model—voluntary societies gathered together for association, but unable to access the immediacy of mysticism.

To a second generation, unlike those who wrote early testimonies or kept journals and diaries and made much of the value of their communal class experience as a vital regular means of growth in grace and holiness, it was possession of the ticket and the social standing that came with it that offered value. The class was necessary, but not of primary importance. It had offered much to the first generation of Methodists, but did not offer much to later generations. Thus John Kent is correct when he writes:

> After the first wave of Wesleyanism the societies gradually lost their appetite for ecstatic experience, because members were beginning to feel themselves in control of their social and personal circumstances.[117]

A simple example of this early experiential meeting is noted in an oath, made against the Methodists in 1747.

> This informant on his oath voluntarily saith that he formerly attended the meetings of those persons who called themselves Methodists being invited so to do by one of their preachers called Cownley and that they divide themselves into different classes where they meet in private homes that a husband and wife cant be of the same Class nor Father & Daughter, nor father & son, nor a brother and sister, that they often pretend to receive the Spirit & they that receive it (as they say) just above the room & ask others if they don't feel the Spirit: and that he is credibly in-

---

117. Kent, *Wesley and the Wesleyans*, 42.

formed that one Joseph Heber of the said Parish . . . reported he was in a trance or deep sleep when an angel appeared to him.[118]

This quotation, from an anti-Methodist oath, shows how experiential or highly charged Methodist class meetings were. The settled Methodists of the later eighteenth century were not enamored of the highly charged and emotive writings in journals and diaries of the first Methodists, who pioneered the movement across England. Not only did they not identify with such charged meetings, they did not identify with the writings of these early men and women.

John Kent, in his discussion of Methodism's earliest phase, primary religion, summarizes Wesley's lifelong reliance on his own experience and understanding of religious practice. He quotes V. H. H. Green:

> His life was built around his own experience, an experience glazed and insulated from the outside world by his confidence in God and in himself. Completely selfless and yet intensely egoistic, he had come to identify himself with his own creation.[119]

In this was Wesley's major failing, that he could not see that those who had come into a settled Methodism did not have his primary religious affection. The class was not the melting pot of an exuberant and vibrant faith after the first generation's experience had faded to memory.

Roy Hattersley's biography of Wesley approaches the change from mysticism to sect by showing how Wesley became concerned with the need for unity across the Connexion in the 1760s. He does not consider the move toward a laxity of doctrine in favor of a broader organization reliant on rules of behavior within the framework of Troeltsch's model, but this fits well within it. The need for unity expressed in Hattersley's view in the *Large Minutes* created a body of doctrine that "still bound Methodism to the Church of England."[120] Yet by the time of their publication, Methodism was broader than these minutes and required skillful handling to remain one body, albeit with a loose connection to Anglicanism. Hattersley suggests that it was the maintenance of

---

118. Lambeth Palace Archives *Archbishops Papers–Secker Papers*, Volume 8, *(Methodists) 1738-57*. This was An oath sworn before J Snow by Thomas Lovell (25th May 1747), 8 in folio. This oath was part of Lavington's information gathering exercise against the Methodists.

119. Kent, *Wesley and the Wesleyans*, 43.

120. Hattersley, *A Brand from the Burning: The Life of John Wesley*, 299.

Methodist unity that overrode the need to remain as a reforming body within the Anglican Communion.

In the change from mysticism to sect, under the model expounded by Roy Hattersley, the emerging, confident grouping known as Methodism required an identity that bound them together. That identity was no longer based on the earlier experiential model, but on a regulated, "national" set of rules and expectations imposed from Conference.

For Hattersley, these changes in Methodism's printed rules and doctrines, contained in the *Large Minutes* and other publications, set the second generation on a course that would inevitably lead to separation from the Church of England. A regulated, national organization had moved away from the early years of ad hoc local decisions, and later generations were joining a broader Methodism. These generations were seeking the order of Methodism as a sect, and all it offered: regulation, doctrine, respectability, and organization. Roy Hattersley gives a sense of this when he writes:

> In his sixtieth year Wesley continued to pay necessary respect to the Thirty-Nine Articles and the Church of England's homilies. But he was laying down articles and homilies of his own. By choice and by design, year by year, Methodism was creating its own position within the spectrum of Protestant Christianity.[121]

The first generation who had come into a locally organized society and class, or whose religious society had been taken over by the Wesleys, would have recognized only the form of their class by the 1760s. That which was a small element of a small and somewhat informal Connexion was by this period a highly organized national group. The east-west axis of 1740 had long since given way to a complex Connexion that could not be disciplined by an itinerant Wesley working alone. The leadership that had developed to service the Connexion was drawn from primary-stage Methodists, working with the remnants of that group, but commonly with a secondary generation, who did not identify easily with their leaders' experience.

The earliest testimonies, journals, and diaries highlighted the process toward conversion, and a daily, almost obsessive measurement of spiritual fervor, coupled with ecstatic experience, or at least the hope thereof. William Holder regularly reviewed his spiritual state, which var-

---

121. Ibid., 298.

ied from depression to near ecstasy. Toward the end of 1768, he shared his writing with a family with whom he was staying:

> I breakfast (sic) with P Newman was still pressed by the enemy, after breakfast I read some things of my Journal to them, particularly how I was before, at the time, & after my deliverance.[122]

The result of his reading was to "open the eyes" of a woman present at the time.

Anti-Methodist polemic serves to show how those not sympathetic to the Methodist cause used the model of testimonial spiritual journaling and diarying to good effect. One writer, using the pseudonym "Nathaniel Snip,"[123] admirably uses the voices and ecstatic experiences of the early Methodists to show them as enthusiasts and anti-enlightenment people. For "Snip" a Methodist was an individual who rejected all forms of entertainment, dressed soberly, and saw God in every aspect of human life and natural event. Although "Snip" had no time for Methodists, his short *Journal* lampooning the more serious Methodist journals and diaries indicates what turned second generation Methodists away from their earlier counterparts. All was supernatural and highly Dissenting.

John Walsh helps to make the reason for these highly charged writings pertinent to a first generation, but by default also serves to explain why a later generation found them, and the experiential class meeting, less relevant. "The Methodists offered the poor a salvation which they felt to be within their reach, immediately attainable and recognizable."[124] This is highlighted in a letter of 1747 to the Bishop of Exeter, who was compiling a dossier on Methodist activity. The authors wrote to the bishop:

> A set of people who stile (sic) themselves Methodists have infus'd their enthusiastick (sic) notions in to the minds of vast numbers of the meaner sort of people in the western part of this County, they are very strenuously endeavouring to propagate them all over it: several have assembled frequently . . . the preacher they are so very fond of, is no better than a mean illiterate Tinner, and what is more surprising, but a boy of nineteen years old.[125]

---

122. Holder, *The Diary of William Holder*, entry for 29th November 1768. MA 1977/238.

123. Snip, *A Journal of the Travels of Nathaniel Snip a Methodist Teacher of the Word*.

124. Walsh, " 'Methodism' and the Origins of English Speaking Evangelicalism," 31.

125. Lambeth Palace Archives "Bishops Meetings: Papers of Bishop Lavington of

It is no wonder that a generation, who joined Methodism as a means of social pretence or respectability, or the children of those who had been amongst the poor, felt no sympathy or empathy with the earlier Methodists. The class meeting had served its life in one generation; for a later generation another model of meeting was required, but none was forthcoming.

This book is not concerned with the changes made within Methodism from 1749, when the basic organization was in place. However, knowingly or otherwise, Wesley was actively involved in making a second generation of Methodists part of an organization, not a movement. To have had an experiential second generation required Methodism to remain committed to a movement, which inevitably meant constant change.

Frank Baker addresses this in *John Wesley and the Church of England*. Through his discussion of the Deed of Declaration, settled in 1784, he opens the chapter with the ominous words: "If ever there was a year when Wesley could be said to have irrevocably severed himself and Methodism from the Church of England it was 1784."[126] The Deed, however, merely regularised the reality of Methodism, setting out what would happen after his death. Myles noted in his précis of the Conference for 1784 that there were preachers whose names were not included as members of the "Legal Hundred." Those named by Myles[127] left the Methodist Connexion, and in doing so, left behind the men happy to be numbered amongst an emerging Methodist Church.

Wesley had made his movement uniform in 1749; he had abandoned hope of reconciliation with evangelical Anglicans in the 1760s. Methodist properties were established on a Model Trust Deed, and the doctrinal standards for all Methodists were settled as Wesley's *Forty Four Sermons* and his *Notes on the New Testament*. Wesley also published a form of worship for the Methodists and ordained men to supply the sacramental life of the Methodists.

Exeter," *Archbishops Papers–Secker Papers*, Volume 8, *(Methodists) 1738–57*. Letter from J. Birkhead and J. Tremayne to the Bishop of Exeter, (23rd May 1747). 4 in folio. See also T. Hext's letter to the Bishop of Exeter dated the 23rd February 1748. Same folio, 64–65.

126. Baker, *John Wesley and the Church of England*, 218.

127. Myles, *A Chronological History*, 158. Myles names the men who left as John Hampson Sen., John Hampson Jr., William Eells, Joseph Pillmore, and a few others.

In these actions, which Baker asserts Wesley recognized as acts of separation, but hoped for a way through them that would not actually lead to physical separation,[128] the Methodists fundamentally changed as an organization. The small experiential classes of 1742, which met to raise funds to alleviate poverty (as well as settle debts), one of the great Pietstic acts of the Methodists, were now part of a larger Connexional structure.

Class money was used to support the Itinerants and thereby Methodist structure, as Wesley accepted in correspondence to his brother as early as 1751.[129] Charles' objection to this was that paying the preachers in this way maintained his brother's authority over them,[130] a charge John Wesley denied. Perhaps by not maintaining the preachers, the movement's sharp edge could have been maintained and held the experiential nature of the movement for a longer period.

However, Wesley's control has to be an important factor in the decline of the class. This is discussed fully in the previous chapters, but it can be seen here that as the emphasis shifted from movement to organization, the survival of the jobs of the "employees," those in local, circuit, and Connexional leadership became the primary focus of the leadership *per se*. Charles Wesley noted this change in the 1750s. "Unless a sudden remedy be found, the preachers will destroy the work of God. What has wellnigh ruined many of them is their being taken from their trades . . . the tinner, barber, thatcher, forgot himself, and set up for a gentleman, and looked out for a fortune, having lost the only way of maintaining himself."[131]

Opponents of Methodism laid before Wesley the charge that men were seeking a life beyond their station. Howard Snyder quotes Augustus Toplady, an Anglican Calvinist, who advised Wesley to: "Let his cobblers keep to their stalls. Let his tinkers mend their vessels. Let his barbers confine themselves to their blocks and basons. Let his bakers stand to their kneading-troughs. Let his blacksmiths blow more suitable coals than those of controversy."[132]

---

128. Baker, *John Wesley and the Church of England*, 218.

129. Wesley, *Works [BE]*, Vol. 26, 479. See also Whitehead, *The Life of the Rev John Wesley M.A.*, 342. This is a transcript of the *Large Minutes* and allowed an annual collection from the Classes for the building of new Preaching Houses. (Q49)

130. Ibid.,fn5

131. Baker, *Charles Wesley as Revealed by his Letters*, 84–85.

132. Snyder, *The Radical Wesley*, 64.

If classes were supporting (to Charles' disgust) the new itinerancy, then their focus was of itself changing in line with a new "professional" group emerging among them. The class was the ground from which these preachers had come, and from which new preachers would arise. The mystical life of the movement, or primary religion was giving way to the emerging sect or secondary religion, and as Kent maintains, "by the late 1760s the Wesleyan leaders had to ease the pressure of their idiosyncratic theology on daily life; they were responding more cautiously to the religious situation they had created."[133] Quite simply, as Methodism grew as a voluntary association, and the organization required more than a sheet of rules to govern belonging and behavior, Wesley tempered his idiosyncrasies to bring forth a more socially acceptable Methodism. The passage of time led to a change in the emphasis of the class's life, from experiential to catechetical, from confessional to fellowship meeting. This change suited a leadership which was settling into a regulated and increasingly respectable lifestyle: a lifestyle that eschewed emotionalism, which led to marginalization by the local community, in favor of "fellowship" leading to acceptance by the local community.

Added to this has to be the changing world view of the Methodist people themselves. Early Methodists shared John Wesley's desire to band together into societies, where mystery, visions, and rapture were part of the way of life. Wesley's quest for primitive religion, continued beyond his purpose for traveling to America, and through his life Wesley managed to walk a tightrope between enthusiasm and reason. In 1750, Wesley was reading the French Prophet John Lacy[134] and although he denied their claim to direct revelation, he accepted their claim that the Montanists were really scriptural Christians.[135] Wesley denied the enthusiasm he saw in their claim to particular revelation, but was willing to allow a claim to early Christian roots. Likewise, John Wesley's ready acceptance of the accounts of divine providence from his people could be countered by his denial that Methodists had any claim to unique religious revelation as David Hempton has argued.[136]

---

133. Kent, *Wesley and the Wesleyans*, 105.

134. Lacy's book was *The General Delusion of Christians with Regard to prophecy*.

135. See Schwartz, *The French Prophets*, 205. The *Journal* entry is Wesley, *Works [BE]*, Vol. 20, 356.

136. Hempton, *Methodism*, 32–54.

Amongst the early Methodists, primitive religion reigned, and in that, the experiential class meeting was paramount, supplying sufficient subculture for Wesley to maintain at the opening of the New Chapel in City Road in 1778 that Methodism was "the old religion, the religion of the Bible, the religion of the primitive church, the religion of the Church of England."[137] Some 36 years after the first class meeting in Bristol he could not allow that any shift of emphasis had taken place for his people. Kent correctly describes the ecstatic events surrounding the class and early Methodists, and indeed Wesley's own ecstatic experiences:

> When he described these events he did not question what had happened, he defined and approved what took place as divinely prompted. He did not hesitate to use the language of perfect holiness to stir up others, he was always demanding that they "go on to perfection." And he believed their claims that they had achieved a state of perfect love in which the self was possessed by a divine spirit.[138]

The Methodists moved on without him. At the earliest period, the very nature of being members of a voluntary religious group gave impetus and purpose when attacks by a mob or attempts to suppress field preaching through the judiciary were stock-in-trade for small and oppressed local societies. Leslie Church's writing on persecution graphically accounts the early problems encountered by fledgling Methodist societies:

> Towards the end of May (1743) mobs from Darlaston, Walsall and Bilston attacked the Wednesbury Methodists. Houses were wrecked and looted, and "even pregnant women were beaten with clubs and otherwise abused."[139]

Perhaps most effective in forming the homogenous and closely knit class or society were the verbal and physical attacks upon the Methodists

---

137. Wesley, *Works [BE]*, Vol. 3, 585. Sermon 112, *On laying the Foundation Stone for the New Chapel*. See also the essay by Carveley, "From Glory to Glory: The Renewal of All Things in Christ. Maximus the Confessor and John Wesley," 173–88. Kenneth Carveley quotes this passage from Wesley sermon in his essay.

138. Kent, *Wesley and the Wesleyans*, 191–92.

139. Church, *More about the Early Methodist People*, 74. See also Wesley, *Works [BE]*, Vol. 11, 282–89. Wesley recounted in *A Farther Appeal to Men of Reason and Religion*, Part III, the attacks made upon the Methodists in Darlaston, West Bromwich and Wednesbury.

led by local clergy or bishops. Notable in this was the Bishop of Exeter,[140] who in the early years of Methodism used a form of intelligence-gathering to discredit Methodism, and he was not averse to using the judiciary to suppress the Methodists. Opposition can be described as a further factor which drew the earliest Methodist people together. I have shown elsewhere that the use of violence, threat, or even another doctrine or the trial of a fellow Methodist could cause a society to bond, or regroup. Equally, however, in the face of local opposition, members would leave the Methodists. This is most clearly seen in the *Journal* entry of March 1743.[141]

As time progressed, however, the desire to be respected and respectable (an inherent trait of Methodist people who followed Wesley's prescriptive dress and behavior code) grew amongst the people who called themselves Methodists. With the falling away of the mob and magistrate, the people who by the time of Wesley's death were interested in their own buildings and place in society left behind the primitive religion that Wesley believed he had founded and sought a settled, communal model of being.

To the generation of primitive religion belonged the experiential class meeting: to a later generation belonged the respected society. Charles Wesley's acerbic comment of the preachers setting themselves up as "respectable" men illustrates this point well. Whether he was concerned that the emerging working class was seeking to settle at a point above their natural station in life, or whether he was noticing that the leadership was "divorcing" from the people is impossible to tell. The one point from it is this: Methodism as a voluntary meeting of men and women focused upon the effects of meeting in class, relied on hostile external forces to give purpose and impetus. Once hostility ceased, the class for the reasons outlined in this section lost purpose and impetus.

The class worked as an effective meeting for the first Methodist people, eager to share in the experiential religion that included them as potential leaders, and willing to submit to the local authority of John and Charles Wesley. Later generations, who revered the Wesleys as founders of their chosen faith structure, but who were not so closely controlled

---

140. This was Bishop Lavington, whose papers are now held at Lambeth Palace Library in the *Secker Papers*.

141. See Wesley, *Works [BE]*, Vol. 19, 318. Amongst those who left was one person as people were rude in the street, twelve because their parents were not willing for them to attend, and five because others spoke badly of the society.

by them directly (but by the itinerants without the same gravitas of authority), did not pick up on the experiential "heritage" of their recent predecessors, preferring not mysticism but organization.

The class meeting could not satisfy the generations beyond the earliest mystical or primary phase as fully as it needed to do to maintain its principal functions: fellowship, conversion and discipleship, financial accountability, and discipline. The use of a class as a catechetical group, and its oversize led to a failure in effectiveness. Further, using the class as a means of eliciting funds to support the emerging leadership relegated its purpose from experiential to functional.

The class became part of a broad organization, not the kingpin of a movement into which every prospective Methodist entered as the starting point for a life changed by faith, and shared in common with others whose own conversion supported, encouraged, and challenged the new member. The life-changes the class required for the first generation were not as stringent for men and women who had grown up within Methodism and who had learned behavior from an early age, or for those who wished to join an organization that offered a respectable model of life within a faith structure.

The following conclusion will examine the class both as crown and cross in the light of Wesley's inheritance of faith and its relatively short effective lifespan prior to Wesley's death in 1791.

9

Conclusion

At the end of chapter 2, I drew attention to the well-known term relating to Wesley's structure of belief, "the quadrilateral."[1] This term, coined by Albert Outler, is used to describe Wesley's theology through Scripture, tradition, reason, and experience. However, I agreed with David Hempton that quadrilateral is inadequate when used in relation to Wesley himself. As Hempton states:

> the attempt to boil Wesley's theology down to a simple formula, such as the much-peddled quadrilateral . . . spectacularly misses the point. A forensic appeal to geometrical precision, of all the approaches to Wesley's theology, is the one least likely to capture its essence.[2]

Hempton's term, "vortex" is more descriptive of Wesley's faith structure. For Wesley, the experience of life to conversion on May 24th 1738 was indeed a vortex, or whirlpool of fast-moving life and spiritual experience. Through his reading, conversation, practice, and witness, Wesley was experiencing, assimilating and rejecting the models of faith with which he came into contact.

This process is most famously known in his rejection of the mystics, but he also disagreed with aspects of Law's and à Kempis' writings amongst others. In *The Christian Library*, intended for the Methodists, primarily the assistants, Wesley abridged many authors, leaving only those aspects of their writing to which he could assent. Likewise, though he held a high regard for de Renty, Wesley still abridged St Jure's biography, ensuring only that de Renty's practices, acceptable to Wesley became known amongst the literate Methodists.

1. See last paragraph of chapter 2.
2. Hempton, *Methodism Empire of the Spirit*, 57.

However, a vortex requires a continuous flow of water into the whirling pool for it to remain a fast-moving, spiralling, vital pool of water. It is undoubtedly true that Hempton's descriptor is accurate for John Wesley, and his brother Charles. They both experienced classic Pietst conversions, through readings of Luther's preface to the Romans (John) and the Commentary on Galatians (Charles), but those came at the end of a long and tortuous journey, especially for the elder Wesley.

The moment of conversion crystalized the journey that had taken since 1725 for John Wesley, and similarly 1729 for his brother. I have already outlined in detail the variety of theologies, doctrines, and periods that Wesley accessed in order to create what was to become the Wesleyan schema, subsequently offered to those who were willing to follow his pattern of Christian living from 1740. The vortex of Wesley's theology was delivered into the Methodist Movement as a given scheme of spirituality. He offered to the society, class, and bands that which he had come to accept and would subsequently teach and seek to hand as a legacy to his people.

I have argued in this book that the fullness of Wesley's theology was found within the class meeting in its earliest years from 1742, and shown that the experiential, expressive, and accountable small group which was the class could offer a faith encounter that was not dissimilar to Wesley's own. Awakening was frequently highly charged with feelings of uncertainty and helplessness, and conversion was a sense of the fullness of God, coupled with visions, voices, and ecstatic experiences.

The four elements of class membership I have drawn out in this book—fellowship, conversion and discipleship, financial accountability, and discipline—were integral to Wesleyan spirituality, and each can be discovered from aspects of the system of faith that Wesley had himself created over a period of 13 years. Each of these aspects is best understood when the vortex of Wesley's system is at its most lively.

From Spener's *Collegia Pietatis*, the later Unitary societies and Fetter Lane Society, fellowship was a vital element of associational life found within the religious life of Pietsts, Anglicans, and Moravians. For each of these traditions the need to deepen fellowship was fundamental to increasing spiritual life, and in some Unitary societies at least might have offered a means of improving in business. At its most meaningful, fellowship required class members to recognize themselves personally accountable, not only for their attendance at class, but also for their use of time and money. This accountability was also to be expressed in the class as members openly and honestly discussed their spiritual state before their peers.

Conversion and discipleship can similarly be identified from earlier traditions. Alongside the Pietists, Anglicans, and Moravians, the Puritans also sought to convert and disciple men and women, in a variety of ways, through the pursuit of godliness and holiness, through the use of journals and diaries, and by teaching that there were degrees of faith. Discipleship was further expressed in Pietstic works of mercy.

Financial accountability appears in the Unitary societies, and young men were encouraged to pay into their society funds to cover the support of the poor. The Methodists were encouraged to support their own poor, as well as those beyond the society's boundaries. Wesley drew on the Unitary society model in which those who were not themselves rich supported their peers in their distress and also reached into the community to assist the poor within the wider community. This accountability diversified beyond the Unitary societies aims as monies gathered began to be used for the support of an emerging stipendiary leadership.

The key to these three strands of the class's life was discipline. Again, Wesley's own highly disciplined life and experience fed into the class meeting all he learned from other traditions. Discipline was central to the Puritan model of faithful living, the Pietsts of both Moravian and Halle traditions and the membership of the Unitary societies. This discipline was not, as Dean[3] suggested, simply a means of ensuring that class members were held in a "repressive" atmosphere under which continuing membership was dependent on submitting to authority. I hold that the discipline of the class was mutual. Members assented to a discipline, shown most clearly in the *Directions* and *Rules*.[4]

Overarching these aspects of communal life were mysticism and the means of grace. Mysticism was found in Wesley's belief that men and women could experience perfection in this life. He drew this aspect of his spirituality from the Puritans, the mystics—both Eastern and continental—and from his high Anglican roots. The class meeting was not the primary place in which perfection was sought, but it was a meeting to which those who had been made perfect would belong. In essence, men and women who had been awakened but had not received assurance, could meet with and see at firsthand those who were perfected in love.

3. Dean, "Disciplined Fellowship."
4. See Appendices 10, 11, and 12.

In stating this, I am aware that Dean understood the bands' primary function to be the "vision of perfection."[5] He then relates the rationale of the class as disciplinary. I disagree that this is so, as the perfected members of the society would have a place in the class meeting. Their presence alone lifts the purpose of the class beyond discipline.

Wesley's personal reliance on the means of grace spilled into every aspect of societal life, and was an element of class life. At one level this reliance was simply to ensure church order, and prevent Methodism being seen as Dissent. At another level this reliance reflected Wesley's high Tory Anglicanism, his understanding of Christian life prior to the Commonwealth and the early church. His insistence on the observance of the fasts of the church,[6] and the baptism[7] or rebaptism of Dissenters is another element of his denial of Dissent and reliance on the Anglican Church as the bedrock of a faithful life.

In Hempton's "vortex model," the class meeting for the earliest generation of Methodists was the same swift-moving, vibrant, and experiential system of faith contained in a small group. The term "vortex" describes well the pattern of Methodist life when those coming into the movement were either previously unchurched, Dissenters seeking a fresh expression of faith, Anglicans moving from traditional Unitary societies, or women, who had previously had their Christian expression confined to the Parish church, or to family prayers.

Some of the earliest testimonies, predominantly from females, elucidate the exciting change of life that Methodism offered. Social status beyond the class remained unaltered, yet within it women and men found that a voice could be expressed which had previously been ignored, and a status was offered that gave opportunity to lead and direct a peer group. I hold therefore that Wesley's quadruple approach—Scripture, tradition, reason, and experience—was a vortex for early Methodists, too.

Hempton clearly states why this might be so. "Any model that lacks dynamic movement toward holiness and its growth within individuals

---

5. Dean, "Disciplined Fellowship," 180.

6. See Appendix 10: Rule 6; Appendix 12: Rule III, part 5.

7. See Wesley's correspondence with Sarah Perrin. Perrin was unbaptized (and may have previously been a Quaker), who despite being allied to Wesley's work in Bristol from 1740 was not baptized until October 1743. This meant her involvement in societal life was limited until that point. See especially letter: Sarah Perrin to John Wesley. October 1743. From: *Letters Chiefly to the Wesley's Volume II.*

and its dissemination throughout the world is clearly inadequate."[8] For the earliest followers of the Methodist model of spirituality within the milieu of the Evangelical Revival this is true. The primary purpose of class membership was fellowship with God. This was found in the context of a dynamic relationship with one's peers under God.

Each individual was able to enter the class aware of his or her unawakened state, and through that recognize the need for salvation, a change of lifestyle and life-pattern and through conversion and discipleship learn the Wesleyan way of faith. This way of faith offered at a significantly deep level not just godliness (what to do), but also holiness (how to be). This can be described simply as a serious turn to works of piety and works of mercy for every Methodist.

The Wesleyan model of organization is remarkably similar to the Moravian model. The Moravians began to organize themselves more rigidly after the experience of 11-year-old Susanne Kühnel in 1727.[9] Over time, classes were introduced, and bands drawn from them. Bands were segregated in the same way as the Methodist bands, which Wesley copied from the Fetter Lane organizational structure. Wesley's classes, which were not introduced until 1742, took the same place within the movement's structure as the Herrnhut classes did in the Moravian structure. Unlike Herrnhut's classes, however, Methodists met in class without segregation by age, sex or marital status.

The settled Moravian model at Herrnhut was unable, even within a short period of time, to maintain ecumenical unity. Wesleyanism drew men and women from a variety of religious backgrounds and it may be that without the closeness of a community rule, Methodism was more easily able to hold in tension varieties of religious understanding.

The caveat, however, is that Wesley imposed his own model of spirituality on the people called Methodists. Perhaps it was easier to do this with a group of people who were voluntarily joining a non-communal movement than in a communal movement made up of a number of traditions. Herrnhut imposed communal rules, but Zinzendorf did not insist that Lutherans, Moravians, and others should accept one model of faith.

It may also be true that Wesley did not attempt communal living for Methodists, as the Fetter Lane experiment with the House "Shiloh"[10]

8. Hempton, *Methodism Empire of the Spirit*, 57.
9. See chapter 1, note 34.
10. See chapter 4, note 254.

in Islington was unsuccessful. This book does not discuss the communal experiment in detail, but its lifespan was short and while Wesley attended meetings at the House, he clearly did not see that this was a model for his own movement, preferring his people not to live in community, separate from society, but in society itself. His firsthand experience of Hernhut might also have led him to see community living as a separation from the world. Despite the Moravians' rejection of mysticism themselves, this manner of living was reminiscent of the mystical desire for the annihilation of the will, with the believer ultimately lost in God.

While John Wesley considered communal living at Kingswood,[11] and built the Orphan House in Newcastle, there is no evidence that either building provided this. Rack[12] adduces that plans were laid for some form of communal living, especially in the holding of "common stock"[13] amongst select society members, but these plans do not seem to have been brought to fruition. While communal living might have fulfilled Wesley's interest in primitive Christianity, held over from his involvement with the Manchester Non-Jurors, the reality was that men and women of the social level Methodism reached could not abandon work and trades for such a lifestyle.

It is unarguable that the earliest years of Methodism, with its highly organized connexional structure, and emerging system of unpaid and subsequently paid leaders, was unique within the Evangelical Revival of the eighteenth century. George Whitefield, Wesley's Calvinist "rival," was constantly traveling between England and America. He left behind him no formal structures. This meant there was no supervised organization for him to return to from America. Early in Wesley's career as a Methodist proper, he took over the building and subsequent running of Kingswood School,[14] on the outskirts of Bristol. Wesley had no qualms in doing this, despite the foundation being Whitefield's, and the fact that his preaching tours were in part a means of raising funds for the school. The Countess of Huntingdon's attempts within the Calvinist branch of the Revival in

11. See Wesley, *Works [BE]*, Vol. 25, 667. Whitefield wrote to Wesley and was clearly upset. In this letter he asked whether it was intended that "the house at Kingswood is intended hereafter for the brethren to dwell in as at Herrnhut?"

12. Rack, *Reasonable Enthusiast*, 364–65.

13. See Wesley, *Works [BE]*, Vol. 9, 270. *A Plain Account of the People Called Methodist*. Wesley outlines the brief rules for the Select Societies in this open letter to the Reverend Mr. Perronet.

14. See Rack, *Reasonable Enthusiast*, 201.

founding Trevecka College in 1768 to train Calvinist ministers was too late to counter Wesley's associational network of lay-led societies.

The voraciousness of Methodism in assimilating other societies—Grimshaw's Howarth societies for example, or taking over Unitary societies, as Wesley did in Bristol, and in Cornwall, and his refusal to reach a rapprochement with Anglican colleagues such as Samuel Walker in Truro, or Henry Venn in Huddersfield—was a strong factor in the success of the emerging movement.[15] In short, while Wesley traveled tirelessly, converts to Methodism, who were also traveling, could begin a new society in their locality, not simply modeled on Wesley's pattern, but as a replica of the pattern.[16] These new societies then became Wesley's. Hence the later need for a single Model Trust Deed on which all preaching houses were to be settled to prevent local societies claiming ownership. This gave the added benefit that Methodists who traveled were able to attend, or join identical societies. Thomas Olivers[17] attended the society in Bristol, and then moved to Bradford upon Avon. He was able to move from one society to another without having to go through a new learning process of the society's meetings.

The Methodists as a movement existed until around 1749. At that point, with the introduction by John Bennet of the circuit meeting in Todmorden, the movement became an organization proper. Wesley added no further layers of structure into the Methodist system, and from that point, he worked on a clearly defined system: conference, circuit, society, class, band, select bands (perfect and penitents). I have not included the select societies into this structure for two reasons. First, they were clearly people taken "from" Methodist life to act as advisors to Wesley personally. Secondly, there is no evidence that these actually functioned beyond Wesley's earliest references to them. I would propose that from 1744 the Conference fulfilled this advisory role.

Into this defined organization, the people called Methodist fitted as their abilities and promotion gave rise: band leaders, class leaders, society leaders, and stewards, local preachers, and assistants, all came to recognize their role within a given structure. Movement through the ele-

15. See chapter 3, note 85. The Unitary society in St Ives became Methodist in 1743

16. An example of a differing pattern was found by Samuel Bradburn in Wales. In the societies to which he was appointed, there were no classes, and he began divisions, later named classes. See Bradburn, *A Memorandum Book, volume I*, September 1775. MA 1977/296.

17. Olivers, "The Life of Thomas Olivers," 82. See also 85.

ments of the organization can be called promotion, and with promotion and ensuing responsibility came a desire, as Weber argued, for the organization to survive to maintain their place. Once the Methodists began supporting assistants on stipends, however small,[18] then routinization was taking hold. Wesley was the charismatic leader, but he was rarely present in circuits and societies. Local leadership therefore took the initiative to maintain Methodism as an organization. It is here I would argue that Hempton's definition of Wesley's spirituality fails. A vortex cannot settle, yet that is what happened with the Methodist organization. It is accurate to replace *vortex* with *quadrilateral* at this point, since an organized and settled Methodism required a set form of spirituality that each Methodist could access, accept, and develop through.

Until a settled pattern emerged and was imposed across the Connexion, a vortex was indeed a helpful descriptor. The earliest Methodists found themselves subjected to verbal, printed, and physical abuse. The earliest Methodists relied upon highly charged experiential moments of awakening and conversion. The first Methodists, who came from a variety of backgrounds needed a place in which to assimilate; the class was that place. Later Methodists joined for different reasons.

The quadrilateral model aptly fits later "secondary" Methodists. These received the Methodist system from a well-regulated organization. Through publications, Wesley's occasional personal visits, and the power of the assistants, the spirituality which Wesley held personally was handed to the people as a given scheme. For these Methodists, the quadrilateral model is a helpful descriptor, primarily because they saw the relationship between Scripture, tradition, reason, and experience, not as a fast swirling pool of moving spirituality, but as a body of belief handed from a previous generation, or discovered through the preacher's sermons, Wesley's writings, or the intimacy of the class.

The hymns of Charles Wesley provided a backdrop against which Methodists could reference their lives. Hymnody gave a means of expressing hopes, expectations, and experiences in a communal manner. Equally, however, these same hymns, set within the context of Scripture, or based upon a desired experience, became integral to the Wesleyan manner of spirituality. Whether sung lustily, or read privately, the hymns published in various forms from 1739 gave to the Wesleys' followers a way of assimilating their spirituality in a common form. Undoubtedly

---

18. See Crowther, *A True and Complete Portraiture of Methodism*, 253–54.

a vital element to the success of the Wesleyan movement, they equally stood as a way in which the quadrilateral of faith could be learned. The hymns expressed what was believed, from awakening to sanctification, and modeled the journey from one to the other. As a settled organization emerged from the early years of a tumultuous movement, hymnody provided a way in which, perhaps more than any other Wesleyan teaching method, spirituality could be assimilated as a schema of belief.

The book has discussed emerging spirituality over a period of more than 200 years. Beginning with the Puritans who returned to England after Mary Tudor's death, and discussing the emergence of piety in Europe, I have shown how Wesley drew upon a variety of religious affections, and assimilated those he found acceptable into his own body of belief. Within that period, each strand of religious belief came to be routinized, in that each became recognizable as a system of belief to which an individual could be held. Methodism was no different. While each strand of belief represented a new mode from that which existed previously, no new strand entirely replaced that which had preceded it.

In the Evangelical Revival, Methodism was one single strand, albeit the most carefully organized and highly regulated. Therefore, the routinization that occurred within Methodism could be identified in other strands, with which this book is not concerned. Notably, routinization affected the class meeting most severely. As Wesley's Methodists organized, leaders began to emerge from the class who saw their future within the organization, and in time their control over the local societies and circuits grew. Wesley became a figurehead, rather than the controlling charismatic leader of the earliest period.

As I evidenced in chapter 6, the membership reacted to routinization by non-attendance at class meetings and drawing away from the openness required of them week by week. The elective affinity originally given to the class, through manner, dress, language, and behavior, was not maintained as affinity occurred within the life of the society, the larger, less demanding meeting. The centrality of the class therefore declined.

In a similar vein, totemism added to the class's decline. As Wesley became more distant from the Methodist people, yet held the importance of meeting in a class, especially in his letters and publications aimed at leaders rather than members, the class took on an iconic status, helped by Wesley's spiritual language addressed to the foundation of the class, not least that it was a "prudential" means of grace.

As was shown in the article about Kim Il Sung,[19] the process of totemism is occurring in part because the leadership are willing to afford him such status, and in part because the people themselves are willing to accept that this status is being placed upon Kim Il Sung. Similarly, the leadership of Methodism accepted that Wesley held a high regard for the class, and therefore undertook their part in maintaining the class in a system which had outgrown it. Unlike the acceptance of the totemic status of Kim Il Sung by the North Korean people, the Methodist people expressed their lack of interest in the class by not attending, or by coming to faith through other mediums in Methodism, notably the prayer meeting.

Within the discussion of totemism in chapter 7, I noted that, as the class meeting was used as the only means of entry into the society, it had to survive, even as a shell of its original purpose, to fulfill that function. As an ideal, made known to the people through Wesley's publications, the totemic class was the ideal place to be awakened, converted, and discipled, and it created a model through which affective religion could be discovered.

The discussion of homogeneity within chapter 7 addressed the "them and us" syndrome that an homogenous unit (the class meeting) required for a level of success. Once Methodism settled, the emphasis of the homogenous unit moved from the experiential class to the routine society. The class meeting required a specific mode of entry; the society required only an acceptance of broad Methodist values.

Finally, in chapter 8, I evidenced the manner in which the class was wholly operational for only one generation—those who joined while Methodism was under attack, or those who desired to change their life and lifestyle. The use of Troeltsch's and Kent's terminology assisted the description of the process in which later generations moved away from a mystical understanding of faith and life, expressed in the experiential class meeting, to a sect-like settled understanding of faith and life in which being a Methodist was not to be derided, but a welcomed and accepted model of religious life, even though outside the state religion.

The earliest Methodists entered into a mystical or primary religious view of the world through the Methodist movement. Mysticism featured in Wesley's reasoning for leaving England for Georgia in 1735, and was the teaching he would abandon because of the lack of "concrete" faith it offered. The Methodists of the 1740s onwards discovered a mystical

---

19. See chapter 7, note 19.

"world of ideas" within the class meeting, offering the possibility of an immediate experience of God in the here and now. For them, mysticism was tempered by adherence to the means of grace, and by continuing to reside within the communities from which they had come—unlike Wesley, who had more or less fled England and all that was secure.

Later Methodist men and women sought the secondary or sect-like experience of religious life, offering an established routine of religious life, within a culture that was no longer as distrustful of the Methodists. The matured lifestyle of the people, exampled by Ruth's account of the decline of the American Methodist love feast, accounted for the loss of interest of later generations in the full meaning of class, a meaning that could be read about, sung of, and testified to through Wesley's constant publications and his leaders' regular exhortations, but which no longer spoke personally to the people called Methodists who were finding their way to God.

The place of Methodism in the Evangelical Revival is unparalleled, even though the emergence of Methodism within it was one new model of religious experience among many. This new model or discontinuity was not recognized as such by Wesley or his brother. Both considered themselves constant priests in the Church of England, and they demanded their members gave allegiance to the same mother Church. However, Wesley drew into his own system of belief more elements of other religious strands or traditions than any other leader. Other traditions were plundered by Wesley and assimilated into his own schema, under the overarching umbrella of Anglican allegiance within Methodism.

In time, Methodism experienced settlement and regulation and became a recognized and organized branch of the Evangelical Revival that it had broken into with such vigor in 1740. Just as Wesley drew from established schemas of belief, so his own schema matured and Methodism added to the fullness of the body of English belief, giving a name to a particular strand. Methodist became as recognizable as Pietist, Puritan, Moravian, or Anglican.

The class meeting became a casualty of the maturation of the movement into an organization because it was the single group to which everyone belonged, and it was the single group that demanded a particular form of religious experience to work. The band and subsets of the band required members to actively seek holiness, and it is true they also declined and failed,[20] but there was never a requirement for any Methodist

---

20. See "Advice to Preachers," in *A History of the Methodist Church in Great Britain*, 214. In 1786 Wesley exhorted the assistants to re-establish the bands and select societies.

to belong; just a hope on Wesley's part that some would persevere toward perfection. The class's importance as a prudential means of grace gave it a place that was hard to dislodge. With the earliest Methodist people, there undoubtedly was a prudential element to the meeting; for God's prevenient grace had drawn together a disparate group into one body.

Later Methodists, who entered a routinized, idealized, and totemized class became "second generation" Methodists, who could not understand why such value was placed upon a meeting in which secrecy was paramount, and the verbal expression of temptation and sin, with the resultant chiding or praise was required.

In all, the decline of the class from crown to cross was, as I have argued through this book, inexorable and inevitable. Expressed in the context of "vortex" and "quadrilateral" in this conclusion, I have shown how the Methodists matured in spite of Wesley's inability to change as his people's circumstances changed—giving rise in part to the constant stream of correspondence and publications urging class observance. The question remains, however: would Methodism have experienced success in its earliest "primary" period if the class meeting had not become the portal into the movement? I assert that it would not.

The class meeting offered a small, highly affective, experiential group meeting, in which each individual was wholly included, for each person's experience spoke to another's. This "prudential means" offered a place for the inarticulate and illiterate as much as the rising artisan classes, who were otherwise excluded from Anglican religious observance, or members of Dissenting groups. Personal experience which could not be found in Dissent or the Church of England could be spoken of and heard about in class, giving to each newly awakened searching individual not just the possibility but the promise of the same awareness of faith.

Hempton once more assists in this conclusion. Writing on the centrality of scriptural holiness, he draws out the importance for the Methodists of self-determination in faith:

> What is distinctive about Methodist Spirituality, however, is its remorseless emphasis on scriptural holiness and on the need for human beings to take control of their spiritual destinies, not as passive respondents to the iron will of God, but as active agents in "working out our own salvation" or what one scholar has aptly called "responsible grace."[21]

21. Hempton, *Methodism Empire of the Spirit*, 58. Randy Maddox used the term "responsible grace." See Maddox, *Responsible Grace. John Wesley's Practical Theology*.

This self-determinism, drawn by Hempton from the journey of scriptural holiness, was the crown of the class meeting—that each member was responsible for his or her personal development. Equally it describes the class's decline—that later Methodists sought their self-determination within the less rigorous society meeting. The Methodists of the secondary period did not see their life as any less dedicated to scriptural holiness, but the context in which that was worked out was in a more public arena.

The class meeting was the crown of the first Methodists' experiential lives; it became the cross of the later Methodists' settled, regulated, and socially acceptable lives. The class was a reminder to those outside Methodism of its earlier, more separatist period, when the mystical life was present for those who joined. It was also a reminder, for Wesley particularly, of a period that might be described as a "golden age," when immediate access to God was discovered by a mainly unchurched population in the context of a small prudentially ordained group. While for the general population in the later period, the decline of the class made Methodism less difficult to enter, and more acceptable to join; for Wesley it removed, or dulled, the primary reason for entering Methodism, a desire to flee from the wrath to come.

The class did not convert the millions that Henderson asserted in the introduction. It did, however, give to the movement an initial impetus that no other grouping had: a welcoming and peer-based meeting that offered and delivered access to an experience of God's grace, leading to conversion, and embarking upon the path toward perfection in Christ. When the class declined, the single most effective evangelistic tool available to the Methodists was lost forever. In the process of organization and with the generational gap between the foundation of the movement and the present widening, only Wesley's insistence on the efficacy of the class continued to maintain its place as the entry point for the Methodist people.

The class meeting was the crown of the movement, and the cross of the organization that was Methodism in the eighteenth century. This book started out to illustrate how the class altered within a set period of time, and how the people who accessed the class altered their understanding of its purpose. Through it I have shown how the inheritance of John Wesley, brought into a schema of spirituality in Methodism, could be accessed most meaningfully in the class meeting. I have indicated how that spirituality offered the first generation of Methodists a radical model of Christian faith different from any other, especially through established Anglicanism, and how that model became unpopular as Methodists ceased to want to share in such an experiential manner of Christian formation, preferring the society, which offered a style of worship, which, while distinctive, was not entirely dissimilar to Anglicanism, or Dissent.

Here, then, was the rise and decline of the class meeting taking place in the 49 years before Wesley's death. With the class's functional demise, Methodism embarked on a path that led to its acceptance within the mainstream of English religious life. The class remained in name, and in reality continued to be the nominal entrance into the society into the late nineteenth century, but no attempt to reinvigorate the class would succeed. In 1865, correspondence on the issue of class-attendance as a condition of membership compared English and American models of society-admission, with the English Methodists continuing to insist on class-observance. One correspondent, "A Liberal," gave voice to the reality that would shortly occur:

> I believe that Methodism would gain both in spirituality and in power, were meeting in a Class allowed to become voluntary instead of compulsory, that I am inclined to think our American brethren are ahead of us in this matter, and that we might take a leaf out of their book with advantage to ourselves.[22]

The author could not have known that within a few short years the attachment of membership to class attendance would be irrevocably severed; however, the reality was that the membership had chosen to distance themselves from the class meeting a century before the leadership assented to the actuality.

---

22. See "The Class Meeting in Decline," 531.

Appendix 1

The Rules of Anthony Horneck's Savoy Society[1]

1. All that enter into such a Society shall resolve upon a holy and serious life.
2. No person shall be admitted into the Society until he has arrived at the age of sixteen, and has been first confirmed by the bishop, and solemnly taken upon himself his baptismal vow.
3. They shall choose a minister of the Church of England to direct them.
4. They shall not be allowed, in their meetings, to discourse of any controverted point of divinity.
5. Neither shall they discourse of the government of Church or State.
6. In their meetings they shall use no prayers but those of the Church, such as the Litany and Collects, and other prescribed prayers; but still they shall not use any that peculiarly belong to the minister, as the absolution.
7. The minister, whom they choose, shall direct what practical divinity shall be read at these meetings.
8. They may have liberty, after prayer and reading, to sing a psalm.
9. After all is done, if there be any time left, they may discourse each other about their spiritual concerns; but this shall not be a standing exercise which any shall be obliged to attend unto.

---

1. From: F. W. B. Bullock. *Voluntary Religious Societies 1520–1799.*

10 One day in the week shall be appointed for this meeting, for such as cannot come on the Lord's day; and he that absents himself without cause shall pay three-pence to the box.

11 Every time they meet, every one shall give six-pence to the box.

12 On a certain day in the year, viz. Whit-Tuesday, two stewards shall be chosen, and a moderate dinner provided, and a sermon preached; and the money distributed (necessary charges deducted) to the poor.

13 A book shall be bought, in which these orders shall be written.

14 None shall be admitted into this Society, without the consent of the minister who presides over it; and no apprentice shall be capable of being chosen.

15 If a case of conscience shall arise, it shall be brought before the minister.

16 If any member think fit to leave the Society, he shall pay five shillings to the stock.

17 The major part of the Society shall conclude the rest.

18 The following rules are more especially recommended, to the members of the Society, viz. To love one another. When reviled, not to revile again. To speak evil of no man. To wrong no man. To pray, if possible, seven times a day. To keep close to the Church of England. To transact all things peaceably and gently. To be helpful to each other. To use themselves to holy thoughts in their coming in and going out. To examine themselves every night. To give every one their due. To obey superiors, both spiritual and temporal.

Appendix 2

The Poplar Regulations[1]

1. That the sole design of this Society being to promote real holiness of heart and life: it is absolutely necessary that the persons, who enter into it, do seriously resolve, by the grace of God, to apply themselves in good earnest to all means proper to make them wise unto salvation. (1 Pet. i.15; Josh xxiv.15; 2 Tim. iii.15)

2. That in order to their being of one heart in this design, every member of this Society shall own and manifest himself to be of the Church of England, and frequent the liturgy, and other public holy exercises of the same. And that they be careful withal to express due Christian charity, candour and moderation towards all such Dissenters as are of good conversation. (Rom. xv.5, 6: Phil. ii.2: 1 Pet. ii.13; Eph. iv.2; Rom xii.18)

3. That the members of this Society shall meet together one evening in the week at a convenient place, in order to encourage each other in practical holiness, by discoursing on spiritual subjects, and read God's holy word, and to pray to Almighty God, and praise Name together. And to this assembly any serious person may be admitted upon request. (1 Thess. v.14; Rom. xiv.19; psalm xxxiv.3)

4. That at such meetings there be no hot disputes about controversial points, State affairs, or the concerns of trade, and worldly things; but that the whole bent of the discourse be to glorify God, and edify one another in love. (Rom xv.6; Eph iv.16)

---

1. Reproduced from F. W. B. Bullock. *Voluntary Religious Societies 1520–1799*. 140–2.

5. That it be left to every person's discretion to contribute at every weekly meeting, what he thinks fit towards a public stock for pious and charitable uses; and the money thus collected shall be kept by the two stewards to the Society, who shall be chosen by majority of votes once a years, or oftener, to be disposed of by the consent of the major part of the Society, for the uses above-mentioned. And the said stewards shall keep a faithful register of what is thus collected and distributed, to be perused by any member of the Society, at his request. (1 Cor. xvi.2)

6. That any respective member may recommend any object of charity to the stewards, who shall (with the consent of the rest) give out of the common stock, according as the occasion requires. And in a case of extraordinary necessity, every particular person shall be desired to contribute farther, as he thinks fit.

7. That every one who absents himself four meetings together (without giving a satisfactory account to the stewards) shall be looked upon as disaffected to the Society.

8. That none shall be admitted into this Society, without giving due notice thereof to the stewards, who shall acquaint the whole Society therewith. And after due inquiring into their religious purposes and manner of life, the stewards may admit them if the major part of the Society allows it, and not otherwise. And with the like joint consent, they may exclude and member proved guilty of any mis-behaviour, after due admonition, unless he gives sufficient testimony of his repentance and amendment, before the whole Society.

9. It is hereby recommended to every person concerned in this Society, to consider the many inconveniences (and many times sins), which attend ale-house-games, and wholly decline them. And to shun all unnecessary resort to such houses and taverns, and wholly to avoid lewd play-houses. (Gal, v.13; 1 Thess. v.22)

10. That whereas the following duties have been too much neglected to the scandal and reproach of our holy religion, they do resolve, by the grace of God, to make it their serious endeavour,

To be just in all their dealing, even to exemplary strictness. (1 Thess. iv.6)

To pray many times every day: remembering our continual dependence upon God, both for spiritual and temporal things. (1 Thess. v.7)

To partake of the Lord's Supper at least once a month, if not prevented by a reasonable impediment. (1 Cor. xi.26; Luke xxii.19)

To practise the profoundest meekness and humility. (Matth. xi.29)

To watch against censuring others. (Matth. vii.1)

To accustom themselves to holy thoughts in all places. (Psalm cxxxix.23)

To be helpful to one another. (1 Cor. xii.25)

To exercise tenderness, patience, and compassion towards all men. (Tit. iii.2)

To make reflections on themselves when they read the Holy Bible, or other good books, and when they hear sermons. (1 Cor. x.11)

To shun all foreseen occasions of evil: as evil company, known temptations, etc. (1 Thess. v.22)

To think often on the different estates of the glorified and the damned, in the unchangeable eternity, to which we are hastening. (Luke xvi.25)

To examine themselves every night, what good or evil they have done in the day past. (2 Cor. xiii.5)

To keep a private fast once a month (especially near their approaching the Lord's table), if at their own disposal; or to fast from some meals when they may conveniently. (Matt. vi.16; Luke v.35)

To mortify the flesh, with its affections and lusts. (Gal. V. 19, 24)

To advance in heavenly-mindedness and in all grace. (1 Pet. iii.8)

To shun spiritual pride, and the effects of it; as railing, anger peevishness, and impatience of contradiction, and the like.

To pray for the whole Society in their private prayers. (James v.16)

To read pious books often for their edification, but especially the Holy Bible (John v. 39); and herein particularly, Matt. v, vi, vii,;

Luke xv, xvi; Rom. xii, xiii; Eph. v, vi; 1 Thess. v; Rev. i, ii, iii, xxi, xxii. And in the Old Testament, Levit. Xxvi; Deut. Xxviii; Is. Liii; Ezek.xxxvi.

To be continually mindful of the great obligation of this special profession of religion; and to walk so circumspectly, that none may be offended or discouraged from it by what they see in them; nor occasion given to any to speak reproachfully of it.

To shun all manner of affectation and moroseness, and be of a civil and obliging deportment to all me.

11. That they often consider (with an awful dread of God's wrath) the sad height to which the sins of many are advanced in this our nation; and the bleeding divisions thereof in Church and State. And that every member be ready to do what, upon consulting with each other, shall be thought advisable, towards the punishment of public profaneness, according to the good laws of our land, required to be put in execution by the King's and the late Queen's special order. And to do what befits them in their stations, in order to the cementing of our divisions. (Mal. iii. 16; Judg. v. 15; Deut. xiii. 8; Levit.xxiv. 11)

12. That each member shall encourage the catechising of young and ignorant people in their respective families, according to their stations and abilities: and shall observe all manner of religious family-duties. (Deut. vi. 7; Josh. Xxiv. 15)

13. That the major part of the Society shall have power to make a new order to bind the whole, when need requires; if it be approved by three pious and learned ministers of the Church of England, nominated by the whole Society.

14. That these orders shall be read over at least four times in the year, by one of the Stewards; and that with such deliberation, that each member may have time to examine himself by them, or to speak his mind in anything relating to them.

15. lastly, that every member of this Society shall (after mature deliberation and due trial), express his approbation of these orders, and his resolution to endeavour to live up to them. In order to which, he shall constantly keep a copy of them by him.

The end of the Orders

Appendix 3

Samuel Wesley's Rule for the Epworth Society[1]

THIS SOCIETY FIRST MET on the 1ˢᵗ February 1701–1702

I Every week at set hours, when 2 or 3, or more do meet together for this intent, First to pray to God; Secondly to read the Holy Scriptures, and discourse upon Religious Matters for their mutual Edification; and Thirdly, to deliberate about the Edification of our neighbour, and the promoting it.

II Those that do thus meet together, are above all things solicitous about the Salvation of their neighbour, yea they make it their business to be Christians not only in name but in deed: least they should strive rashly to pull out the Mote from the Eies of others, not observing the Beam in their own; and lest while they preach to others themselves should become castaways.

III For this reason they do not admit every body promiscuously, but if any one desires to be of their Society, it must be done by the consent of all; and therefore his piety ought to be known to all, lest a little leven should spoil the whole lump, For they take it for Granted that things will then fall out well, when each of them shall be of that mind, as that it may be affirm'd upon good Grounds that This is Emmanuel that dwells through Faith, of the power of God, in the Heart of every One, as in his Temple.

IIII Nor do they allow that the number of their members should encrease too much, lest this Religious design should fall with its

---

1. W. O. B. Allen and E. McCLure. *Two Hundred Years: The History of The Society for Promoting Christian Knowledge, 1698–1898*. London: S.P.C.K., 1898, 89–93. See also D. L. Watson. *The early Methodist Class Meeting*. Nashville: Discipleship Resources, 1985, 194–6.

own weight, or at least be marr'd. Therefore when they have twelve Members they admitt no more. But if God shall stir up more, two shall desire the same Edification with them, they seperate two members from them, to form a new Society with those that desire it, till that also grow's up to the number of Twelve, and so another new Society be form'd out of it.

V A Society or two now being set up; the think it may be practicable to take such in persons only, in whom there may be hopes, that by such a pious Conversation, they may be brought to a real and serious denying of the World, yet not to admit above 2 or 3 at the most of such Members, of whose solid piety they are not yet sufficiently appris'd lest by any unwary Charity towards all it may happen by degrees, that Darkness might begin to get ground.

VI But if they of whose Conversion to God there may be hopes, shall not blush to devote themselves to Vice and Wickedness and thereby become a scandal to their neighbour: they are no longer look'd as a part of the Society lest those who are sincere should e drawn to partake either of the Vice or of the Scandal.

VII All Debates about the Corruption of Manners which have crept into the Church, of Amending or Reforming the Church point of Manners, is referr'd to the first Society. The other Societies are contented with their own Edification and if any one knows what will tend to the publick Edification, he discover's it to the first Society, that so it may be consider'd by all the Members thereof, how it does conduce towards the common design, and may be reduced into practice.

VIII But this first Society does in no wise assume any prerogative to itself: but the Debating about the publick Edification is for this reason; least one Society should hinder another, and because all are not fitt to be Counsellors. Hence it is that this Society is obliged to be carefull to take in such Members alone, as are able to help the Church by their wisdom and good advices.

VIIII They do not take in any Women into these Societies, in order to avoid scandal and all other abuses the more easily, to which promiscuous meeting cannot be but liable. Women may hear their Husbands at Home, and Girls their parents: for tis a duty incumbent upon every Member of these Societies, next to his own soul to be chiefly solicitous for those of his Family. And if there be any one who is a Master of a Family, yet by his grace Conversation he may be very beneficial to those amongst whom he lives, tis very necessary that by living Examples men may see what a true Christian is, who still is very hard to meet with.

X   they carry on a subscription in every Society, towards which every Member contributes each Meeting, according to his Charity and ability. The money so collected is to be expended no other way than in promoting the designs of the Societies, or for reforming the Church.

XI   Their first care is to set Schools for the Poor, wherein Children (or if need be, Adult Persons,) may be instructed in the Fundamentals of Christianity by en of known and approv'd Piety.

XII   Their second design is to procure little Practical Treatises from Holland, England, and Germany, &c. to translate them into the Vulgar Tounge, print them, and so to give or lend them to those who are less solicitous of their own and others Edification.

XIII   The Third is to establish a Correspondence with such Societies in England, Germany, &c. that so they may mutually Edify one another: especially since they have learn'd that by keeping up a Correspondence, as they gain knowledge and experience in Edifying the whole Church: so their wholesome advices will thereby be forwarded and the better reduced to practise.

XIIII   The Fourth is to take Care of the Sick and other Poor, and to afford them Spiritual as well as Corporal Helps. When their Stock is sufficiently large to carry on these pious Designs, they deliberate of some other proper method of disposing of that which remains. The means will not fail to be present, if all things shall be done of God, in God and thro' God.

Appendix 4

The Rules of the Rev Samuel Walker's Truro Society[1]

THE DESIGN IS THREEFOLD-TO glorify God-to quicken and confirm ourselves in faith and holiness-and to render us more useful among our neighbours.

First. As a Society, we shall be better able to glorify God; for hereby we shall bear a more public and convincing testimony to the cause of Christ, and make a more avowed profession of his name and gospel in these evil days, than we could do when separate. Every one of you desires that his kingdom may be further enlarged, and better established than it is, which, by joining your hands together to promote so desirable an end, will be most effectually brought about. Take then these cautions for this purpose.

Let each look upon himself as associated with others, to promote the honour of their common master.

Never therefore be ashamed of him, or his doctrines, or your fellow Christians in this Society.

Demean yourselves, every one, as his disciples, by walking in all humility, meekness, heavenly mindedness, and charity, after his blessed example.

Keep yourselves heedfully fro all things that may disgrace your profession, or this Society-such as pride, in a conceit of your own knowledge and attainments, or that you are admitted members of this Society-valuing yourselves on any distinction of place or circumstances, sinking into a worldly frame, or declining into sloth and idleness, practising at least dishonesty, or conniving at it in others; making sinful compliances

---

1. Reproduced from F. W. B. Bullock. *Voluntary religious Societies 1520-1799*. 206-9.

to avoid shame, or promote your temporal interests, falling into lukewarmness, and losing your first love, and absenting yourselves from, or slighting public ordinances.

Often, especially before or after temptations to any of these, reflect that you belong to a Religious Society, instituted to promote the honour of Christ.

Secondly. The second design of this Society is to quicken, comfort and build up yourselves, and one another in your holy faith. By this means, we shall be better able to maintain the war against our enemies, who are all united against us, and to grow in grace; as we may hope, by this association, we shall have the Spirit to assist and strengthen us; we shall have the benefit of mutual advice, and reproof; shall be more hardy in opposing temptations besetting us from a wicked world: shall walk under a peculiarly happy restraint, from the observation and eyes of our brethren upon us, and be assisted by the mutual prayers of each for the rest. To this end,

Watch over one another in love.

Be willing to hear of your faults, and thankful for reproof.

Watch against any disgust against any of your brethren, and if any arise, without delay tell the party, and if that fail, the director.

Desire the prayers of one another, and pray for one another.

Be sure not to rest on being members of this Society, as if that could be your security either from falling here, or for heaven hereafter.

Guard against the least decay in your love for Christ, zeal for his honour, and love to souls.

Preserve continually in your mind, your obligations to these things, from your relation to us as members of this Society.

Thirdly. The third design of this Society is to promote our usefulness among our neighbours. Hereby we make ourselves more discernable. People cannot so easily be quiet in their sins, when they see United Societies testifying against them by their practice. Good examples are naturally more prevalent than reproof or advice, especially if the first be wanting. To this end,

Be careful to set such examples to all about you.

Think not to gain any by sinful compliances.

Discountenance all things which may be snares to your neighbours, such as public-houses, gaming, and many diversions and sports, which are not convenient nor of good report.

Shew all love to men's souls, and enforce that by a care of their bodies.

Avoid all quarrels and disputes, which usually begin in pride or impatience, and end in anger, malice, and revenge.

Do not be angry with those who blame this Society. If they point out anything wrong, reform it; if not, meekly and silently bear with them.

Despise none in your hearts, because not members with you.

Shew no valuing of yourselves because you are.

Let the following motives encourage you to observe the rules:

Real disciples must do more than nominal professors.

The Spirit is promised to comfort and assit those who walk by these rules.

You will have peace and satisfaction in your own consciences.

You are engaged in the most honourable service.

You will hereby promote the best of interests, and honour the best of masters.

He will acknowledge you as his servants, and reward your labours and perseverance, in the day of his appearing.

~

The Orders for the Religious Societies at Truro, under the direction of the Rev Mr. S.W.–Instituted February, 1754, read as follows: -

In the single men's Society, no woman to be admitted.

In the married men's, their wives and other women, but no single men.

That the sole design of this Society, is to promote real holiness in the heart and life of all who belong to it, in a dependence upon the Divine Power, and the conduct of the Holy Spirit, through our Lord Jesus Christ, to advance and perfect all good in us.

That in order to our being of one heart, and one mind, and to prevent whatever may engender strife as well as to remove all occasion of offence being taken against us, no person be admitted a member of this Society, or be allowed to continue such, who is a member of any other religious meeting, or follows any other preaching than that of the established ministry in this town. That none be admitted members, but such as are inhabitants here and communicants, and that no person at any time be introduced, but at the request of the director.

That the members of this Society do meet together at a convenient place, one evening in every week, and that they go home at nine o'clock.

That every member endeavour to give constant attendance, and be present at the hour of meeting precisely, and that whoever absents himself four meetings together, without giving satisfactory reason to the Society, shall be looked upon as disaffected to it.

That to prevent confusion, no person be removed from the Society but by the director, who shall be present on such occasion, and that any person do apply to him in cases where he judges such removal needful; and that a disorderly carriage, or a proud contentious, disputing temper (the greatest bane to Christian love and peace) be sufficient ground for such complaint and removal.

N.B. By a disorderly carriage, we mean not only the commission of gross and scandalous sins, but also what are esteemed matters of little moment in the eyes of the world, such as light use of the words, Lord, God, Jesus etc. in ordinary conversation, which we cannot but interpret as an evidence of the want of God's presence in the heart. The buying and selling of goods which have not paid custom. The doing of needless work on the Lord's day. The frequenting ale-houses or taverns without necessary business.

And considering the said consequences of vain amusements so generally practised, we do in charity to the souls of others, as well as to avoid the danger of such things to ourselves, think ourselves obliged to use particular caution, with respect to many of them, however innocent they may be, or are esteemed, to be in themselves; such as cards, dancing, clubs for entertainment, play-houses, sports at festivals and parish feasts, and as much as may be parish feasts themselves; lest by joining therein, we are a hindrance to ourselves and others. And that no person may remove from one place or Society to another, without the consent of the director.

That with the concurrence of the director, the major part of the Society may have power to make new orders, when need shall require it, but that the proposal for this purpose be made by the director, and that any member may consult him about it before the day of the meeting.

That every member do esteem himself peculiarly obliged to live in an inoffensive and orderly manner, to the glory of God and the edification of his neighbours; that he study to advance himself and others, humility and meekness, faith in our Lord Jesus Christ, love to God, gospel repentance, and new obedience, in which things Christian edification consists, and not in vain janglings. And that in all his conversation and articles of his faith, he stick close to the plain and obvious sense of Holy Scripture, carefully avoiding all intricate niceties and refinements upon it.

That these orders shall be read over at least four times a year by the director, and that with such deliberation, that each member may have time to examine his own conduct by them.

Appendix 5

Articles of the Religious Societies at Truro[1]

1st Men's Society	Society of married men
That no woman be admitted to this Society	their wives and other women no unmarried man be admitted to this society

2d That the sole design of this Society is to promote real holiness in heart and life trusting in the Divine Power and gracious conduct of the Holy Spirit thro' our Lord Jesus Christ to excite, advance and perfect all good in us.

3d That in order to our being of one heart and one mind and to prevent all things which may gender strifes as well as to remove all occasions of offence being taken at us, no person be admitted a member of this society or be allow'd to continue such who is a member of any other meeting or follows any other preaching than that of the established ministry of this town, that none be members of this society than are inhabitants of this town and communicants and that no person at any time be introduced but by the request of the Director.

4th That no person be admitted member but upon the recommendation of the Director or with the consent of the majority of the members so present and that they Director be the Rev'd Mr. Samuel Walker curate of this town.

5 That the members of this society will meet together one evening of the week at a convenient place and that they go home at 9 o'clock and that the Director do appoint a deputy to transact all necessary affairs and to read in his absence who shall be changed at pleasure and that all matters of business be done before the sentences begin.

1. Taken from the Lavington Papers at Lambeth Palace Library. Seck 8.16.

6 That every member will labour to give constant attendance and to be present at the House of Meeting precisely and that whoever absents himself four nights successively without giving a satisfactory account to the Deputy which shall by him be communicated to the Society shall be looked upon as disaffected the Society.

7 That to prevent confusion no person be removed from this Society but by the Director, who if possible shall be present upon such occasions and that any member do beforehand apply to the Director if he judge such removal needful–shall a disorderly carriage, a proud contentious and disputing temper (the greatest adversary of Christian love and peace) be sufficient grounds for such complaints and removal and that no person may remove from one society to another without the Director's consent.

8 That with the consent of the director the major part of the Society have power to make a new order when need requires but thatg the Proposal for this purpose be made by the Director or someone deputed by him and that any person may consult him thereon before the day of meeting.

9 That every member do consider himself as peculiarly obliged to live in an inoffensive and orderly manner to the glory of God and the edifying of his neighbours that he study to advance in himself and others humility, faith in our Lord Jesus Christ, love to God, Gospel repentance and new obedience, wherein Christian edification doth consist; and in all plain and obvious sense to the Holy Scriptures carefully avoiding all niceties and refinements upon them.

10 That the orders shall be read over at least four times in the year by the Director or Deputy and that with such deliberation that each member may have time to examine himself by them

11 That the membership of this Society do meekly & humbly join together in the following exercises, the Director or in his absence the Deputy shall read the following sentences –

> God is greatly to be feared &c

Then shall be said these three Collects all kneeling

> Prevent us &c
> O most blessed &c

> O God for as much &c

Then all seating themselves shall be read a portion of Scripture with Mr. Ruskitts exposition appointed by the Director–

Then all kneeling down they shall joyn in the Confession of sin

> O Almighty God &c
> Our Father &c

After which the Director alone shall say

> Almighty and everlasting God &c
> O most holy & blessed God &c

Then all standing up a psalm shall be sung and a sermon read to be appointed by the Director, after which shall be read some suitable prayers he shall judge fit.

Then all standing up this Exhortation and Humility shall be read

> My brethren since the great God &c

And a Psalm being sung the Reader shall say

> It is very meet &c

All shall joyn

> Therefore with angels &c

The Reader alone

> May the Grace of God & C

Appendix 6 (Rules A)

The Rules of the Fetter Lane Society[1]

"THE RULES and orders of a religious Society meeting AT PRESENT IN A ROOM in Fetter Lane. THE MEMBERS CONSISTING OF PERSONS IN COMMUNION WITH THE ESTABLISHED CHURCH, GLORY TO GOD IN THE HIGHEST ON EARTH PEACE GOOD WILL TOWARDS MEN. LITTLE CHILDREN LET US LOVE ONE ANOTHER

MAY 1 1738

In obedience to the command of God by St James (5:16) and by the advice of Peter Boehler: (a It was agreed by John Bray, Brazier; Sheperd Wolf, Barber; John Edmonds, Poulterer; James Hutton, Bookseller; William Oxlee, Clogmaker; William Clarke, Barber; John Shaw (late) attorney & John Wesley, Clerk–All members of the Church of England

That they will meet together once a week, to confess their faults one to another, And pray for one another, that they may be healed.

That any others of whose sincerity they are well assured, may if they desire it, meet with them for that Purpose and May 29th it was agreed:

That the persons desirous to meet together for that Purpose, be divided into several bands or little societies.

That none of these consist of fewer than five or more than ten persons.

That some one person in each band be desired to interrogate the rest in order, who may be called the Leader of the Band.

---

1. W. M. Trousdale. "The Moravian Society. Fetter lane–London", in *Proceedings*, Vol. XVII, part II, 30.

Appendix 6 307

Tuesday Sept. 20

It was agreed

That John Bray, Shepherd Wolf, John Edmonds, James Hutton, William Oxlee, William Hervey, John Shaw, John Wesley, John Brown and the Leaders of the New Bands meet together at McBray's at 6½ every Wednesday evening. That each Leader then give an Account of the State of each Person in his Band. That a person and time then fixed, for doing what may then appear necessary; of which an account is to be given in the beginning of the Next Meeting. That in Particular a Person and time be then fixed, for settling and visiting female bands.

Monday Sept 26

It was agreed

That each of the Bands meet twice in a week; once on Monday Evenings, the Second time, when it is most convenient for each Band.

That every person come punctually at the hour appointed, without some extraordinary Reason.

That those that are present, begin exactly at that hour.

That every meeting be begun & ended with Singing and prayer.

That each Person in order speak as freely, plainly, and concisely as he can, the Real State of his Heart, with his several Temptations and Deliverances since the last time of meeting.

That all the Bands have a Conference at 8 every Wednesday evening, begun and ended with Singing and prayer.

That whosoever speaks in this Conference stand up, & that none else speak till he is sat down.

That nothing which is said in this Conference be by any means mentioned out of it.

That every Member of this Society who is a Member of any Other, prefer the Meeting with this & with his Particular Band, before the Meeting with any other Society or Company whatever.

That if any Person absent himself without some Extraordinary Reason, either from his Band or from any Meeting of the whole Society, he be first privately admonished, & if He absent again, be reproved before the whole Society.

That such women as have entered their names the Friday before, if there be no objection against them, may meet in the Society Room, every Wednesday from six to eight in the evening.

That no men be present except their Respective Husbands, & the Persons who pray and Expound the Scriptures.

That any who desire to be admitted into the Society be ask'd,

What are your reasons for desiring this?

Will you be entirely open?

Using no kind of Reserve, least of all in the case of Love or Courtship.

Will you strive against Desire of Ruling, of being first in your Company, of having your own way?

Have you any objections to any of our orders?

The orders may then be read to them.

That those who answer these Questions in the Affirmative, be proposed every Fourth Wednesday.

That everyone then present speak clearly and fully, whatever objection he has to any Person proposed to be a member.

That those against whom any Reasonable Objections appears, be acquainted with that Objection, & the admitting them upon Trial postponed, 'till that Objection is removed.

That those against whom no Reasonable Objection appears or remains, be in order for their trial, immediately formed into distinct Bands & some Person agreed on to assist them.

That if no New Objection then appears, they be after a month's Trial admitted into the Society.

That every fourth Saturday be observed as a Day of General Intercession, which may continue from 12 to 2, from 3 to 5 & from 6 to 8.

That on Sunday se'ennight following be a general lovefeast from 7 to 10 in the evening.

That a Collection be made towards a Common Stock, in each Band on Monday Evening, at 6 and 8 on Wednesday s, at 8 on Friday & on the General Thanksgiving Day.

That out of this be defrayed the expenses of the Lovefeasts, of Letters, & whatever else relates to the Society in General.

That in order to a Continual Intercession every Member of this Society chuse some Hour either of the day or night, to spend in Prayer chiefly for his Brethren.

That in order to a Continual Fast three of the Members of the Society fast every Day (as their health permits) Sundays and Holidays excepted, and spend as much as they can of that Day, in Retirement from Business & Prayer."

Appendix 7 (Rules B)

The Rules of the Fetter Lane Society[1]

ORDERS OF A RELIGIOUS SOCIETY MEETING IN FETTER LANE.

"In obedience to the command of God by St James, and by the advice of Peter Boehler, May 1, 1738, it was agreed,

That they will meet together once in a week, to confess their faults one to another, And pray for one Another, that they may be healed.

That any others, of whose Sincerity they are well assured, may, if they desire it, meet with them for that purpose. And May 29, it was agreed,

That the Persons desirous to meet together for that Purpose, be divided into several Bands or little Societies.

That none of these consist of fewer than five, or more than ten persons.

That some person in each Band be desired to interrogate the rest in order, who may be called the Leader of that Band.

And on Monday, September 26, it was agreed,

That each Band meet twice in a week; once on Monday Evenings, the second Time, when it is most convenient for each Band.

That every person come punctually at the hour appointed, without some extraordinary Reason.

That those that are present, begin exactly at the hours.

That every meeting be begun & ended with Singing and prayer.

---

1. D. Benham. *Memoirs of James Hutton*. London: Hamilton Adams & Co, 1856.

That every one in order speak as freely, plainly, and concisely as he can, the Real State of his Heart, with his several Temptations and Deliverances since the last time of meeting.

That all Bands have a Conference at eight every Wednesday evening, begun and ended with Singing and prayer.

That at nine of the Clock the names of the Members be called over, and the absenters set down.

That notice of any extraordinary Meeting be given on the Wednesday Night preceding such Meeting.

That exactly at ten, if the business of the Night be not finished, a short concluding prayer be used, that those may go who are in haste, but that all depart the Room by half an hour after ten.

That whosoever speaks in this Conference stand up, and that none else speak till he is set down

That nothing which is mentioned in this Conference, be by any means mentioned out of it.

That every Member of this Society, who is a Member of any other, prefer the Meeting with this, and with his Particular Band, before the Meeting with any other Society or Company whatsoever.

That if any Person absent himself without some Extraordinary Reason, either from his Band or from any Meeting of the whole Society, he be first privately admonished; and if He be absent again, reproved before the whole Society.

That any Person who desires, or designs to take any Journey, shall first, if possible, have the Approbation of the Bands.

That all our Members who are in Clubs, be desired to withdraw their names, as being Meetings nowise conducing to the Glory of God.

That any who desire to be admitted into this Society, be asked, What are your reasons for desiring this? Will you be entirely open using no kind of Reserve, least of all in the case of Love or Courtship? Will you strive against Desire of ruling, of being first in your Company, or having your own way? Will you submit to be placed in what Band the Leaders shall choose for you? Have you any Objections to any of our orders? The orders may then be read to them.

That those who answer these Questions in the Affirmative, be proposed every Fourth Wednesday.

That everyone then present speak clearly and fully, whatever Objection he has to any Person proposed to be a member.

That those against whom any Reasonable Objection appears, be acquainted with that Objection, and the admitting them upon Trial postponed till that Objection is removed.

That those against whom no Reasonable Objection appears or remains, be, in order for their Trial, formed into distinct Bands & some Person agreed to assist them.

That if no new Objection then appear, they be, after two month's Trial admitted into the Society.

That every fourth Saturday be observed as a Day of General Intercession, which may continue from twelve to two, from three to five & from six to eight.

That on Sunday se'en-Night following be a general lovefeast from seven till ten in the evening.

That in order to a continual Intercession, every Member of this Society choose some Hour, either of the Day or Night, to spend in Prayer chiefly for his Brethren.

That in order to a continual Fast, three of the Members of the Society Fast every Day (as their health permits), Sundays and Holidays excepted, and spend as much as they can of that Day, in Retirement from Business, and Prayer.

That each Person give Notice to the Leader of his Band how much he is willing to subscribe towards the general Charge of the Bands, and that each person's Money be paid into the Leader of his Band once a Month at farthest.

That no particular Person be allowed to act in any Thing contrary to any Order of the Society, but that every One, without Distinction, submit to the Determination of his Brethren; and that if any Person or Persons do not after being thrice admonished, conform to the Society, they be not esteemed any longer as Members.

That any Person whom the whole Society shall approve, may be accounted a correspondent Member, and as such, may be admitted at our general Meetings, provided he correspond with the Society once in a Month at least."

Appendix 8 (Rules C)

The Rules of the Fetter Lane Society[1]

THIS EVENING OUR LITTLE society began, which afterwards met in Fetter Lane. Our fundamental rules were as follow:

In obedience to the command of God by St James, and by the advice of Peter Böhler, it is agreed by us,

That we will meet together once a week to 'confess our faults to one another, and pray for one another, that we may be healed.'

That the persons so meeting be divided into several bands, or little companies, none of them consisting of fewer than five or more than ten persons.

That every one in order speak as freely, plainly and concisely as he can, the real state of his heart, with his several temptations and deliverances, since the last time of meeting.

That all the bands have a conference at eight every Wednesday evening, begun and ended with singing and prayer.

That any who desire to be admitted into the society be asked, 'What are your reasons for desiring this? Will you be entirely open; using no kind of reserve? Have you any objection to any of our orders?' (which may then be read).

That when any new member is proposed, every one present speak clearly and freely whatever objection he has to him.

That those against whom no reasonable objection appears be, in order for their trial, formed into one or more distinct bands, and some person agreed on to assist him.

That after two months' trial, if no objection then appear, they may be admitted into the society.

---

1. J. Wesley. *Works [BE]*, Vol. 18, 236–7.

That every fourth Saturday be observed as a day of general intercession.

That on the Saturday seven-night following be a general lovefeast, from seven till ten in the evening.

That no particular member be allowed to act in anything contrary to any order of the society; and that if any persons, after being thrice admonished, do not conform thereto, they be not any longer esteemed as members.

Appendix 9

Religious Societies from John Wesley's Diary

Minories

Sun 17th September 1738 5pm -- preached, sang, prayed: Sun 24th September 6pm

Bear Yard

Tues 19th September 1738 7.30: 3rd October 8pm: Tue 24th October 8pm:

Tue 31st October 8.15pm: Tue 7th November 8pm

Savoy

Thu 21st September 1738 7.45pm: Thu 28th September 8.30pm:

Thu 19th October 8pm: Thu 26th October 8pm: Thu 2nd November 8.15pm: Thu 21st December 8pm: Thu 28th December 8pm: Thu 4th January 1739 8pm: Thu 11th January 8pm: Thu 18th January 8pm: Thu 25th January 8pm:

Thu 1st February 8pm: Thu 8th February 8pm: Thu 22nd February 8.30pm:

Thu 22nd March 8pm: Thu 6th September 8pm: Thu 8th November 8pm

Westminster

Fri 20th October 1738 7.30pm: Fri 12th January 1739 7.30pm

St Anne's Lane

Fri 29th December 1738 8pm: 5th January 1739 7.45pm

Appendix 9   315

BLENDON

Tue 24th October 1738 10am

WAPPING

Fri 27th October 1738: Fri 16th March 1739 6pm:
Fri 15th June (26 present [comforted])): Fri 6th June 1740 6.30pm:
Fri 20th June 6.30pm: Fri 18th June 6.30pm

ST BRIDE'S

Sun 29th October 1738: 24th December 1738 5.30pm

SOUTHWARK

Wed 1st November 1738 7pm: 15th December 7pm:
Sun 18th February 1739 5.15pm: 18th March 5pm:
3rd September 4.45pm (visited): 30th June 1740 5.45pm: Mon 14th July 7pm

GUTTER LANE

Thu 2nd November 1738 6pm

BLACKFRIARS

Thu 14th December 1738 8pm

GOODMAN FIELDS

Fri 22nd December 11am

BLOOMSBURY

Fri 22nd December 1738 12.15pm

DEADMAN'S FIELDS

1st January 1739 7.30pm

CREED CHURCH SOCIETY

(St Katherine Cree) 7th January 1739 5.15pm

BEECH LANE

13th January 1739 6pm: 17th February 6pm: Fri 23rd February 7pm

Appendix 9

ALDERSGATE

17th September 1738: 11th February 1739 3pm

GRAVEL LANE

12th February 1739 8pm: Mon 19th February 8pm: Mon 26th February 8.15pm: Mon 19th March 8pm: Mon 26th March 8pm (many angry!)

DOWGATE HILL

13th February 1739 7.30pm: Tue 20th February 8pm: 11th September 8pm: 6th November 7pm

THE GREEN MAN

14th June 1739 8pm (possibly with George Whitefield)

LAMBETH MARSH

9th September 1739: 16th September 7pm: Sun 23rd September 6.30pm

PLAISTOW

(The Ship) 10th September 1739 4pm

PLAISTOW

(The House) Mon 10th September 1739 5pm in the House 7.30pm: at the House Fri 14th September 5.30pm: at the house Mon 24th September 4.30pm: 16th June 1740 4.15pm: at the House, the bands Mon 23rd June 4.30pm: at the house

THE THREE CUPS

Sat 22nd September 1739 1pm

CARNABY MARKET

Mon 24th September 1739 8.30pm

St James's

25th September 1739 4pm: Tue 6th November 4pm

WINCHESTER YARD

25th September 1739 8pm: Sun 4th November 5pm: Mon 5th November 7.30pm (many ill)

Deptford
27th Sept 1739 3pm

Turner's Hall
27th September 1739 6pm

Bowe's Society
7th June 1740 5pm

Long lane
28th June 1740 6.30pm: 7th July 7pm: Sat 12th July 6.30pm: Sat 19th July 6.30pm

Marylebone
2nd July 1740 6pm: Wed 16th July 1740 6pm

Whitechapel Society
Sat 5th July 1740 6.15pm

Appendix 10

The Nature, Design, and General Rules of the United Societies

IN LONDON, BRISTOL, KINGSWOOD AND NEWCASTLE UPON TYNE

(1743)

1. In the latter end of the year 1739 eight or ten persons came to me in London who appeared to be deeply convinced of sin, and earnestly groaning for redemption. They desired (as did three more the next day) that I would spend some time with them in prayer, and advise them how to flee from the wrath to come,[1] which they saw continually hanging over their heads. That we might have more time for this great work I appointed a day when they might all come together, which from thenceforward they did every week, namely on Thursday, in the evening. To these, and as many more as desired to join with them (for their number increased daily), I gave those advices from time to time which I judged most needful for them; and we always concluded our meeting with prayer suited to their several necessities.

2. This was the rise of the United Society, first at London, and then in other places. Such as Society is no other than a 'company of men "having the form, and seeking the power of godliness,"[2] united in order to pray together, to receive the word of exhortation, and to

---

1. Matt. 3:7.
2. Cf. 2 Tim. 3:5.

watch over one another in love, that they may help each other to work out their salvation.'[3]

3. That it may the more easily be discerned whether they are indeed working out their own salvation, each society is divided into smaller companies, called Classes, according to their respective places of abode. There are about twelve persons in every class, one of whom is styled the Leader. It is his business:

(1) To see each person in his class once a week at the least; in order

> To receive what they are willing to give toward the relief of the poor;
>
> To inquire how their souls prosper;
>
> To advise, reprove, comfort or exhort, as occasion may require.

(2) To meet the Minister and the stewards of the Society once a week, in order:

> To pay in to the stewards what they have received of their several classes in the week preceding;
>
> To show their account of what each person has contributed; and
>
> To inform the Minister of any that are sick, or of any that walk disorderly and will not be reproved.

4. There is only one condition previously required in those who desire admission into these societies, 'a desire to flee from the wrath to come'[4], to be saved from their sins'[5]. But wherever this is really fixed in the soul it will be shown by its fruits. It is therefore expected of all who continue therein that they should continue to evidence their desire of salvation.

First, By doing no harm, by avoiding evil in every kind–especially that which is most generally practised. Such is–

> The taking the name of God in vain.[6]

---

3. See Phil. 2:12.
4. Matt. 3:7.
5. Cf. Matt 1:21.
6. See Exod. 20:7, etc.

The profaning the day of the Lord, either by doing ordinary work thereon, or by buying or selling.

Drunkenness, buying and selling spirituous liquors; or drinking them (unless in case of extreme necessity).

Fighting, quarrelling, brawling; brother 'going to law[7]' with brother; returning evil for evil,[8] or railing for railing; the 'using many words'[9] in buying or selling.

> The buying or selling uncustomed goods.
> The giving or taking of things on usury.[10]

Uncharitable or unprofitable conversation, especially speaking evil of ministers or those in authority.

> Doing to others as we would not they should do unto us.[11]
> Doing what we know is not for the glory of God, as

The 'putting on of gold or costly apparel,' particularly the wearing of calashes, high-heads or enormous bonnets;

> The taking such diversions as cannot be used in the name of the Lord Jesus,

The singing of those songs, or reading those books, which do not tend to the knowledge or love of God;

> Softness, and needles of self indulgence;
> Laying up treasures upon earth;

Borrowing without a probability of paying: or taking up goods without a probability of paying for them.

5. It is expected of all who continue in these societies that they should continue to evidence their desire of salvation,

Secondly, By doing good, by being in every kind merciful after their power, as they have opportunity doing good of every possible sort and as far as possible to all men:[12]

---

7. Cf. 1 Cor. 6:6.
8. See 1 Pet. 3:9.
9. See Ecclus. 20:8 also Ecclus. 13:11.
10. Cf. Lev 25:36; Isa. 24:2 ,etc.
11. See Matt. 7:12, etc.
12. See Gal. 6:10.

To their bodies, of the ability which God giveth, by giving food to the hungry, by clothing the naked, by visiting or helping them that are sick, or in prison.[13]

To their souls, by instructing, reproving, or exhorting all they have of any intercourse with; trampling under foot that enthusiastic doctrine of devils, that 'we are not to do good unless our heart be free to it.'

By doing good especially to them that are of the household of faith,[14] or groaning so to be; employing them preferably to others, buying one of another, helping each other in business–and that so much the more because the world will love its own, and them only.

> By all possible diligence and frugality, that the gospel be not blamed.

By running with patience the race that is set before them;[15] 'denying themselves, and taking up their cross daily';[16] submitting to bear the reproach of Christ, to be as the filth and offscouring of the world;[17] and looking that men should 'say all manner of evil of them falsely, for their Lord's sake.'[18]

6. It is expected of all who desire to continue in these societies that they should continue to evidence their desire of salvation,

> Thirdly, By attending upon all the ordinances of God. Such are:
> The public worship of God;
> The ministry of the word, either read or expounded;
> The supper of the Lord;
> Family and private prayer;
> Searching the Scriptures;[19] and
> Fasting, or abstinence.

7. These are the *General Rules* of our societies; all which we are taught of God to observe, even in his written Word, the only rule, and

---

13. See Matt. 25:35–39.
14. See Gal. 6:10.
15. See Heb. 12:1.
16. Cf. Luke 9:23.
17. See 1 Cor. 4:13.
18. Cf. Matt. 5:11.
19. See John 5:39; Acts 17:11.

the sufficient rule, both of our faith and practice. And all these we know his Spirit writes on every truly awakened heart. If there be any among us who observe them not, who habitually break any one of them, let it be made known unto them who watch over that soul, as they that must give account. We will admonish him of the error of his ways. We will bear with him for a season. But if then he repent not, he hath no more place among us. We have delivered our own souls. [20]

John Wesley
Charles Wesley
May 1, 1743

---

20. See Ezek. 3:19, etc.

Appendix 11

Rules of the Band Societies

(DRAWN UP DECEMBER 25TH 1738)

THE DESIGN OF OUR meeting is to obey that command of God, 'Confess your faults one to another, and pray one for another that ye may be healed.'[21]

To this end we intend:

- To meet once a week, at the least.
- To come punctually at the hour appointed, without some extraordinary reason.
- To begin (those of us who are present) exactly at the hour, with singing or prayer.
- To speak, each of us in order, freely and plainly the true state of our souls, with the faults we have committed in thought, word or deed, and the temptations we have felt since our last meeting.
- To end every meeting with prayer, suited to the state of each person present.
- To desire some person among us to speak *his*[22] own state first, and then to ask the rest in order as many and as searching questions as may be concerning their state, sins, and temptations.

---

21. Jas. 5:16.
22. The italics indicate that the alternative "her" might be used.

Some of the questions proposed to every one before he is admitted amongst us may be to this effect:

Have you the forgiveness of your sins?

Have you peace with God, through our Lord Jesus Christ?[23]

Have you the witness of God's Spirit with your spirit that you are a child of God?[24]

Is the love of God shed abroad in your heart?[25]

Has no sin, inward or outward, dominion over you?[26]

Do you desire to be told of your faults?

Do you desire to be told of all your faults, and that plain and home?

Do you desire that every one of us should tell you from time to time whatsoever is in his heart concerning you?

Consider! Do you desire we should tell you whatsoever we think, whatsoever we fear, whatsoever we hear, concerning you?

Do you desire that in doing this we should come as close as possible, that we should cut to the quick, and search your heart to the bottom?

Is it your desire and design to be on this and all other occasions entirely open, so as to speak everything that is in your heart, without exception, without disguise, and without reserve?

Any of the preceding questions may be asked as often as occasion offers; the five following at every meeting:

What known sins have you committed since our last meeting?

What temptations have you met with?

How was you delivered?

What have you thought, said or done, of which you doubt whether it be sin or not?

Have you nothing you desire to keep secret?[27]

---

23. See Rom 5:1.
24. See Rom 8:16.
25. See Rom 5:5.
26. See Rom 6:14.
27. This question was removed from later editions, in around 1779 or 1780.

Appendix 12

Directions given to the Band Societies

DEC. 25, 1744

You are supposed to have the 'faith that overcometh the world'[1]. To you therefore it is not grievous,

I. Carefully to abstain from doing evil; in particular.

   Neither to buy nor sell anything at all on the Lord's Day.
   To taste no spirituous liquor, no dram of any kind, unless prescribed by a physician
   To be at a word both in buying and selling.
   To pawn nothing, no, not to save life.
   Not to mention the fault of any behind his back, and to stop those short that do.
   To wear no needless ornaments, such as rings, ear-rings, necklaces, lace, ruffles.
   To use no needless self-indulgence, such as taking snuff or tobacco, unless prescribed by a physician.

II. Zealously to maintain good works; in particular,

   To give alms of such things as you possess, and that to the uttermost of your power.
   To reprove all that sin in your sight, and that in love, and meekness of wisdom.[2]

---

1. Cf. 1 John 5:4.
2. See Luke 9:23.

To be patterns of diligence and frugality, of self-denial, and taking up the cross daily.[3]

III. Constantly to attend on all the ordinances of God; in particular,

To be at church, and at the Lord's table, every week, and at every public meeting of the bands.

To attend the ministry of the Word every morning, unless distance, business, or sickness prevent.

To use private prayer every day, and family prayer if you are the head of a family.

To read the Scriptures, and meditate thereon, at every vacant hour. And,

To observe as days of fasting or abstinence all Fridays in the year.

---

3. Jas 3:13.

Appendix 13

Of the right METHOD of meeting CLASSES and BANDS, in the Methodist-Societies[1]

(BY THE LATE MR. CHARLES PERRONET[2])

IN GENERAL, THE METHOD proper for meeting the one is proper for meeting the other. The particular design of the Classes is,

To know who continue members of the Society;

To inspect their Outward Walking,

To inquire of their inward State;

To learn, what are their Trials? And how they fall by, or conquer them?

To instruct the ignorant in the first Principles of Religion: if need be, to repeat, explain, or enforce, what has been said in public Preaching.

To stir them up to believe, love, obey; and to check the first spark of Offence or Discord.

The particular design of the Bands is,

To inquire, whether they now believe? Now enjoy the life of God? Whether they grow herein, or decay? If they decay, what is the cause! And what the cure?

Whether they aim at being wholly devoted to God; or would keep something back?

---

1. Arminian Magainzine, Volume IV.
2. Charles Perronet died on August 12th 1776.

Whether they see God's hand in all that befals [sic] them? And how they bear what he lays upon them?

Whether they take up their cross daily? Resist the bent of Nature? Oppose self-love in all its hidden forms, and discover it, through all its disguises?

Whether they humble themselves in everything? Are willing to be blamed and despised for well-doing? Account it the greatest honour, that Christ appoints them to walk with himself, in the paths that are peculiarly his own? To examine closely, whether they are willing to drink of his cup, and to be baptized with his baptism?

Whether they can cordially love those that despitefully use them! Justify the ways of God in thus dealing with them? And in all they suffer, seek the destruction of inward Idolatry, or Pride, Self-will and Impatience?

How they conquer Self-will, in its spiritual forms? See through all its disguises, seeking itself, when it pretends to seek nothing but the glory of God?

Whether they are simple, open, free, and without reserve in speaking? And see it their duty and privilege so to be?

To inquire concerning Prayer, the Answers to Prayer, Faith in Christ, Distrust of themselves, Consciousness of their own witness and nothingness:

How they improve their talents? What zeal they have for doing good, in all they do, or suffer, or receive from God?

Whether they live above it, making Christ their All, and offering up to God nothing for acceptance, but his Life and Death?

Whether they have a clear, full, abiding conviction, that without inward, compleat, universal Holiness, no man shall see the Lord? That Christ was sacrificed for us, that we might be a whole burnt-sacrifice to God; and that they having received the Lord Jesus Christ will profit us nothing, unless we steadily and uniformly walk in him?

C.P.

I earnestly exhort all Leaders of Classes and Bands, seriously to consider the preceding Observations, and to put them in execution with all the Understanding and courage that God has given them.

J. W.

Bibliography

Addison, William G. *The Renewed Church of the United Brethren 1722-1930*. London: SPCK, 1932.

Alexander, Disney. *Reasons for Methodism Briefly Stated in Three Letters to a Friend*. Halifax: J. Nicholson & Co, 1795.

Allchin, Arthur M. *Participation in God. A Forgotten Strand in Anglican Tradition*. London: Darton, Longman & Todd, 1988.

Allen, W. Osborn B., and McClure, Edmund. *Two Hundred Years: The History of the Society for the Promotion of Christian Knowledge. 1698-1898*. London: SPCK, 1898.

Articles of the Religious Societies at Truro. Lambeth Palace Library.

Askey, Reginald. *Muskets and Altars Jeremy Taylor and the Last of the Anglicans*. London: Mowbray, 1997.

Austen, M., to Wesley, C., Letter, 19th May 1740. Early Methodist Volume. *John Rylands University Library (Methodist Archives)*.

Austin, Margaret. Testimony, 19th May 1740. Early Methodist Volume. *John Rylands University Library (Methodist Archives)*.

Author of the Last Century. *An Address to the Heads of Families on the Necessity of Family Religion; Also an Interesting Discourse on Weekly Class meetings*. Leeds: A. Newsom, 1797.

Baddiley, E., to Wesley, J., Letter, 31st December 1741. Wesley College Archives D5/69/2. *Wesley College Archives, Bristol*.

Baker, Frank. *Charles Wesley as Revealed by his Letters*. London: Epworth Press, 1948.

———. *John Wesley and the Church of England*. London: Epworth Press, 1970.

———. *William Grimshaw 1708-63*. London: Epworth Press, 1963.

Baker, Frank. "The People Called Methodists 3: Polity." In *A History of the Methodist Church in Great Britain*, Volume 1, edited by Rupert Davies and Gordon Rupp. London: Epworth Press, 1965.

Balmer, Randall. *Mine Eyes Have Seen the Glory. A Journey into the Evangelical Subculture in America*. New York: Oxford University Press, 1989.

Barber, Joanna, Death account, February 1752. Early Methodist Volume. *John Rylands University Library (Methodist Archive)*.

Barber, S., to Wesley, C., Letter, May 1740. Early Methodist Volume. *John Rylands University Library (Methodist Archives)*.

Bebbington, David W. *Evangelicalism in Modern Britain. A History from the 1730s to the 1980s*. London: Routledge, 1989.

Beckham, William A. *The Second Reformation. Reshaping the Church for the 21st Century*. Houston: Touch Publications, 1995.

Benham, Daniel. *Memoirs of James Hutton*. London: Hamilton Adams & Co, 1856.

Bennet, John. *John Bennet's Copy of the Minutes of the Conferences of 1744, 1745, 1747 and 1748 Publications of the Wesley Historical Society. Number 1*. London: Charles Kelly, 1896.

———. *Mirror of the Soul: The Diary of an Early Methodist Preacher John Bennet 1714-1754*, edited by Simon R. Valentine. Peterborough: Methodist Publishing House, 2002.

Bhattacharji, Santha. "Julian of Norwich." In *Dictionary of National Biography*, Volume 30, edited by H. C. G. Matthew and B. Harrison. Oxford: Oxford University Press, 2004.

Bierstedt, Robert. *Emile Durkheim*, London: Weidenfield & Nicolson, 1966.

Birkhead, J., & Tremayne, J., to Lavington, G., Bishop of Exeter. Letter, 23rd May 1747. Archbishop's Papers: Secker Papers. Volume 8 (Methodists). 1738-57. Folio 4. *Lambeth Palace Library*.

Birnbaum, Norman, and Gudrun Lenzer (editors). *Sociology and Religion: A Book of Readings*. New Jersey: Prentice Hall. 1969.

Böhler, Peter. *Diary* (copy) Moravian Archive Book AB43.A.3. *Moravian Church House Archive*.

Bosch, David. *Transforming Mission. Paradigm Shifts in the Theology of Mission*. New York: Orbis, 1994.

Bowmer, John C. *The Sacrament of the Lord's Supper in Early Methodism*. London: Dacre Press, 1951.

Bradburn, Samuel. *A Memorandum Book Containing a List of the Places I have been in and the Texts of Scripture I have Preached on, with the Times of Preaching in each place: Since May 31 1774*. Early Methodist Diaries Collection: MA 1977/296. *John Rylands University Library (Methodist Archives)*.

Bretherton, Francis F. "Mrs Fletcher's Class Paper." In *Proceedings of the Wesley Historical Society Volume XXI*, PWHS Archives, 1938.

Brod, Max. "A Radical Network in the English Revolution: John Pordage and His Circle, 1646-54." In *English Historical Review*, Volume CXIX, Part 484, edited by G. W. Bernard et al. Oxford: Oxford University Press, 2004.

Brown, Rupert. *Group Processes*. Oxford: Blackwell, 1988.

Bruaer, J. C., "Puritan Mysticism and the Development of Liberalism." In *Church History*, Volume 19, Part 5, edited by W. S. Hudson et al. Chicago: American Society of Church History, 1950.

Bullock, Frederick W. B. *Voluntary Religious Societies 1520-1799*. St Leonard's on Sea: Budd & Gillatt, 1963.

———. *Evangelical Conversion in Great Britain 1516-1695*. St Leonard's on Sea: Budd & Gillatt, 1966.

Calamy, Edmund. *A Continuation of the Account of the Minsters, Lecturers . . . who were ejected and slenced after the Restoration in 1660, by or before the Act for Uniformity. To which is added the Church and Dissenters compar'd as to persecution, in some remarks on Dr.Walkers attempt to recover the names and sufferings of the clergy that were sequestered, &c Between 1640 and 1660, And also some free remarks on the twenty-eighth of Dr. E. Bennets Essay on the 39 Article of Religion*. London: R. Ford, 1727.

Cambell, Ted A. *The Religion of the Heart. A Study of European Religious Life in the Seventeenth and Eighteenth Centuries*. Columbia: University of South Carolina Press, 1991.

Carter, Joseph. Testimony, November 1741. Early Methodist Volume. *John Rylands University Library (Methodist Archive)*.
Carter, J., to Wesley, C., Letter, 9th June 1743. Letters Chiefly to the Wesleys. Volume II. *John Rylands University Library (Methodist Archives)*.
Carveley, Kenneth. "From Glory to Glory: The Renewal of All Things in Christ. Maximus the Confessor and John Wesley." In *Orthodox and Wesleyan Spirituality*, edited by Stephen T. Kimbrough, Jr. New York: St. Vladimir's University Press, 2002.
Chilcote, Paul W. *Wesleyan Tradition A Paradigm for Renewal*. Nashville: Abingdon Press, 2002.
Church, Leslie F. *The Early Methodist People*. London: Epworth Press, 1948.
———. *More About the Early Methodist People*. London: Epworth Press, 1949.
Claggett, Mrs., undated testimony. Early Methodist Volume. *John Rylands University Library (Methodist Archives)*.
Clapper, Gregory S. *John Wesley on Religious Affections*. Metuchen: The Scarecrow Press, 1989.
Clark, John P. H. "Hilton, Walter." In *Dictionary of National Biography*, Volume 27, edited by Matthew H. C. G. and Harrison Brian. Oxford: Oxford University Press, 2004.
Clark, Peter. *British Clubs and Societies 1580-1800*. Oxford: Clarendon Press, 2000.
Coats, Robert H. *Types of English Piety*. Edinburgh: T&T Clark, 1912.
Cooney, D. A. L. "Bell, George." In *A Dictionary of Methodism in Britain and Ireland*, edited by John A. Vickers. Peterborough: Epworth Press Ltd, 2000.
Cragg, Gerald R. *The Church & the Age of Reason 1648-1789*. Middlesex: Penguin, 1960.
Croft, Steve, et al. "A Future for Housegroups." In *Grove Pastoral Series 66*, edited by Paul Simmonds. Cambridge: Grove Books Ltd, 1996.
Cross, Frank L., and Livingstone, Elizabeth A. "Boehme, Jakob." In *The Oxford Dictionary of the Christian Church*, edited by Frank L. Cross and Elizabeth A. Livingstone. Oxford: Oxford University Press, 1974.
Crowther, Jonathan. *A True and Complete Portrait of Methodism*. London: Richard Edwards, 1811.
Dale, Graham. *God's Politicians*. London: Harper Collins, 2000.
Dallimore, Arthur. *A Heart Set Free-The Life of Charles Wesley*. Darlington: Evangelical Press, 1988.
Dean, William W. "The Methodist Class Meeting. The Significance of its Decline." In *Proceedings of the Wesley Historical Society*, Volume XLIII, Part 2. Wesley Historical Society: Cheshire, 1981.
———. "Disciplined Fellowship: The Rise and Decline of Cell Groups in British Methodism." PhD diss., University of Iowa, 1985.
Dugdale, Bennet. *The Diary of Bennet Dugdale*. Early Methodist Diaries Collection: MA 1977/216. *John Rylands University Library (Methodist Archives)*.
Durkheim, Emile. *The Elementary Forms of the Religious Life*, translated by Carol Cosman. Oxford: Oxford University Press, 2001.
East, David. "My Dear Sally: The Life of Sarah Mallet One of John Wesley's Preachers." In *More People Called Methodists No. 6*. Loughborough: WMHS Publications, 2003.
Edwards, Maldwyn. "John Wesley." In *A History of the Methodist Church in Great Britain*: Volume 1, edited by Rupert Davies and Gordon Rupp. London: Epworth Press, 1965.

Field, Clive D. "The Social Composition of English Methodism to 1830: A Membership Analysis." In *The Bulletin of the John Rylands Library*, Volume 76, edited by Dorothy Graham. Manchester: John Rylands University of Manchester, 1994.

Filney, Ann, Baptismal entry for 14th November 1738, St Mary's Anglican Church, Islington. X085/079. *London Metropolitan Archives.*

Finney, John. *Finding Faith Today*. Swindon: British and Foreign Bible Society, 1992.

———. *Fading Splendour? A New Model of Renewal*. London: Darton, Longman & Todd, 2000.

Fletcher, Mary. Class Meeting Notes. Fletcher Tooth Collection. MA FI 38.3. *John Rylands University Library (Methodist Archives).*

Foster, H. J. "Bristol Methodist Notes V. - Who was Captain Foy?" In *Proceedings of the Wesley Historical Society*, Volume III. No Publication Details. 1902.

French, Alfred T. *The World in the Church; A Contribution to the Class-Meeting Question*. London: T.Woolmer, 1889.

Gardner, Joseph, Baptismal entry for 11th March 1739, St Mary's Anglican Church, Islington. X085/079. *London Metropolitan Archives.*

Giddens, Anthony. *Durkheim*. London: Fontana, 1978.

Gilbert, Catherine. Testimony, 1740. Early Methodist Volume. *John Rylands University Library (Methodist Archives).*

Gill, Frederick C. *Charles Wesley the First Methodist*. London: Lutterworth Press, 1964.

Goldhawk, Norman P. "The Methodist People in the Early Victorian Age: Spirituality and Worship." In *A History of the Methodist Church in Great Britain*: Volume 2, edited by Rupert Davies and Gordon Rupp. London: Epworth Press, 1978.

Goodfellow, John. *The Diary of John Goodfellow*. Early Methodist Diaries Collection: MA 1977/236. *John Rylands University Library (Methodist Archives).*

Goss, William A. "Early Methodism in Bristol with Special Reference to John Wesley's Visits to the City 1739–1790, and their Impressions on the People." PhD diss., No University stated, 1932.

Green, Vivian H. H. *The Young Mr Wesley*. London: Epworth Press, 1963.

Hardt, Philip F. *The Soul of Methodism. The Class Meeting in Early New York Methodism*. Maryland: University Press of America, 2000.

Heitzenrater, Richard P. *Wesley and the People Called Methodists*. Nashville: Abingdon Press, 1995.

———. The *Elusive Mr Wesley. John Wesley his own Biographer*, Volume I. Nashville: Abingdon Press, 1984.

———. *Mirror and Memory*. Nashville: Kingswood Books, 1989.

Hext, T., to Lavington G., Bishop of Exeter. Letter, 23rd February 1748. Archbishop's Papers: Secker Papers. Volume 8 (Methodists). 1738–57. Folio 4. *Lambeth Palace Library.*

Hindmarsh, D. Bryan. *The Evangelical Conversion Narrative. Spiritual Autobiography in Early Modern England*. Oxford: Oxford University Press, 2005.

Hempton, David. *Methodism: Empire of the Spirit*. New Haven: Yale University Press, 2005.

Henderson, D.Michael. *John Wesley's Class Meeting: A Model for Making Disciples*. Nappanee: Evangel Publishing House, 1997.

Hill, Christopher. *Society and Puritanism in Pre-Revolutionary England*. London: Mercury Books, 1964.

Hill, Michael. *A Sociology of Religion*. London: Heinmann Educational Books, 1973.

Hogg, Michael A., and Terry, Deborah J. *Social Identity Processes in Organizational Contexts*. Philadelphia: Psychology Press, 2001.

Holder, William. *The Diary of William Holder, who was Born in Painswick (Glos) and Died in London January 17th 1810 aged 70*. Early Methodist Diaries Collection: MA 1977/238. *John Rylands University Library (Methodist Archives)*.

Holland, Bernard G. *Baptism in Early Methodism*. London: Epworth Press, 1970.

Holland, William. *Extract of a Short Account in Some Few Matters Relating to the Work of the Lord in England 1745*. No publication details.

Howdle, Susan R. "Class meeting." In *A Dictionary of Methodism in Britain and Ireland*, edited by John A. Vickers. Peterborough: Epworth Press, 2000.

Hughes, Jonathan. "Rolle, Richard." In *Dictionary of National Biography*, Volume 47, edited by H. C. G. Matthew and B. Harrison. Oxford: Oxford University Press, 2004.

Hunter, George G. *The Celtic Way of Evangelism*. Nashville: Abingdon Press, 2000.

Hutchings, J., to Hutton, J., Letter, 23rd July 1738. Moravian Archive Book p88A.A.3 (folder 13). *Moravian Church House Archive*.

Ingham, B., to Hutton, J., Letter, 23rd June 1738. Moravian Archive Book p88A.A.3 (folder 14). *Moravian Church House Archive*.

Jackson, Thomas. *Recollections of my Own Life and Times*, edited by B. Frankland. London: Wesleyan Conference Office, 1873.

———, (editor). *The Lives of the Early Methodist Preachers Chiefly Written by Themselves*, (6 volumes). London: Wesleyan Conference Office, 1872.

Johnson, John. Baptismal entry for 11th March 1739, St Mary's Anglican Church, Islington. X085/079. *London Metropolitan Archives*.

Käsler, Dirk. *Max Weber. An Introduction to his Life and Work*. Oxford: Polity Press, 1988.

Kent, John. *Wesley and the Wesleyans: Religion in Eighteenth Century Britain*. Cambridge: Cambridge University Press, 2002.

Kinchin, C., to Zinzendorf, N.L., Letter, 15th October 1740. Moravian Archive Book p43A.3. *Moravian Church House Archives*.

La Capra, D. *Emile Durkheim Sociologist and Philosopher*. Ithaca: Cornell University Press, 1972.

Lackington, James. *Memoirs of the first Forty Five Years of the Life of James Lackington*. Bristol: W. Bulgin, 1791.

Lake, Peter, with Questier, Michael. *The Antichrist's Lewd Hat. Protestants, Papists and Players in Post-Reformation England*. New Haven: Yale, 2002.

Langford, Thomas A. "Charles Wesley as Theologian." In *Charles Wesley: Poet and Theologian*, edited by Stephen T. Kimbrough. Nashville: Kingswood Books, 1992.

———. *Methodist Theology*. Peterborough: Epworth Press, 1998.

Lavington Papers: Archbishop's Papers: Secker Papers. Volume 8: Folio 16. 'Articles of the Religious Societies at Truro'. *Lambeth Palace Library*

Lawton, George. *John Wesley's English. A Study of His Literary Style*. London: George Allen & Unwin, 1962.

Lee, Sidney. "John Westley." In *The Dictionary of National Biography: Volume LX, Watson-Whewell*, edited by S. Lee. London: Smith, Elder & Co. 1899.

Lewis, Arthur J. *Zinzendorf the Ecumenical Pioneer*. London: SCM, 1962.

Libby, James N. "James Hutton's Account of 'The Beginnings of the Lord's Work in England to 1741.'" In *Proceedings of the Wesley Historical Society*, Volume X, Part 7. Burnley: Ashworth Nuttall, 1926.

———. "The Personnel of the Fetter Lane Society." In *Proceedings of the Wesley Historical Society*, Volume XVI. Burnley: Ashworth Nuttall, 1926.

Lineham, P. J., "Charles Delamotte." In *Dictionary of Evangelical Biography 1730–1860*. Volume 1, edited by D. M. Lewis. Oxford: Blackwell, 1995.

Lloyd, Gareth. "Repression and Resistance: Wesleyan Female Public Ministry in the generation after 1791." In *Proceedings of the Wesley Historical Society*, Volume 55, Part 3. Birmingham: Westpoint Publishing Company Ltd, 2005.

———. "Charles Wesley: A New Evaluation of His Life and Ministry." PhD diss., Liverpool Hope University, 2002.

Maddox, Randy L. *Responsible Grace. John Wesley's Practical Theology*. Nashville: Kingswood Books, 1994.

Marshall, Peter, and Ryrie, Alec. *The Beginnings of English Protestantism*. Cambridge: Cambridge University Press, 2002.

Martin, Hugh. *Puritanism and Richard Baxter*. London: SCM Press, 1954.

Matthaei, Sondra H. *Making Disciples: Faith Formation in the Wesleyan Tradition*. Nashville: Abingdon Press, 2000.

McCabe, Richard A. "Joseph Hall." In *Oxford Dictionary of National Biography* Volume 24, *Grigg-Hanboys*, edited by H. C. G. Matthew and B. Harrison. Oxford: Oxford University Press, 2004.

McGonigle, Herbert B. *Sufficient Saving Grace John Wesley's Evangelical Arminianism*. Carlisle: Paternoster Press, 2000.

———. "Maxfield, Thomas." In *A Dictionary of Methodism in Britain and Ireland*, edited by John A. Vickers. Peterborough: Epworth Press Ltd, 2000.

———. "Valton, John." In *A Dictionary of Methodism in Britain and Ireland*, edited by John A. Vickers. Peterborough: Epworth Press Ltd, 2000.

Meistadt, Tore. "The Missiology of Charles Wesley and its Links to the Eastern Church." In *Orthodox and Wesleyan Spirituality*, edited by Stephen T. Kimbrough Jr. New York: St. Vladimir's University Press, 2002.

Miller, Perry, and Johnson, Thomas H. *The Puritans*. New York: American Book Company, 1938.

Molther, Philip H. "The Life of Philip Henry Molther." In *Moravian Messenger*. London: Moravian Publication Office, 1876.

———. Letter to the Fetter Lane Society 20th October 1740. Moravian Archive Book p43A.3. *Moravian Church House Archives*.

Monk, Robert C. *John Wesley and his Puritan Heritage*. Nashville: Abingdon Press, 1966.

Monod, Paul K. *The Power of Kings. Monarchy and Religion in Europe 1589–1715*. Michigan: Yale, 1999.

Moravian Prayer Day Meeting Notes, 17th September 1740. Moravian Archive Book p43A.3. *Moravian Church House Archives*.

Morgan, Kenneth. "Methodist Testimonials for Bristol Collected by Charles Wesley in 1742." In *Reformation and Revival in Eighteenth Century Bristol*, Volume XLV, edited by Jonathan Barry and Kenneth Morgan. Stroud: Bristol Record Society, 1994.

Mursell, Gordon. *English Spirituality from Earliest Times to 1700*. London: SPCK, 2000.

Myles, William. *A Chronological History of the People Called Methodist of the Connexion of the Late John Wesley from their rise on 1729 to their Last Conference in 1802.* London: Wesleyan Conference Office, 1803.

Nelson, John. "The Journal of John Nelson." In *The Lives of the Early Methodist Preachers*, Volume I, edited by Thomas Jackson. London: Wesleyan Conference Office, 1871.

Niebuhr, H. Richard. *Christ and Culture.* New York: HarperSanFrancisco, 1951.

Nightingale, Joseph. *A Portraiture of Methodism being an Impartial View of the Rise, Progress, Doctrines, Discipline and Manners of the Wesleyan Methodists in a Series of Letter Addressed to a Lady.* London: Longman, Hurst, Rees and Orme, 1807.

Noblemen's Chaplains, Register of. Shelf Mark: FV/I/X. *Lambeth Palace Library.*

O'Brien, Susan. "Eighteenth Century Publishing Networks in the First Years of Transatlantic Evangelicalism." In *Evangelicalism*, edited by Mark A. Noll et al. New York: Oxford University Press, 1994.

Orcibal, Jean. "The Theological Originality of John Wesley and Continental Spirituality." In *A History of the Methodist Church in Great Britain:* Volume 1, edited by Rupert Davies and Gordon Rupp. London: Epworth Press, 1965.

Pawson, John. *The Letters of John Pawson (Methodist Itinerant 1762-1806).* Volume I, *to the Conference of 1794*, edited by Bowmer, John C., and Vickers, John A. Peterborough: Wesleyan Methodist Historical Society Publications, 1994.

———. "The Life of John Pawson." In *The Lives of the Early Methodist Preachers*, Volume IV, edited by Thomas Jackson. London: Wesleyan Conference Office, 1872.

Pearsell, J. "Gnomic." In *The Concise Oxford English Dictionary*, edited by J. Pearsell. Oxford: Oxford University Press, 1911.

Penketh, Ann. "God is Dead. Long Live Kim Il Sung." In *The Independent*, edited by Simon Kellner. Watford: Independent News & Media Ltd, 2004.

Perrin, S., to Wesley, J., Letter, 9th June 1743. Letters Chiefly to the Wesleys. Volume II. *John Rylands University Library (Methodist Archives).*

———. to Wesley, J., Letter, October 1743. Letters Chiefly to the Wesleys. Volume II. *John Rylands University Library (Methodist Archives).*

———. to Wesley, J., Letter, June 1744. Letters Chiefly to the Wesleys. Volume II. *John Rylands University Library (Methodist Archives).*

Pickering, William S. F. *Durkheim on Religion.* London: Routledge & Kegan Paul, 1975.

Piette, Maximin. *John Wesley in the Evolution of Piety.* London: Sheed & Ward, 1937.

Podmore, Colin. *The Moravian Church in England 1728-1780.* Oxford: Clarendon Press, 1998.

———. "John Gambold." In *Dictionary of Evangelical Biography 1730-1860.* Volume I, edited by D. M. Lewis. Oxford: Blackwell, 1986.

———. "The Fetter Lane Society." In *Proceedings of the Wesley Historical Society Volume XLVII.* Ilford: Robert Odcombe Associates, 1990.

Polemical Tracts: Methodist Apology (Various Dates). Wesley College Archives IC3/D6/5. *Wesley College Archives, Bristol.*

Portus, Garnet V. *Caritas Anglicana.* London: A. R. Mowbray & Co. Ltd, 1912.

Rack, Henry D. *Reasonable Enthusiast: John Wesley and the Rise of Methodism*, London: Epworth Press, 1989.

———. "Religious Societies and the Origins of Methodism." In *The Journal of Ecclesiastical History*, Volume 38, number 4. Cambridge: Cambridge University Press, 1987.

———. "The Decline of the Class Meeting and the Problem of Church-Membership in Nineteenth-Century Wesleyanism." In *Proceedings of the Wesley Historical Society*, Volume XXXIX, Part 1, Wesley Historical Society, 1973.

———. "Wesleyan Methodism." In *A History of the Methodist Church in Great Britain*, Volume 3, edited by Rupert Davies et al. London: Epworth Press, 1983.

Rattenbury, J.Ernest. *The Conversion of the Wesley's*. London: Epworth Press, 1938.

———. *The Evangelical Doctrines of Charles Wesley's Hymns*. London: Epworth Press, 1941.

Riddy, F. "Kempe (nee Brunham), Margery." In *Dictionary of National Biography*, Volume 31, edited by H. C. G. Matthew and B. Harrison. Oxford: Oxford University Press, 2004.

Rigall, M., 'Richard Viney's Diary,' in *Proceedings of the Wesley Historical Society*, Volume XIV, PWHS Archive, 1924.

Rigg, J.M. "Francis Rous." In *The Dictionary of National Biography*, Volume XVII, *Robinson-Sheares*, edited by Leslie Stephen and Sidney Lee. Oxford: Oxford University Press, 1917.

Rose, E. Alan. "Benjamin Ingham." In *Dictionary of Evangelical Biography 1760-1860*, Volume 1, edited by D. M. Lewis. Oxford: Blackwell. 1986.

Rupp, Gordon. "Introductory Essay." In *A History of the Methodist Church in Great Britain*. Volume I, edited by Rupert Davies and Gordon Rupp. London: Epworth Press, 1965.

Russell, Norman. "Cloud of Unknowing, The." In *A Dictionary of Christian Spirituality*, edited by Gordon Wakefield. London: SCM Press Ltd, 1983.

Ruth, Lester. *A Little Heaven Below. Worship at Early Methodist Quarterly Meetings*. Nashville: Kingswood Books, 2000.

Schmidt, Martin. *John Wesley A Theological Biography*, Volume I. London: Epworth Press, 1971.

———. *John Wesley A Theological Biography*, Volume II Part I. London: Epworth Press, 1971.

Schwartz, Hillel. *The French Prophets: The History of a Millenarian Group in Eighteenth-Century England*. Berkeley: University of California Press, 1980.

Seward, W., to Hutton, J., Letter, 11th March 1738. Moravian Archive Book AB101. A3.4.13. *Moravian Church House Archive*.

Simon, John S. *John Wesley and the Methodist Societies*. London: Epworth Press, 1923.

———. "The Letters of Joseph Sanderson." In *Proceedings of the Wesley Historical Society*, Volume X, PWHS Archive, 1916.

Simpson, J. A., & Weiner, E. S. C. "Movement." In *The Oxford English Dictionary: Second Edition*. Volume X. Oxford: Clarendon Press, 1989.

———. "Organization." In *The Oxford English Dictionary: Second Edition*. Volume X. Oxford: Clarendon Press, 1989.

Skevington-Wood, Arthur. "John Hutchings." In *Dictionary of National Biography 1730-1860*, Volume I, edited by D. M. Lewis. Oxford: Blackwell, 1986.

Smith, George. *History of Wesleyan Methodism. Volume II, the Middle Age*. London: Longman, Brown, Green, Longmans & Roberts, 1858.

Snip, Nathaniel. *A Journal of the Travels of Nathaniel Snip a Methodist Teacher of the Word*. London: W. Bristow & M. Cooper, 1761.

Snow, J., Oath, 25th May 1747. Archbishop's Papers: Secker Papers. Volume 8 (Methodists). 1738-57. Folio 8. *Lambeth Palace Library*.

Snyder, Howard A. *The Radical Wesley and Patterns for Church Renewal*. Eugene,OR: Wipf and Stock, 1996.
Stephen, Leslie. "Samuel Annesley." In *The Dictionary of National Biography*: Volume II, *Annesley-Baird*, edited by Leslie Stephen. London: Smith, Elder & Co. 1885.
Stoeffler, Fred E. *The Rise of Evangelical Pietism*. Leiden: E. J. Brill, 1971.
Stranks, Charles J. *The Life and Writings of Jeremy Taylor*. London: SPCK, 1952.
Sugden, E. H. "A Wesley Class." In *Proceedings of the Wesley Historical Society*, Volume XII, PWHS Archives, 1920.
Symonds, John. *Thomas Brown and the Angels*. London: Hutchison & Co, 1961.
Taft, Zachariah. *Biographical Sketches of the Lives and Public Ministry of various Holy Women, whose Eminent Usefulness and Successful Labours in the Church of Christ, Have entitled them to be enrolled among the great benefactors of Mankind: In which are included Several Letters from the Rev J. Wesley never before published*, Volume I. London: H. Cullingworth, 1828. Facsimile reproduction. Peterborough: Methodist Publishing House, 1992.
———. *Biographical Sketches of the Lives and Public Ministry of various Holy Women, whose Eminent Usefulness and Successful Labours in the Church of Christ, Have entitled them to be enrolled among the great benefactors of Mankind: In which are included Several Letters from the Rev J. Wesley never before published*, Volume II. London: H. Cullingworth, 1828. Facsimile reproduction. Peterborough: Methodist Publishing House, 1992.
Taggart, N. W. "Clarke, Dr. Adam." In *A Dictionary of Methodism in Britain and Ireland*, edited by J. A. Vickers. Peterborough: Epworth Press Ltd, 2000.
Taylor, Jeremy. *The Rule and Exercises for Holy Living in which are described The Meanes and Instruments of obtaining every Vertue; and the Remedies against every Vice, and Considerations serving the resisting all temptations. Together with Prayers containing the whole duty of Christians, and the parts of Devotion fitted to all occasions and furnish'd for all Neccessities*. London: R. Royston, 1650.
———. *The Rules and Exercises of Holy Dying, in which are described The Means and Instruments of preparing ourselves, and others respectively for a blessed death: and the remedies against the evils and temptations proper to the state of sicknesse. Together with Prayers and acts of Vertue to be used by sick and dying persons, or by others standing in their attendance. To which are added Rules for the visitiation of the sick, and offices proper for that Ministry*. London: R. Royston, 1651.
Thompson, David M. *Nonconformity in the Nineteenth Century*. London: Routledge and Kegan Paul, 1972.
Thorold, J., to Hutton, J., Letter, 23rd October 1738. Moravian Archive Book p88A.A.3 (folder 13). *Moravian Church House Archives*.
Tooth, Mary. Class Meeting Notes. Fletcher Tooth Collection. MA FI 38.1. *John Rylands University Library (Methodist Archives)*.
Tucker, Ruth A. *From Jerusalem to Irian Jaya*. Grand Rapids: Academie, 1983.
Turner, Bryan. "The Decline of Methodism: An Analysis of Religious Commitment and Organisation." PhD diss., University of Leeds, 1970.
Turner, John M. *Conflict and Reconciliation: Studies in Methodism and Ecumenism in England 1740-1982*. London: Epworth Press, 1985.
———. *John Wesley: The Evangelical Revival and the Rise of Methodism in England*. Peterborough: Epworth Press, 2002.
Tuttle Robert G., Jr. *John Wesley his Life and Theology*. Grand Rapids: Zondervan, 1978.

Unknown Author. Class Meeting Notes. Fletcher Tooth Collection. MA FI 38.9. *John Rylands University Library (Methodist Archives)*.

Valentine, Simon R. *John Bennet and the Origins of Methodism and the Evangelical Revival in England*. Lanham: The Scarecrow Press, 1997.

Valton, John. *The Christian Experience of the Late Rev. John Valton; A Clerk in the Ordinance Office; Afterwards a Most Zealous Minister in the Late Mr Wesley's Connection*. Volume 1. (1764). Early Methodist Diaries Collection: MA 1977/293. *John Rylands University Library (Methodist Archives)*.

———. *The Christian Experience of the Late Rev. John Valton; A Clerk in the Ordinance Office; Afterwards a Most Zealous Minister in the Late Mr Wesley's Connection*. Volume 2. (1765). Early Methodist Diaries Collection: MA 1977/293. *John Rylands University Library (Methodist Archives)*.

———. *The Christian Experience of the Late Rev. John Valton; A Clerk in the Ordinance Office; Afterwards a Most Zealous Minister in the Late Mr Wesley's Connection*. Volume 3. (1766). Early Methodist Diaries Collection: MA 1977/293.

Wakefield, Gordon S. *Puritan Devotion*. London: Epworth Press, 1957. *John Rylands University Library (Methodist Archives)*.

———. *Fire of Love. The Spirituality of John Wesley*. London: Darton, Longman & Todd, 1976.

Walsh, John D. "Religious Societies: Methodist and Evangelical 1738–1800." In *Voluntary Religion: Studies in Church History*, Volume 23, edited by W. J. Shiels, and D. Wood. Worcester: Blackwell, 1986.

———. "'Methodism' and the Origins of English Speaking Evangelicalism." In *Evangelicalism*, edited by Mark A Noll et al. New York: Oxford University Press, 1994.

Ward, W. Reginald. *The Protestant Evangelical Awakening*. Cambridge: Cambridge University Press, 1992.

———. *Christianity under the Ançien Regime*. Cambridge: Cambridge University Press 1999.

Watson, David L. *The Early Methodist Class Meeting*. Nashville: Discipleship Resources, 1985.

Watts, Michael. *The Dissenters from the Reformation to the French Revolution*. Oxford: Clarendon Press, 1978.

Webb, Samuel. Testimony, 20th November 1741. Early Methodist Volume. *John Rylands University Library (Methodist Archives)*.

Webb, S., to Wesley, C., Letter, 20th November 1741. Early Methodist Volume. *John Rylands University Library (Methodist Archives)*.

Weber, Max. *Economy and Society an Outline of Interpretive Sociology*, Volume I, edited by Guenther Roth and Claus Wittich. New York: Bedminster Press, 1968.

———. *Economy and Society an Outline of Interpretive Sociology*, Volume II, edited by Guenther Roth and Claus Wittich. New York: Bedminster Press, 1968).

———. *The Sociology of Religion*. London: Methuen & Co. Ltd, 1965.

———. *The Protestant Ethic and the "Spirit" of Capitalism*, edited and translated by Peter Baehr and Gordon C. Wells. London: Penguin, 2002.

Wesley, Charles. *The Journal of the Rev Charles Wesley MA*. Volume I, edited by Thomas Jackson. Reprinted, Kansas City: Beacon Hill Press, 1980.

Wesley, John. *The Arminian Magazine: Consisting of Extracts and Original Treatises on Universal Redemption*. Volume I, *for the Year 1778*. London: J. Fry & Co, 1778.

———. *The Arminian Magazine: Consisting of Extracts and Original Treatises on Universal Redemption*. Volume II, *for the Year 1779*. London: Frys, Couchman & Collier, 1778.

———. *The Arminian Magazine: Consisting of Extracts and Original Treatises on Universal Redemption*. Volume III, *for the Year 1780*. London: J. Paramore, 1780.

———. *The Arminian Magazine: Consisting of Extracts and Original Treatises on Universal Redemption*. Volume IV *for the Year 1781*. London: J. Paramore, 1781.

———. *The Arminian Magazine: Consisting of Extracts and Original Treatises on Universal Redemption*. Volume V *for the Year 1782*. London: J. Paramore. 1782.

———. *The Journal of the Rev John Wesley, A.M*, (8 volumes), edited by Nehemiah Curnock. London: Epworth Press, 1938.

———. *The Letters of the Rev John Wesley AM*, (10 volumes), edited by John Telford. London: Epworth Press, 1931.

———. *The Works of John Wesley*: Volume 1. *Sermons I (1-33)*, edited by Albert Outler. Nashville: Abingdon Press, 1984.

———. *The Works of John Wesley*: Volume 3. *Sermons III (71-114)*, edited by Albert Outler. Nashville: Abingdon Press, 1986.

———. *The Works of John Wesley*: Volume 9. *The Methodist Societies History, Nature and Design*, edited by Rupert E. Davies. Nashville: Abingdon Press, 1989.

———. *The Works of John Wesley*: Volume 11. *The Appeals to Men of Reason and Religion and Certain Related Open Letters*, edited by Gerald R. Cragg. Oxford: Clarendon Press, 1975.

———. *The Works of John Wesley*: Volume 18. *Journals and Diaries I (1735-1738)*, edited by William R. Ward and Richard P. Heitzenrater. Nashville: Abingdon Press, 1988.

———. *The Works of John Wesley*: Volume 19. *Journals and Diaries II (1738-1743)*, edited by William R. Ward and Richard P. Heitzenrater. Nashville: Abingdon Press, 1990.

———. *The Works of John Wesley*: Volume 20. *Journals and Diaries III (1743-1754)*, edited by William R. Ward and Richard P. Heitzenrater. Nashville: Abingdon Press, 1991.

———. *The Works of John Wesley*: Volume 21. *Journals and Diaries IV (1755-1765)*, edited by William R. Ward and Richard P. Heitzenrater. Nashville: Abingdon Press, 1992.

———. *The Works of John Wesley*: Volume 22. *Journals and Diaries V (1765-1775)*, edited by William R. Ward and Richard P. Heitzenrater. Nashville: Abingdon Press, 1993.

———. *The Works of John Wesley*: Volume 23. *Journals and Diaries VI (1776-1786)*, edited by William R. Ward and Richard P. Heitzenrater. Nashville Abingdon Press, 1995.

———. *The Works of John Wesley*: Volume 24. *Journals and Diaries I (1787-1791)*, edited by William R. Ward and Richard P. Heitzenrater. Nashville: Abingdon Press, 2003.

———. *The Works of John Wesley*: Volume 25. *Letters I (1721-1739)*, edited by Frank Baker. Oxford: Clarendon Press, 1980.

———. *The Works of John Wesley*: Volume 26. *Letters II (1740-1755)*, edited by Frank Baker. Oxford: Clarendon Press, 1982.

———. *Cautions and Directions, Given to the Greatest Professors in the Methodist Societies*. London: No publisher given, 1762.

———. *Farther Thoughts Upon Christian Perfection*. London: No publisher given, 1762.

———. *The Minutes of Some Late Conversations Between the Rev Messrs. Wesley and Others*. Bristol: Bulgin & Rosser, 1786.

———. *Minutes of the Methodist Conferences, from the First, Held in London by the Late Rev. John Wesley A.M. in the year 1744*, Volume 1. London: Conference Office, 1812.

———. *Minutes of the Methodist Conferences from the First, Held in London, by the Late Rev. John Wesley, A.M., in the Year 1744*. Volume I. London: John Mason, 1862.
———. *A Plain Account of Christian Perfection*. London: Epworth Press, 1952.
———. *Sermons on Several Occasions*. London: Epworth Press, 1944.
———. to Hutton, J., letter, 26th November 1738. Moravian Archive Book AB100.A.3. *Moravian Church House Archive*.
———. to Hutton, J., Letter, 27th November 1738. Moravian Archive Book AB100.A.3. *Moravian Church House Archive*.
———. to Hutton, J., Letter, 1st December 1738. Moravian Archive Book AB100.A.3. *Moravian Church House Archive*.
Wesleyan Conference Office. "Report of the Committee On Church Membership, as Adopted by the Conference of 1889, Having Special Reference to the Class-Meeting." In *Minutes of Several Conversations at the One Hundred and Forty-Sixth Yearly Conference of the People Called Methodists, in the Connexion Established by the Late Rev. John Wesley, A.M., Begun in Sheffield, on Tuesday, July 23rd, 1889*. London: Wesleyan Methodist Book-Room, 1889.
Wesley, Susanna. *Susanna Wesley: The Complete Writings*, edited by Charles Wallace. New York: Oxford University Press, 1997.
West, John. "Memoirs of Brother John West." In *Moravian Messenger*. London: Moravian Publication Office, 1875.
White, C. E. "The Decline of the Class Meeting." In *Methodist History*, Volume XXXVIII, Number 4, edited by C. Yrigoyen. New Jersey: United Methodist Church. 2000.
Whitefield, G., to Hutton, J., Letter, 22nd March 1738. Moravian Archive Book AB101.A3.4.17. *Moravian Church House Archive*.
———. to Hutton, J., Undated Letter. Moravian Archive Book p88A.A.3 (folder 21). *Moravian Church House Archive*.
———. to Hutton, J., Letter, 14th March 1739. Moravian Archive Book AB106.A3.14.33. *Moravian Church House Archive*.
———. *George Whitefield's Journals*. Guildford: Banner of Truth, 1960.
———. *The Letters of George Whitefield*. Chatham: Banner of Truth Trust, 1976.
Wiseman, F. Luke. *Charles Wesley, Evangelist and Poet* London: Epworth Press, 1933.
Woodward, Josiah. *An Account of the Rise and Progress of the Religious Societies in the City of London & C. And of the Endeavours for the Reformation of Manners Which have been made Therein*. 2d edn. London: R.A. Simpson, 1698.

www.ingramcontent.com/pod-product-compliance
Lightning Source LLC
Chambersburg PA
CBHW061423300426
44114CB00014B/1517